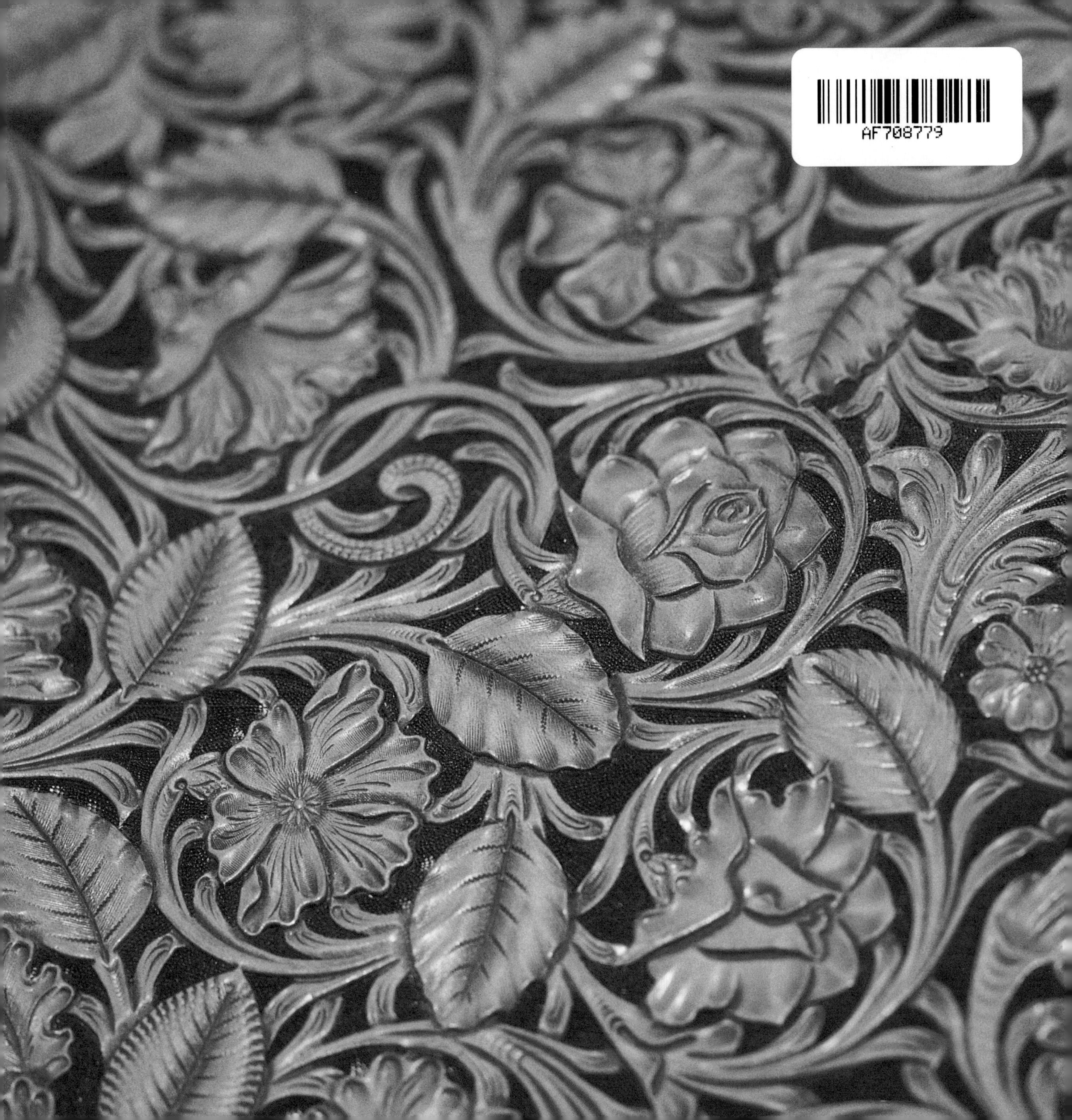

SADDLES OF THE WEST

history, art, culture, function

PHOTOGRAPHY BY DAVID R. STOECKLEIN

To Tom B. Saunders IV

There are a few people who become important in your life—people who influence you and seem to influence everyone they meet. For me, they are men who possess great wisdom, great compassion, and a great passion for life. They are men who live their lives true to themselves, true to their families, true to their friends, and true to their business partners. These rare men pass on their knowledge to others without question and do not ask for a price. They give it freely with love and care.

Tom B is one of these men. He has touched my life in a very profound and positive way. I only hope that I can live up to all that he has given me. Tom is a true Texas cowboy and a man who lives by the real Code of the West.

—David R. Stoecklein

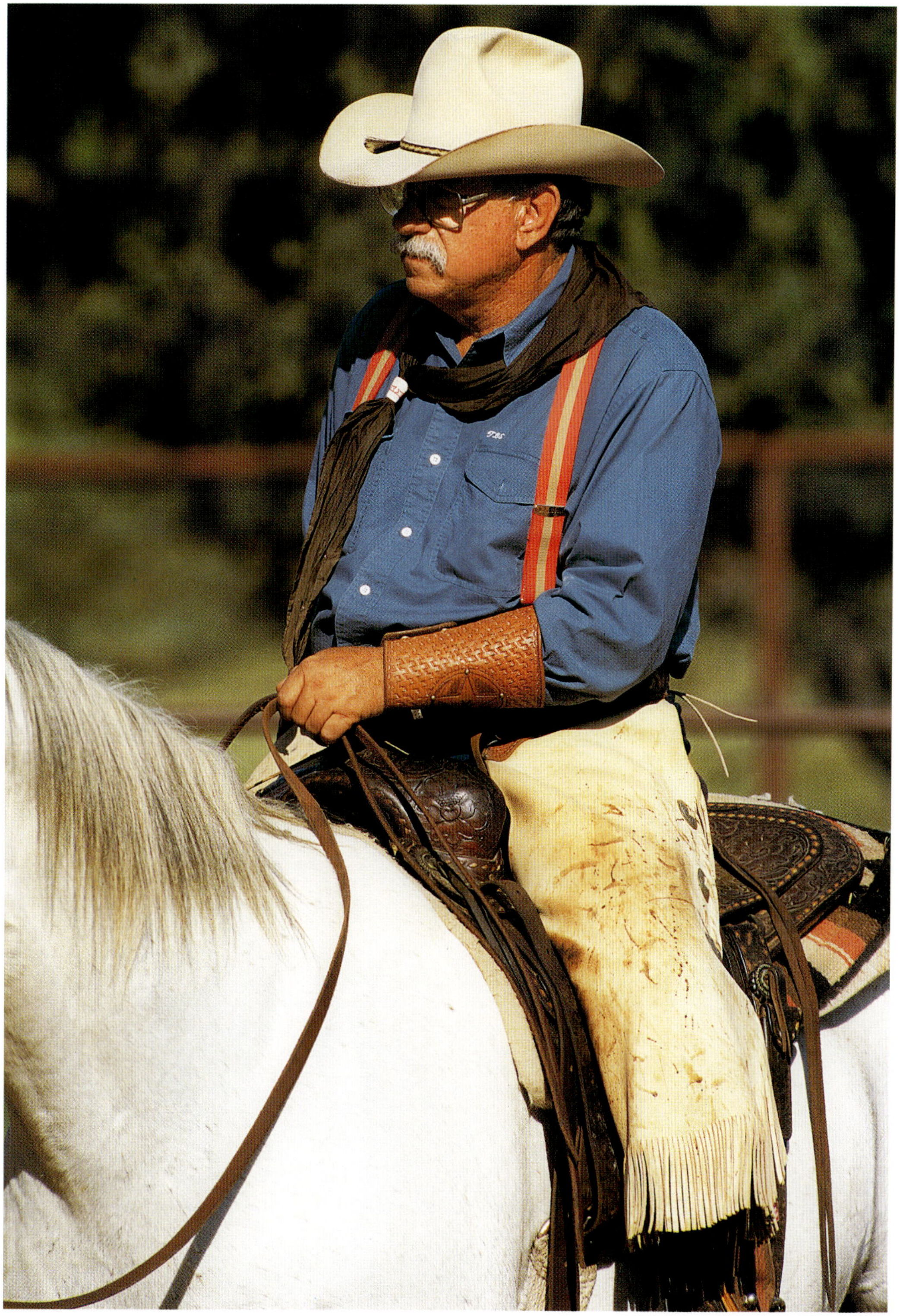

TOM B. SAUNDERS IV RIDING FROSTY, *Weatherford, Texas*

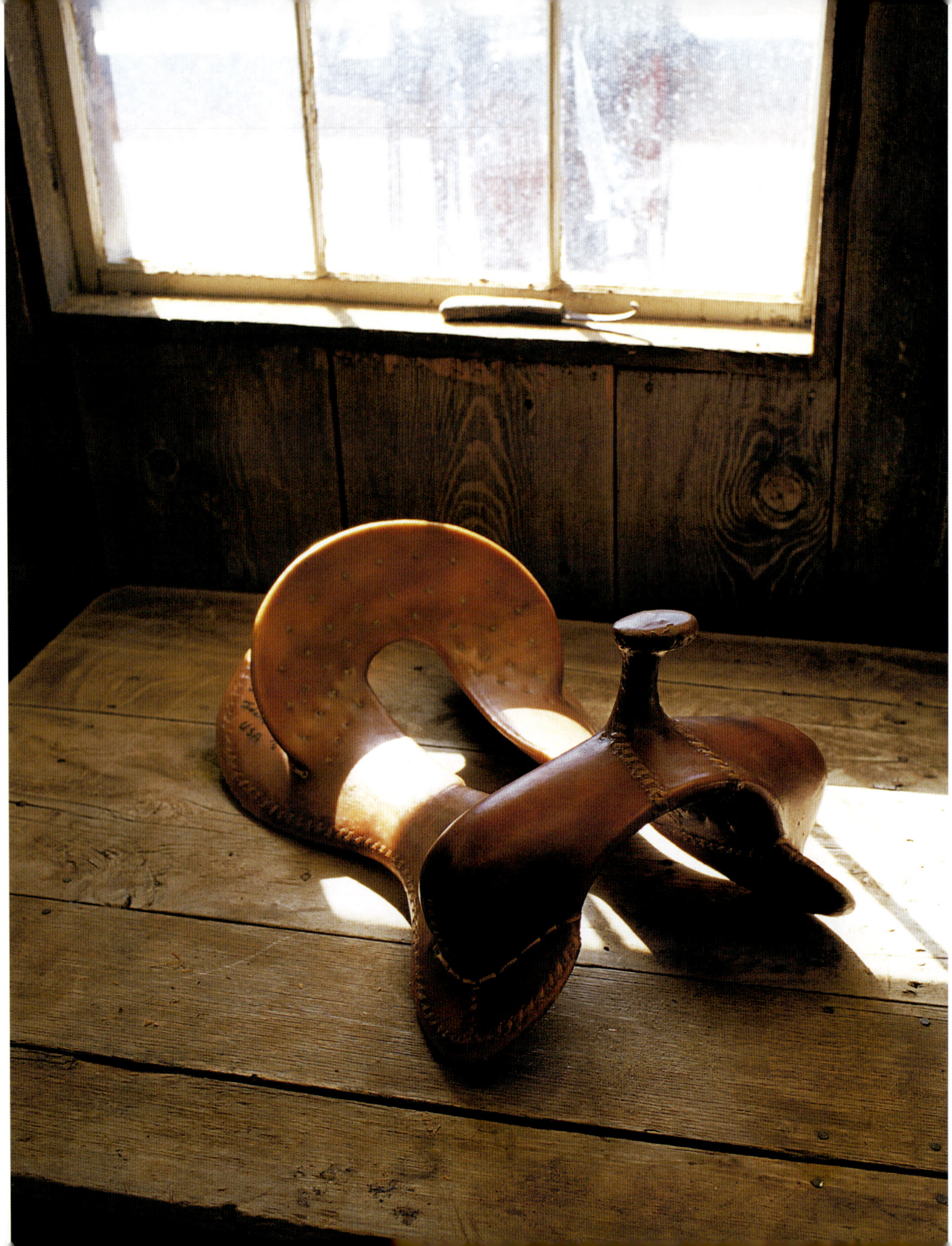

SADDLES OF THE WEST

history, art, culture, function

PHOTOGRAPHY	DAVID R. STOECKLEIN
TEXT	SHIRL WOODSON
EDITOR	CARRIE LIGHTNER
CREATIVE DIRECTOR	DAVID R. STOECKLEIN
ART DIRECTION & DESIGN	T-GRAPHICS

COVER PHOTO: MARC BROGGER SADDLE, *Three Forks, Montana with Cowhorse Equipment, Inc. saddle blanket, Avila's Pro Shop, Pablo, Montana*

All images in this book are available as signed original gallery prints and for stock photography usage. Stoecklein Photography houses an extensive stock library of Western, sports, and lifestyle images. Dave Stoecklein is also an assignment photographer whose clients include Canon, Kodak, Ariat Boots, Merial Pharmaceuticals, USST, Bayer, Hatteras, Marlboro, Chevrolet, Timberland, Ford, Wrangler, Pontiac, and the Cayman Islands.

Other books by Stoecklein Publishing include *The American Quarter Horse, Dude Ranches of the American West, The Cowboy Boot, The Spur, The Western Buckle, Western Fences, Ranch Style, The Cowboy Boot, Cowgirls in Heaven, The Performance Horse, Cow Dogs, Lil' Buckaroos, The American Paint Horse, The Idaho Cowboy, Cowboy Gear, Don't Fence Me In, The Texas Cowboys, The Montana Cowboy, The Western Horse, Cowgirls, Spirit of the West,* and *The California Cowboy.*

Every year, Stoecklein Publishing also produces a line of wall calendars, prints, and cards featuring the Western photography of David R. Stoecklein. For more information or to request a catalog, please contact:

Stoecklein Publishing & Photography
Tenth Street Center, Suite A1
Post Office Box 856 • Ketchum, Idaho 83340
tel 208.726.5191 fax 208.726.9752 toll-free 800.727.5191
www.drsphoto.net

Printed in China

ISBN 1-931153-98-1
Library of Congress Catalog number 2004097258

1 2 3 4 5 6 7 8 9 10 - 09 08 07 06 05

SADDLETREE MADE BY WARREN WRIGHT OF NEW ZEALAND, *waiting for Nancy Hoggan to hang the leather and turn it into a working saddle*

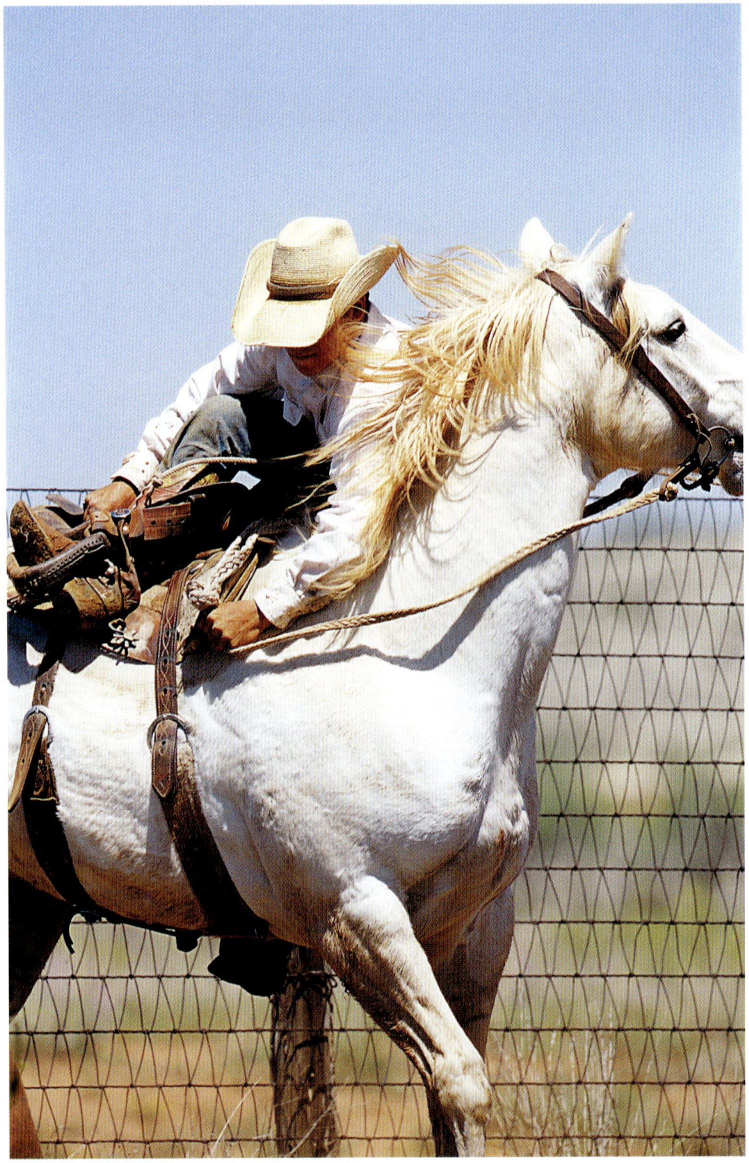

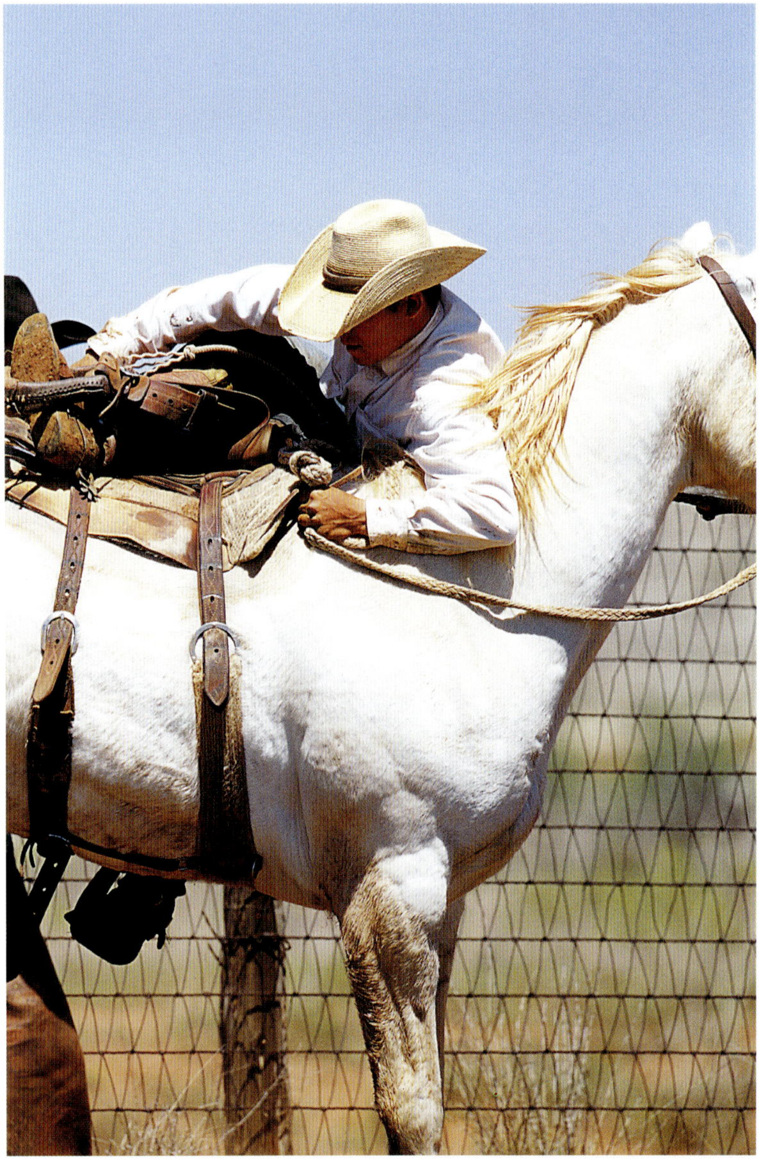

IT IS IMPORTANT *to cinch up your saddle when roping; if you don't, all hell can break loose, Pitchfork Ranch, Guthrie, Texas*

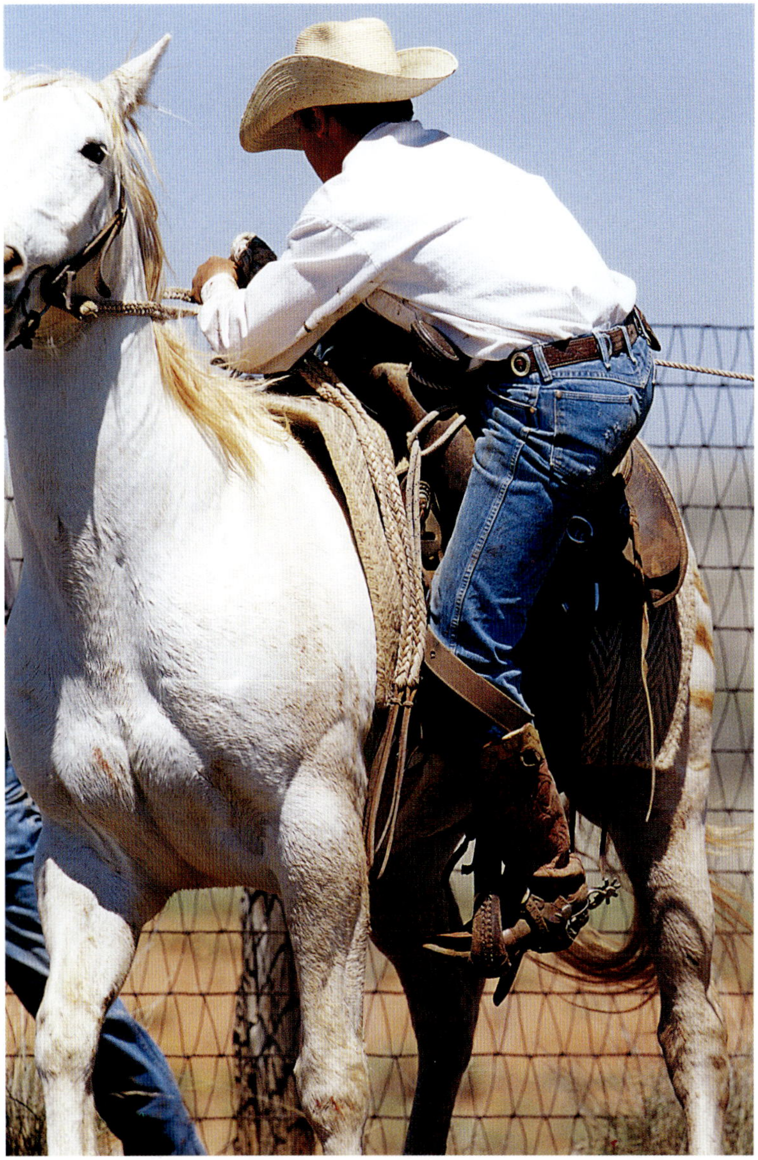

INDEX

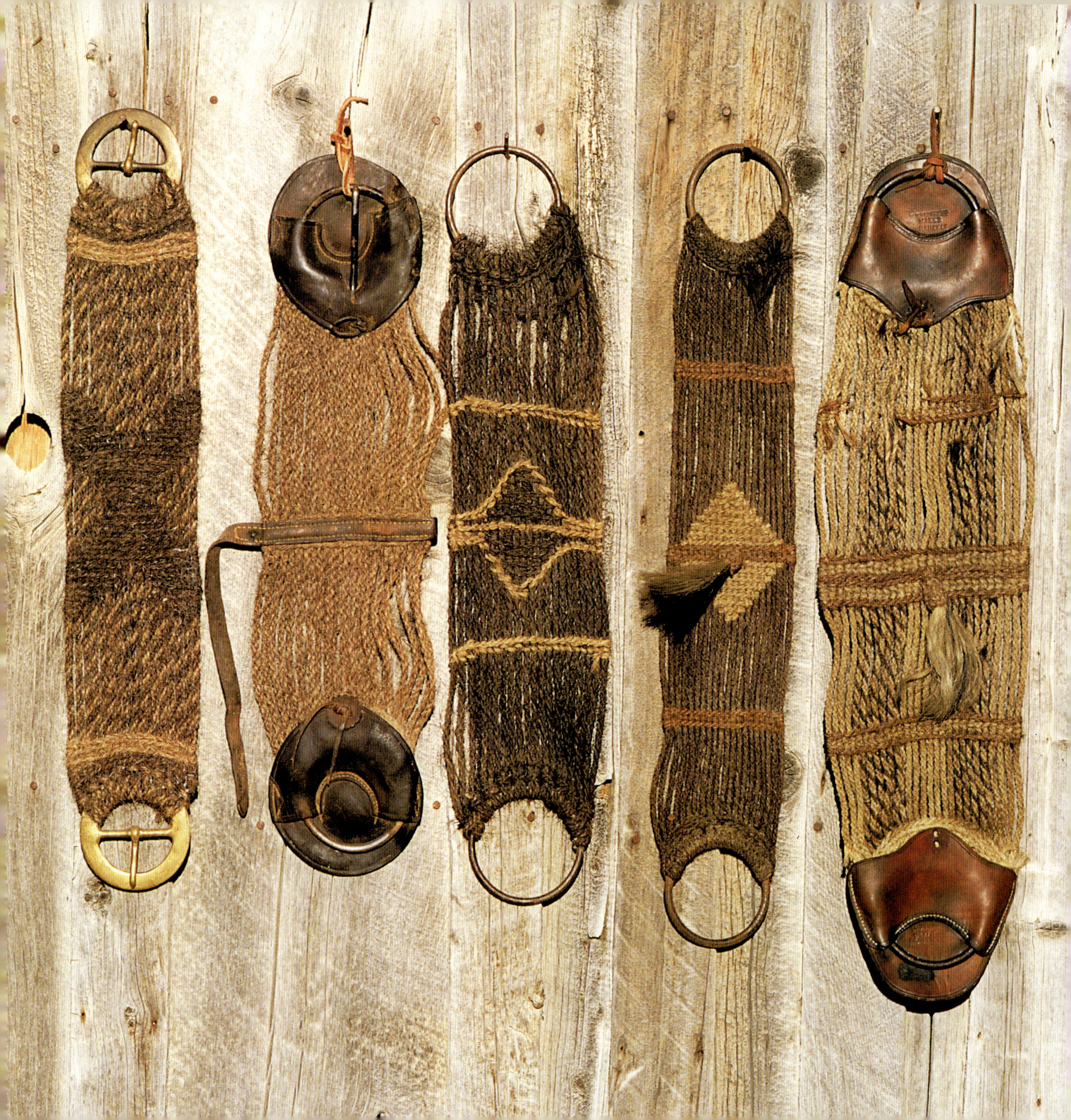

There have been so many books written about saddles—history books, photo books, books on how to build saddles, books about famous saddle makers, and so on. This book is the latest in my series on cowboy gear. As always, my quest is to preserve the West and the Western lifestyle. This book fits right in with that vision. The saddle is as much an icon of the West as is the cowboy. There are sayings such as "a life in the saddle" that suggest a way of life like none other in the world. When you think of a saddle, you immediately think of the West. The saddle is used as a metaphor, not only for the West, but also for craftsmanship of a job well done. The finest saddle leather is often used in high quality products such as automobile seats, furniture, and luggage.

Foreword

With this small volume, I only am only whetting the appetite of the reader. The book offers a small taste of the history of the Western saddle. It shows a few of the great old-time saddle makers and their styles and it takes you through the changes from the very early Western saddle makers to today's most legendary and sought-after makers.

In my books I always try to show the subjects of my photographs in real Western scenes. In this book I have tried to showcase a good cross-section of saddles from Texas to Idaho and California. I know that I have left out some of the great makers and probably some of my readers' favorites, but it is impossible to fit everything in just one book. I apologize in advance for omitting any of the men and women who certainly belong in this book.

I hope you enjoy this book and that you learn from it, just as I did while photographing and producing it.

Keep the spirit of the West alive,

David R. Stoecklein

ANTIQUE HORSEHAIR CINCHES,
David R. Stoecklein Collection

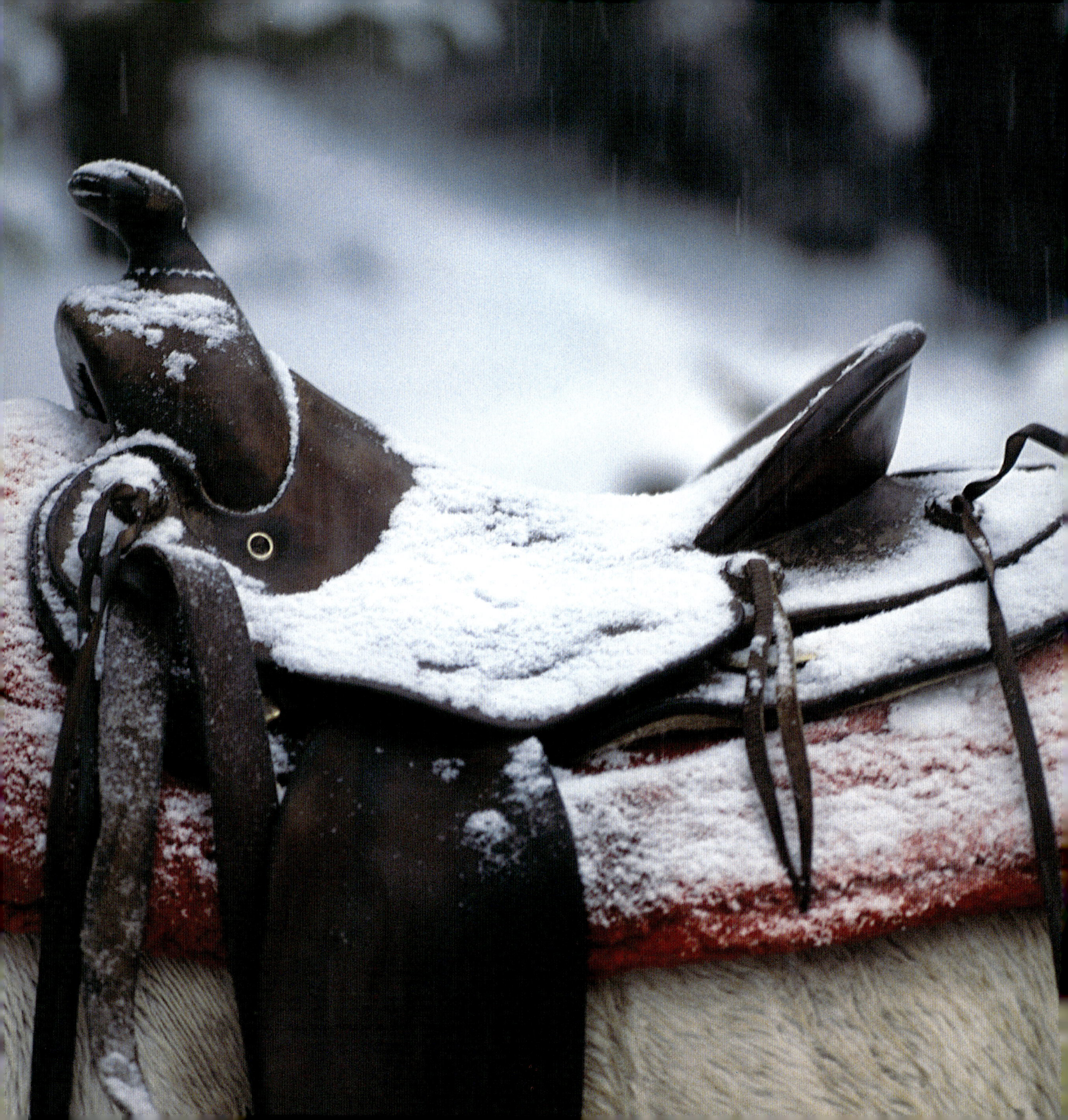

9781931153980

718 718

Location: Room T-Bay 1

COBM.4TM

Title:	Saddles of the West: History, Art, Culture, Function
Cond:	Good
User:	Alyssa
Station:	COAS Receiving7
Date:	2026-05-01 19:22:30 (UTC)
Account:	COAS Books
Orig Loc:	Room T-Bay 1
mSKU:	COBM.4TM
vSKU:	COBV.1931153981.G
Seq#:	718
unit_id:	5274501
width:	1.00 in
rank:	2,569,647
Cond Note:	

COBV.1931153981.G

delist unit# 5274501

XXXXX

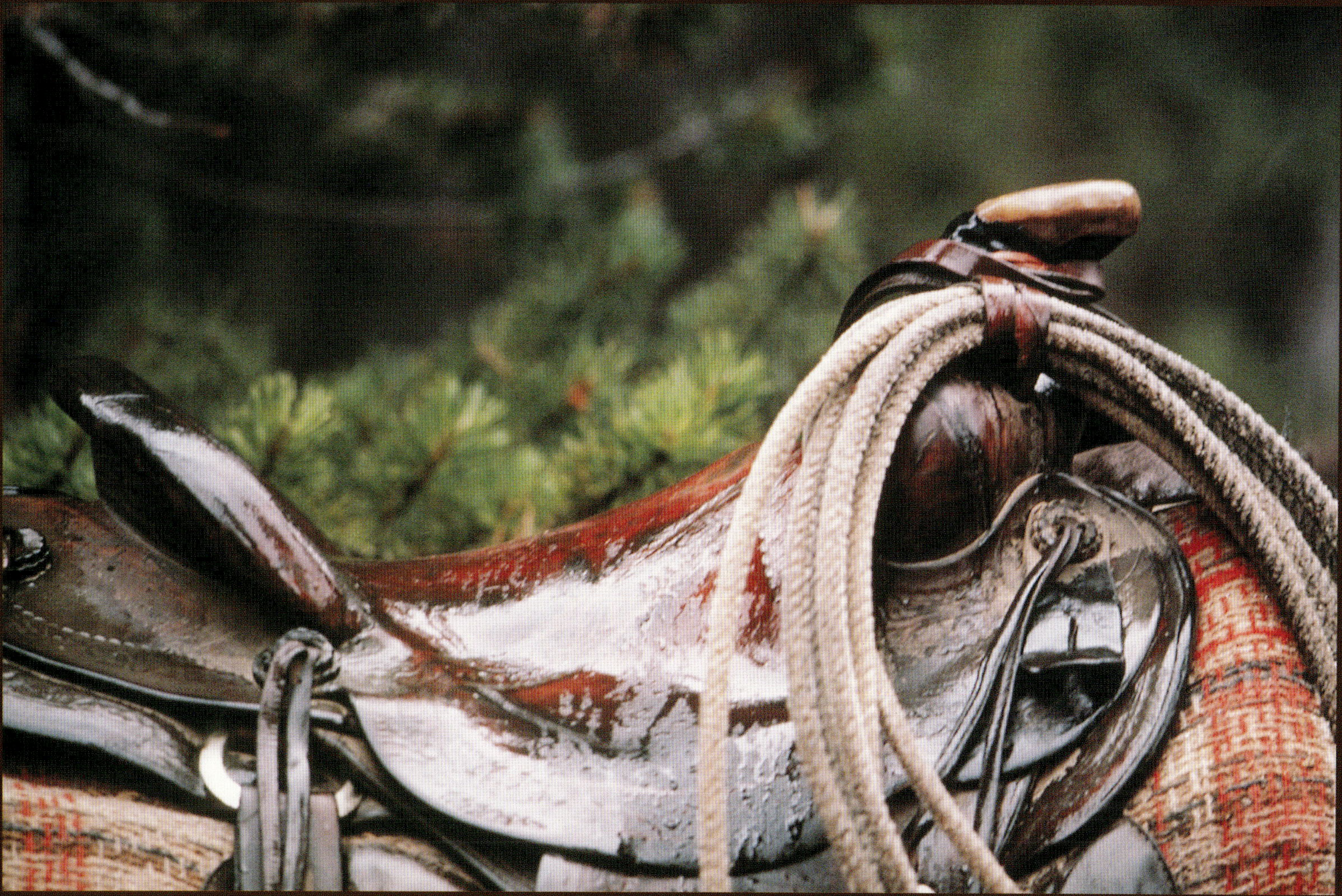

WAITING IN THE RAIN, *1950s Hamley saddle*

A COLD SEAT, *hunting camp,*
Smoky Mountains, Idaho

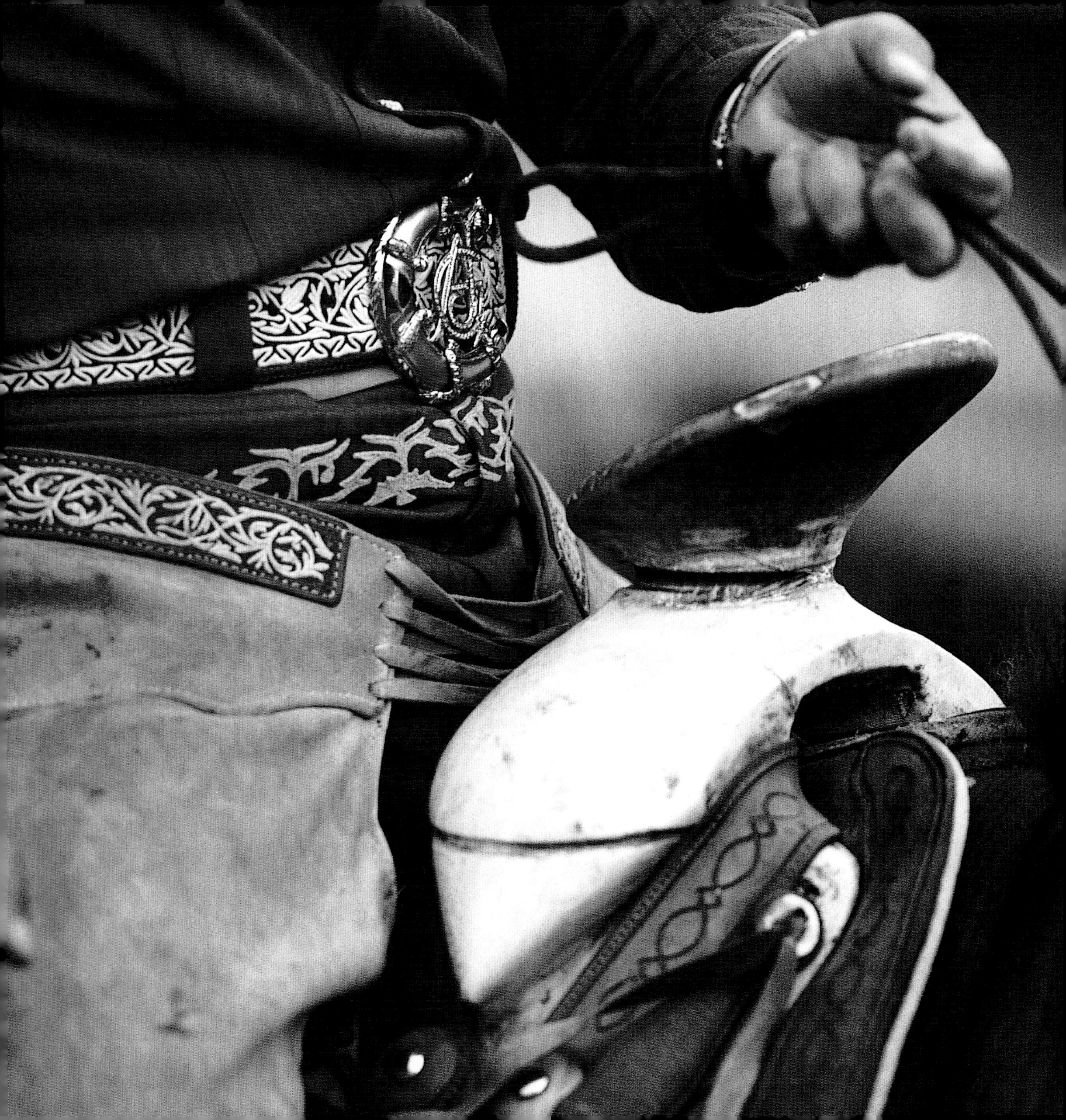

History of the Saddle

by Shirl Woodson

People find saddles in the most unlikely of places. Saddles turn up in dark corners of antique stores or under bright lights of high fashion displays; they can be resting on rafters in cobweb-lined barns or lying in beds of mud-caked trucks. They turn up in museums, homes, and tack rooms in every state. The shapes of saddles are as varied as the spaces they inhabit. They are plain or ornate. They are often decorated with metals as common as nickel or as precious as gold. The most dedicated craftsmen build saddles with the finest natural materials by hand, or they use the cheapest synthetics and mass production. Whatever the shape, whatever the ornamentation, whatever the construction, and wherever the resting place, saddles have one common denominator. A saddle is what merges the bodies of man and horse.

To someone making a living on horseback, a saddle is as important as the boots on his feet and the hat on his head. The most private cowboy reveals hidden aspects of his character when he brings out his saddle—how it was made, where it was made, if it is abused or spoiled, if the cinches are tied up or dragging loose in the dirt, if it is basic and functional, or if it reflects pride of ownership. A cowboy often spends more than a month's wages to get a saddle that suits his fancy.

Cowboys have long been known for the pride they take in their profession and the trappings that go along with it. It is a pride that was passed down to them from Moorish horsemen. After the invasion of Spain, the Moors left behind not only architectural styles from the homeland, but also a unique style of riding and tack. The Spaniards were quick to grasp the benefit in mimicking their conquerors' horsemanship techniques. The Moors used stirrups that were shorter than those of the Spanish soldiers and saddles that were more open in design. The cantles of the Moorish saddles were high like the Spanish, but stood more erect and did not wrap around the rider. This design allowed the horseman greater dexterity in the heat of battle.

The warriors of Spain were impressed by the ability of the Moorish horsemen to maneuver their horses so quickly and with great agility. They soon adopted the reining techniques of the Moors as well as many elements of their tack. Spaniards of this time were riding "al brida" or with long stirrups, which allowed an armored rider to lean against the tall pommel and brace himself in a fight. The shapes of the pommel and cantle created a tight fit and a restrictive seat. Using Moorish inspiration, the Spaniards devised a war saddle that proved to be an asset to the horseman who fought in battles armed with lances and swords. This is the saddle Spain brought to the New World.

As cavalrymen became ranchers, they transformed their saddles of war into saddles for herding stock. These saddles were more streamlined and they consisted of little more than a rawhide tree with simple stirrup leathers to hold carved wooden stirrups. This saddle came to be known as the Spanish Stock Saddle, the "silla de campo" or the "silla de vaquero." The tree of this saddle had a fork and a cantle carved from wood that fastened to fairly thin sidebars. The entire thing was covered in damp rawhide that was sewn into place when it was wet. When the rawhide dried, the tree acquired a new strength.

As colonists followed Father Junipero Serra into Alta, California in the 1700s, they made more changes to the Spanish Stock Saddle to make it suitable for the California vaquero. They lengthened the front rigging strap and shortened the rear rigging strap. This shifted the rigging ring to the center of the saddle, midway between fork and cantle. The exposed tree and center fire rigging was then covered with a large piece of slit leather, allowing the cantle and the horn to protrude. This leather piece was removable and called a "mochila," the sides of which extended down to protect the rider's legs from the sweat of the horse's barrel.

The financial status of the Californios began to change and so did the appearance of the mochila. While most were plain, the wealthier men had mochilas featuring tooled leather or leather embroidered with threads of silk, silver, and gold. The corners of the mochilas were often weighted with metal decoration to prevent them from turning up. For traveling, the mochila was covered with a corono fitted with pockets or cantinas with flaps that were secured by buckles or tied shut.

CHARRO SADDLE, *Saltillo, Mexico*

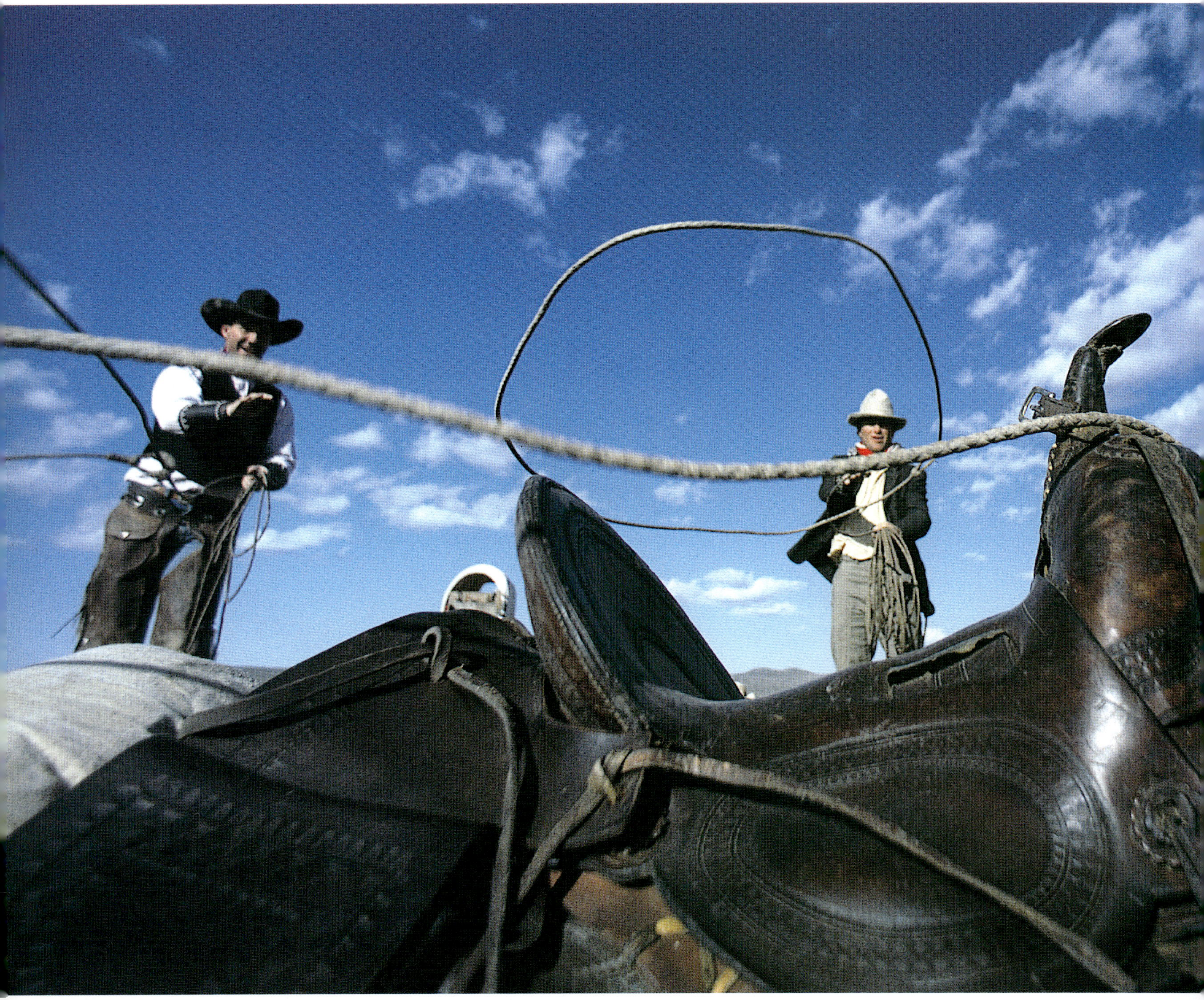

Playtime at the chuck wagon, *Arco Desert, Idaho*

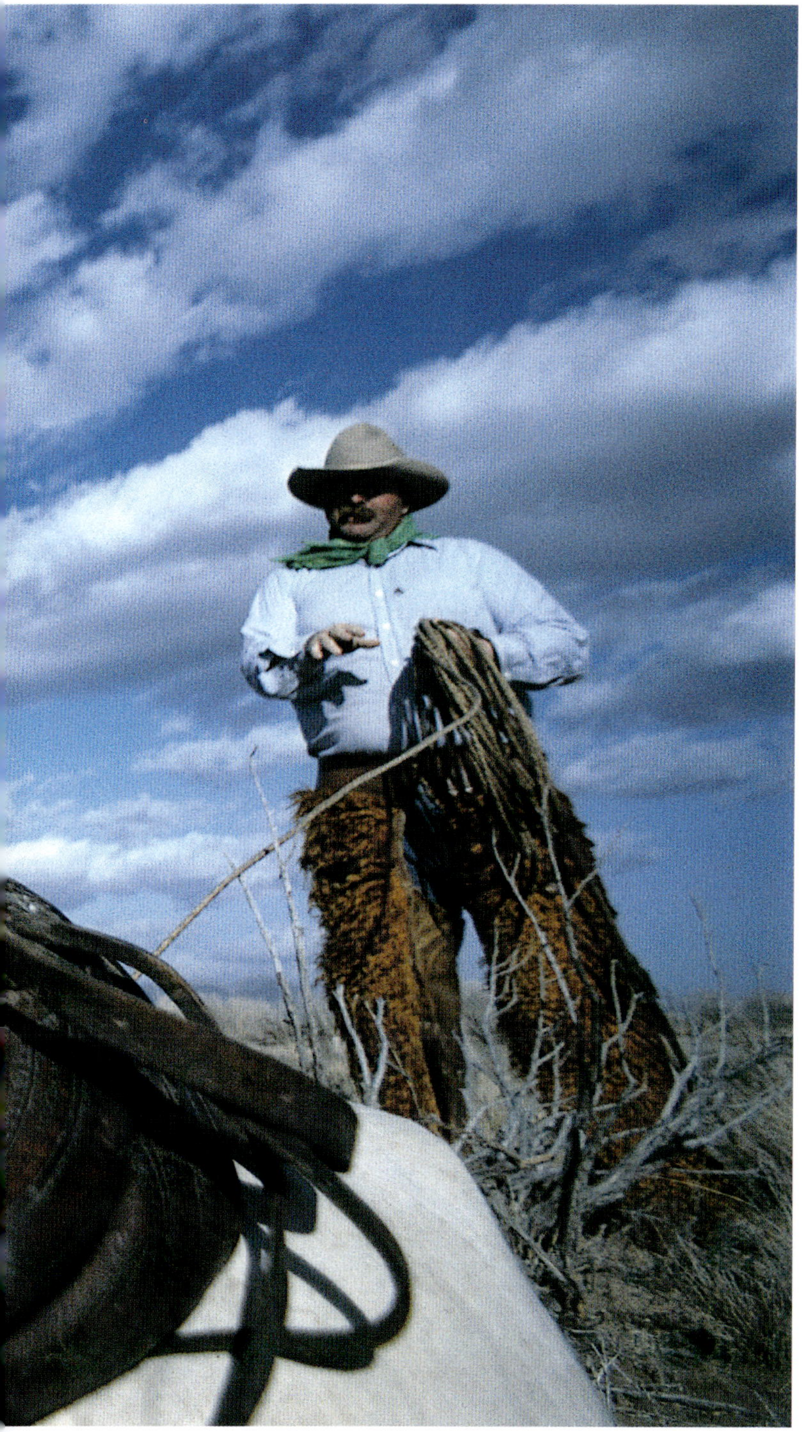

The California Missions were self-sufficient ranchos. The padres taught the mission Indians to make crude versions of the saddles used by the leather jacket soldiers and the Mexican settlers. The mission saddles were carved from four pieces of soft wood, which together formed the fork, cantle, and sidebars. These pieces were lashed with rawhide, but not covered. The seat was split. The Indians often covered the seat with a sheepskin or some type of robe or blanket for cushioning.

Alta, California was not the only area experiencing population growth. Settlements were also formed north of the Rio Grande. By the 1750s, the Spanish Stock Saddle was a coveted item of trade in the land between Texas and Louisiana. As more people came to populate the new lands, the demand for the Spanish Stock Saddle and the California saddle grew. Saddles came in varying degrees of quality. Initially, Texans used saddles found in Mexico, a saddle that was basically a rawhide tree with stirrup straps and strap rigging. Cattle ranching had not yet become a lucrative venture; saddles in Texas from that period were used primarily for transportation. The least expensive were built on Mexican trees made from the dry trunk of a certain type of cactus. It was not long before the Texans began to refer to saddles as "kacks," a term still used today.

Trappers, traders, and other enterprising individuals continued to push into areas of North America previously inhabited only by indigenous people. As traffic in trade goods grew, so grew the demands for the Spanish Stock Saddle. By 1821, traders along the newly opened Santa Fe Trail were bringing saddles with them from as far away as California to exchange for goods in St. Louis.

Emigrants heading West were eager to trade for saddles brought in from the Santa Fe Trail after it opened in 1821. Soon the traders could not keep up with the demand for the saddles. As traffic and trade grew between the eastern and western portions of North America, so did the popularity of the stock saddle. With this growing demand came a need for more saddle makers. To accommodate the desire from customers, saddlers in the gateway towns of St. Louis and St. Joseph soon began to copy the saddles that had been brought in from the West. Literature harking the wonders of the West heralded its unique saddle. So frequently was this saddle mentioned that it began to be known as the

Santa Fe Saddle. The Santa Fe Saddle was basically of the same design as those used by Californios of that period.

Texas was the place where many European men settled, especially Germans who plied the saddlers' trade. In 1826, Atacosita, Texas listed three saddlers in its census report. By 1850 there were 152 saddlers in Texas. In the late 1830s a Texas saddler by the name of Adolphus Hope built a saddle based upon Mexican styles commonly seen in Texas at that time. The tree on the Hope saddle was small, partly exposed, and covered in rawhide. Rather than a mochila, the Hope saddle had a rear jockey, small square skirts, and fenders covering the stirrup leathers that added protection for the rider's leg from dirt and sweat. The Hope saddle of the 1850s and the Santa Fe Saddle as depicted in period art bear a strong resemblance to one another.

Following the Civil War, the nation was in desperate need of beef. Texas was the land of plenty when it came to wild, unbranded cattle. The Texas cowboy tied off to his saddle horn with one end of his rope, leaving the loop end free to capture the wild beasts. To prevent saddles from tipping up in back from extreme weight on the rope, cowboys added a back cinch. The plain saddletree with leather straps began to fade into the past. The mochila morphed into a style known as the "Mother Hubbard." With the birth of the great cattle drives, the evolution of the stock saddle progressed rapidly. Texans began to favor saddletrees fully covered in leather. Their saddles took on a distinctive look with large square skirts attached to the underside of the tree.

With the birth of the great cattle drives, the evolution of the stock saddle progressed rapidly.

In the late 1850s Israel Landis of Independence, Missouri was considered by many to be one of the most accomplished makers of the stock saddle. When Landis received the commission to build saddles for the Pony Express in 1859, he turned the order over to his young assistant Ed L. Gallatin. In 1860, Gallatin convinced Landis to open a second shop in Denver, Colorado to take advantage of commerce during the Colorado Gold Rush. With a pair of four mule teams and laden with wares, they arrived in Denver in June of 1880. The new store was as successful as the original. In 1863, two years after arriving in Denver, Gallatin formed a limited partnership with Francis Gallup and bought out Landis' interest in the Denver store.

In 1865, the shop became known as Gallup & Gallatin. New gold fields were being developed in Montana so Gallatin again loaded a wagon full of goods and headed to Virginia City, Montana where he successfully peddled his merchandise. The next time Gallatin broke trail with his wagonload of wares, he headed for Nebraska City, Nebraska to open another branch of the store. The Union Pacific Railroad reached Cheyenne in 1867. Seeing another golden opportunity, Gallatin opened a shop in Cheyenne but needed a way to distinguish his saddlery. His solution was to put his taxidermy skills to use. He did a full body mount of a horse on a twelve-foot platform. The horse was tacked up in the very best saddle and bridle Gallatin had to offer. The unusual advertising gimmick worked and soon the shop was busy keeping up with orders. The partnership dissolved when Gallup bought out Gallatin in 1873.

In 1868 Ed Gallatin's nephews, Frank and Tom Meanea, arrived in Cheyenne from Missouri. Both young men were saddlers. Nineteen-year-old Frank had previously worked repairing harnesses for the Union Pacific. Tom was a saddletree maker. They both were destined to become legends in stock saddle history. Frank worked with Ed building saddles; Tom stayed in Cheyenne and made trees for Gallatin and his brother for many years. Ed Gallatin sold his Cheyenne shop to his nephew Frank Meanea in the mid 1870s. The name of the business remained E.L. Gallatin and Company until 1881.

Frank Meanea's lasting legacy to the development of the stock saddle was the addition of the "Cheyenne Roll." Meanea saddles had many features of the saddles used on the Texas trail drives. They were double-rigged with square skirts, and cut down to make the saddle weigh less. The marks of Gallatin or Meanea soon came to represent the best quality available in saddles. Like those before him, Meanea understood the value of marketing, but he wanted to reach a market that stretched far beyond Cheyenne. As early as 1874, the Meanea shop produced a catalog of their wares. When Meanea died in 1928 at the age of 79, his former employee T.A. Cobry purchased the business and ran it until the Great Depression forced him to close the doors.

Gallatin and Meanea had competition in Cheyenne from brothers Gilbert and John Collins. The Collins brothers had a successful shop in Omaha, Nebraska. Like Gallatin, they saw opportunity for expansion in the town of Cheyenne. The Collins brothers had put together a chain of saddleries—one in Omaha, two in Montana (Miles City), and one in Cheyenne. They won acclaim by creating a saddletree that fit a horse well without hurting his back. The hard winter of 1886-87 proved disastrous for cattlemen and businessmen alike. After that time, the brothers began selling their three shops. Gilbert retired, but John opened a wholesale saddlery business called Collins and Morrison in Nebraska. The saddle shops under the direction of Gallatin, Meanea, and the Collins brothers in Cheyenne were three of the best during that time. They are credited with creating what was known as the "Cheyenne saddle."

When Kansas instituted a quarantine of Texas cattle, the cow trails moved to the Colorado line. The town of Pueblo, Colorado became a headliner of cow towns. Pueblo gave birth to the shops of the R.T. Frazier Saddlery, the T. Flynn Saddlery, and the S.C. Gallup Saddlery Company. All three shops provided goods to retail and wholesale customers alike. The saddles built in that town soon came to be known as "Pueblo saddles."

In the late 1870s, R.T. Frazier worked in Pete Becker's Leadville, Colorado saddle shop. Becker's clients were mainly those connected to the mining industry. Frazier wanted to build saddles for cowboys, not repair harnesses for miners, so he moved on to Pueblo. By 1880, he was working in the shop of S.C. Gallup. The name changed to Gallup and Frazier after R.T. bought into the firm in 1892. It was not long before Gallup and Frazier became a major force in the manufacturing of cowboy saddles. When the partnership dissolved in 1898, the name returned to S.C. Gallup Saddlery Company. Frazier soon opened his own shop in Pueblo. The use of mail order catalogs made Frazier one of the largest producers of stock saddles in the U.S. In 1917, he had over 50 saddle makers under his employ.

T. Flynn Saddlery was the third of the three great saddle houses associated with the Pueblo saddle. The shop began business in 1892. Mail orders provided Flynn with nearly 100 percent of his customers. The Flynn shop was completely destroyed in the flood of 1921. S.C. Gallup offered space for Flynn to fill his mail orders in his shop. Flynn salvaged what he could and moved three of his saddlers to Gallup's shop until a new location for his business could be found.

S.C. Gallup was the younger brother of Frank Gallup. When S.C. Gallup opened his Pueblo shop in the 1870s, he became the first of the town's saddle makers. Details of his early training have faded away over the years, but it is assumed that S.C. apprenticed in Frank's Denver saddle shop.

S.C. Gallup died shortly after the 20th century arrived. Following his death, James Wimmer stepped as the president of the company. Mrs. Gallup, her sons Hallet and Boone, Karl Kretschmer, and Wimmer all held stock in the business. Wimmer and Kretschmer soon bought out the Gallups. Under their guidance, the business continued to grow. After Wimmer's death, Kretschmer acquired the Gallup mail order lists and most of the equipment. The Depression hit the Gallup profits hard. When Kretschmer told Frank Flynn he would have to close shop, Flynn had a chance to pay back a debt to S.C. Gallup Saddlery. He bought part of the stock and offered his basement to store the remaining stock and fixtures. Kretschmer was given a job as salesman at the Flynn Saddlery where he worked until his death in 1930.

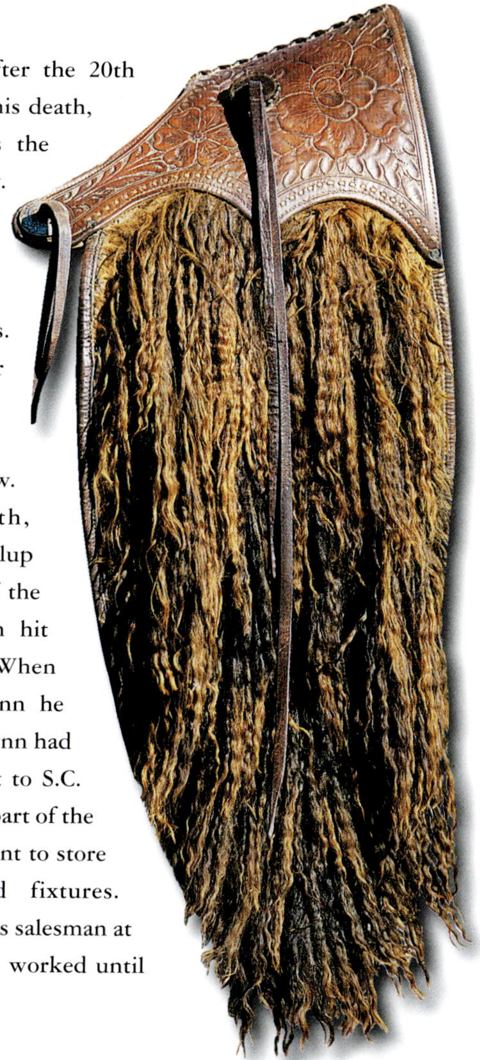

VERY RARE VISALIA ANGORA SADDLE POCKETS, *Stoecklein Collection*

Back in Montana, Hugh and Thomas Moran opened a shop in Milestown in 1879. Hugh had been a saddler in the Montana Territory who took great professional pride in the saddles he built. Long before it was known as Miles City, Milestown marked the end of the cattle trails from Texas. Moran saddles soon became known for outstanding quality. The rigging was connected in a manner that became known as the Sam Stagg Rigging. It was a name left behind by saddler Joseph A. Samstag from New York City who moved to Visalia, California to follow those caught up in the gold fever. This rigging was also called the "naked rigging" or "exposed rigging." It consisted of one piece of leather that looped around the horn and down each side of the fork to the cinch ring.

Montana cowboys saw little need for the double-rigged saddle favored by the Texans. To fit their needs, many cowboys simply removed the back cinch. Moran worked to make alterations in the popular rigging. In addition, Charles E. Coggshall is often credited with making the ultimate refinement of new rigging known as the "three-quarter." The three-quarter rigged saddle was a sound compromise between the full double and the center fire rigs. Coggshall initially partnered with Al Furstnow in what was known as the Goettlich Saddlery. When that partnership dissolved, Coggshall and Furstnow each set up a new business just a few doors away from each other. Moran sold out to Coggshall in the late 1890s, and the business was rechristened as the Coggshall Saddlery.

Coggshall himself was not a saddle maker, yet he had an ability for finding the best craftsmen to make the best products. Coggshall was not only interested in the exposed construction of the saddle, he was determined to build top quality saddletrees. Ever the inventor, after perfecting the three-quarter rig, he designed a swell fork saddle. He eventually sold his shop to two of his saddle makers, Clem Kathmann and Frank Jelinek, and a third man by the name of Bert Coleman in 1909. The name was changed to Miles City Saddlery, makers of original Coggshall Saddles. In 1939, Joe Conway, the shop's bookkeeper, bought the business.

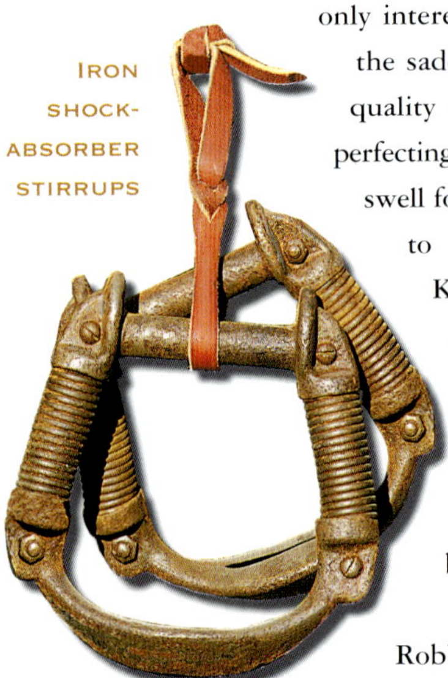
IRON SHOCK-ABSORBER STIRRUPS

Robbins & Lenoi started building saddles in Miles City in 1884. That same year, Al Furstnow was getting his start with Goettlich Saddlery. After his partnership with Coggshall dissolved, Al Furstnow bought out Robbins' business. Like the cities of Cheyenne and Pueblo, Miles City soon became associated with saddles that had unique characteristics. Collectively, the saddles of Moran, Coggshall, Furstnow, Robbins, and Lenoi were called "Miles City Rigs." These saddles demonstrated the influence of their predecessors in Texas, but the three-quarter rigs were lighter and their skirts were smaller. In 1918, the Miles City Saddlery Company alone grossed over $1,000,000. At the peak of the saddle industry in Miles City, as many as 4,000 saddles were turned out annually.

The Cheyenne, Pueblo, and Miles City saddles became the standard for cowboys from the Texas panhandle to the Canadian border for excellence, but saddles in other geographical locations began to make headlines of their own. By the early 1870s Newton Porter had become a full-fledged saddle maker, having learned the trade in St. Louis. Texas to him was the land of opportunity and it was in Taylor, a town near Austin, where he established his shop in 1875. After fire destroyed his shop, he decided to move to the Texas town of Abilene.

Porter's first saddles had large square skirts and were double-rigged, weighing between 40 and 50 pounds. He made the claim in the form of a guarantee that his saddles would not break, sore a horse, or lose a rigging. Porter's business thrived until drought severely affected the economy. He relocated to the state of Washington in the late 1880s. It was not long before he once again relocated his business, this time to Phoenix, Arizona in 1895. As he did when he first came to Texas, Porter built the saddles himself. Soon his sons joined him in learning the craft.

The saddles Porter made in Arizona were influenced more by the styles in California than by those from Texas. When Porter began making lighter, single-rigged saddles he found a niche to fill. After his death in 1906, his sons sent out their first mail order catalog. Like many other saddleries, his wares were not limited to saddles. The store also offered clothing, boots, hats, chaps, and anything else a cowboy needed. A second retail store was opened in Tucson in 1928. The Number 36 Porter catalog of 1951 shows a "Rig in Skirt" rigging. D.O. Diaz, one of Porter's saddle makers, was issued another skirt rigging patent in 1954. Porter's two patents were the results of much effort and experimentation, but they were deemed worthy by those who bought saddles with an in-skirt rigging.

The California Gold Rush of 1848 was a driving force in the development of the stock saddle. Heading up the list of early saddleries on the West Coast is Main & Winchester of San Francisco, California. Charles Main came from Rochester, New Hampshire, and Ezra Winchester hailed from Fall River, Massachusetts. They became acquainted after arriving in California and decided to open a harness repair business together. Their timing was perfect. San Francisco was booming with the influx of gold seekers. It was a merchant's paradise.

The two men bought ready-made goods from Barclays and the business flourished. Main and Winchester were not the only enterprising men dreaming of a successful saddle house during this era. Lucius D. Stone founded his San Francisco saddlery in 1852. Stone featured a full range of saddles, bits, spurs, harnesses, and other assorted tack and hardware. After more than 30 successful years, native San Franciscans Frank M. Gilham and Augustus Kempkey purchased the business in 1888. The enterprise was housed in a five-story building on 417-419 Market Street in San Francisco. Main & Winchester merged with the L.D. Stone Company in 1905. The name then changed to Main, Winchester and Stone until R.P. Grubb bought the company in 1909.

San Francisco's Butchertown was the destination for many herds of cattle covering the California terrain that were primarily tended by vaqueros often of Mexican and Indian descent. These were the men who formed the initial clientele of a saddlery established in the 1870s—the Visalia Stock Saddle Company by Juan Martorell. Two natives of Sonora, Mexico joined him when the doors first opened—master bit and spur maker, Alsalio Herrera and skilled tree maker, Ricardo Mattle. Later on another tree maker, Jesus Salazar, joined the skilled team of men.

Vaqueros brought in saddles for repair that were adaptations of those descended from the mission era. Martorell, along with the men from Sonora, developed a saddle that fit the unique needs of the California horsemen. An early advertisement in a local newspaper for Martorell's shop referred to this saddle as the "Vaquero Saddle." It was lightweight, strong, a good fit for both man and horse, and stylish in appearance.

It was not long before Martorell decided to relocate his shop to the young town of Visalia. After about a year in business there, he realized owning his own business was not working out for him as planned. Shortly after 1870, David E. Walker and Henry Shuham bought the Visalia business from him. They kept Martorell, Herrera, and Mattle on as skilled craftsmen. Although Martorell went to work for another saddler later on, Herrera and Mattle remained at the shop for over 20 years.

Walker was not a newcomer to the saddle business. In 1863, he and and fellow Canadian, Henry Shuham, came to San Francisco to learn the craft of the saddler. They worked for Main & Winchester. Eventually, the two men decided it was time to start their own business. After completing the deal with Martorell, the shop bore the name of Shuham & Walker. They soon added Jose Rodriguez to the staff. Rodriguez had created two new trees that proved favorable to the vaquero—the White River and the Chappo. Rodriguez and Mattle worked together to blend the best qualities of his two trees together with traits Mattle had devised. The blend resulted in the famed Visalia tree.

In 1877 Shuham bought out Walker's interest in the shop. A few days later Walker started a new shop across the street from the old one. The saddles in this shop were marked with the D.E. Walker stamp. By 1879 Shuham decided to sell out to Walker and leave Visalia. Moving back to the old location, Walker resumed business. By buying Shuham's business, Walker not only retained his goodwill, but he also kept his former employees—Martorell, Mattle, and Rodriguez—along with many other skilled craftsmen. As the fame of the saddles grew, so did Walker's need for expansion. He decided to open a second shop in San Francisco. This made it easier to ship the goods since his mail order business was thriving. A San Francisco shop also benefited when vaqueros drove in herds of cattle to Butchertown from far off ranchos. Needing more cash for expansion, Walker took in a business partner in the late 1880s, Mr. Wade. Saddles built in San Francisco during this period were marked "Walker and Wade." The business expanded to include catalogs, handbills, direct mailings, and other methods of advertising.

Vaqueros brought in saddles for repair that were adaptations of those descended from the mission era.

As Walker and Wade grew, so did the need for larger facilities, more employees, and a broader catalog of products. Employees of this period included Dave Anderson, Al Diaz, A. Herrera, Charles Johnson, S. Martranes, and J.A. Samstag. Walker retired in 1887, selling his portion of the business to Edwin Weeks, his nephew. After completing the purchase, Weeks began the process of transferring the business to San Francisco. The old Visalia shop closed its doors for the last time and the Visalia Stock Saddle Company found a new home in San Francisco.

The population growth of California brought about changes to the vast grazing lands of the great ranchos. After 1850, grazing lands were being fenced and the need for open range for cattle was growing. These contributing factors gave birth to California cattlemen who looked elsewhere for locations for great ranches. Cattle were driven north into Oregon and east into Nevada. As the California vaquero created a home for himself in the high desert country, a new horsebacker was created, the buckaroo. Like the cowboy and the vaquero, the buckaroo needed a good saddle.

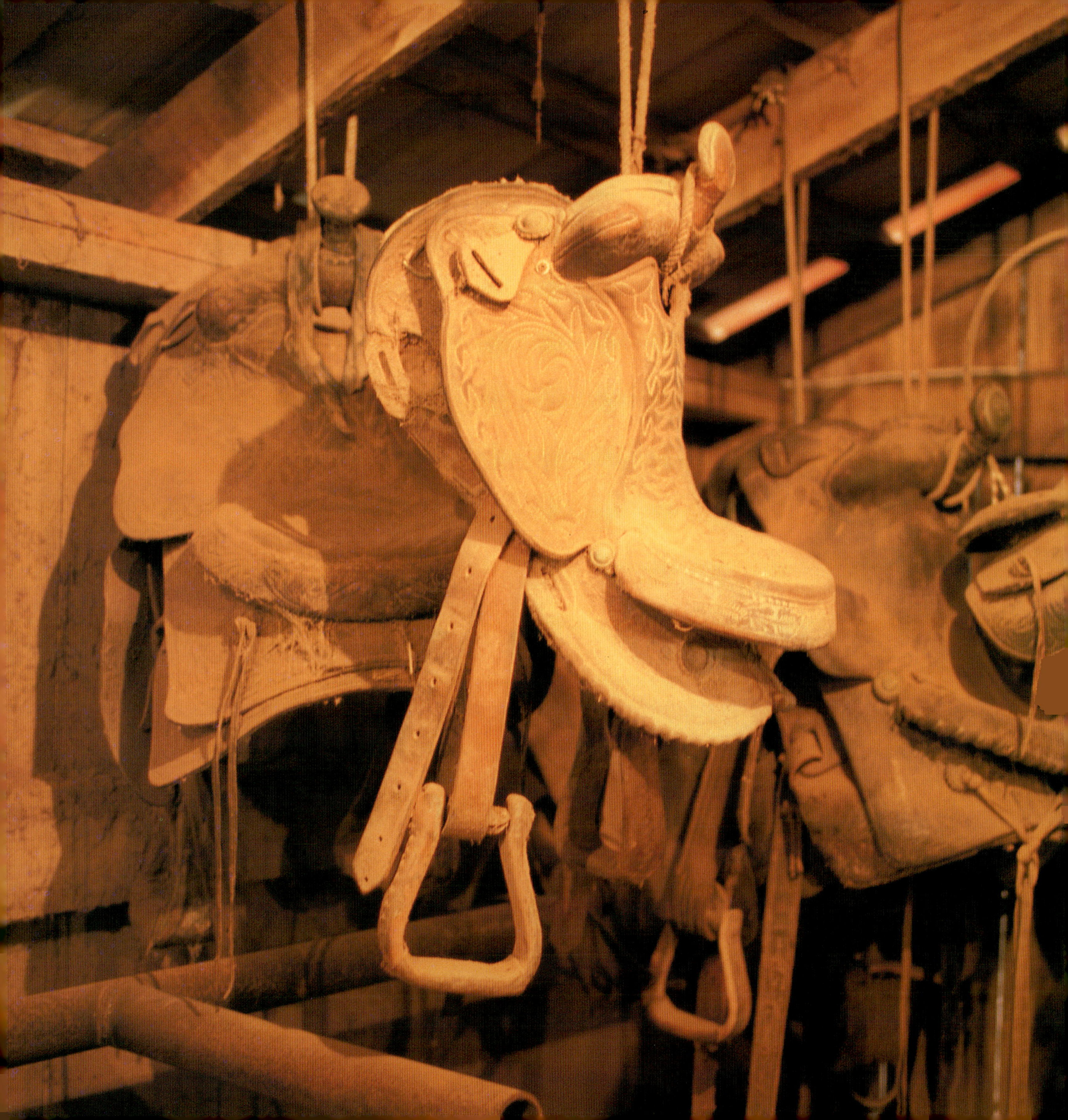

One man with vision in this regard was Guadalupe Garcia of Santa Margarita, California. Like the California cattlemen who were squeezed out of their home ranges, Garcia moved the saddle shop he founded in 1892 in Santa Margarita to Elko, Nevada in 1893. Ever the visionary, Garcia immediately utilized local newspaper advertisements to make the quality of his wares known. A combination of hiring the finest craftsmen as well as extensive marketing made his new business a great success. The climax of his achievements was when he was awarded a gold medal at the 1904 World's Fair Expo in St. Louis, Missouri for creating a stunningly beautiful saddle of leather, gold, silver, and precious gem stones. The Garcia shop closed its doors in Elko in 1938.

Population growth on the West Coast in the 1850s was not limited to California. Portland, Oregon was becoming like San Francisco. It was there that Samuel Sherlock began a small saddlery in 1857. Sherlock had come to the West to ply his trade. The high demand for saddles meant quick expansion for Sherlock's small shop. Joining him in 1874 was his brother-in-law George Lawrence. To serve the remote areas of Oregon, Lawrence hired salesmen and equipped them with catalogs to exhibit his products. Lawrence's aim was to serve the needs of packers and cowboys. Like other saddleries, Lawrence listened to his customers about how to modify the stock saddle. Lawrence is considered the initial designer of the Fremont and the Ellensburg trees.

As the need for more stock saddles and equipment continued to grow, large manufacturers found an eager market for their brand of less personalized service. Main & Winchester were not the only firm operating on a scale far above the small saddlery; Herman H. Heiser of Denver, Colorado, was also doing a booming business. Heiser began modestly in Denver in 1859, marking his product with his triple H logo. Like Main & Winchester, his venture grew at an astounding rate. The shop remained in the Heiser family for 86 years until it was sold to the Denver Drygoods Company. The Keyston Brothers then purchased the Heiser business in 1950.

English saddler Samuel Keyston arrived in New York in 1857 two years before Heiser opened his Denver business. Like so many other immigrants of the day, Keyston keenly felt the call to the West; he moved his family to California in 1868 on a sailing ship. They headed to San Francisco so that Samuel could take advantage of an offer with Main & Winchester. Proficient at his craft, Keyston was the manager of the large saddlery for five years.

Just like other San Francisco saddleries before him, Keyston's business grew quickly. It grew so much that in 1880 the shop offered a full line of saddlery and harness products. That same year, Keyston moved to a Market Street location. The business was extremely successful and continued to grow until it was destroyed in the 1906 earthquake. Even though the quake produced problems for the company, it also created opportunity. Fellow saddler J.C. Johnson and Company soon announced their business was for sale. Keyston seized the opportunity and made the purchase while he continued to grow and diversify. In the 1930s they bought out N. Porter Saddle Company of Phoenix and also had a branch in Fresno, California. In the 1950s Keyston acquired Herman H. Heiser. In the 1960s the company took over the established saddlery of the Lichtenberger-Ferguson Company in Los Angeles. Keyston's current location is in Walnut Creek, California.

Like Keyston, Walker, and Shuham, other men found employment with major saddle houses before opening shops on their own. Al Nolte was employed as a saddler at Main & Winchester prior to working in Walker's San Francisco shop. The time spent in Walker's employ gave Nolte a valuable education in the finer points of saddle making and eight years later he opened his own shop.

By this time, Nolte knew quality workmanship and he knew the clientele of San Francisco's Butchertown very well. The beef packers and the stockyards provided a fresh supply of customers from ranches far outside San Francisco. Although Nolte was an expert craftsman, business and finances were not his forte. For a brief time he partnered with Steve Ybarra, another alumni of D.E. Walker.

Fortunes improved for Nolte when John Olson walked into his shop, Olson decided to order a fancy saddle for one of his show horses from Nolte in 1937 and he walked out as a partner in the shop. In 1939, Nolte sold his remaining half to Olson but stayed on as a saddle maker. Following the death of Al Nolte in 1942, the shop became the Olsen-Nolte Saddle Shop. By 1968, after many ownership exchanges and relocations, consolidation resulted in one store for Olson-Nolte in San Carlos.

Like California, Texas, Montana, Wyoming, and Colorado, Oregon established its own style of saddles. William Hamley was the son of an English

YESTERDAY'S SADDLES, *Gray Ranch, Vinton, Louisiana*

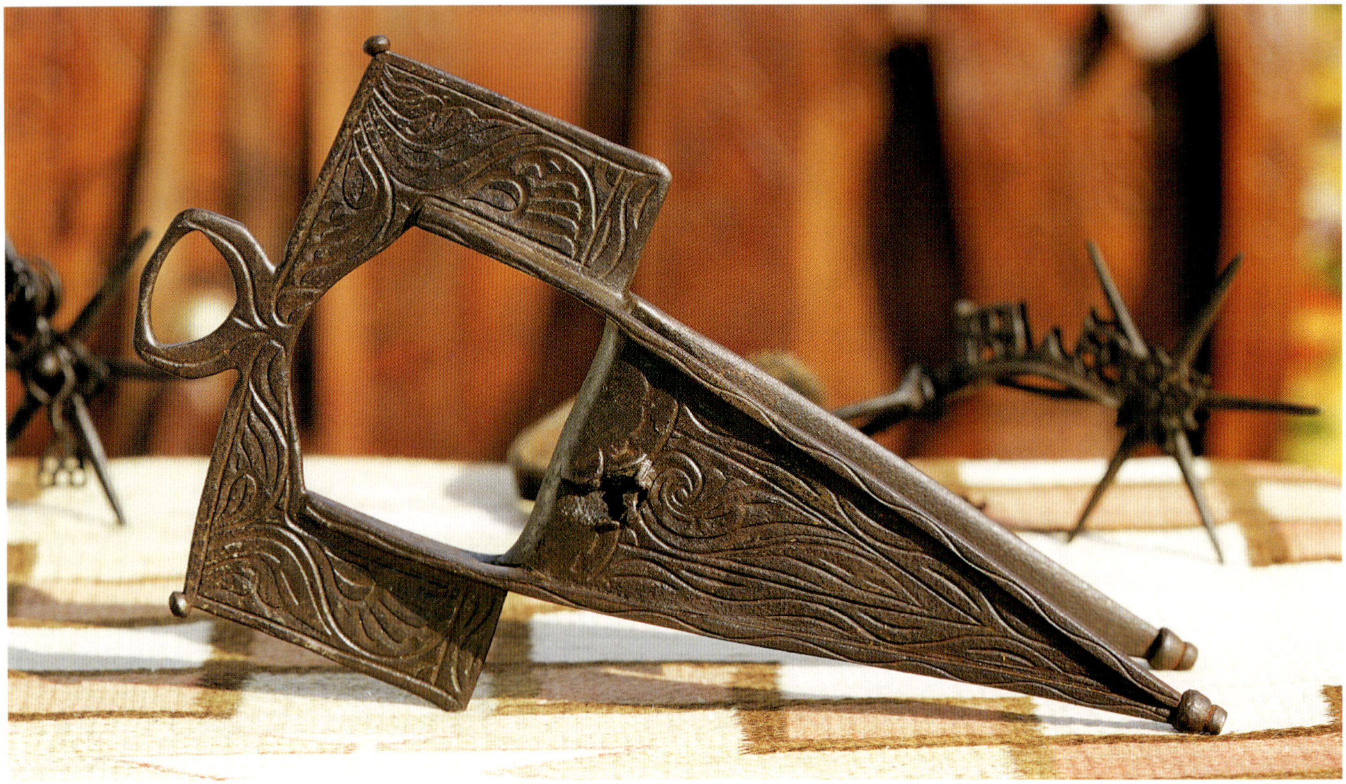

MEXICAN CROSS STIRRUP OR "ESTRIBO DE CRUZ," *Danny Neill Collection*

AS FAR BACK AS THE 12TH CENTURY, *Arab horseman were using an iron stirrup similar to the cross stirrup used in Mexico. When the Moors conquered Spain, they brought the Arab horse, spurs, bits, and cross stirrups with them. After the Moors were driven out of Spain, the cross stirrup was used less and less, eventually ending up in junk markets. Some were purchased for export to Mexico at a time when everything there had to be shipped in, particularly iron. These imported antique stirrups found their way into usage once more and were viewed as stylish by certain kinds of horsemen who had copies locally made, giving rise to the "estribo de cruz." No one knows exactly when the cross stirrups first arrived in Mexico, however many paintings from the 1700s depict them. Metal workers made them even larger and fancier with filigreed animals and flowers, some inlaid with silver. It has been said that some people made fun of the bishop of Mexico, comparing his miter hat to a cross stirrup. The bishop decided that it was not proper to have stirrups that were made in this shape, so he ordered soldiers to cut off the bottoms of all the cross stirrups. The ones that survived were hidden from the bishop and they are very rare and valuable. Very few examples of these hand-forged works of art still exist.* *(courtesy of Danny Neill)*

leather worker. He and his sons John and Henry worked in Ripon, Wisconsin from 1860 to 1880. The boys set out on their own in 1883, dreaming of owning a prosperous saddle shop. The first stop on their journey was in the town of Ashton, South Dakota. They arrived with $10 cash between them and a line of credit for $500. Yet their timing was not ideal for starting a new business. A great drought devastated the country in 1890, drying up the cash flow of their clients as well as the countryside. The brothers pulled up stakes and moved west to Kendrick, Idaho.

By 1891, the Hamleys' business was off to a good start. The strong beginning was snuffed out when a fire destroyed a good portion of the town along with their shop in 1892. Once again, the brothers started over, and once again luck was not on their side. Henry died in 1894 and the Kendrick shop fell victim to fire once again in 1904. John picked up the pieces of his charred business and moved to Pendleton, Oregon. His new enterprise opened its doors on June 3, 1905. By 1909 John's sons Lester H. and John M. joined their father in the family trade.

By 1915 riders were doing all they could to win growing prize money in bucking competitions. Saddles used at the time were not standardized. To gain an advantage, some riders used slick forks; others used a swell fork, and some put on bucking rolls. The popularity and practicality of the swell fork made a saddle of this type the one that most contestants sought out. The problem was that some saddlers and contestants alike were taking the design to the extreme. A freak fork saddle was emerging. The forks extended out in and bent back in grotesque shapes that actually worked to hold a rider in the saddle seat. There were several problems with the freak fork saddles. First, not all riders could be judged fairly due to vastly different saddle shapes, especially when the vise-like saddle was used. Danger to the rider was another consideration. If a horse fell over backwards or rolled over, often the rider was trapped and totally unable to free himself. There were even recordings of riders who were knocked out while in the saddle and were ultimately killed by the beating they took.

Committees from three major Northwest rodeos met with the saddlers to try to put together a uniform saddle for rodeo contestants. Committees from Cheyenne Frontier Days, Boise Rodeo, Pendleton Round-Up, and Walla Walla Frontier Days contacted Hamley with their problem. Keeping with family motto, Hamley listened closely to what the committee had to say. The result was the Hamley Association Saddle. The saddle was and is built on a modified Ellensburg tree. A flank cinch replaced the standard back cinch and it sat further back on the horse's flank to encourage bucking. The Association tree differs with the Ellensburg in that it is not cut out so much at the base of the swell; the swell is more rounded at the base.

Following that initial meeting, Hamley made six of these saddles. The saddle was dubbed the committee saddle, and it was the only saddle to be used in bucking contests at those four rodeos. In the late 1920s, the Rodeo Association of America was formed. The new organization decided the official saddle to be used in their sanctioned events would be the committee saddle. The name was then changed to the Association Saddle. Orders began to flood Hamley from rodeo committees, contestants, and stock contractors alike. Fort Worth, Salinas, New York, Ellensburg, Muskogee Alliance, and North Platte were just a few of the committees ordering the Association Saddle.

Like California, Texas, Montana, Wyoming, and Colorado, Oregon established its own style of saddles.

No longer are the needs of working cowboy the only standard for saddle design. Now there are saddles designed for the trail rider, the endurance rider, the rodeo contestant, the team roper, the barrel racer, the reiner, the cutter, and others. All are images of the saddle from the days when men trained cows.

If you happen upon a saddle lying in some forgotten corner, covered in dust, take a good long look at it. If you are willing to take a few minutes of your time, it will tell you a story about itself. Does its horn show the marks of long ago dallys? Do the fenders and the side jockeys show wear from a rider's body? Are there spur tracks in the seat left from a rider making a last desperate grab at security before he gets dusted? Is its tree broken from a disastrous wreck? Are the saddle strings mangled from a long-dead colt using it as a teething ring? The story is there if you are willing to take a minute or two to think about it.

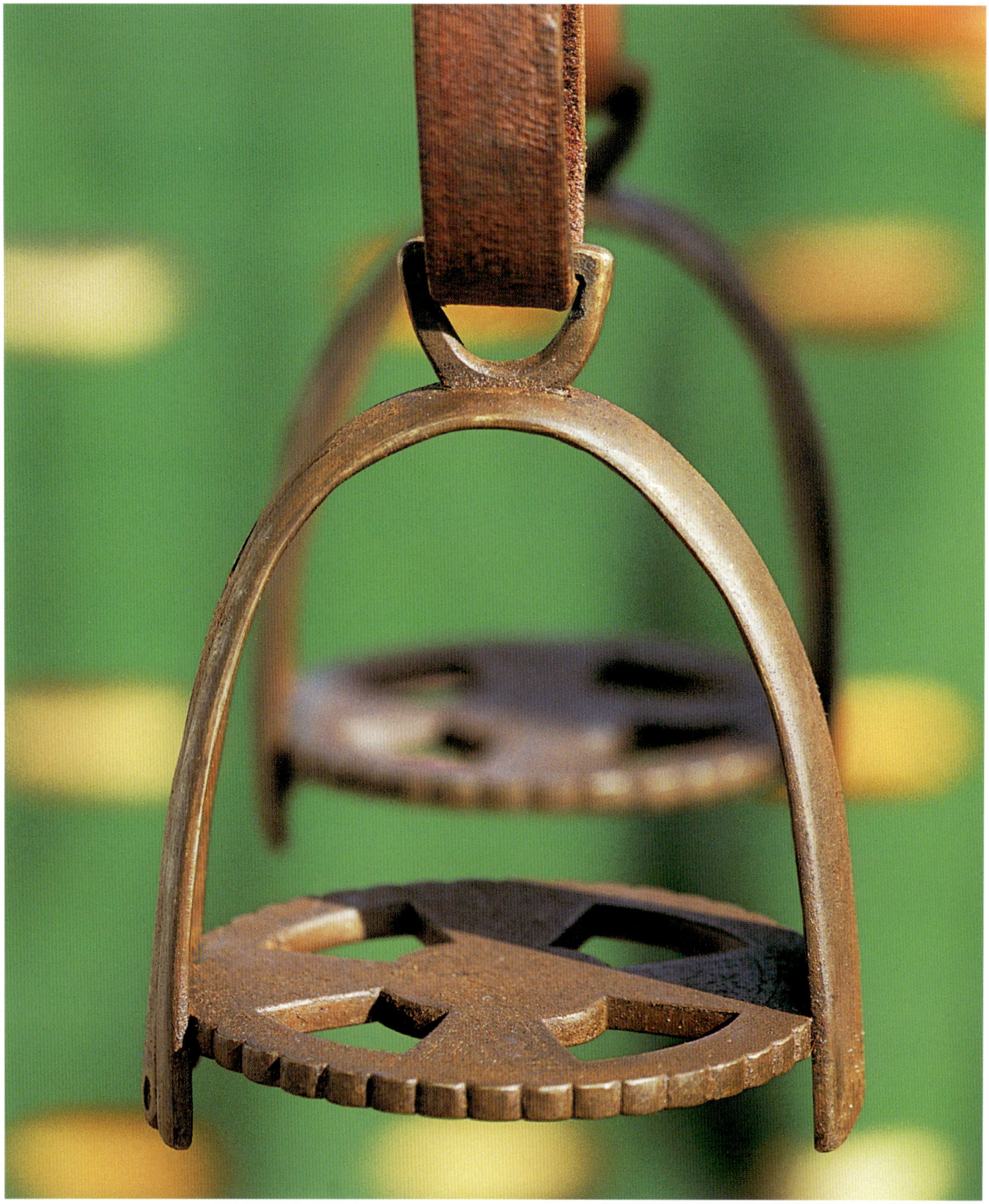

1700s Mexican stirrups, *Neill Collection*

Very rare late 1700s Mexican haciendado saddle—*this style was used by very wealthy haciendados in Texas, New Mexico, and California, Neill Collection*

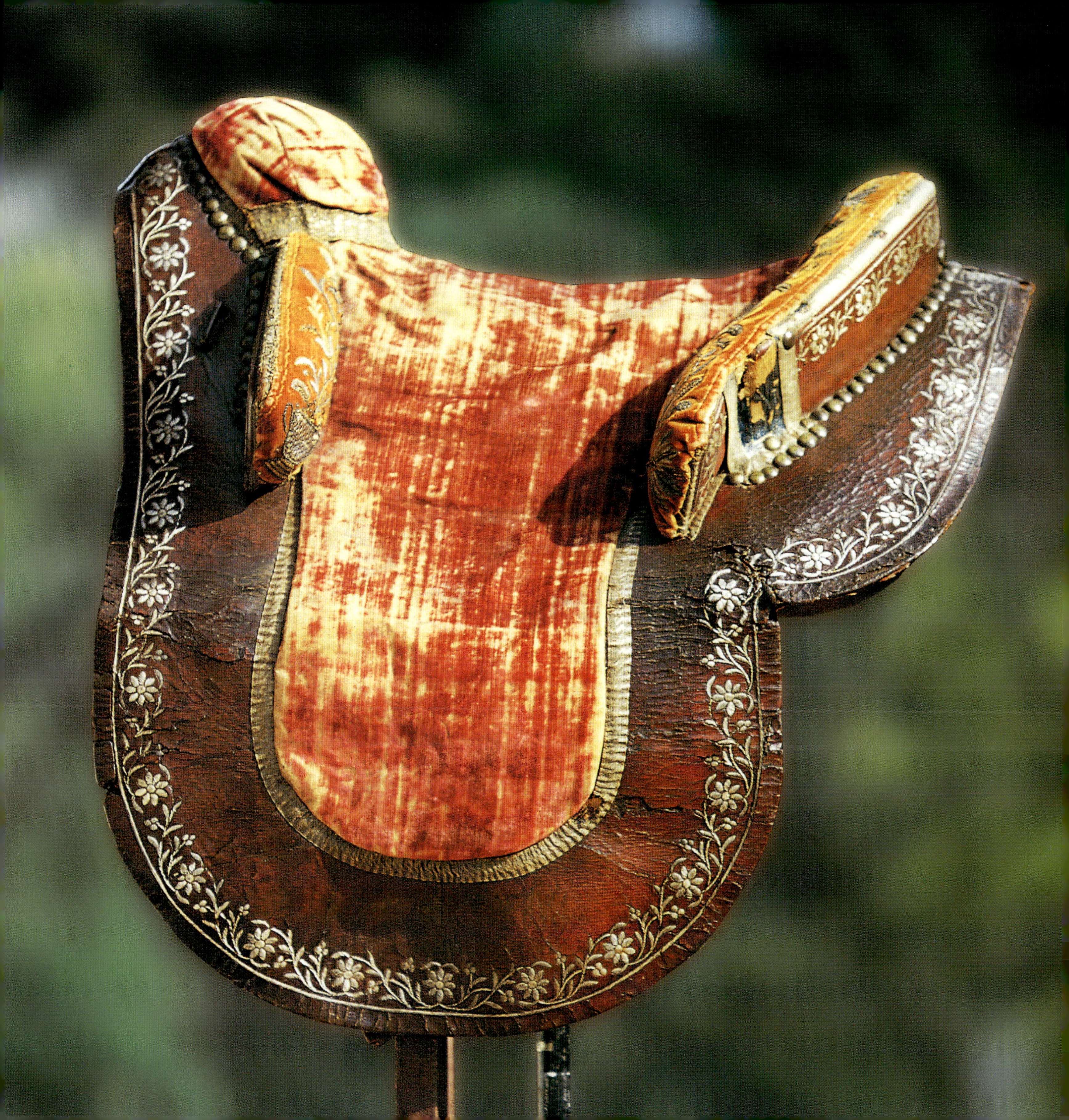

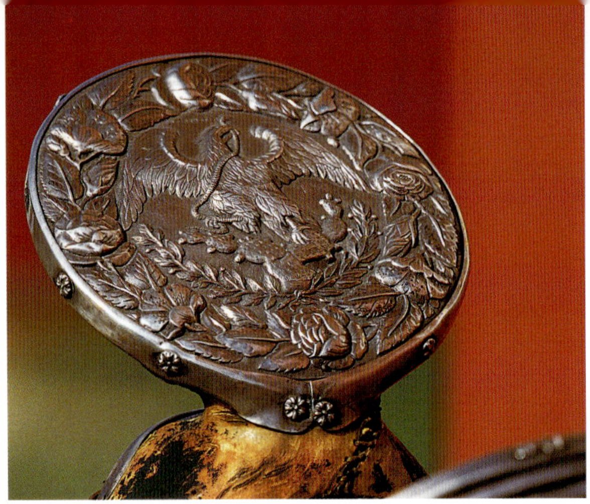

1870s Mexican saddle *with large silver engraved horn, silver cantle binding and silver covered stirrups, jaguar skin seat and black mochila, King Saddlery Museum, Sheridan, Wyoming*

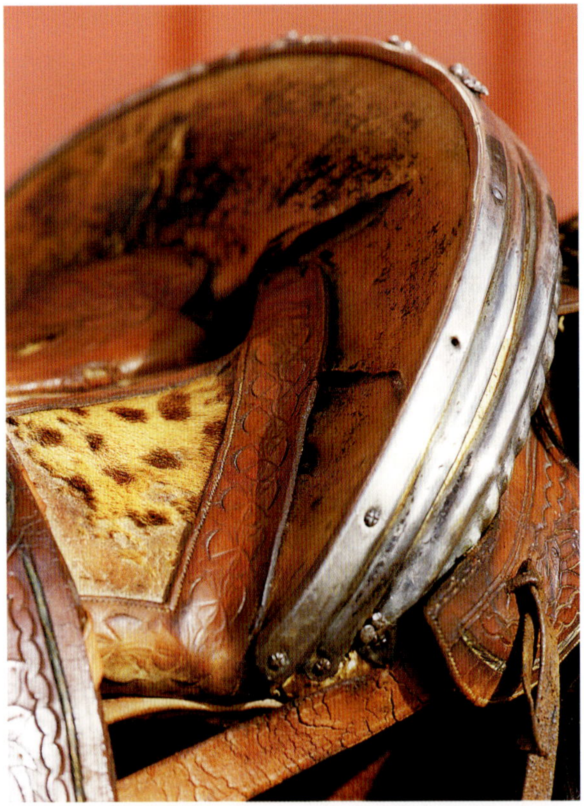

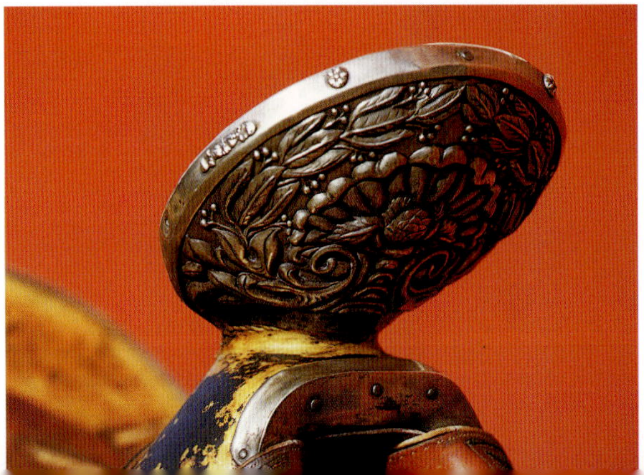

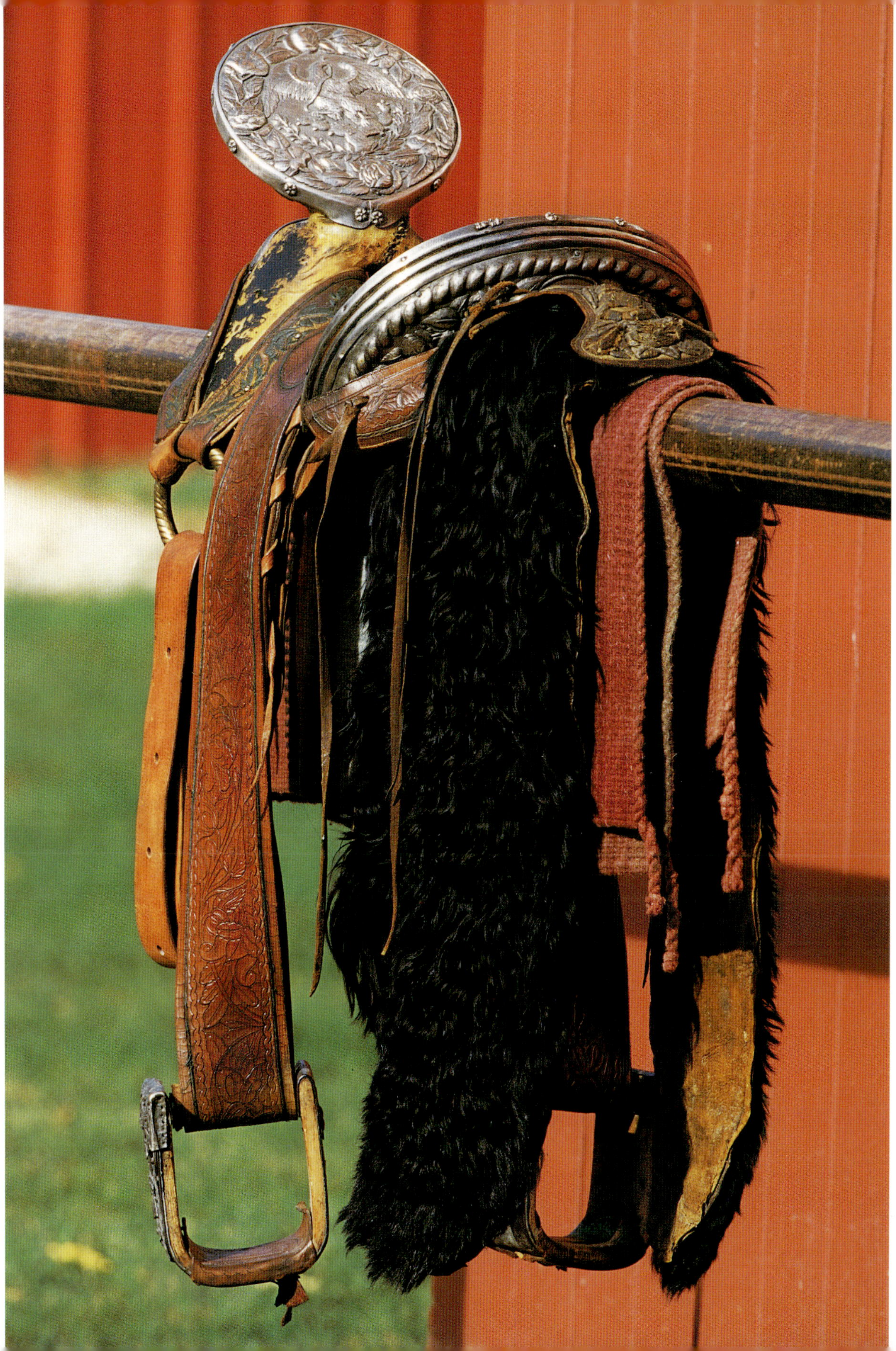

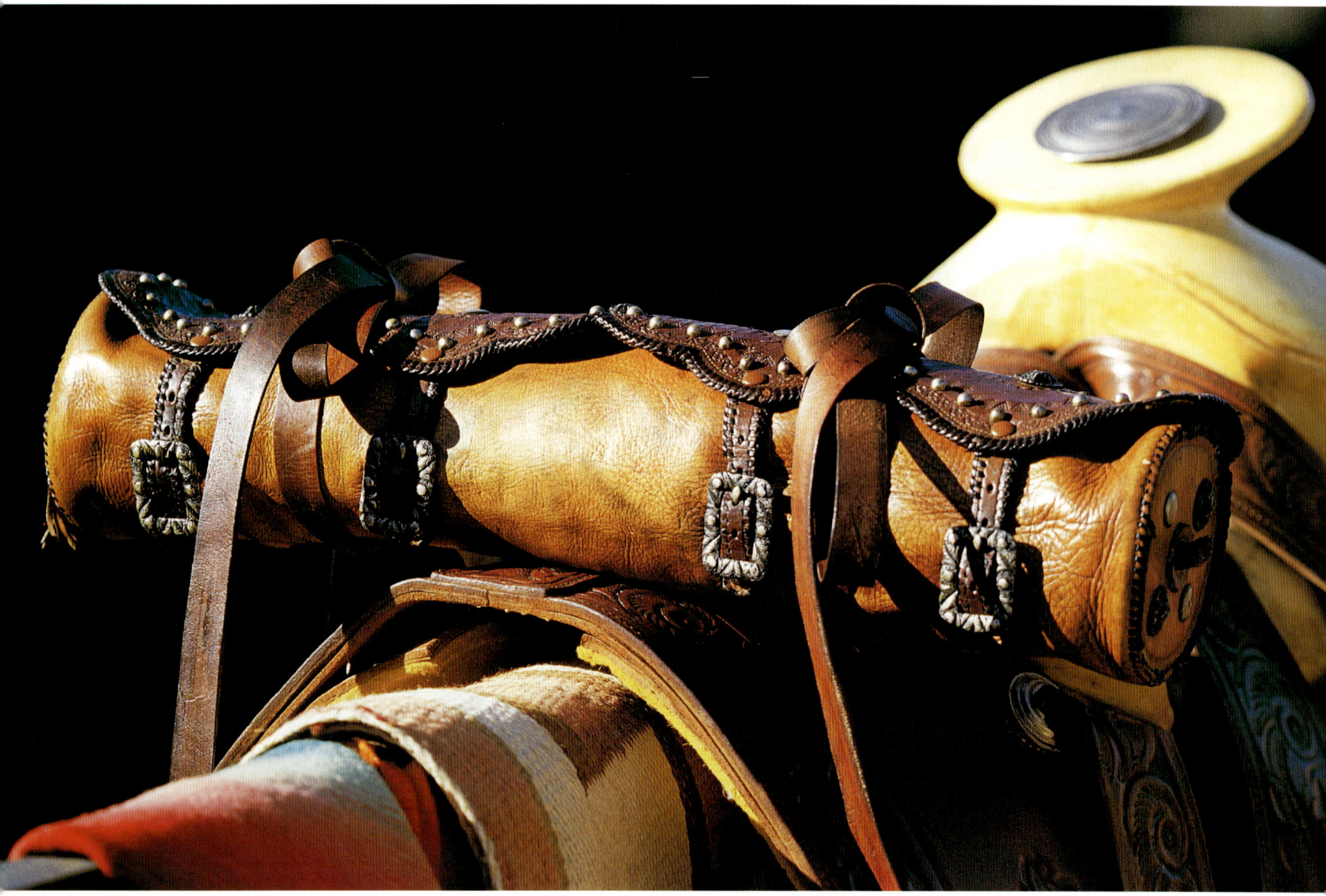

Rare, one of a kind Saltillo case *from old Mexico, Neill Collection*

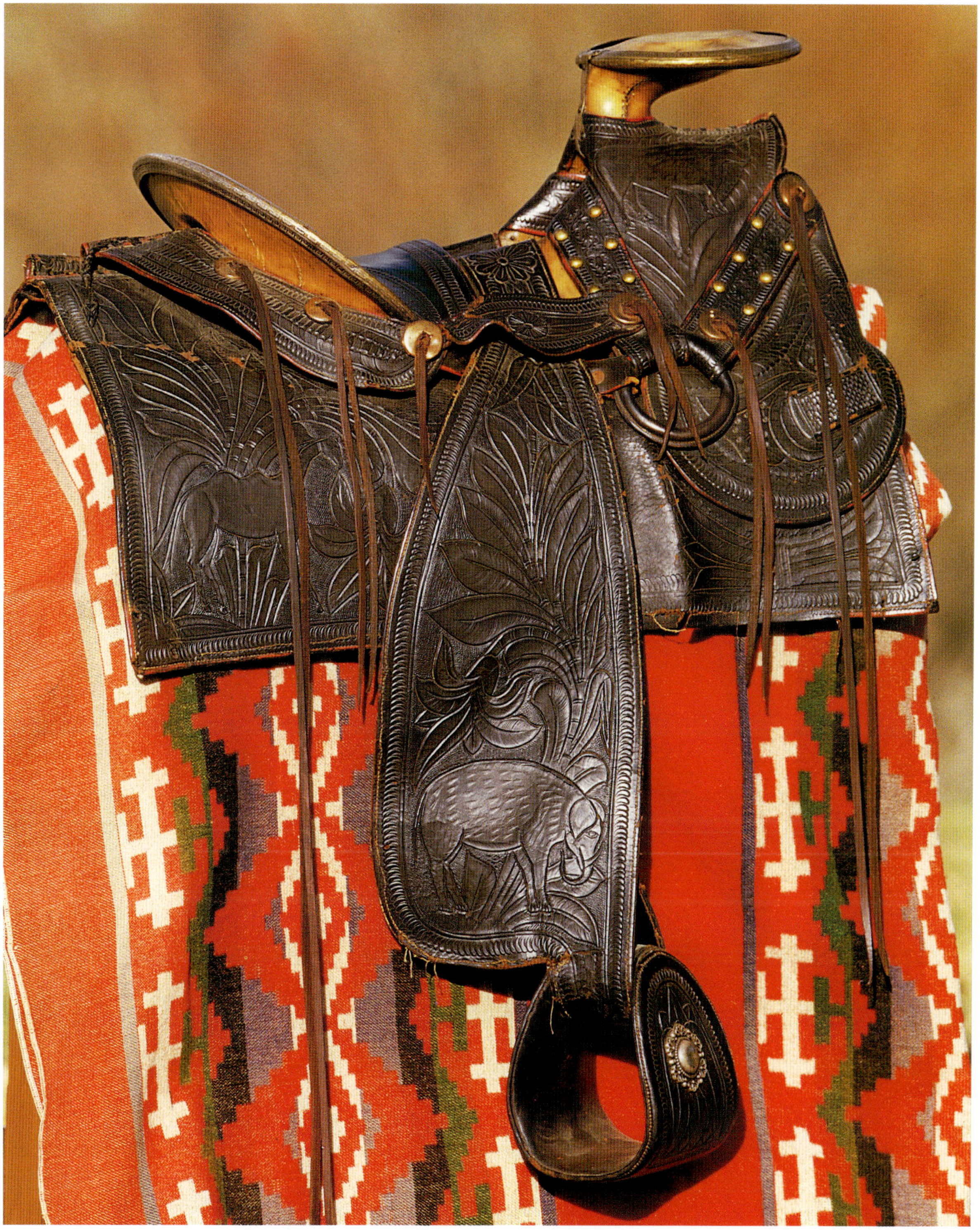

1860 Hope saddle with elephant and giraffe carvings, *most likely owned by a wealthy rancher who spent time in Africa, Stoecklein Collection*

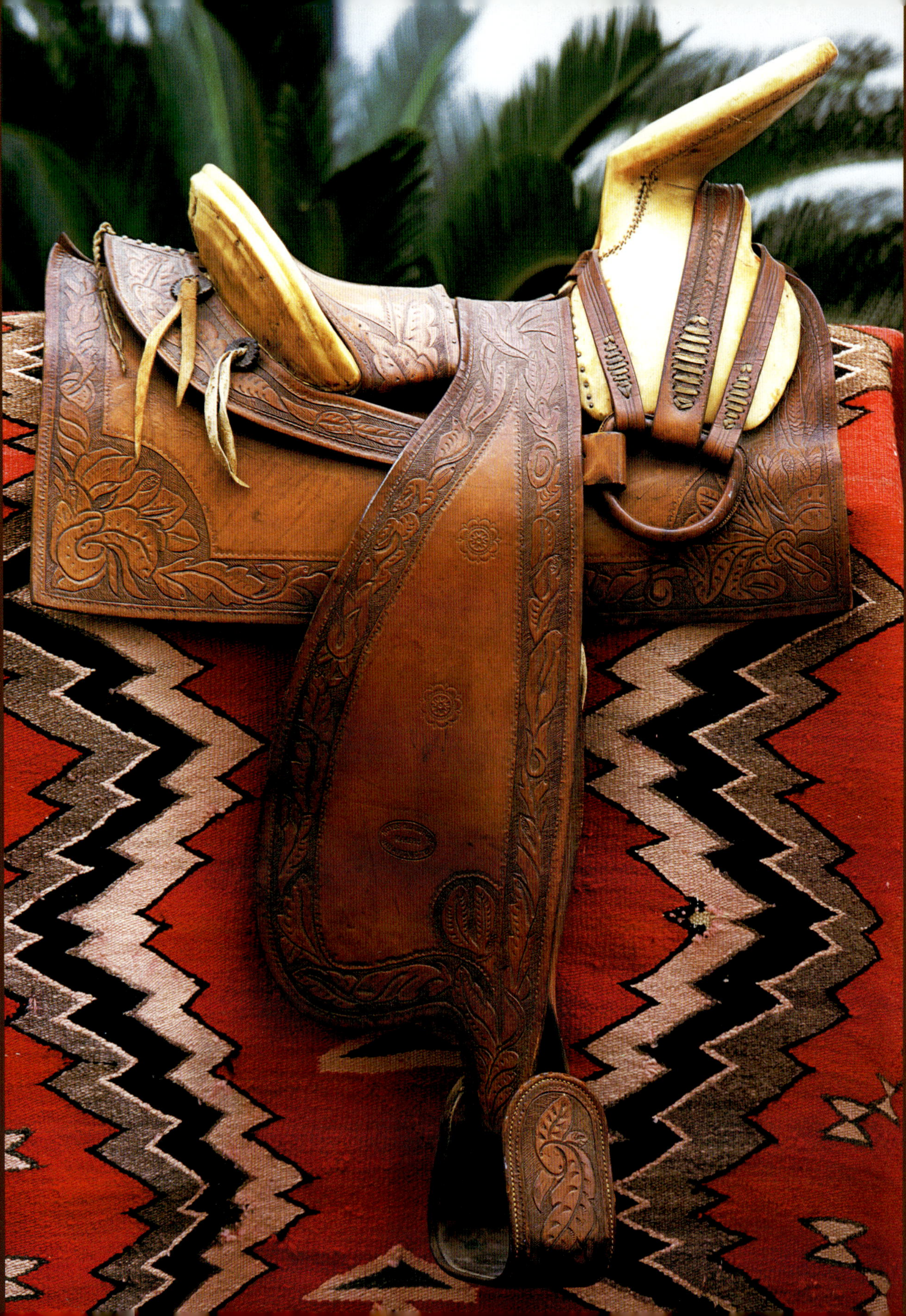

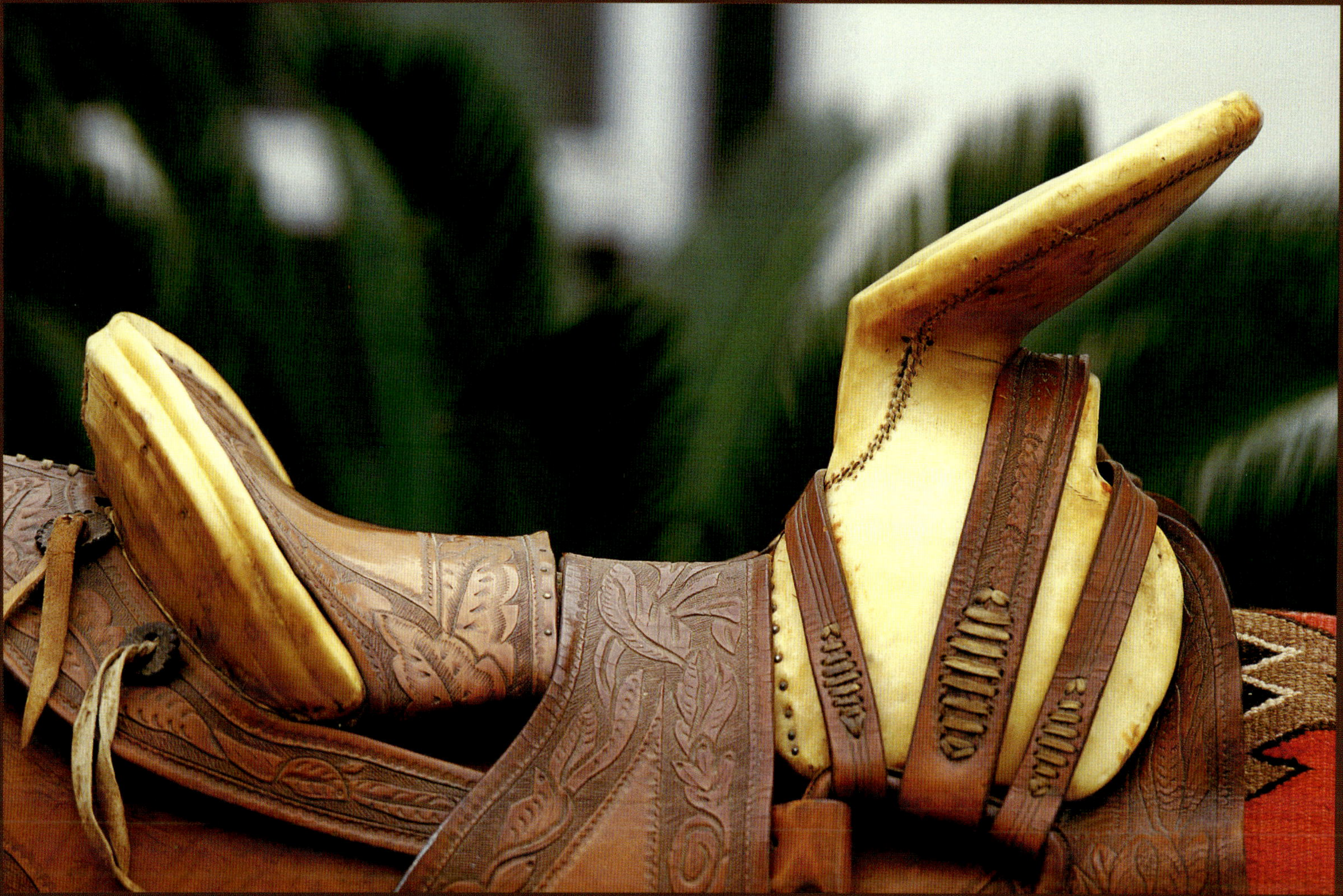

Very early Texas saddle *circa 1880s made by Noyes and Langholz, San Antonio, Texas, Bruce Bartlett Collection*

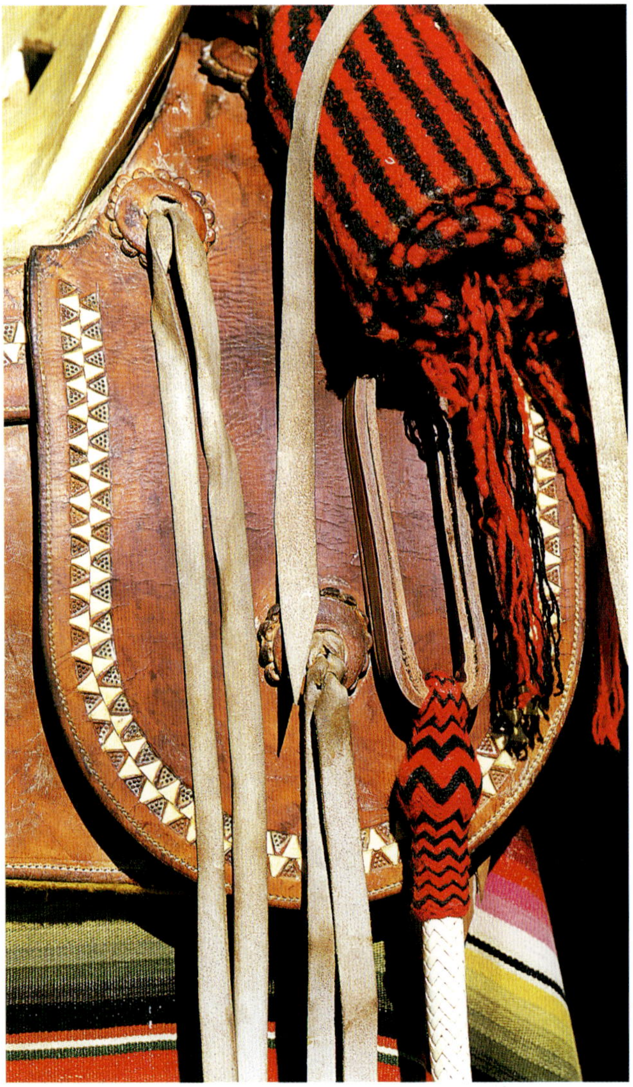

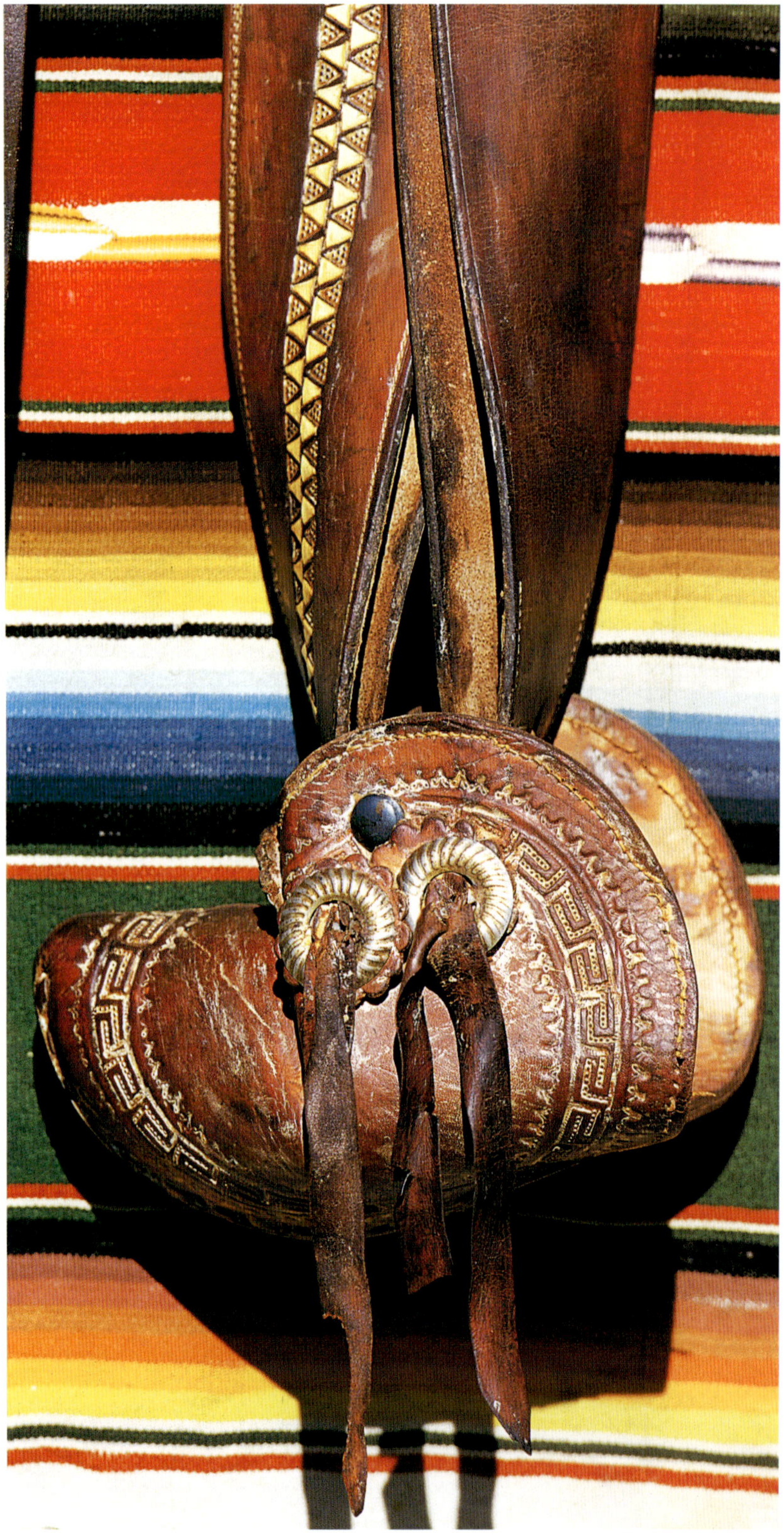

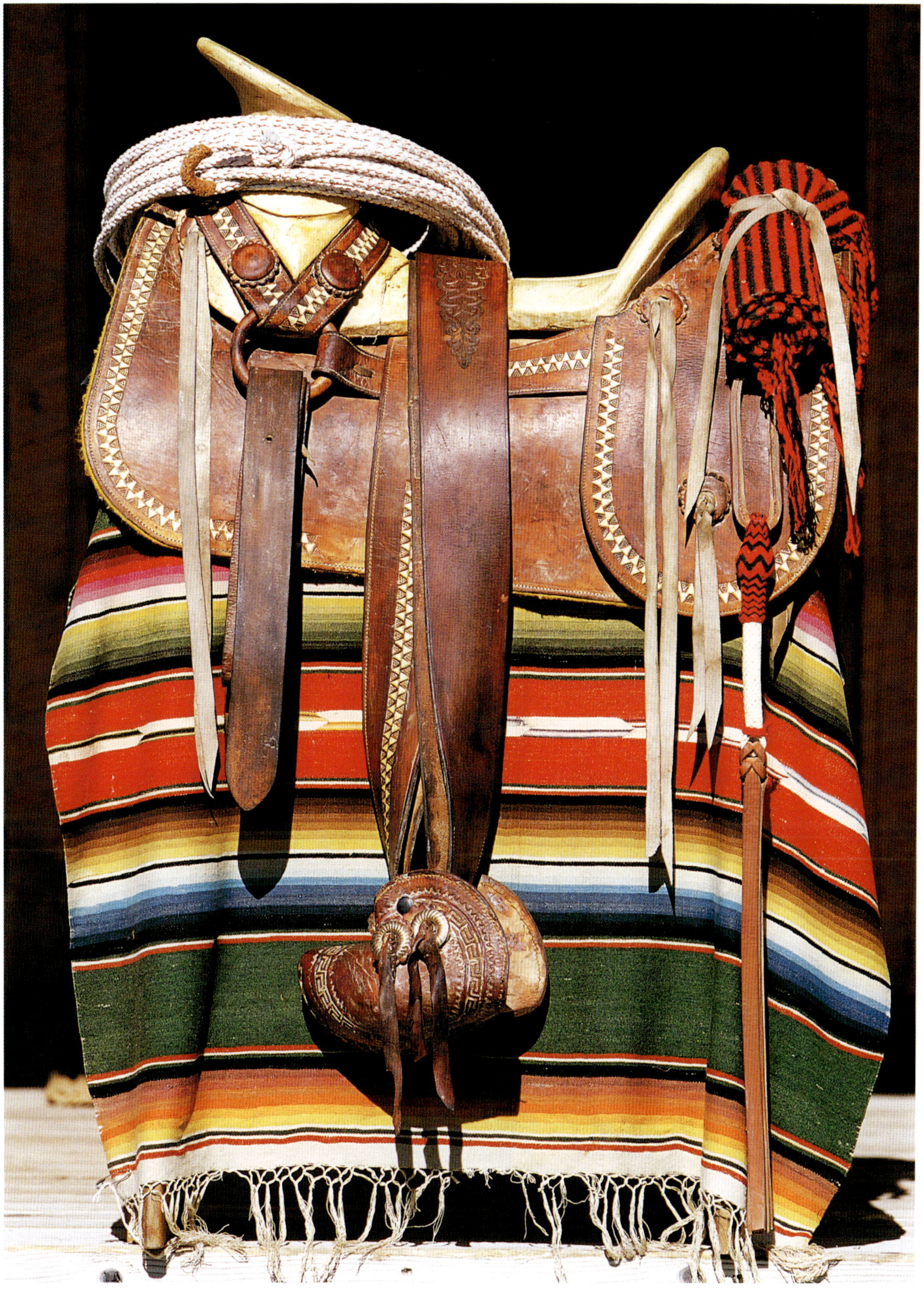

TODAY'S MEXICAN CHARRO SADDLE, *Stoecklein Collection*

Trail Driver Saddles

Today it is very rare to find *a saddle that actually went up the trail with the Texas cowboys. These saddles were ridden hard and spent their entire lives out in the elements. The trail drives started around the end of the Civil War in 1865 and lasted well into the 1890s. The cowboys rode on whatever they could find, most often in the beginning they rode Civil War saddles and old plantation saddles or Mexican saddles. As the trail drives moved along, saddle makers opened up shops at the trailheads and at the end of the trails in Colorado, Kansas, and Miles City, Montana. So in later years, trail drivers had saddles from all over the West. There were catalogs sent out by saddle shops and cowboys ordered them that way. Only the foremen or the herd owners could afford the custom saddles. These saddles had to be tough like their owners. They slept under the stars and worked in the rain, snow, and dust. There was not much care given to the saddles, horses, or men—they all had to survive on their own.*

Mother Hubbard saddle,
circa 1870s, Stoecklein Collection

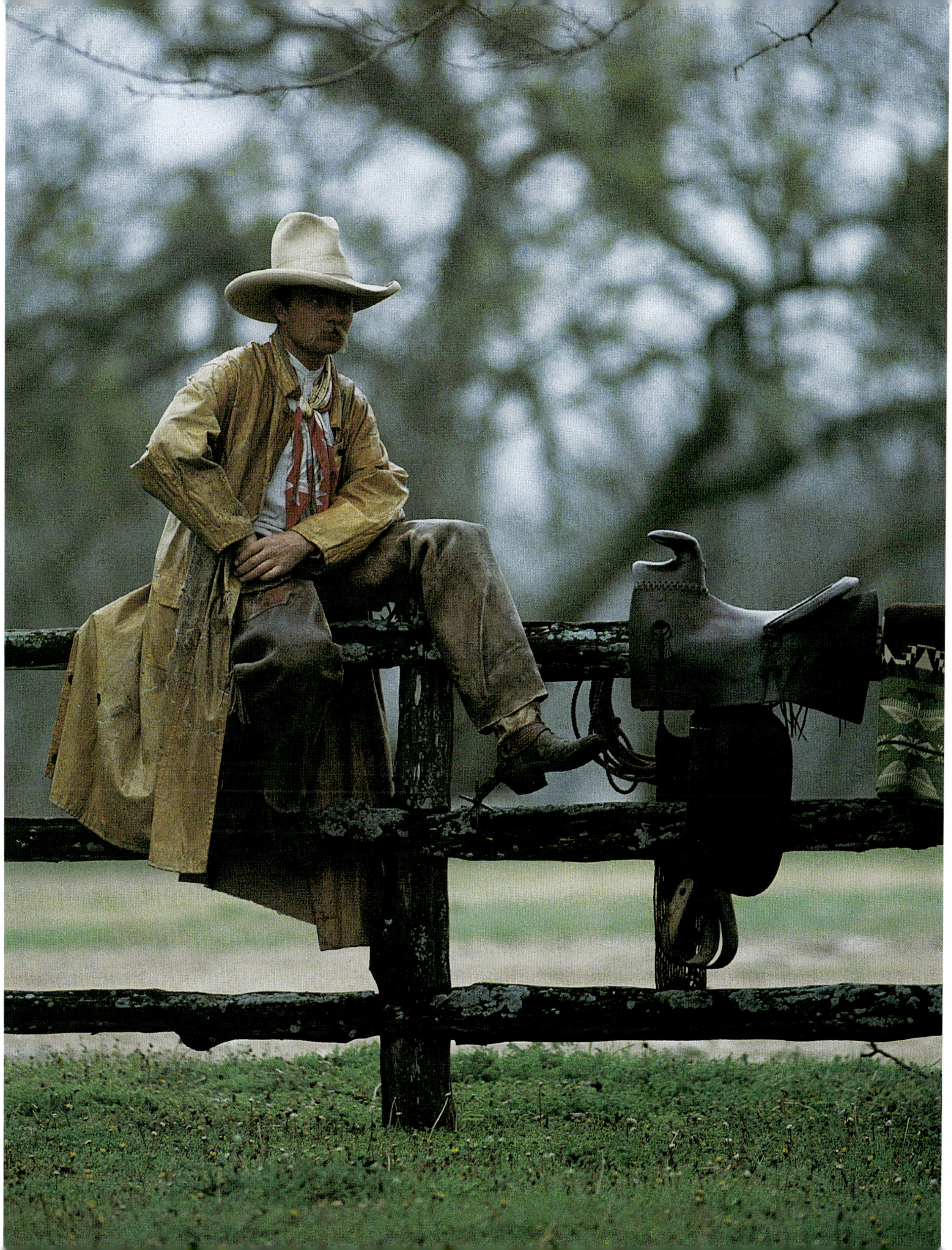

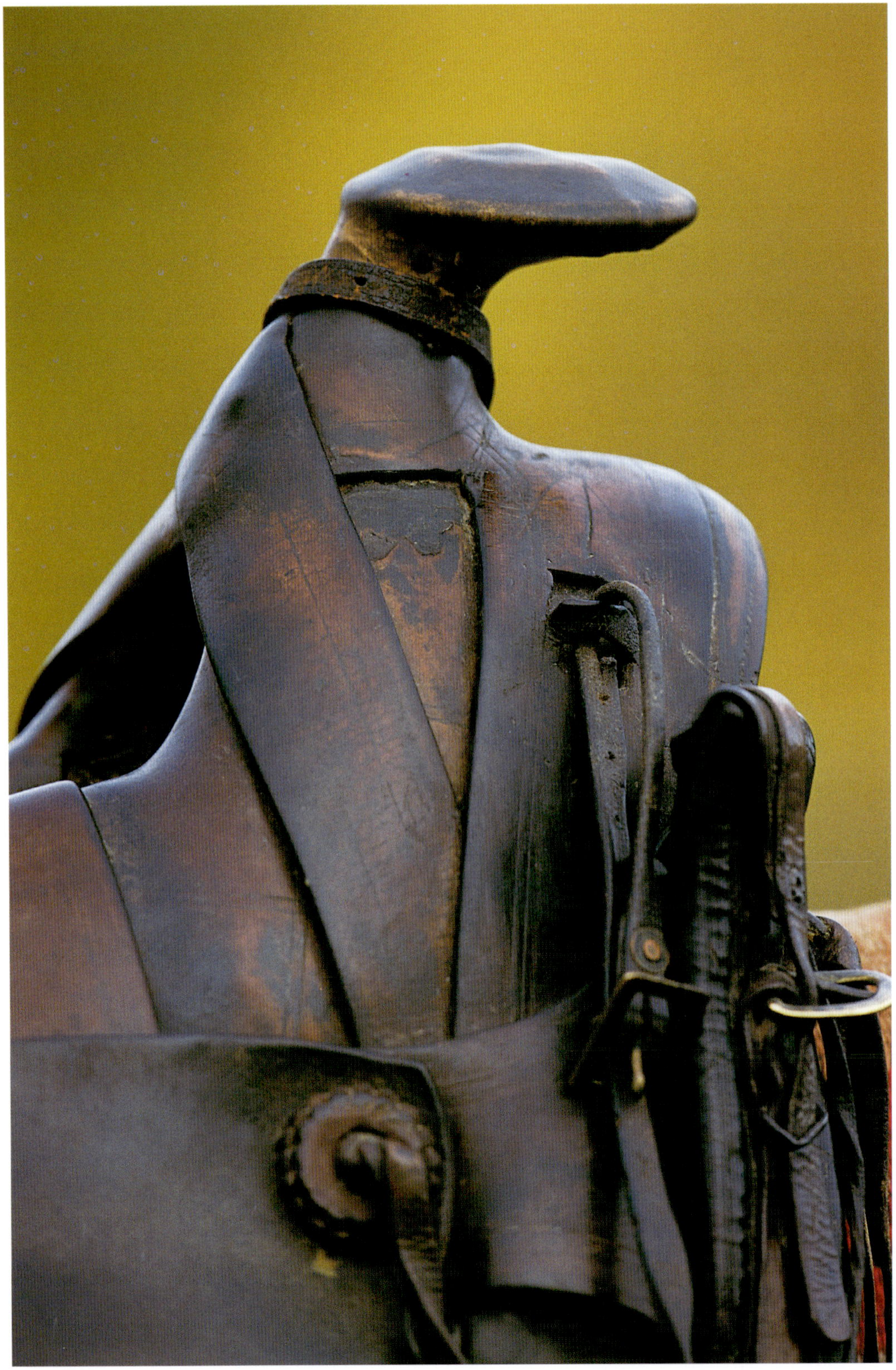

SADDLE OWNED BY DON KING'S GRANDFATHER, GORDON V. FITZHUGH, *made by Collins and Morrison, Omaha, Nebraska, 1860s, King Saddlery Museum, Sheridan, Wyoming*

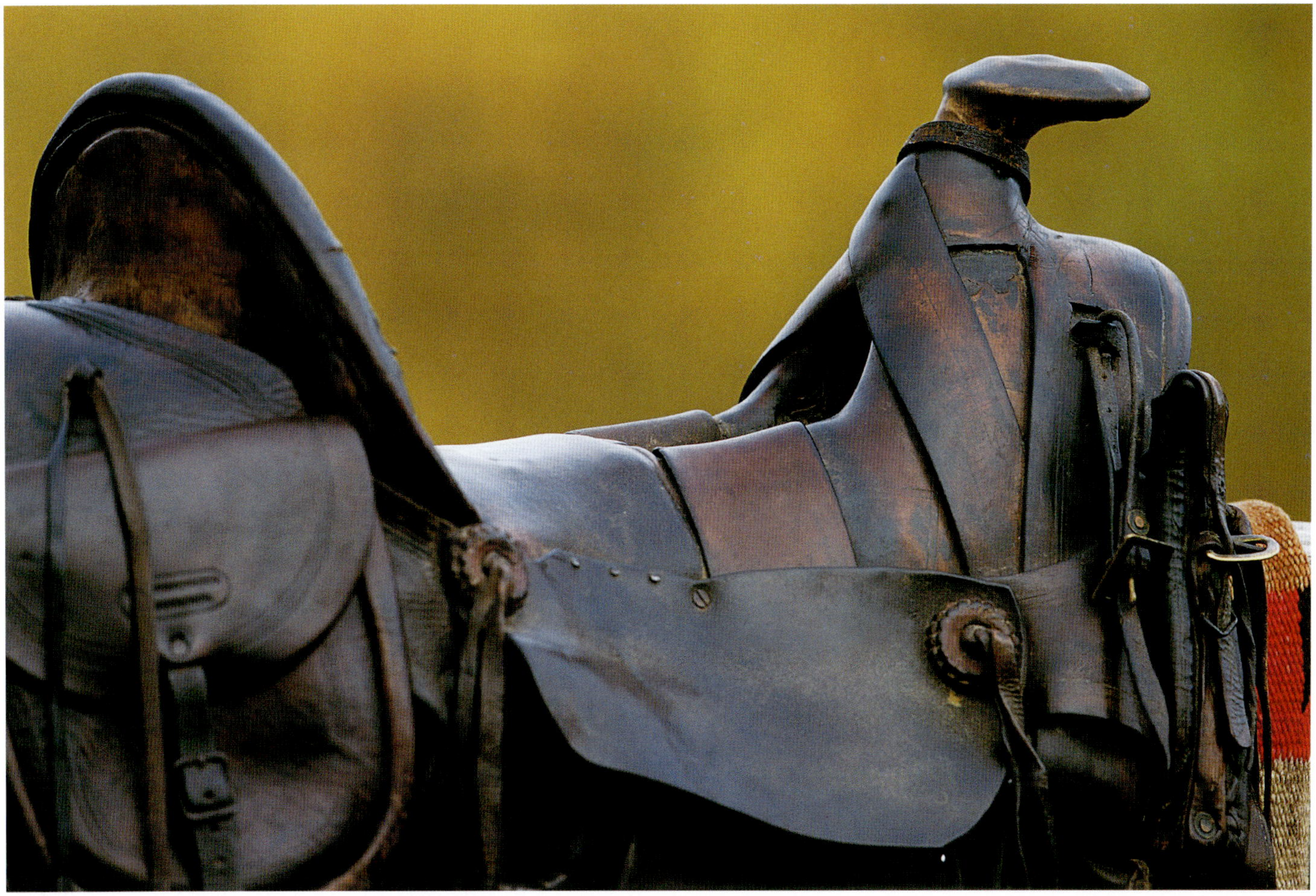

Gordon Fitzhugh rode this saddle *up the trail. He was born in California; his father John ventured west on the Oregon Trail during the 1849 gold rush. Gordon later moved to Texas with his brother. From there they made eight trail drives to Colorado and Wyoming as early as 1876. The last drive was to the Kendrick Ranch near Sheridan, Wyoming. Gordon then became foreman for the Guthrie Brothers at the Colt Track Ranch near Douglas, Wyoming. The Guthrie family ran 50,000 head in the time of no fences. Gordon later homesteaded on Wagon Hound Creek around 1880. The original homestead on the Oregon Trail is still run by the Fitzhughs outside of Douglas, Wyoming.*

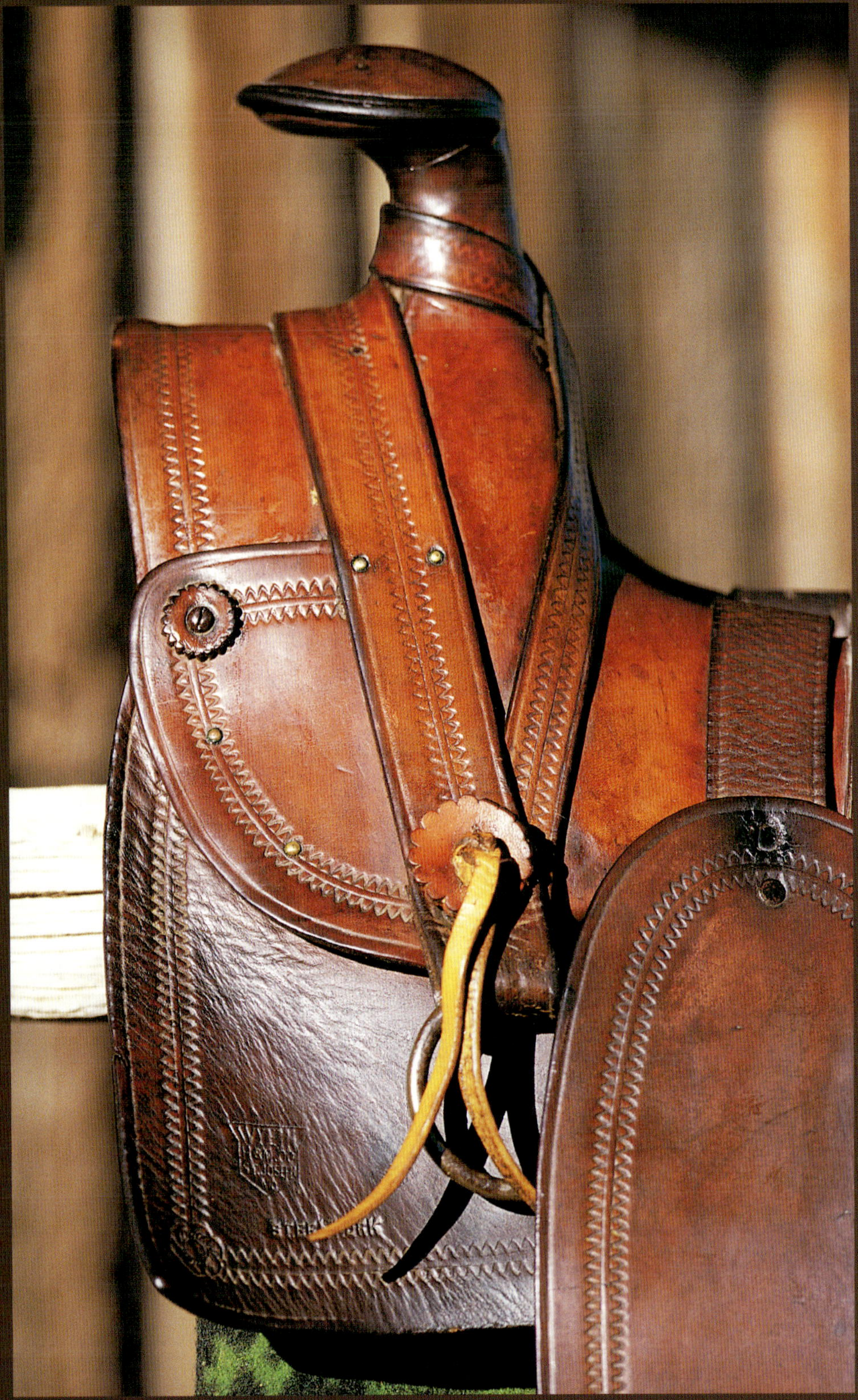

H & M Wyeth saddle *with Sam Stagg rigging, St. Joseph, Missouri, Stoecklein Collection*

Great Plains saddle *built by A.J. Davidson of Helena, Montana Territory in 1885, Charlie Smith Collection*

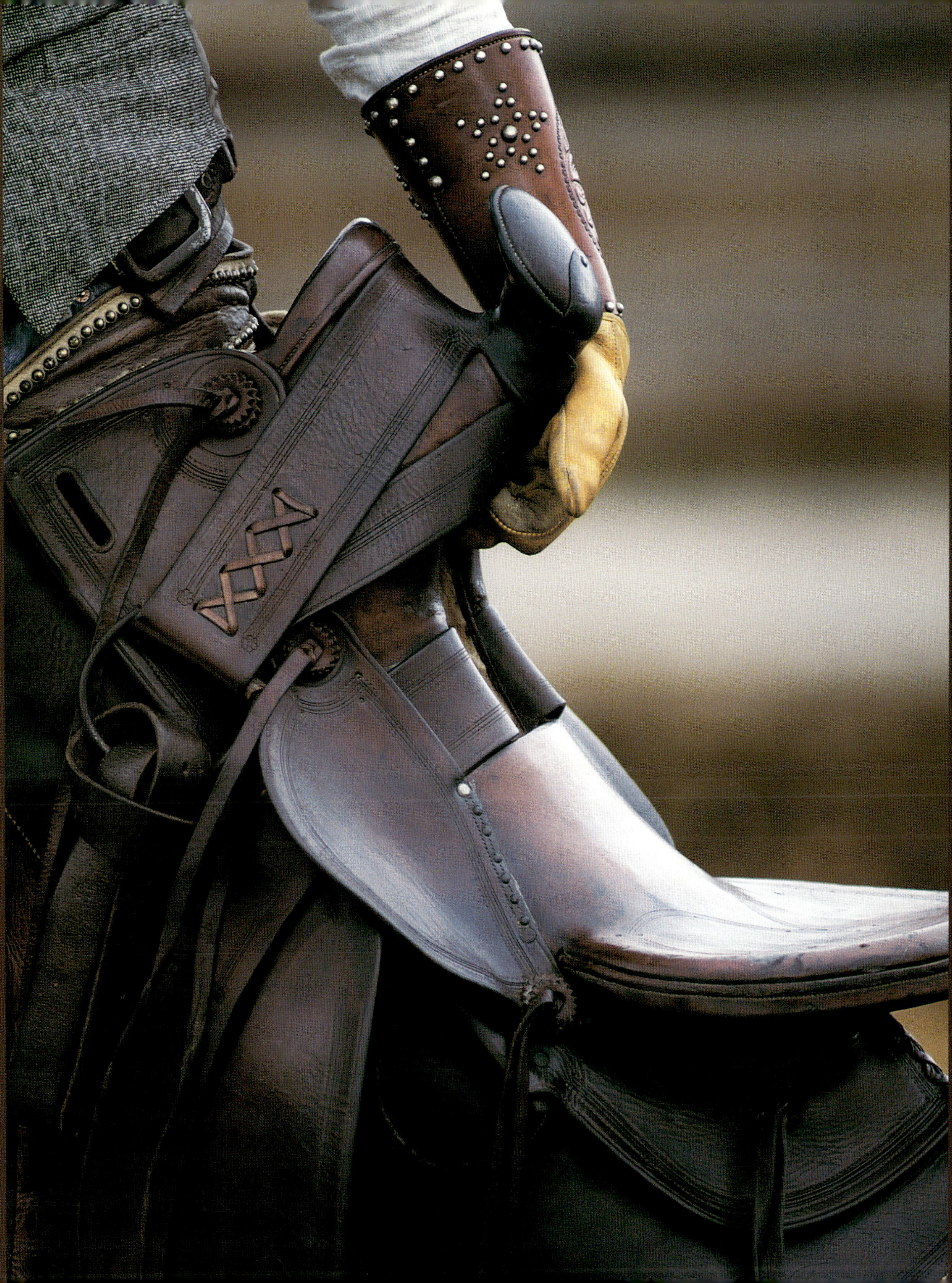

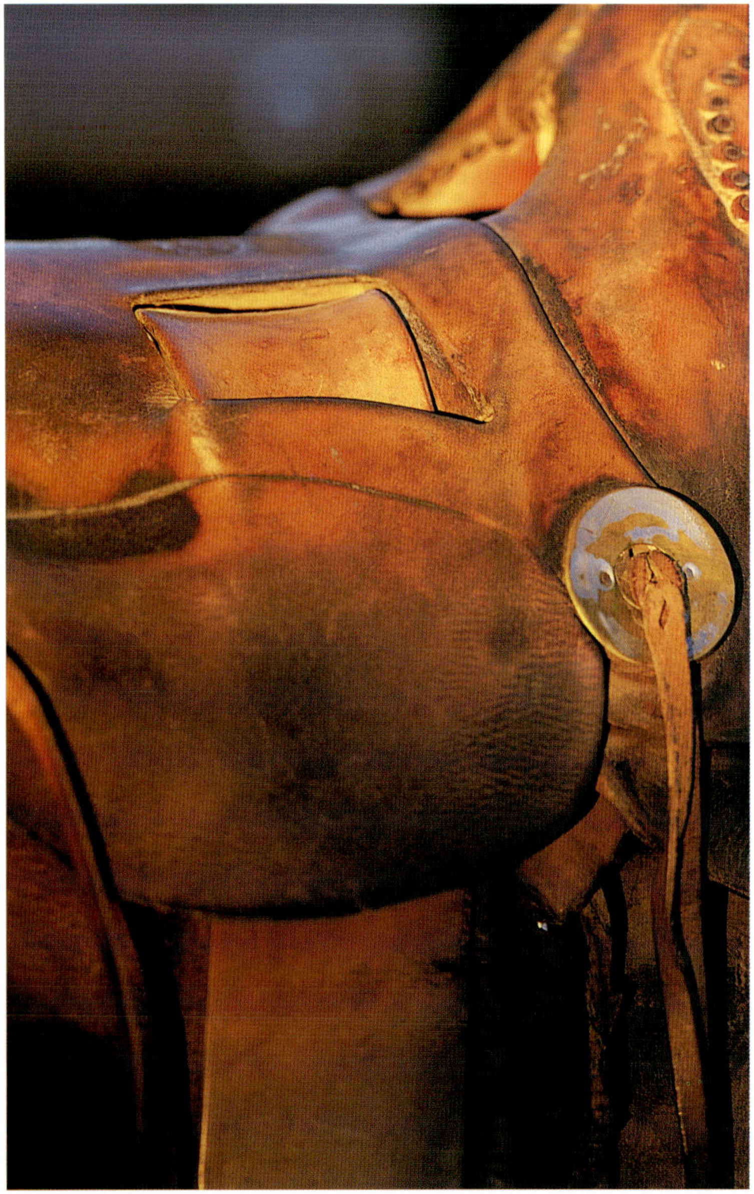

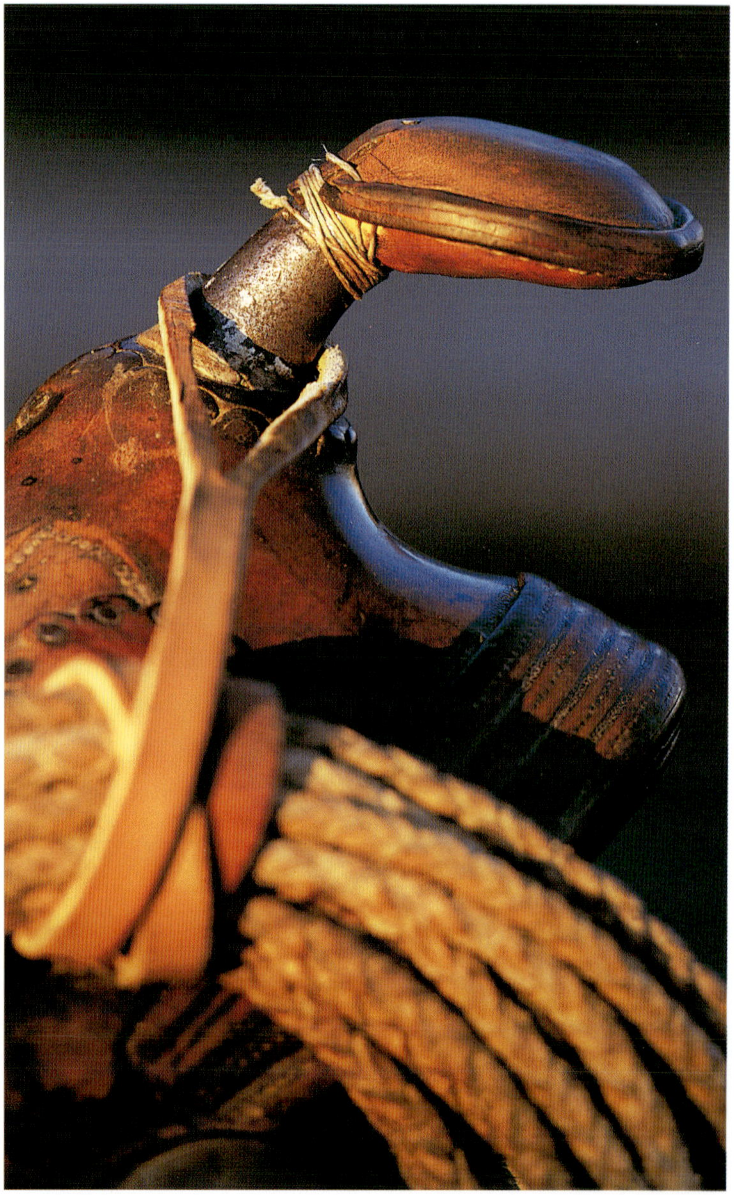

Joseph Sullivan Montana Territorial saddle from Fort Benton, Montana, *cantle most likely carved by a Blackfoot Indian from northern Montana, Stoecklein Collection*

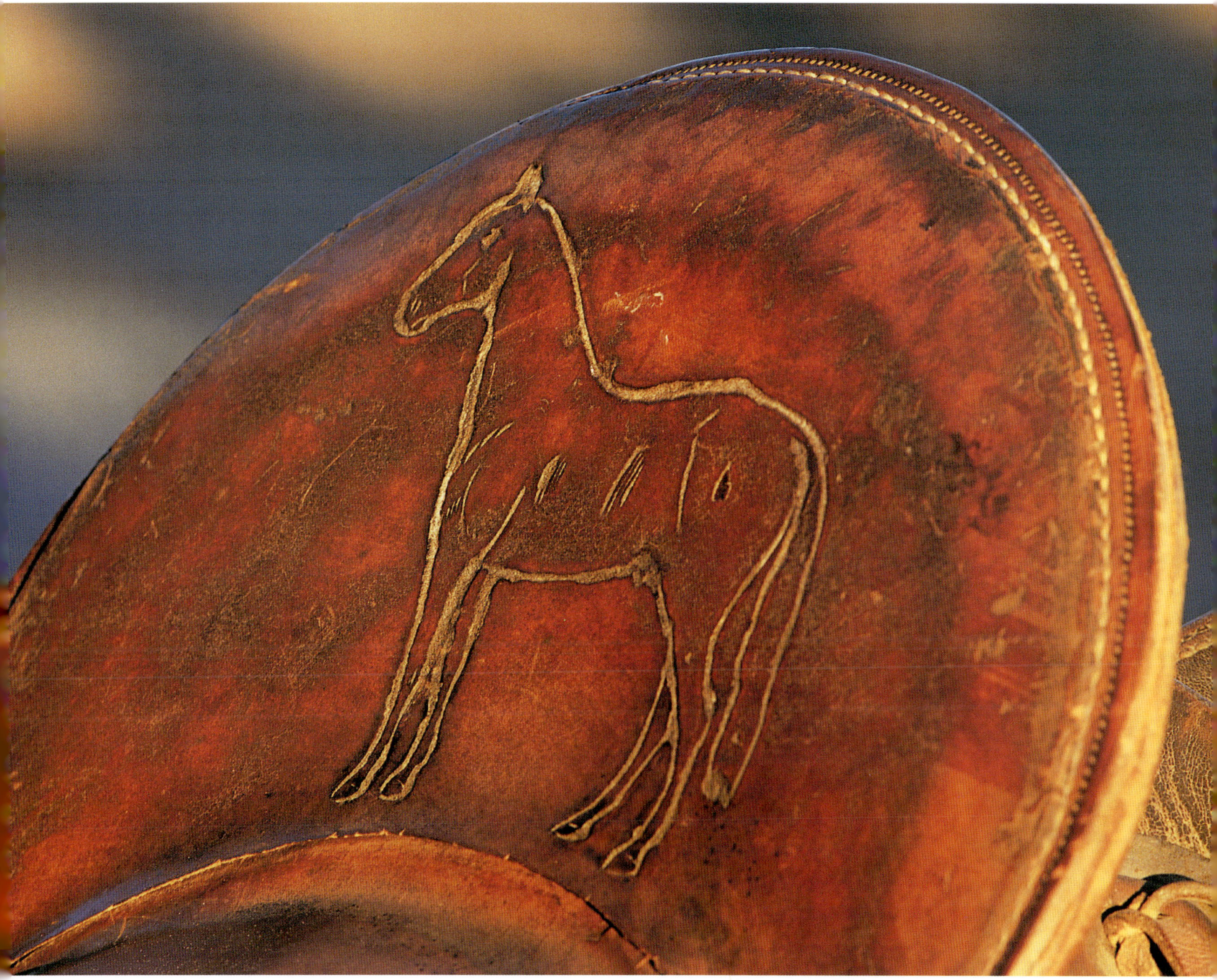

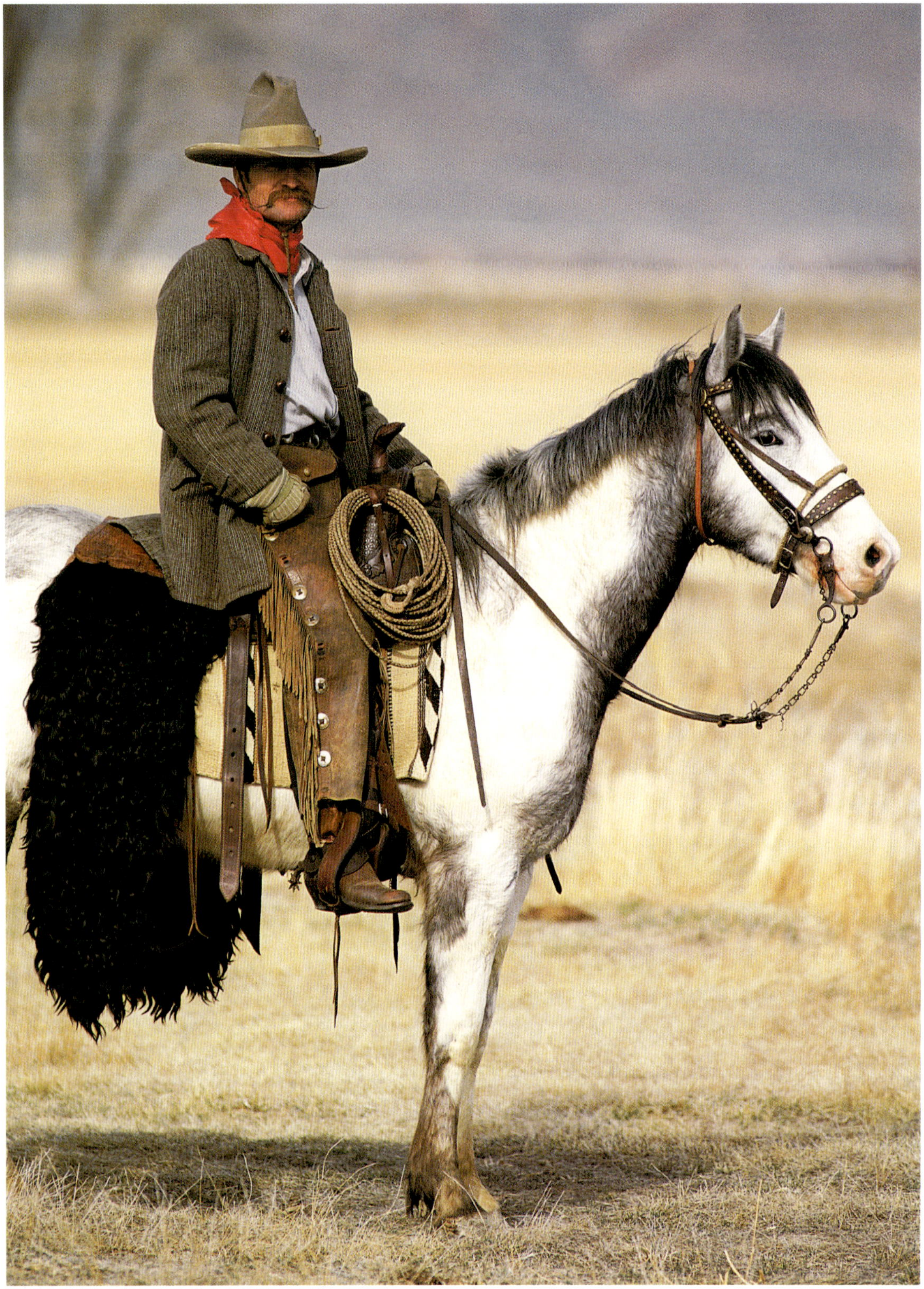

A VERY RARE SERAPE FROM SENTINEL BUTTE SADDLERY, *Montana, circa 1890, Stoecklein Collection*

CANVAS SADDLE BAGS, *circa 1920*

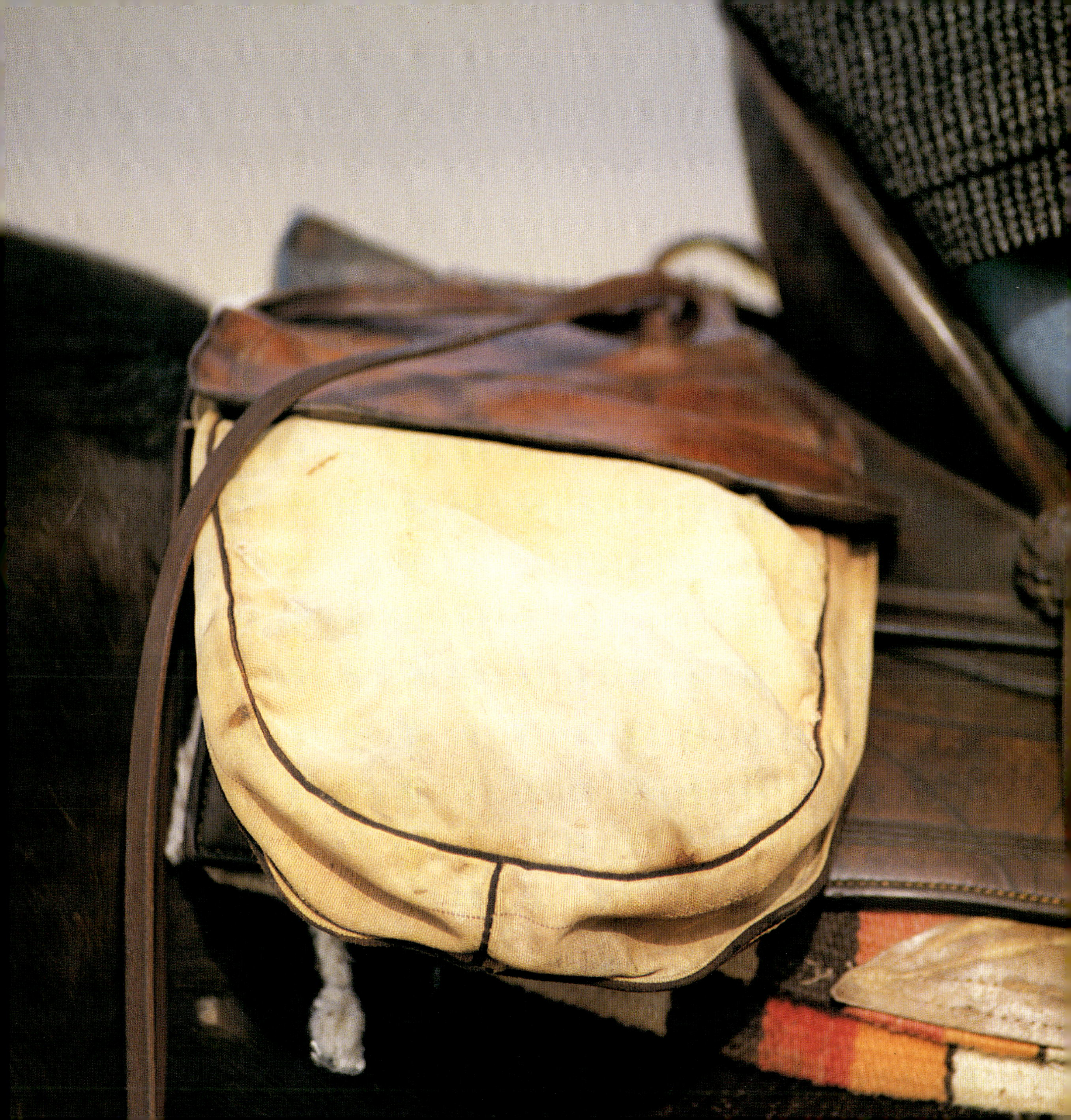

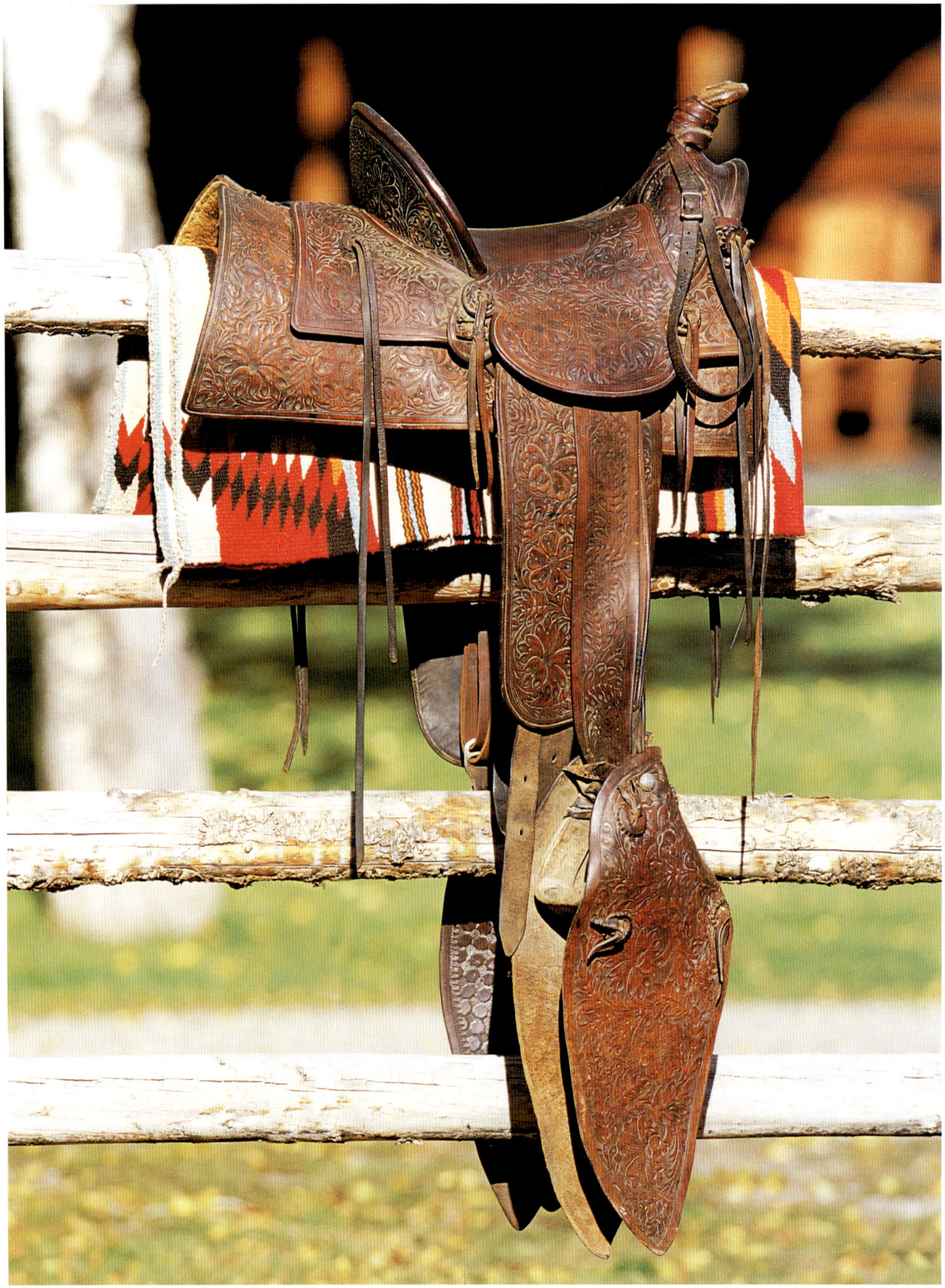

SADDLE MADE BY VISALIA STOCK SADDLE COMPANY, *Flat Creek Saddle Collection, Visalia, California*

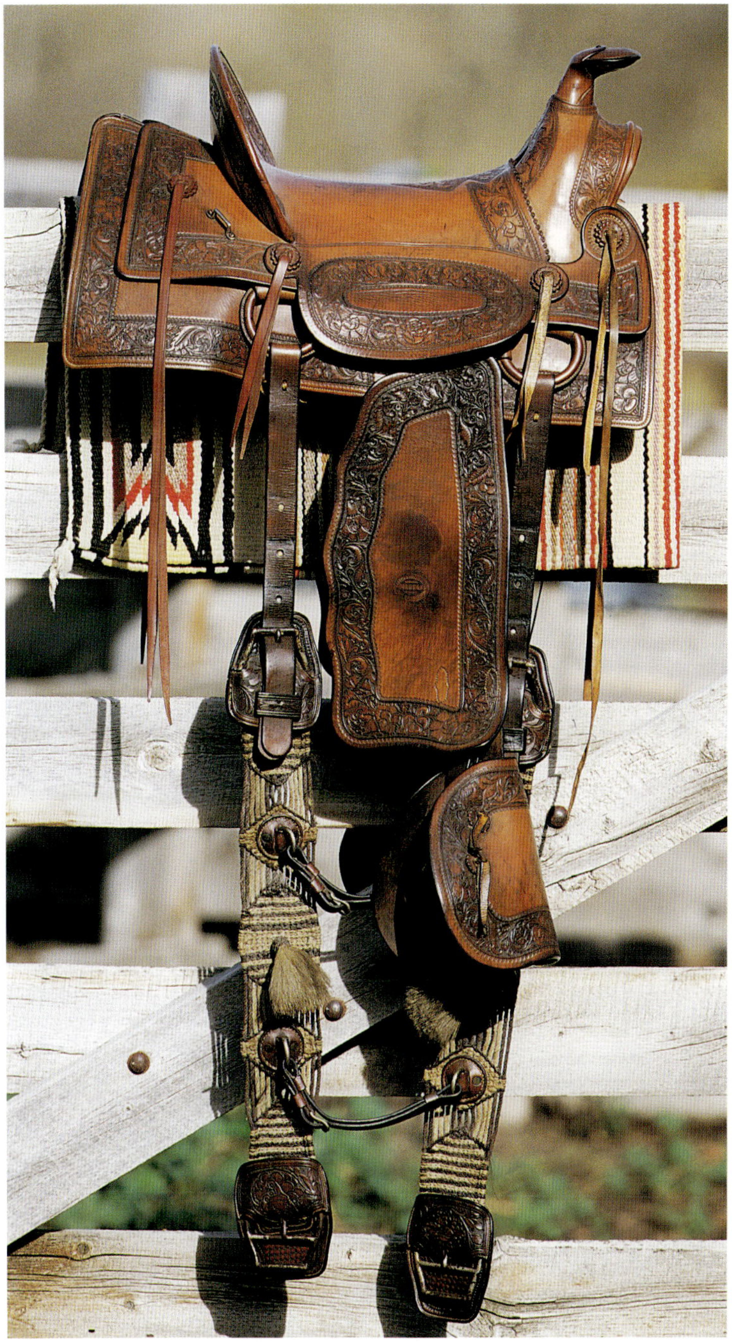

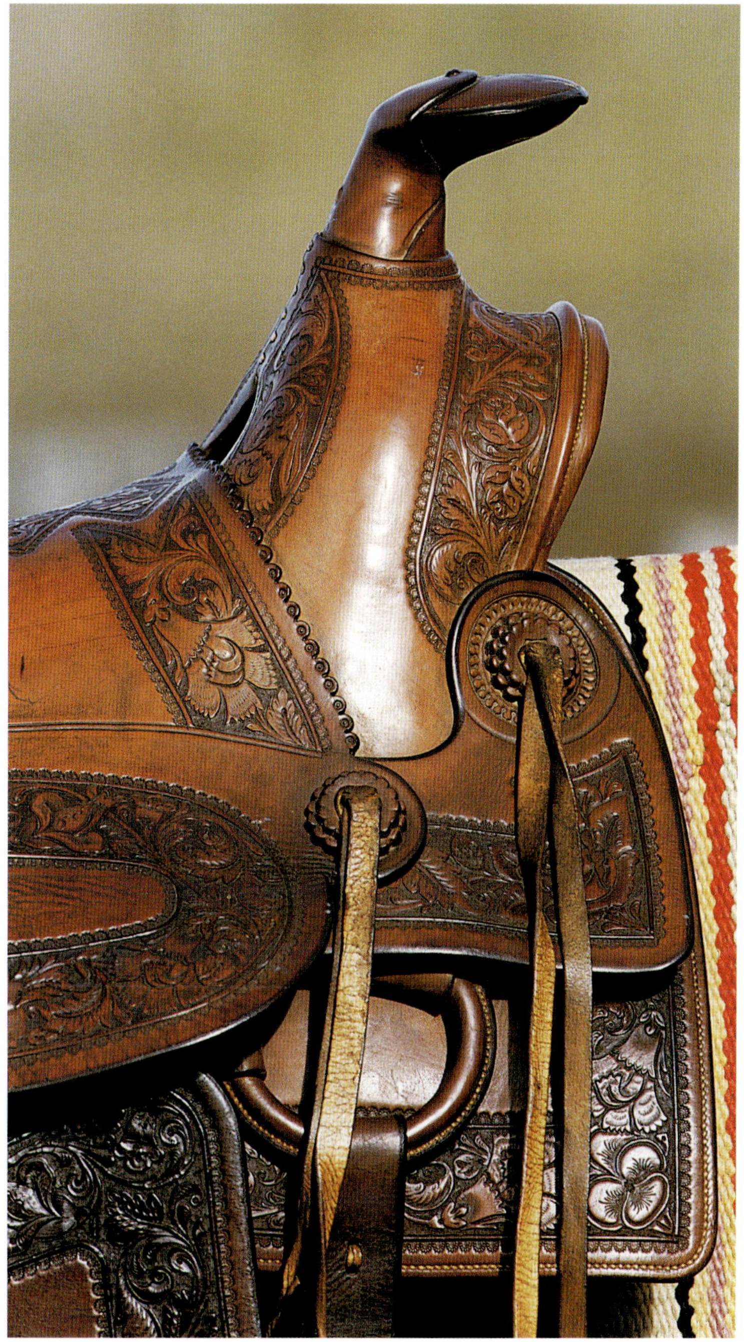

MAIN AND WINCHESTER SADDLE, *circa 1880s,*
Bill King Collection, Bozeman Trail Gallery,
Sheridan, Wyoming

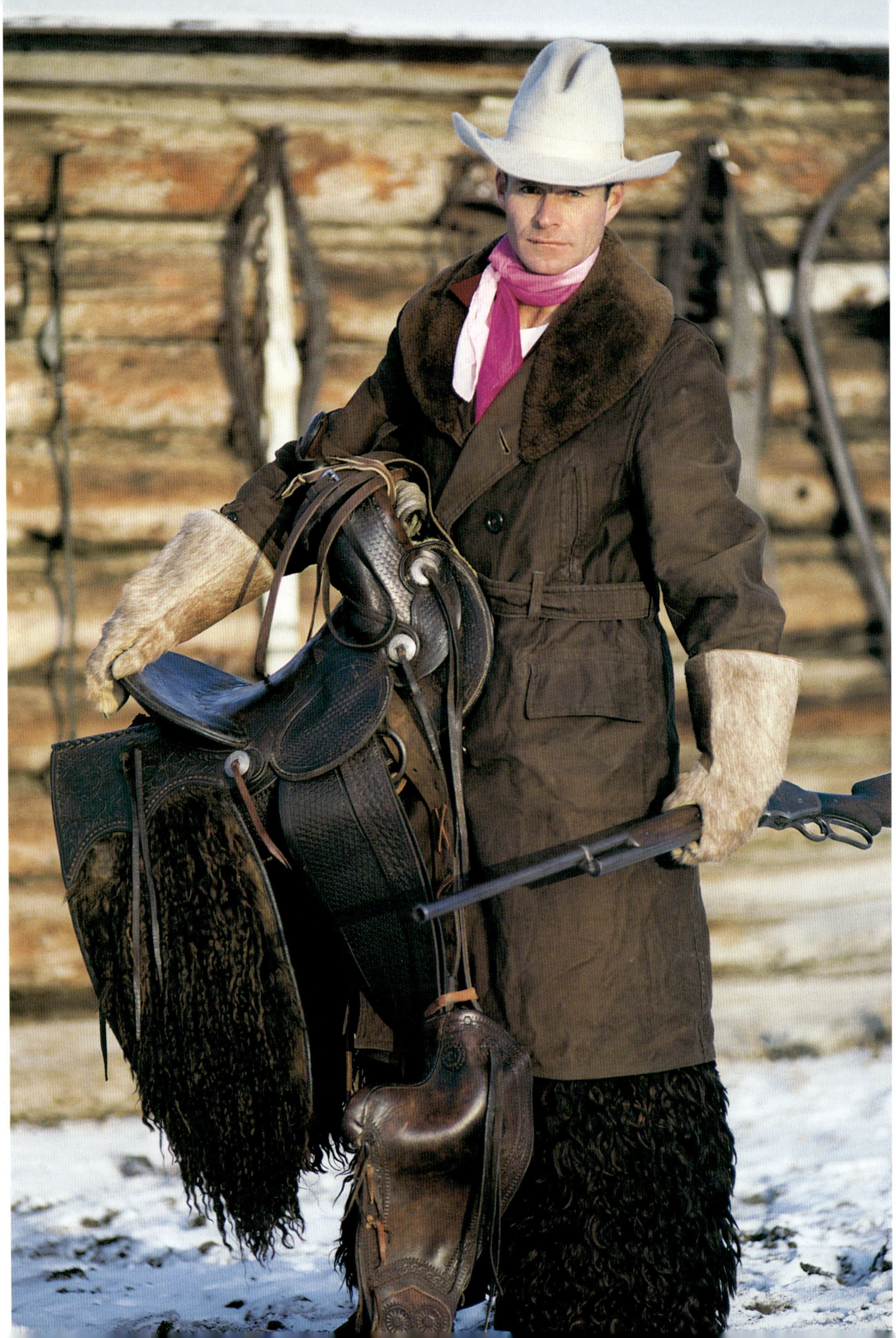

L.D. STONE SADDLE
with eagle-billed tapaderos and Main and Winchester saddle pockets, circa 1880, Stoecklein Collection

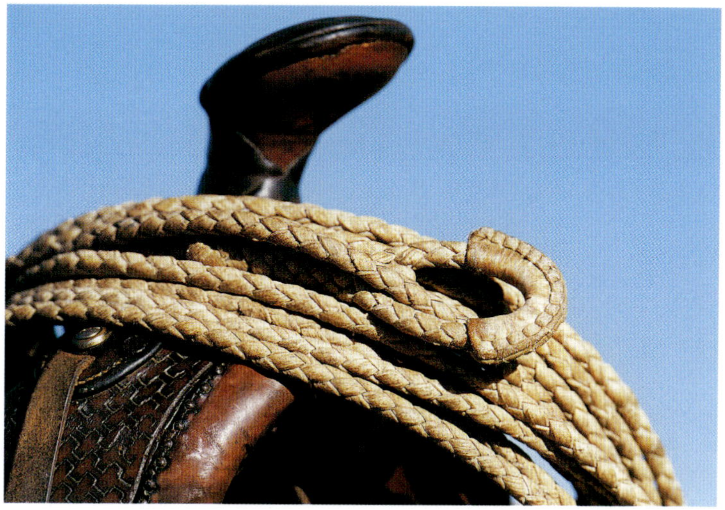

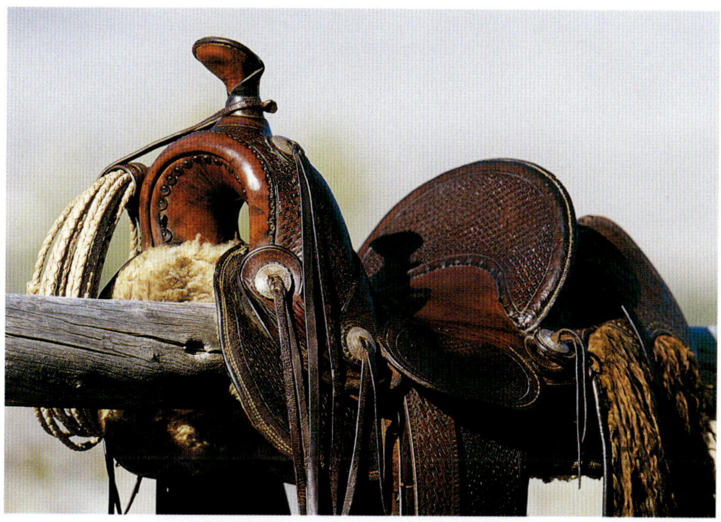

L.D. Stone saddle *with Mexican 1800s silver coins as conchos and handmade reata, circa 1880, San Francisco, California, Stoecklein Collection*

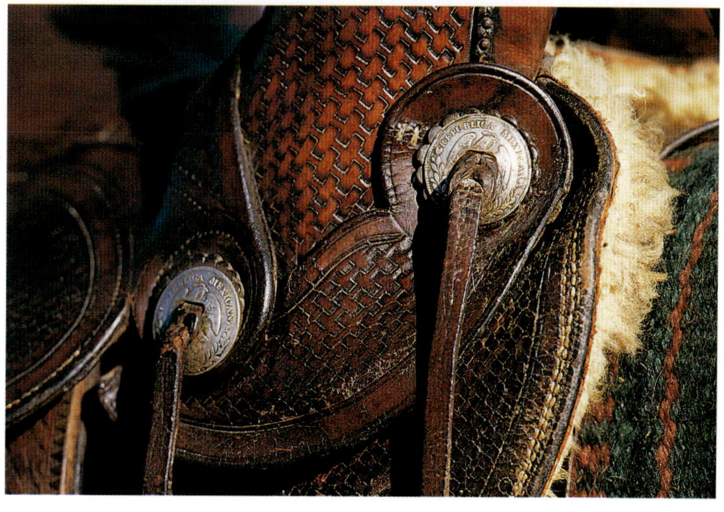

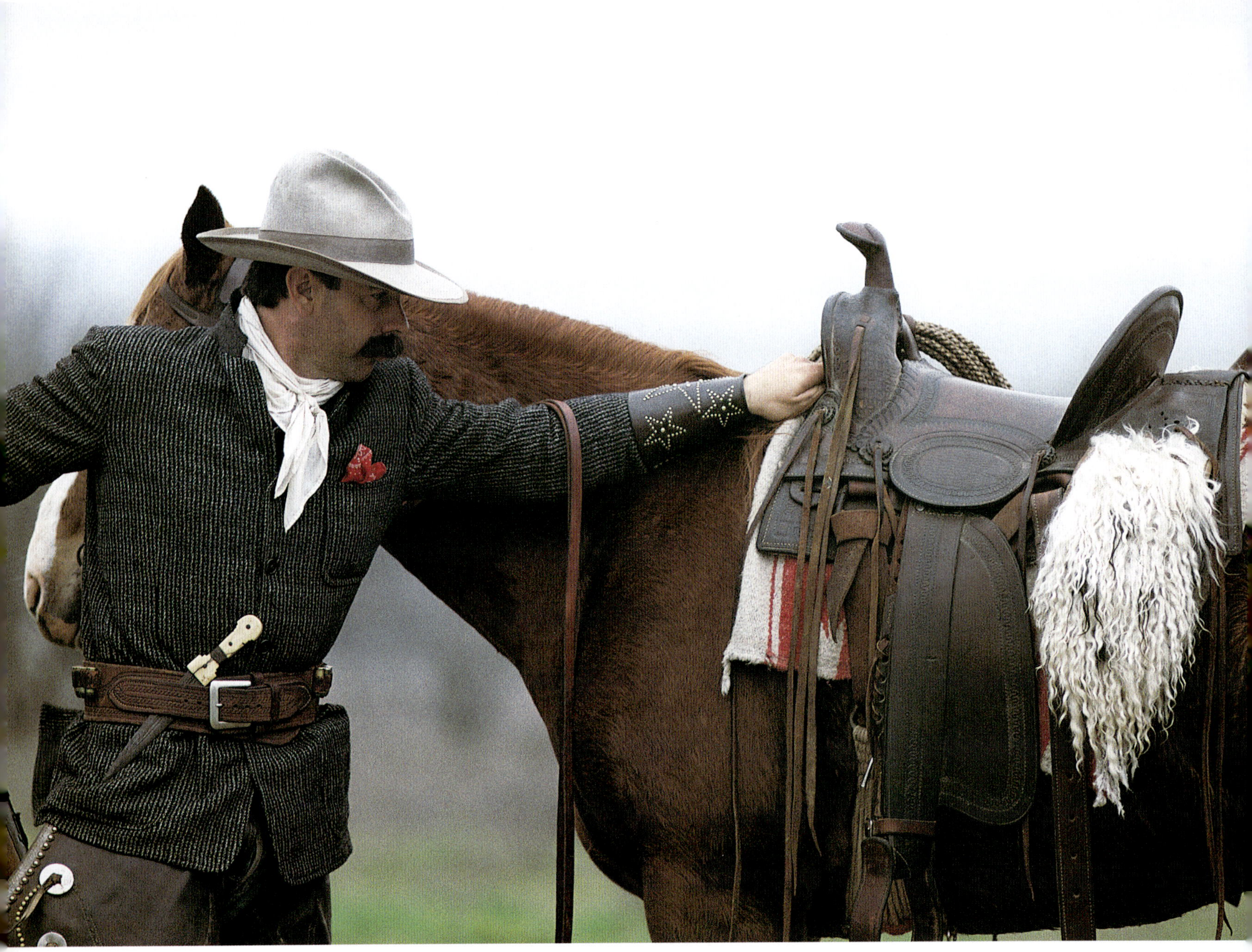

WHITE SPOTTED ANGORA SADDLE POCKETS, *unmarked, Tony McLaughlin Collection*

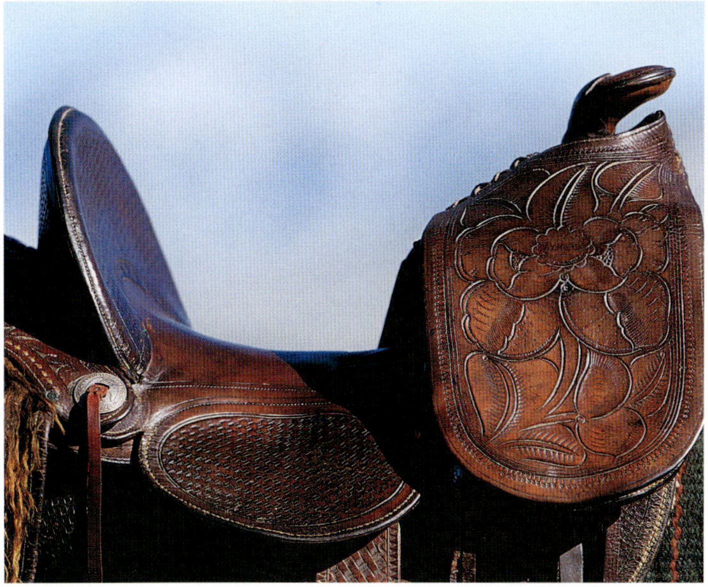

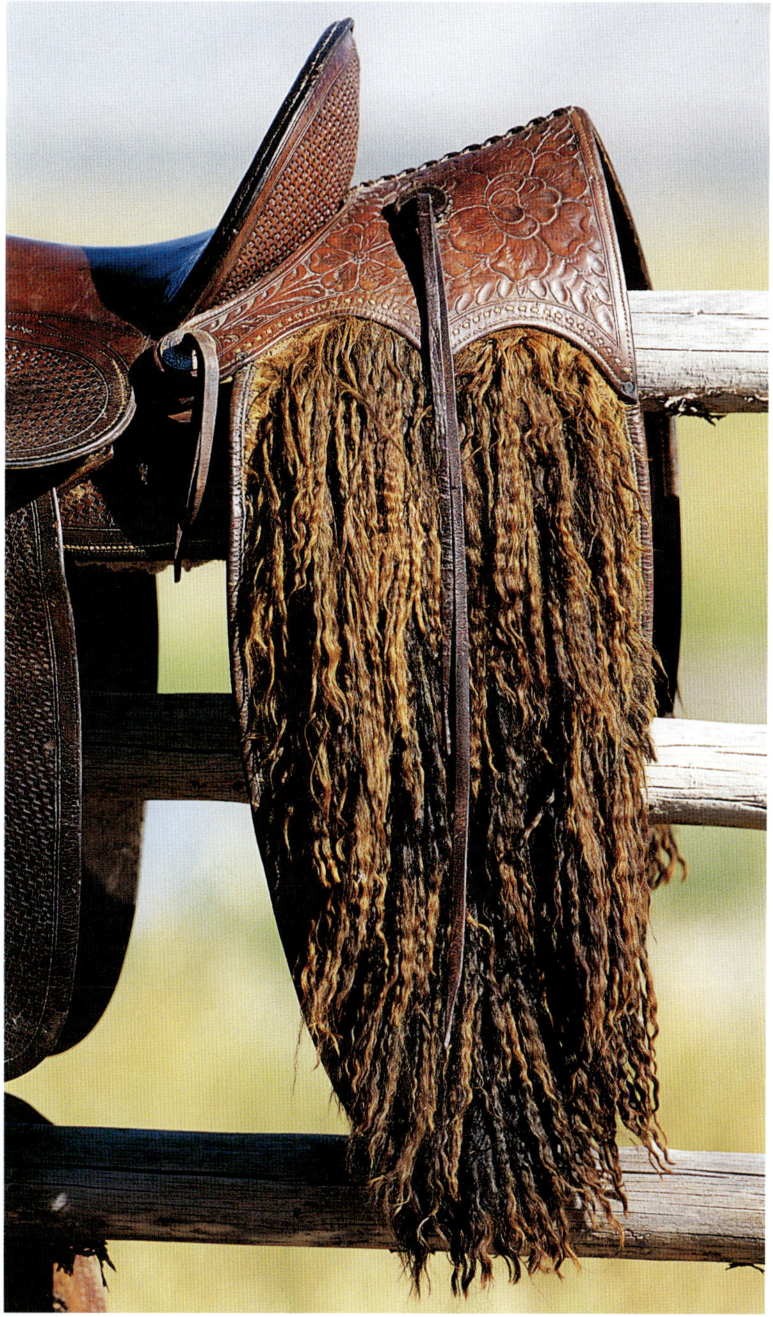

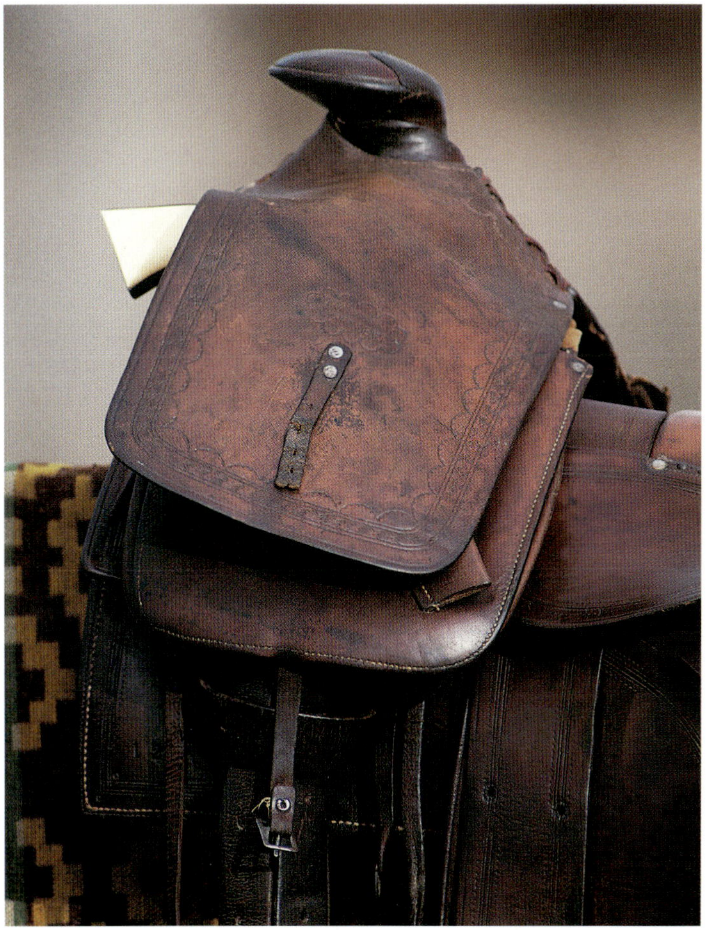

Clockwise from top left

Main and Winchester pommel bags *carved in the early California style, circa 1870s, Stoecklein Collection*

Main and Winchester angora saddle bags

Pommel bags with built-in pistol holster *made by Thomas McAllister, Sprague, Washington Territory, circa 1886, Charlie Smith Collection*

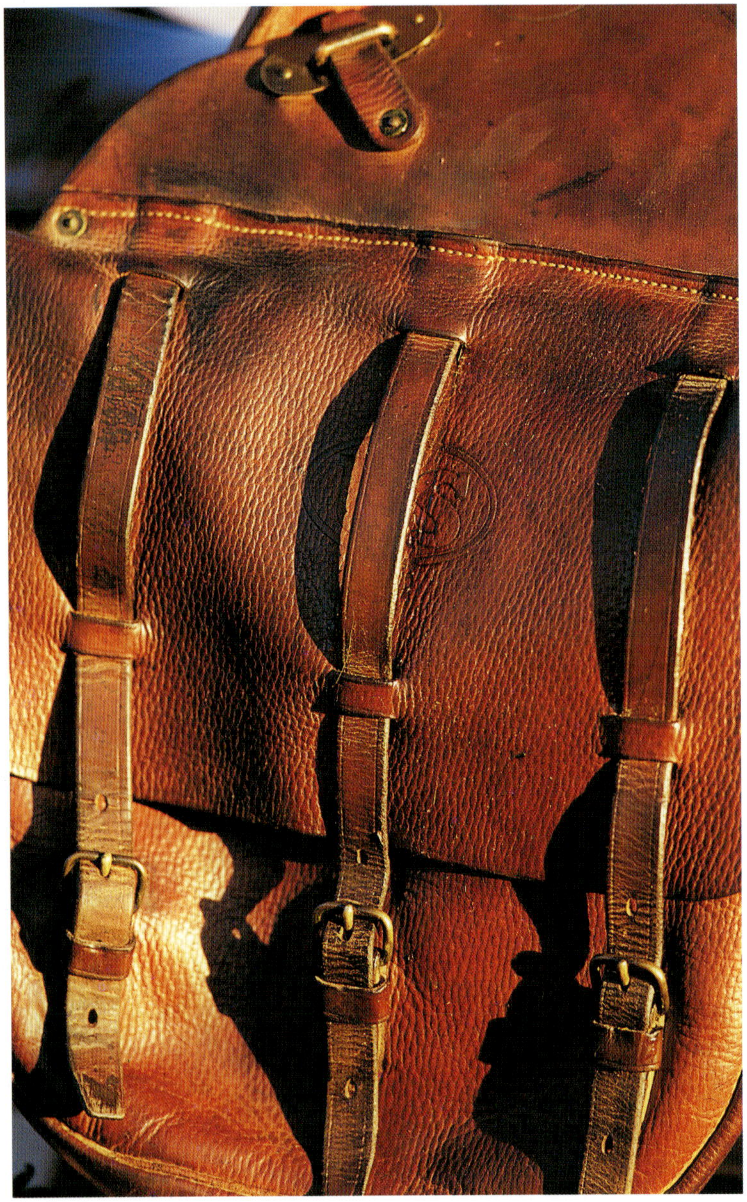

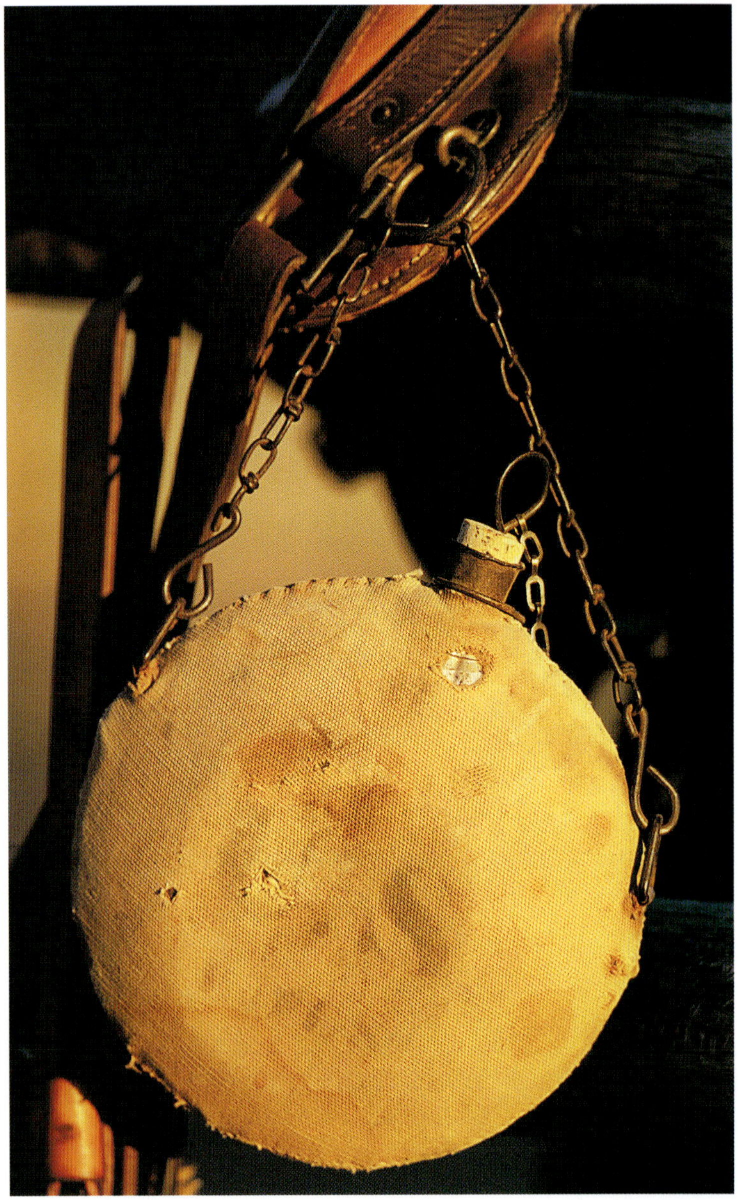

U.S. CAVALRY SADDLE BAGS AND CANTEEN, *Stoecklein Collection*

McCLELLAN CAVALRY SADDLES

were made in the early 1800s and are still made today. The cavalry had to live out of their saddles—it was like their own motor home with everything they needed hanging or strapped to it. They were used by cowboys as well as the cavalry and today are still used by the military. They are also sometimes adapted for such events as endurance riding.

1900s McCLELLAN U.S. MILITARY SADDLE,
Stoecklein Collection

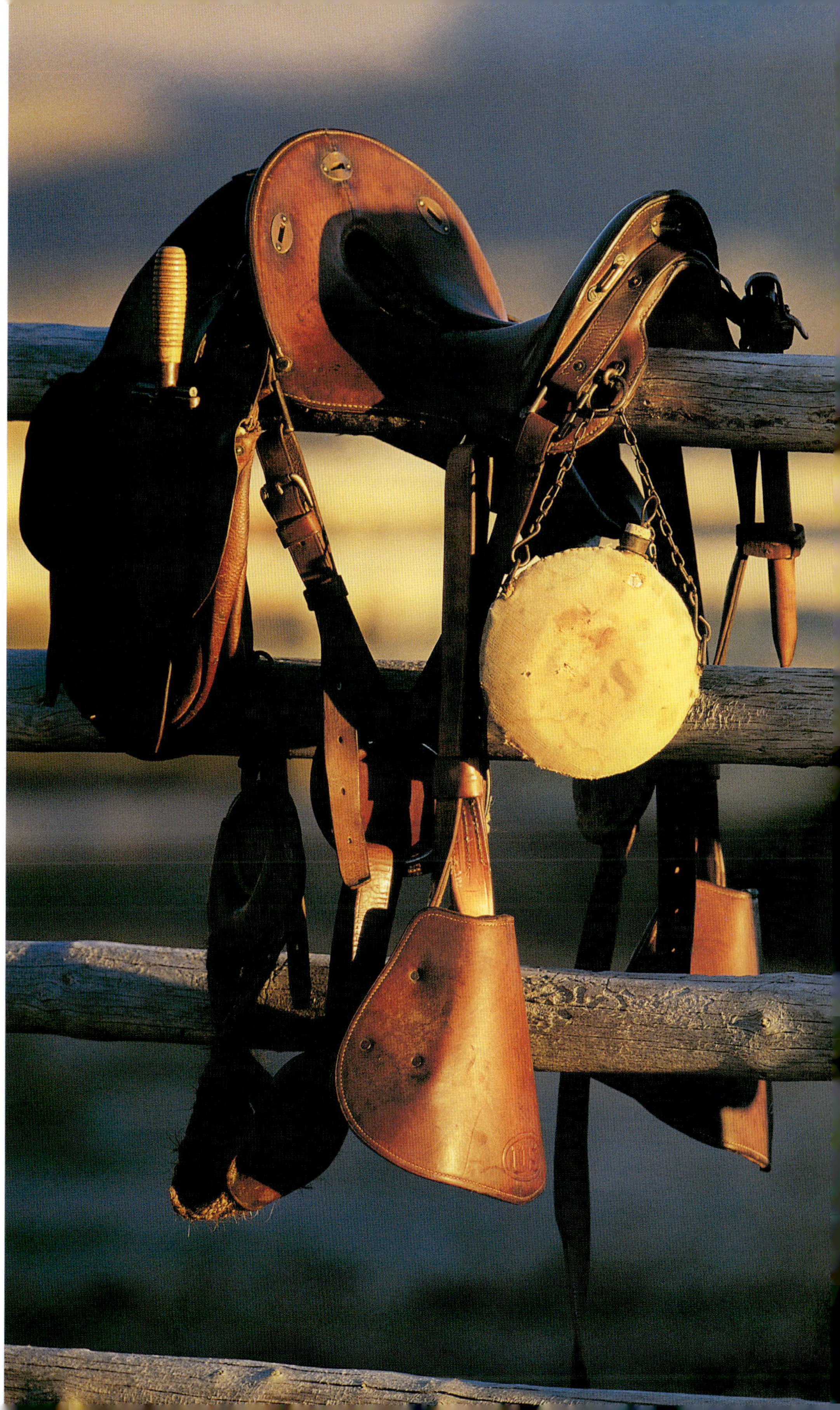

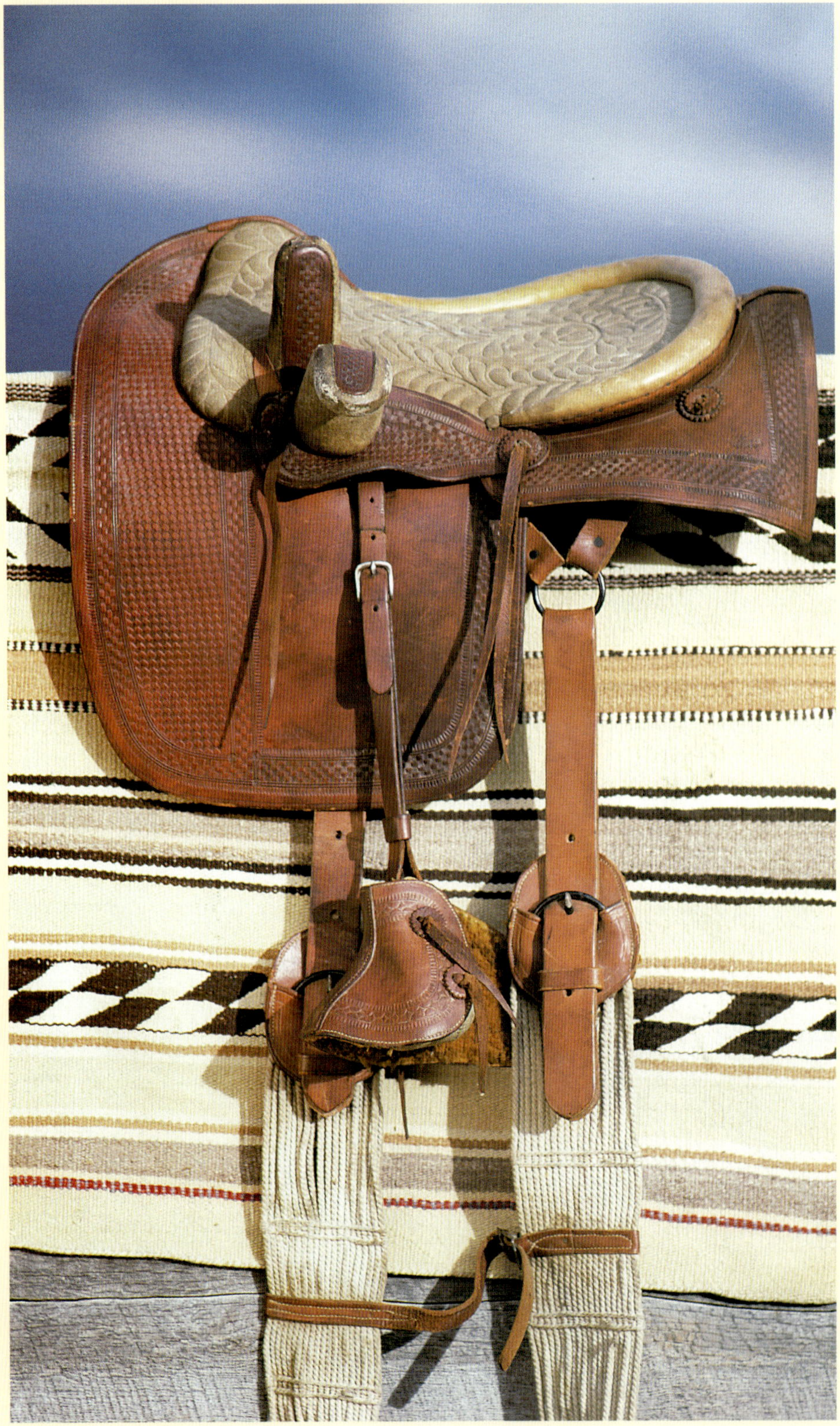

Ladies' sidesaddle *made by Fred Mueller of Denver, Colorado, circa 1890, Charlie Smith Collection*

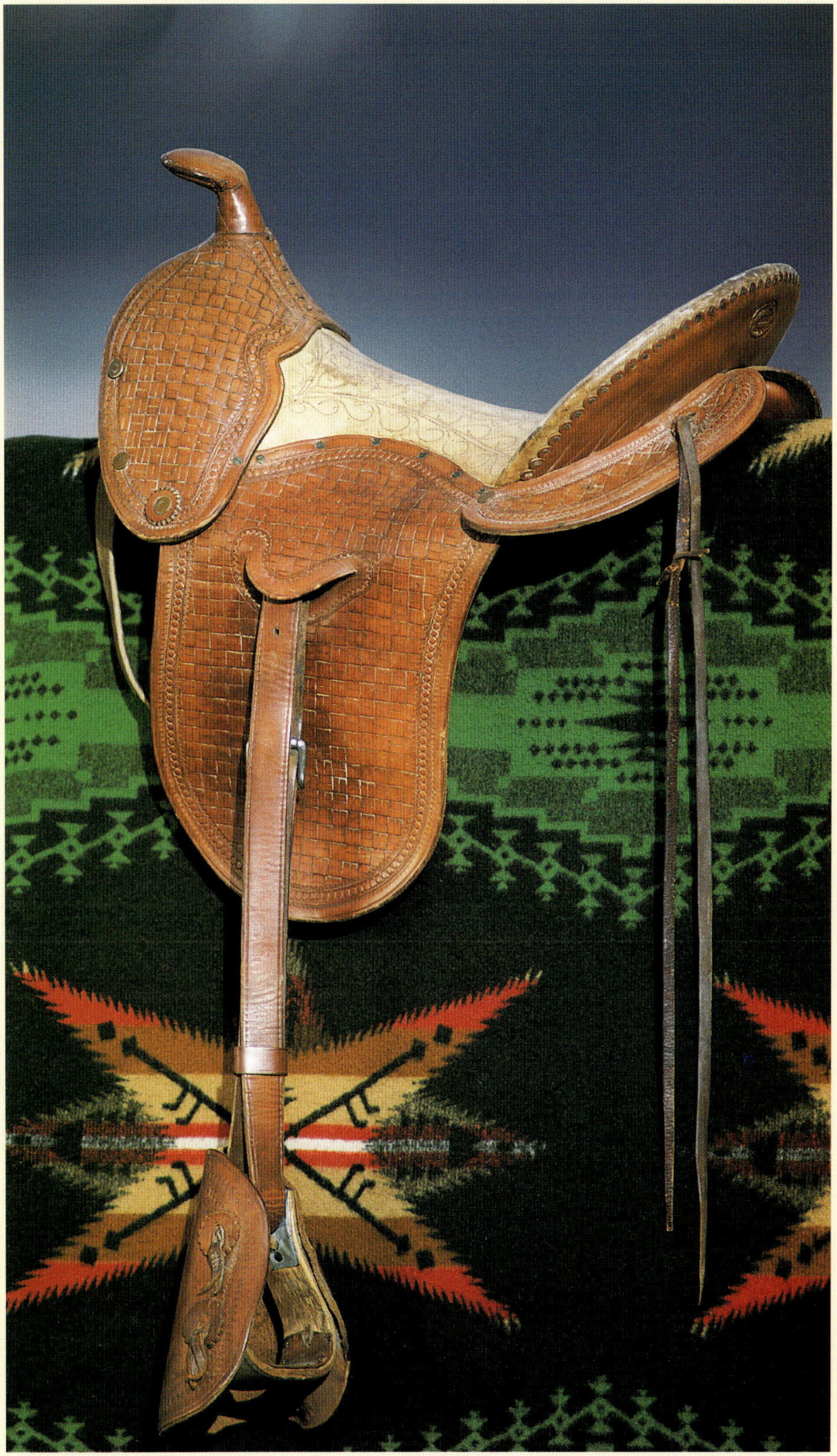

SIDESADDLES *were used throughout most of the 19th century. Women started riding astride saddles after the turn of the century. Today men and women ride the same and sidesaddles are mainly found in collections and are ridden in parades.*

LADIES' ASTRIDE SADDLE *made by Charles Nye of Walla Walla, Washington, Charlie Smith Collection*

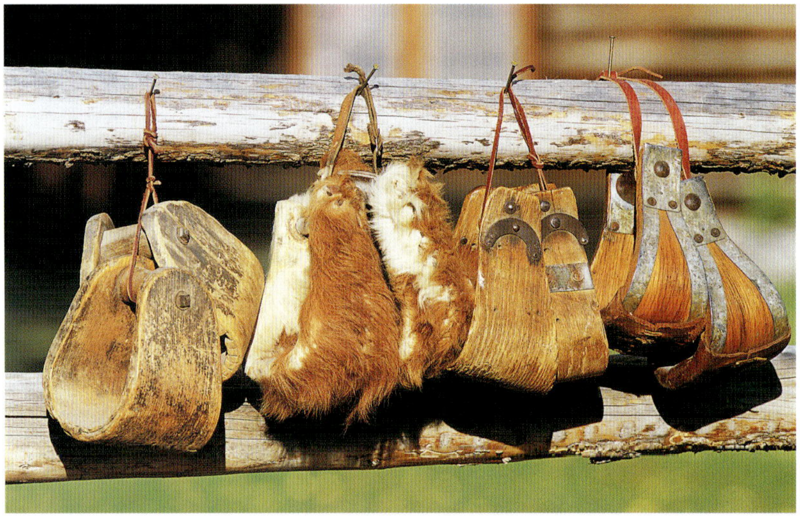

Wood stirrups,
Flat Creek Saddle Collection

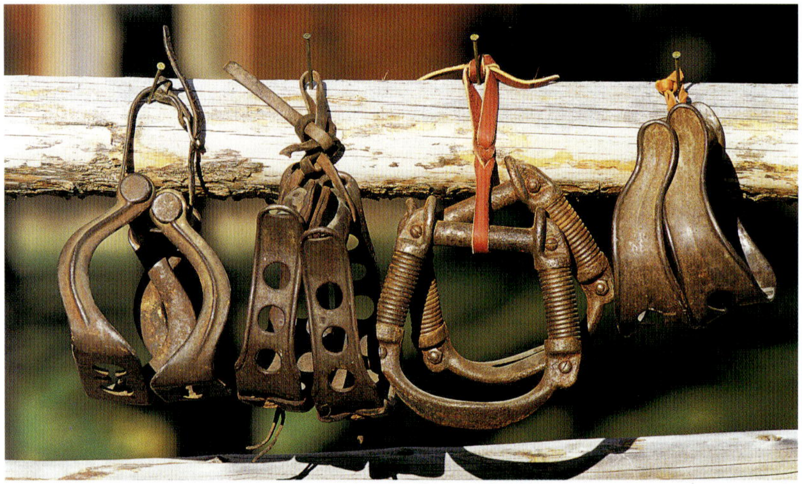

Steel stirrups,
Flat Creek Saddle Collection

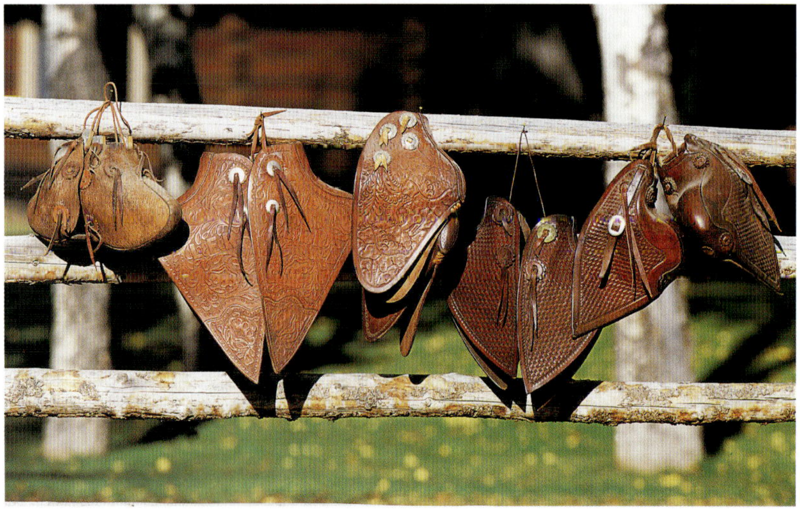

Tapaderos,
Flat Creek Saddle Collection

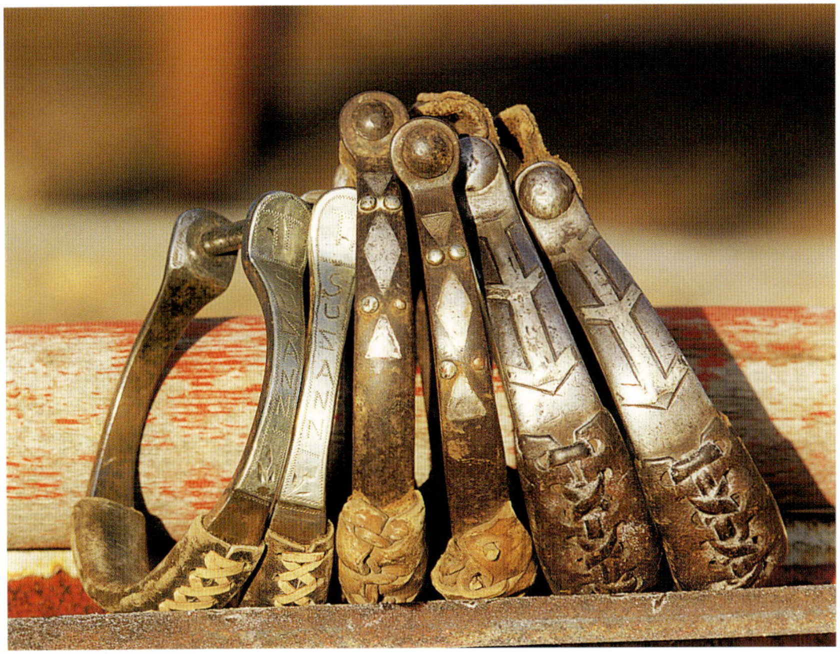

IRON AND SILVER STIRRUPS,
Flat Creek Saddle Collection

THERE HAVE BEEN MORE CHANGES *in stirrups styles and designs than probably any other element of a saddle. Just like shoes and boots, it is a matter first of comfort, then safety, and then style. There have been stirrups made from wood, wood and steel, steel, aluminum, silver and steel, steel and leather, wood and leather, and other combinations. Some stirrups had the owner's name on them and sometimes the owner's brand. Safety is most important. A cowboy's worst nightmare is to be thrown from his horse with his foot caught in the stirrup while the horse drags and kicks him to death. These are just a few examples of all the different types of stirrups.*

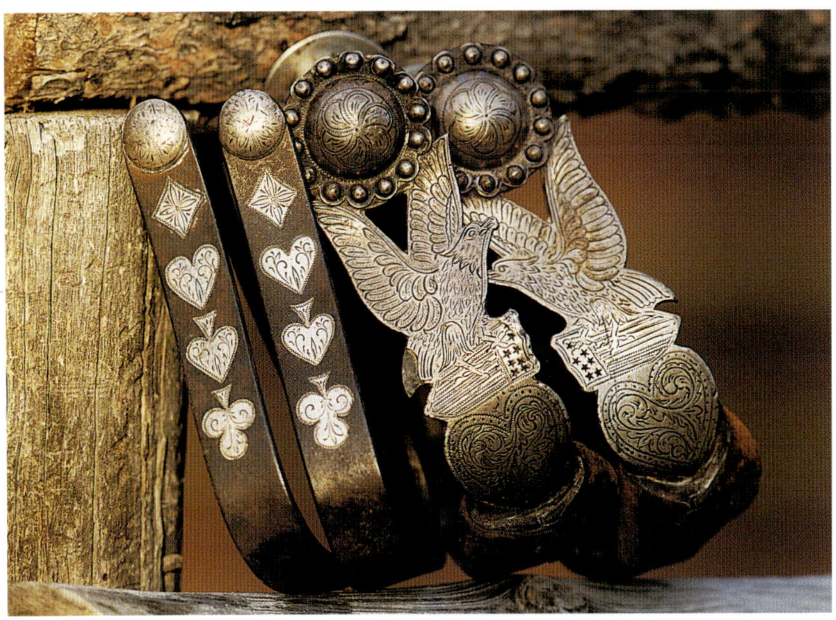

IRON AND SILVER STIRRUPS,
Flat Creek Saddle Collection

Big Swell Saddles

When it comes to saddle style, *one of the most flamboyant and drastic style changes came around in 1915 with the development of the big swell. At first it was supposed to be designed as a safety device to hold a person in the saddle when his horse did not want the rider to be there. As most designs go, this one went a little too far and reached a point where the swells held a rider in even when he wanted to get out, becoming a death trap of sorts. Today these saddles are mostly used as conversation pieces and sit in the saddle rooms of collectors or in museums.*

Swells on saddles today are different according to certain regions. In Idaho, Nevada, Oregon, California, and western Montana, most people ride a slick fork saddle with a bucking roll attached. In Texas and Oklahoma people ride a medium forked saddle with just enough swell to get a leg underneath it. With so much of Western gear, geography plays a big part in what type of equipment and style of equipment is used.

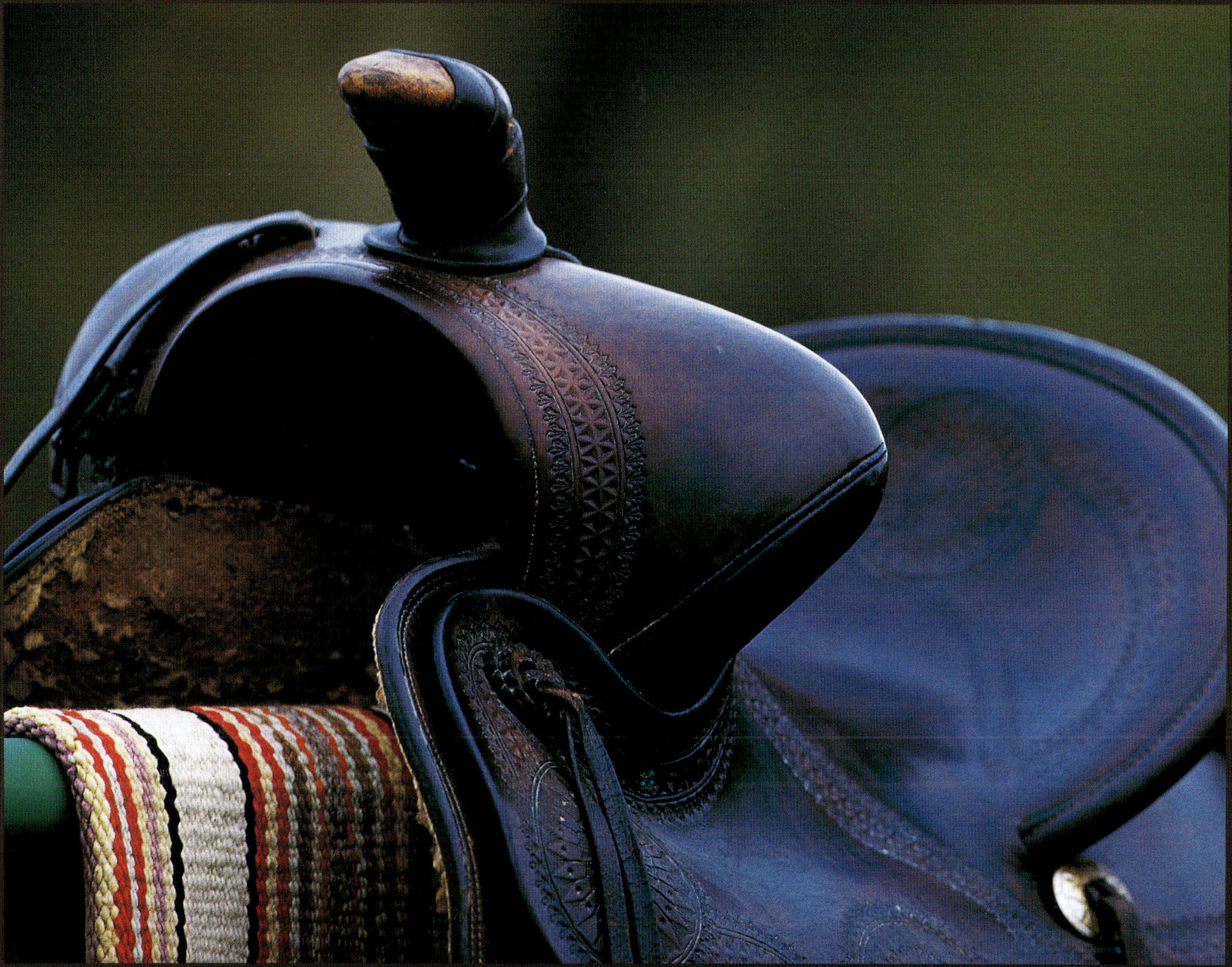

HAMLEY FORM FITTER SADDLE *built in 1930 for R.L. Morton of Detroit, Michigan, King Saddlery Museum, Sheridan, Wyoming*

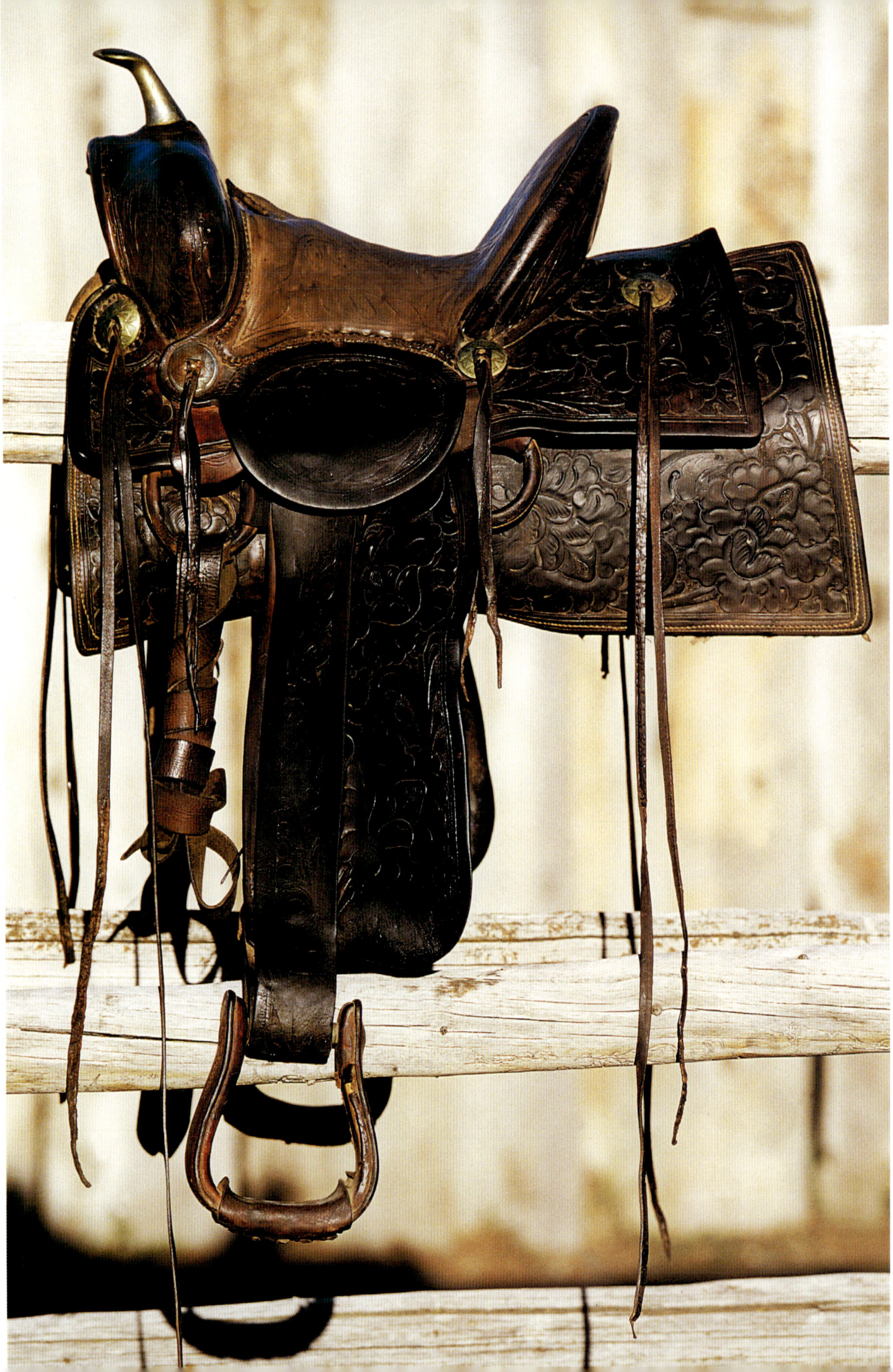

MYRES SADDLE,
El Paso, Texas,
Stoecklein Collection

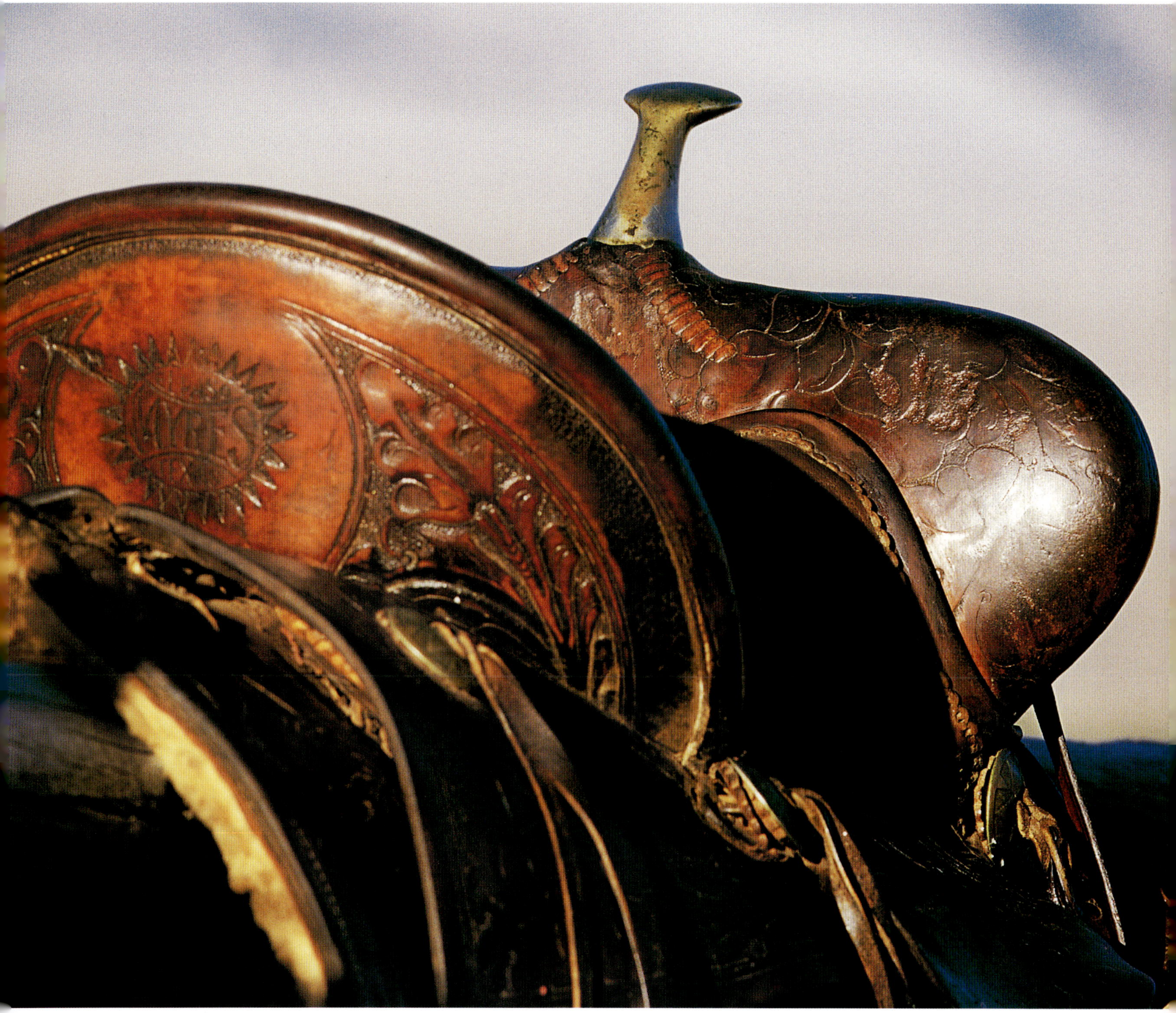

MYRES SADDLE, *El Paso, Texas, Stoecklein Collection*

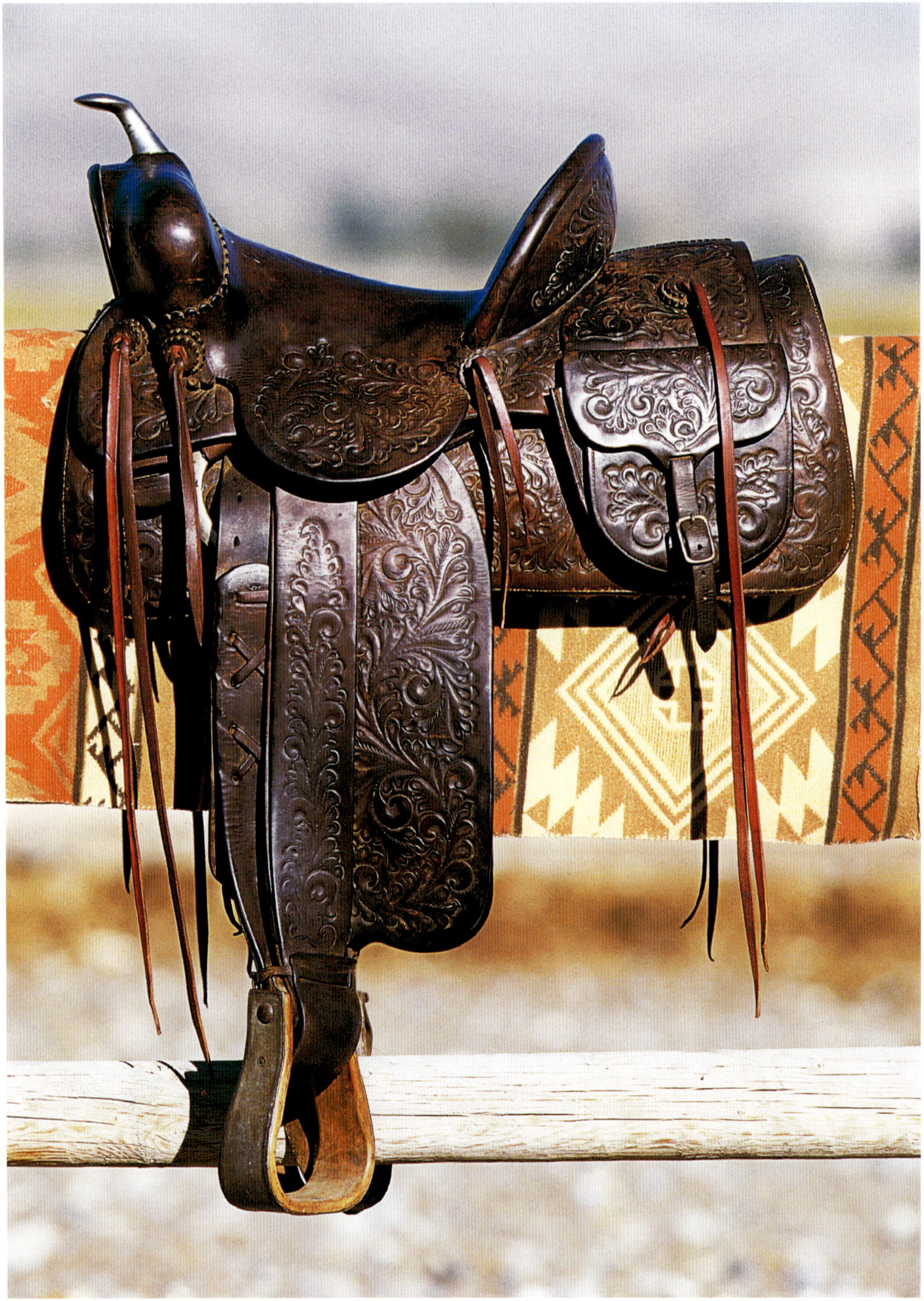

COGGSHALL SADDLE,
Miles City, Montana,
Stoecklein Collection

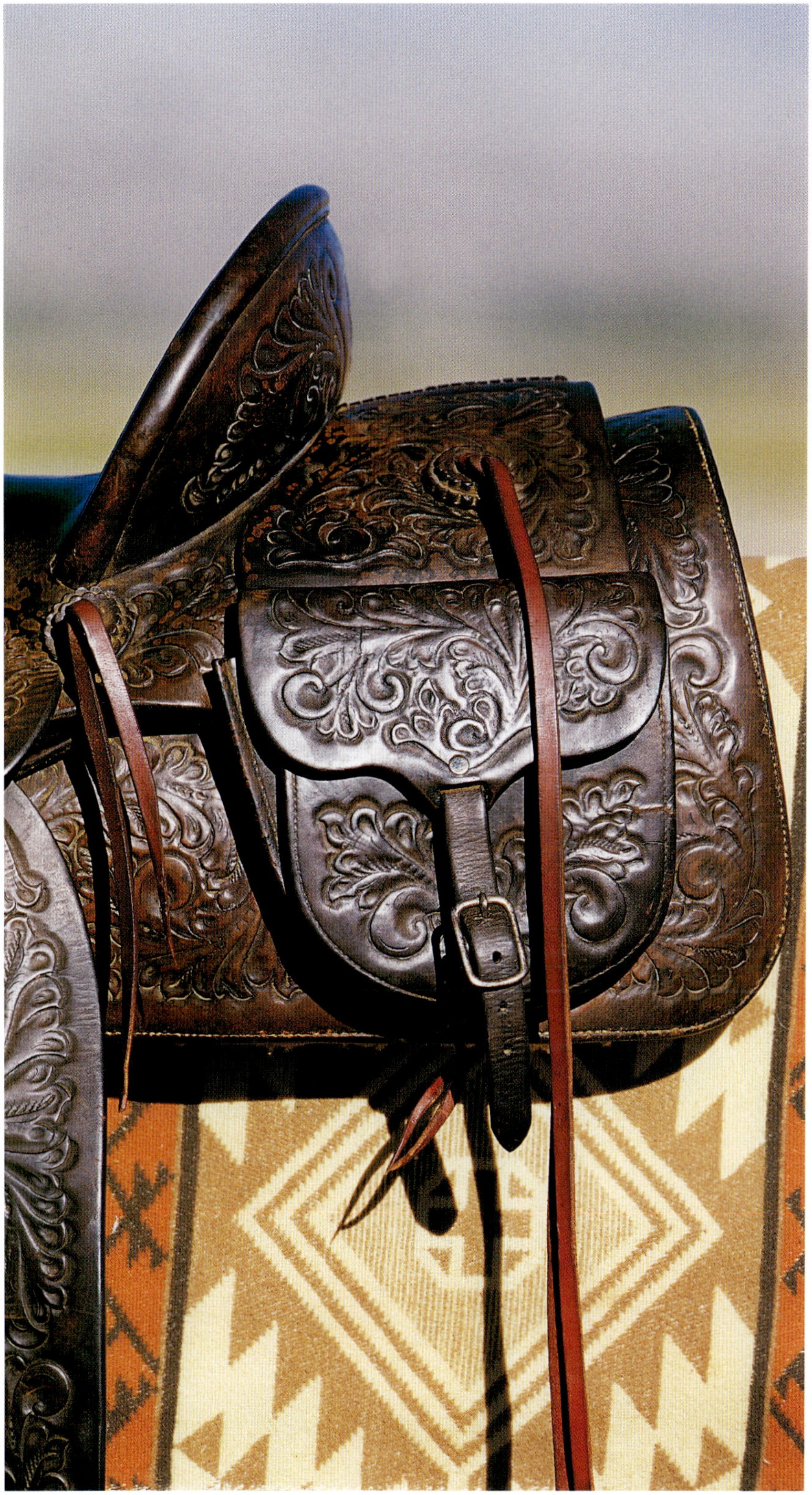

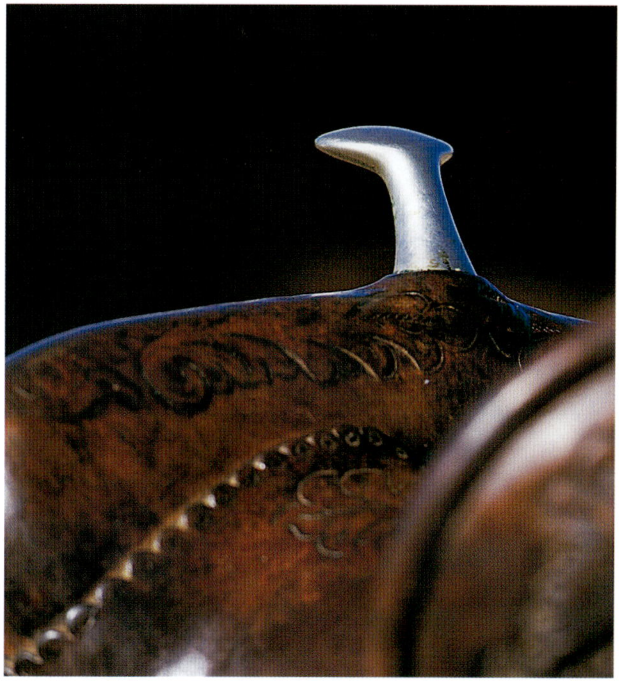

Nickel saddle horn

Coggshall saddle pocket

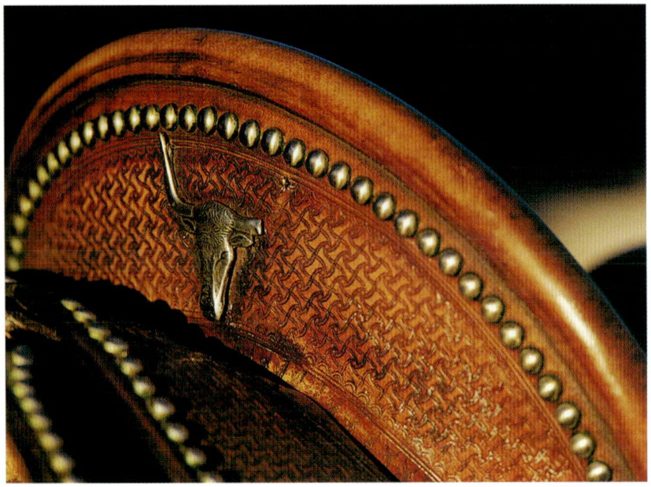
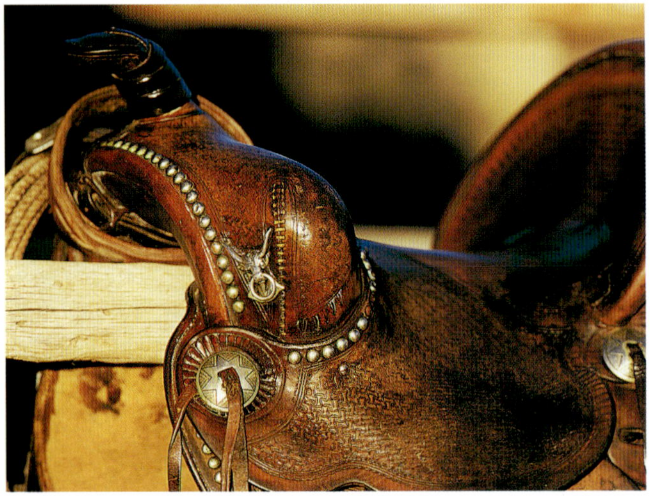
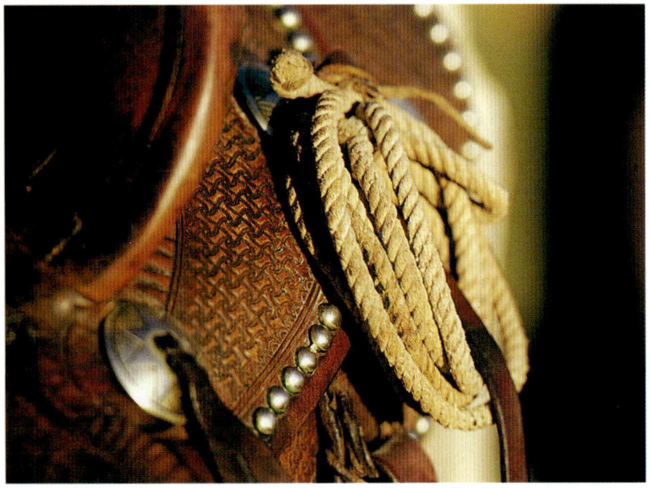
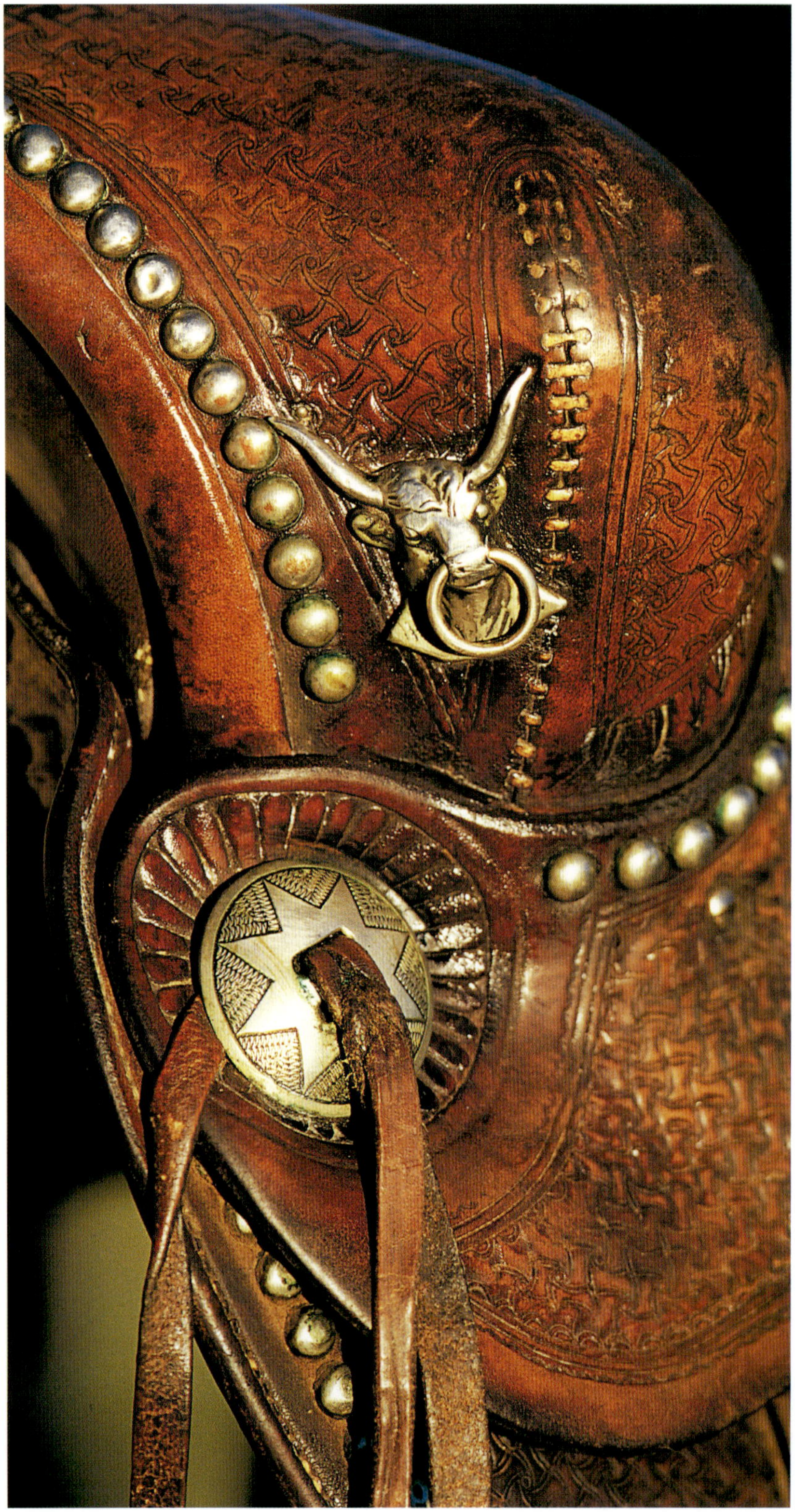

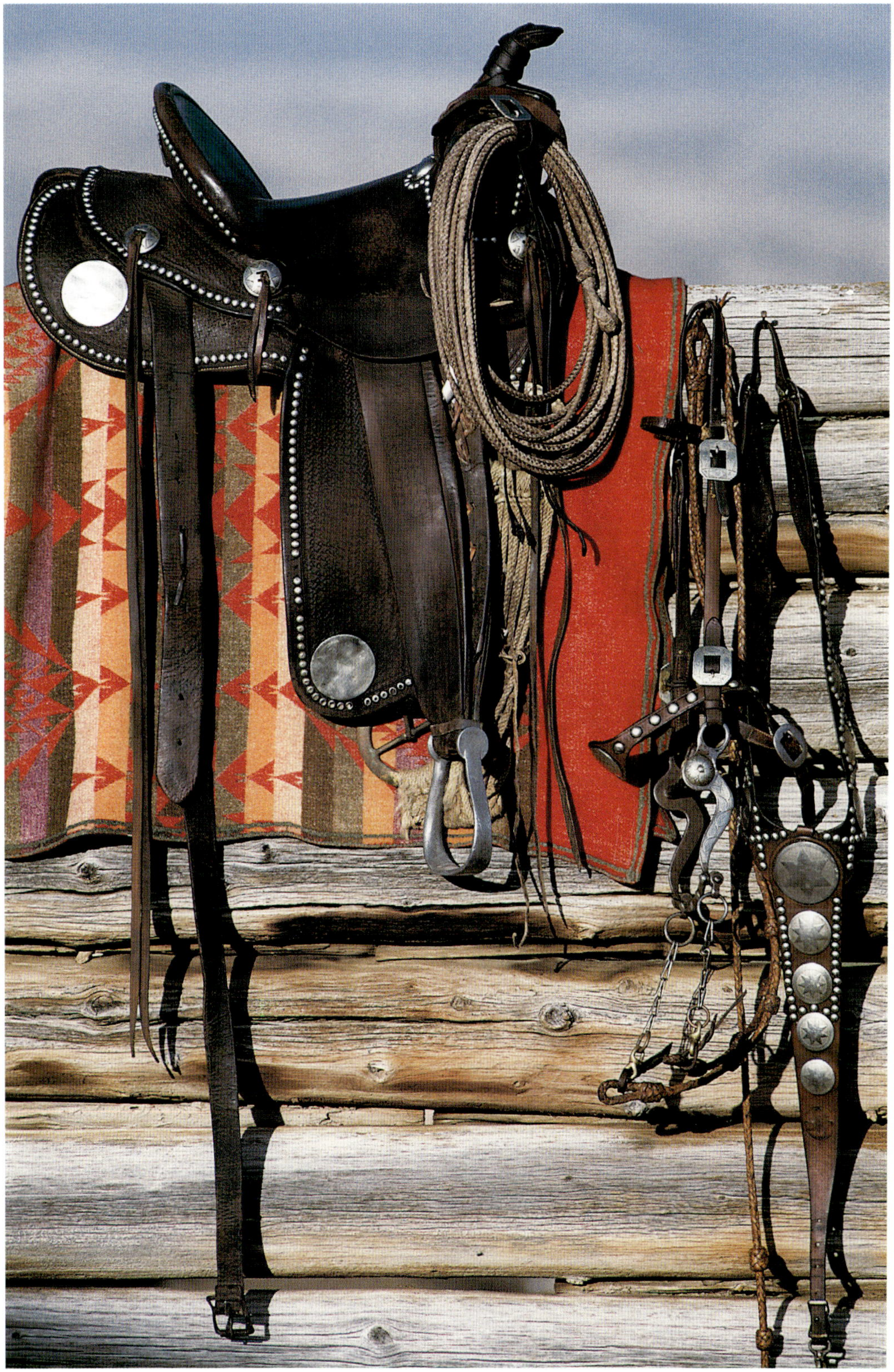

THIS UNIQUE AND RARE *Blake Miller saddle has silver from Canyon City Prison and Visalia, California on the saddle as well as on the breastcollar and headstall. The bridle was also made in Canyon City Prison. The headstall and latigo were made by Frank A. Meanea of Cheyenne, Wyoming. Blake Miller must have purchased the items for a very special client.*

BLAKE MILLER SADDLE, *Cheyenne, Wyoming, Stoecklein Collection*

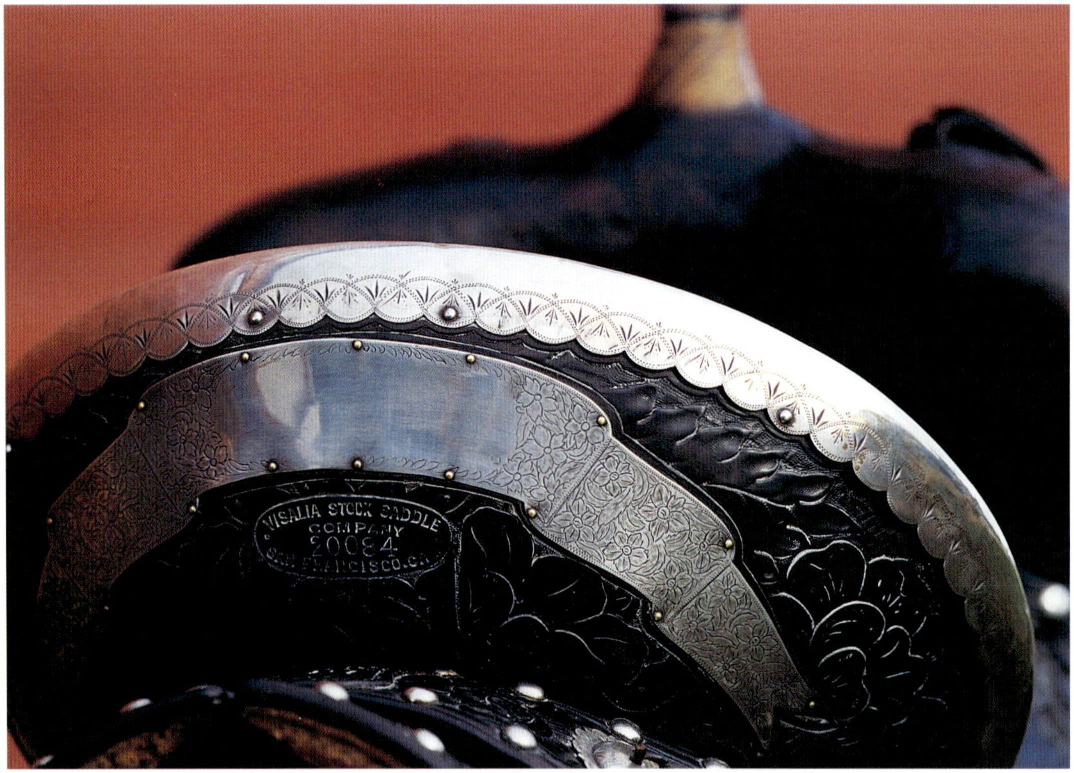

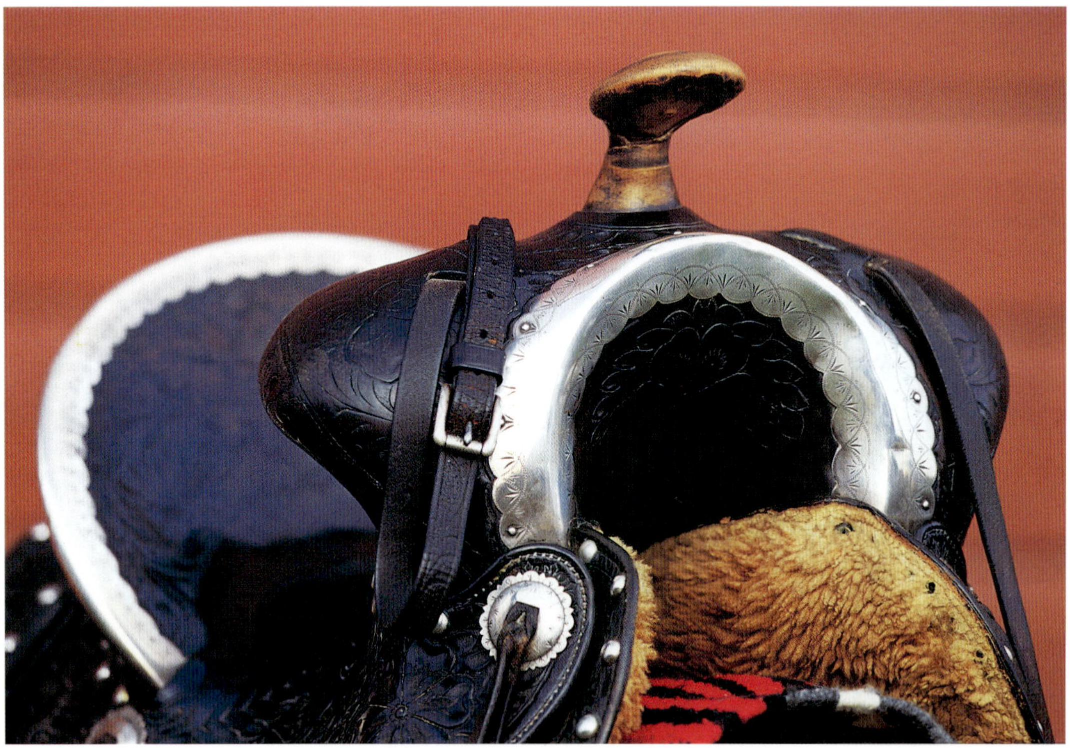

Visalia form fitter saddle, *silver mounted with silver spots, fully flowered with tapaderos and round skirts, originally owned by a "madam" who ran a brothel in California, King Saddlery Museum, Sheridan, Wyoming*

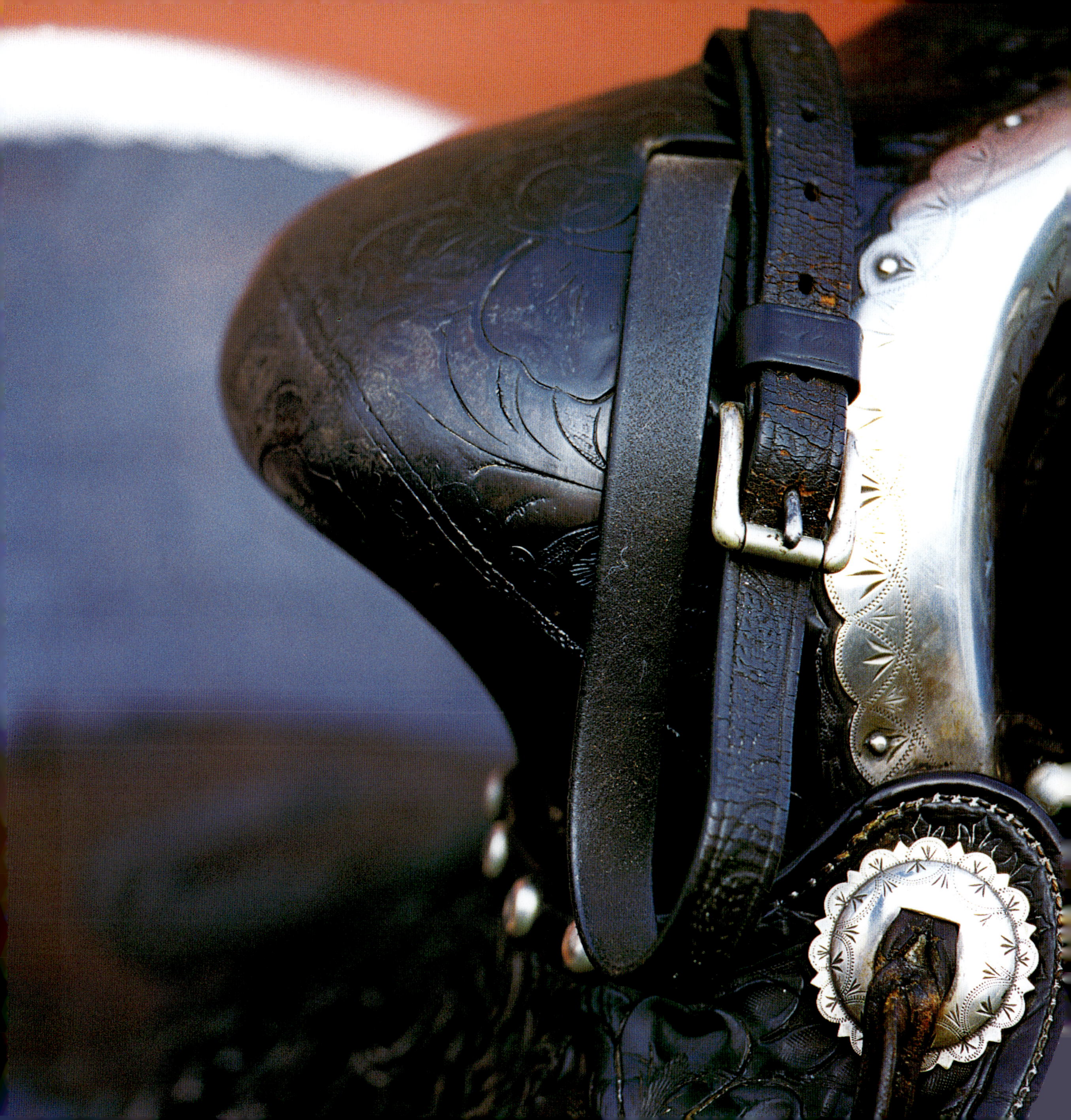

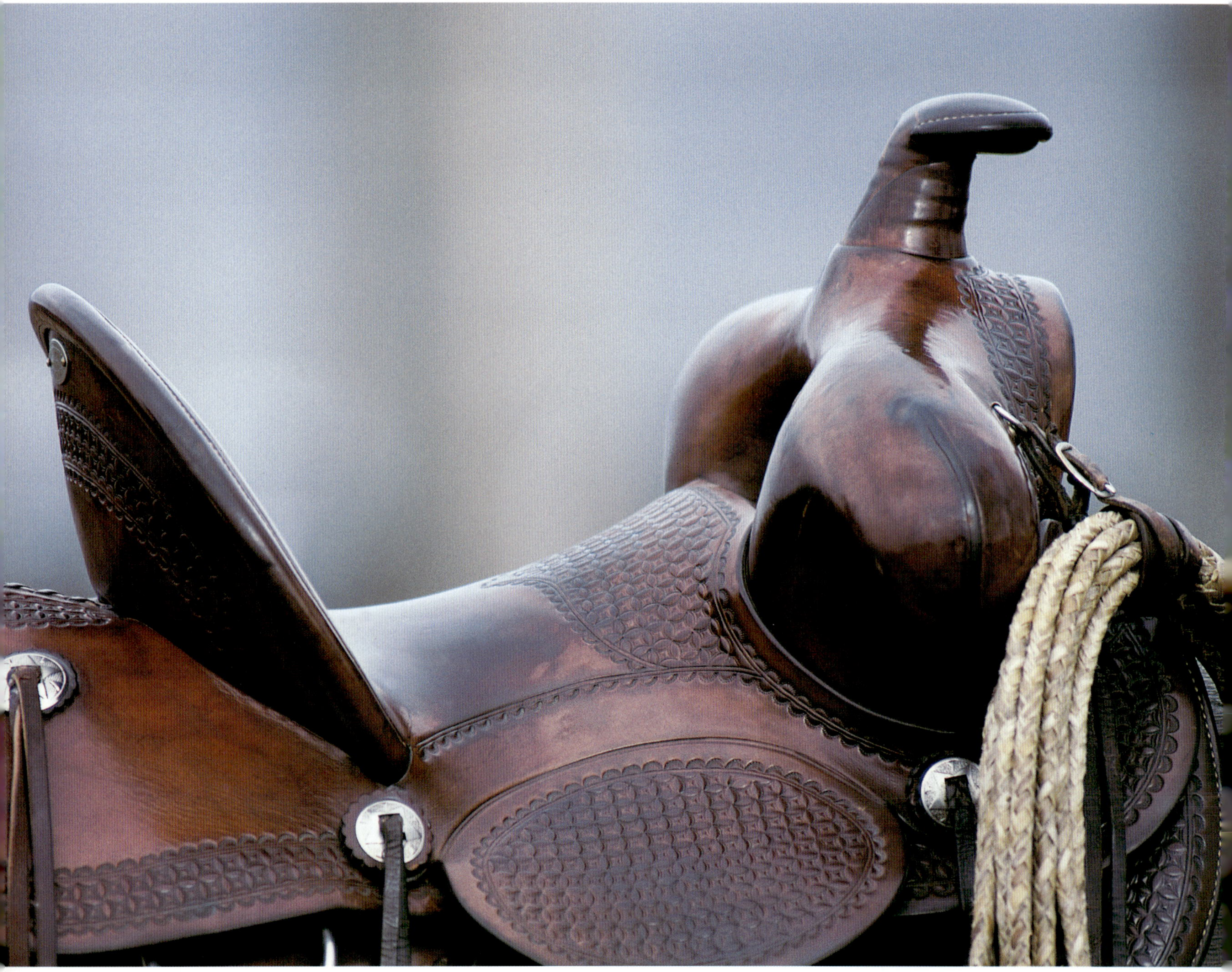

KNOX & TANNER SADDLE, *Los Angeles, California, Ron Gillett Collection*

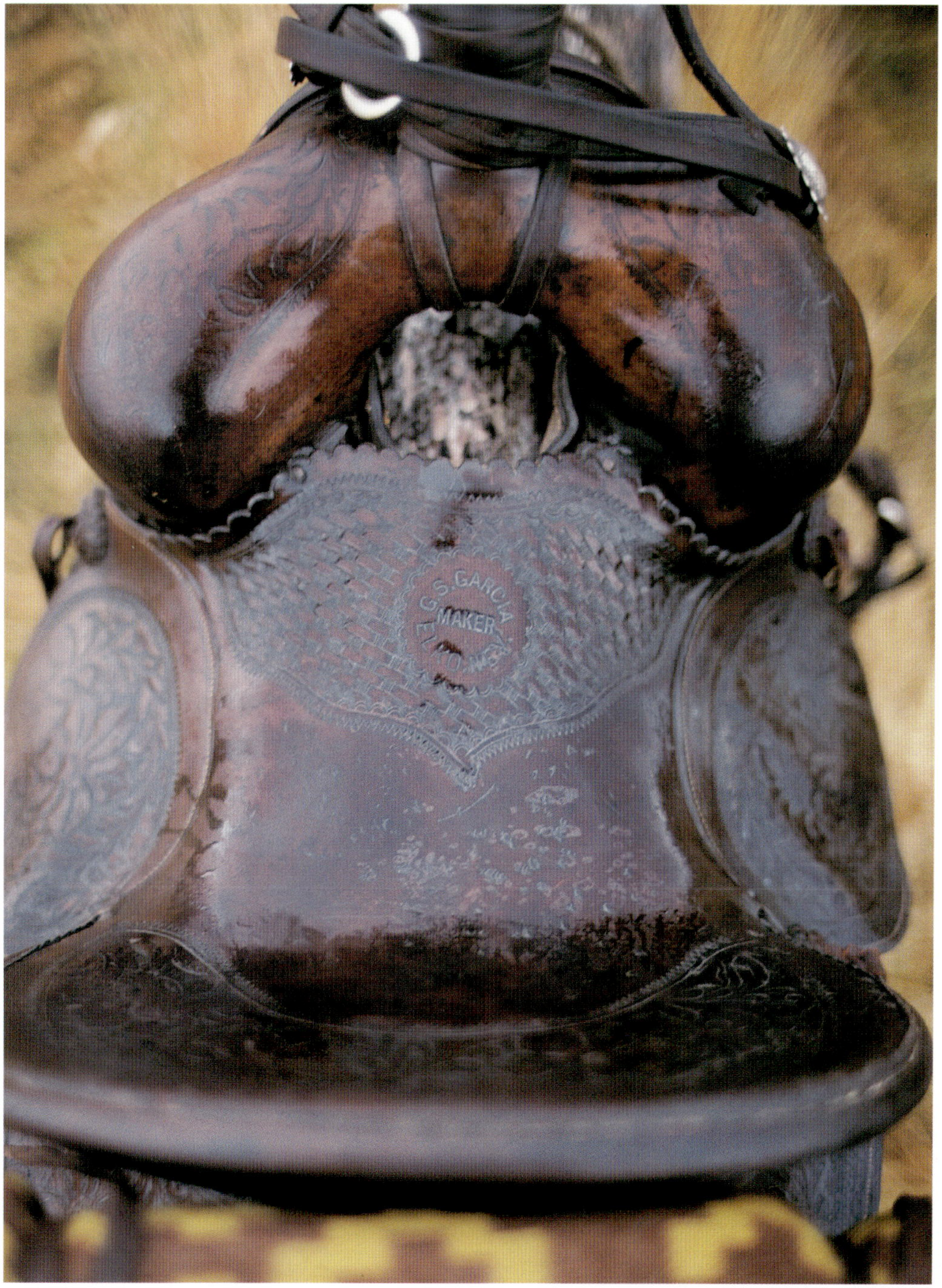

G.S. Garcia saddle, *Elko, Nevada, Ron Gillett Collection*

The Cheyenne Roll *is the lip on the back of the cantle of the saddle. It has been generally agreed that Frank A. Meanea of Cheyenne, Wyoming was the first to put this design element in a saddle and therefore he is credited as the inventor of it.*

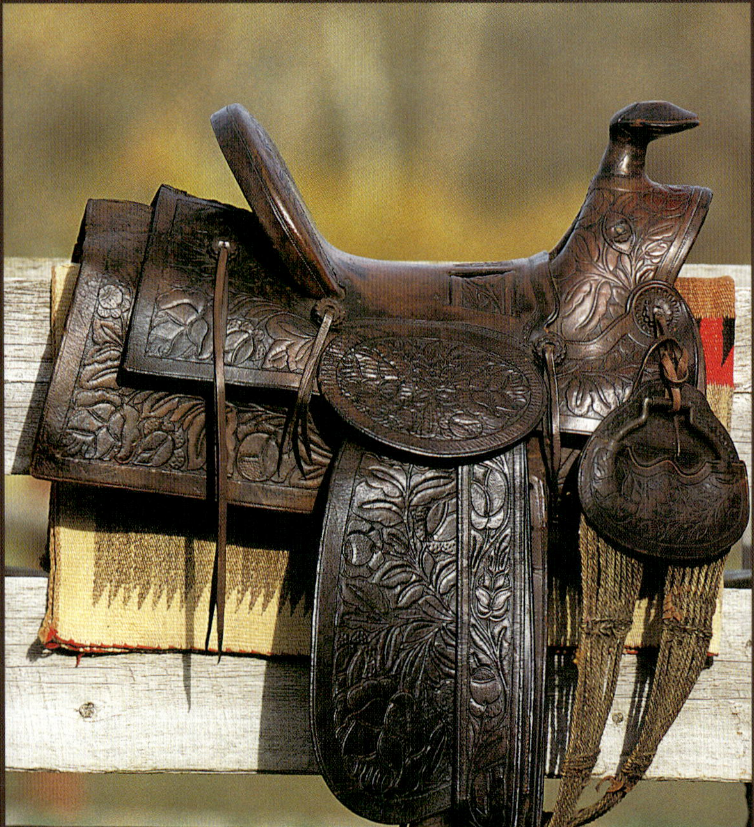

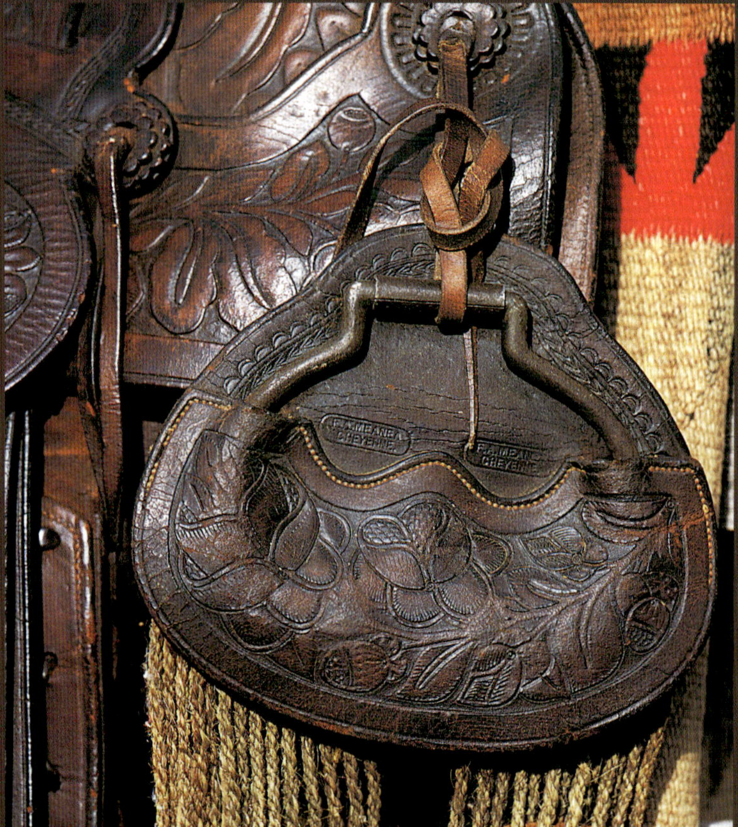

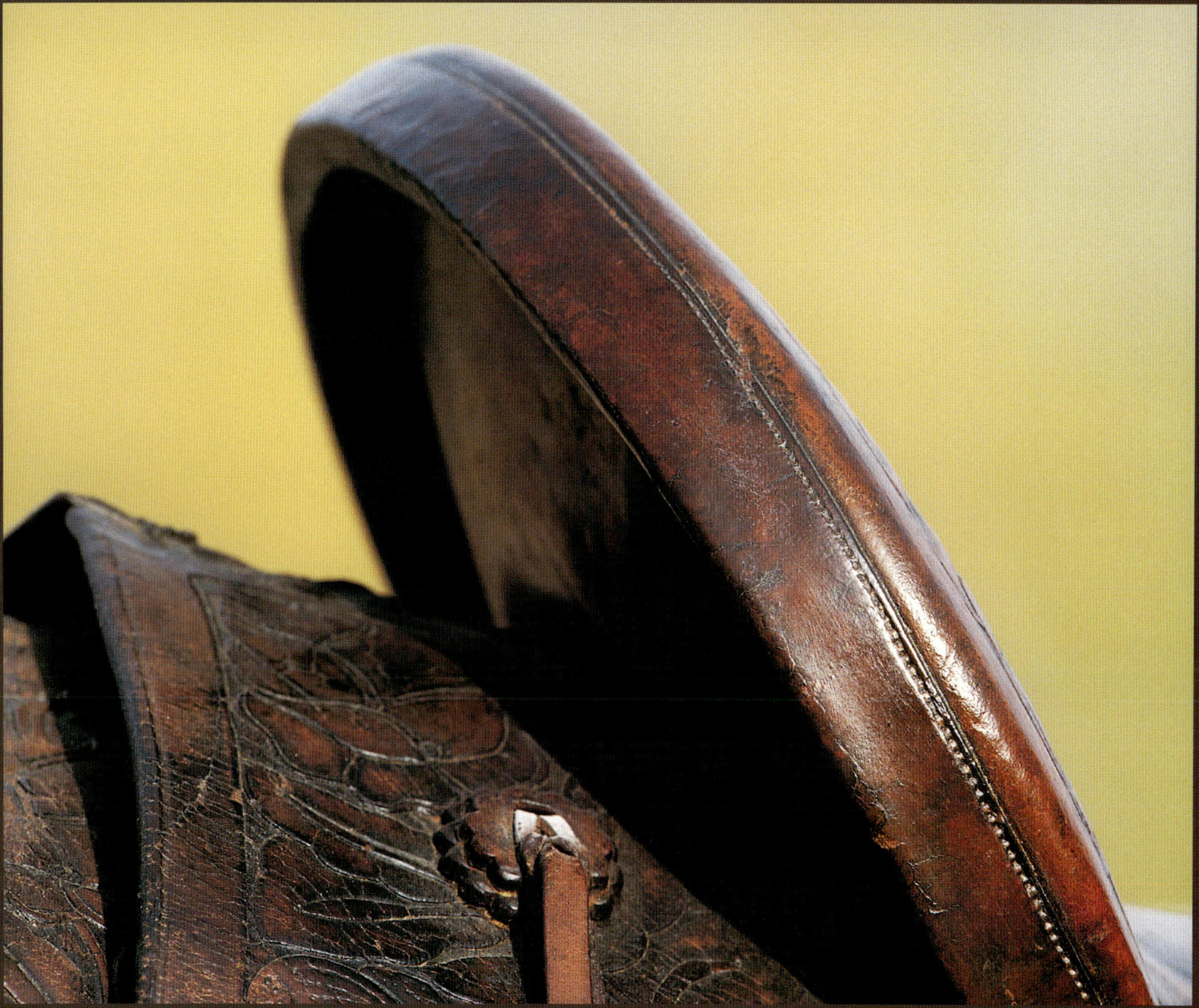

F.A. Meanea *saddle, King Saddlery Museum, Sheridan, Wyoming*

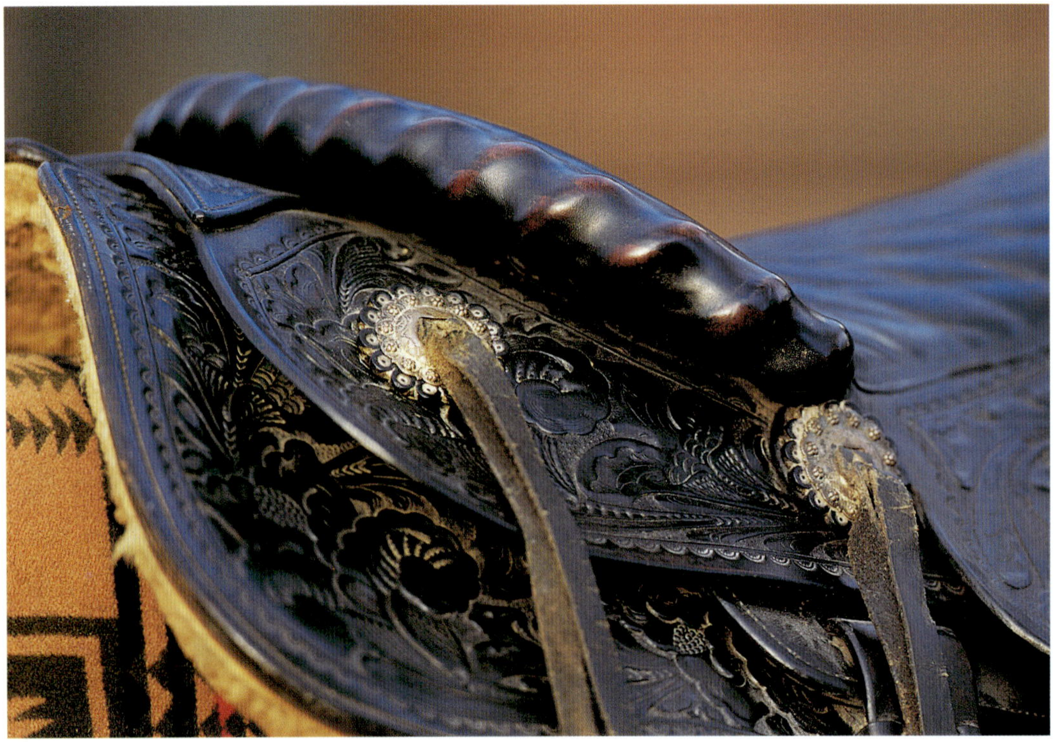

CANTLE WITH ROPE EDGING

PETE VERBECK SADDLE, *Miles City, Montana, circa 1950s, Scott Carter Collection*

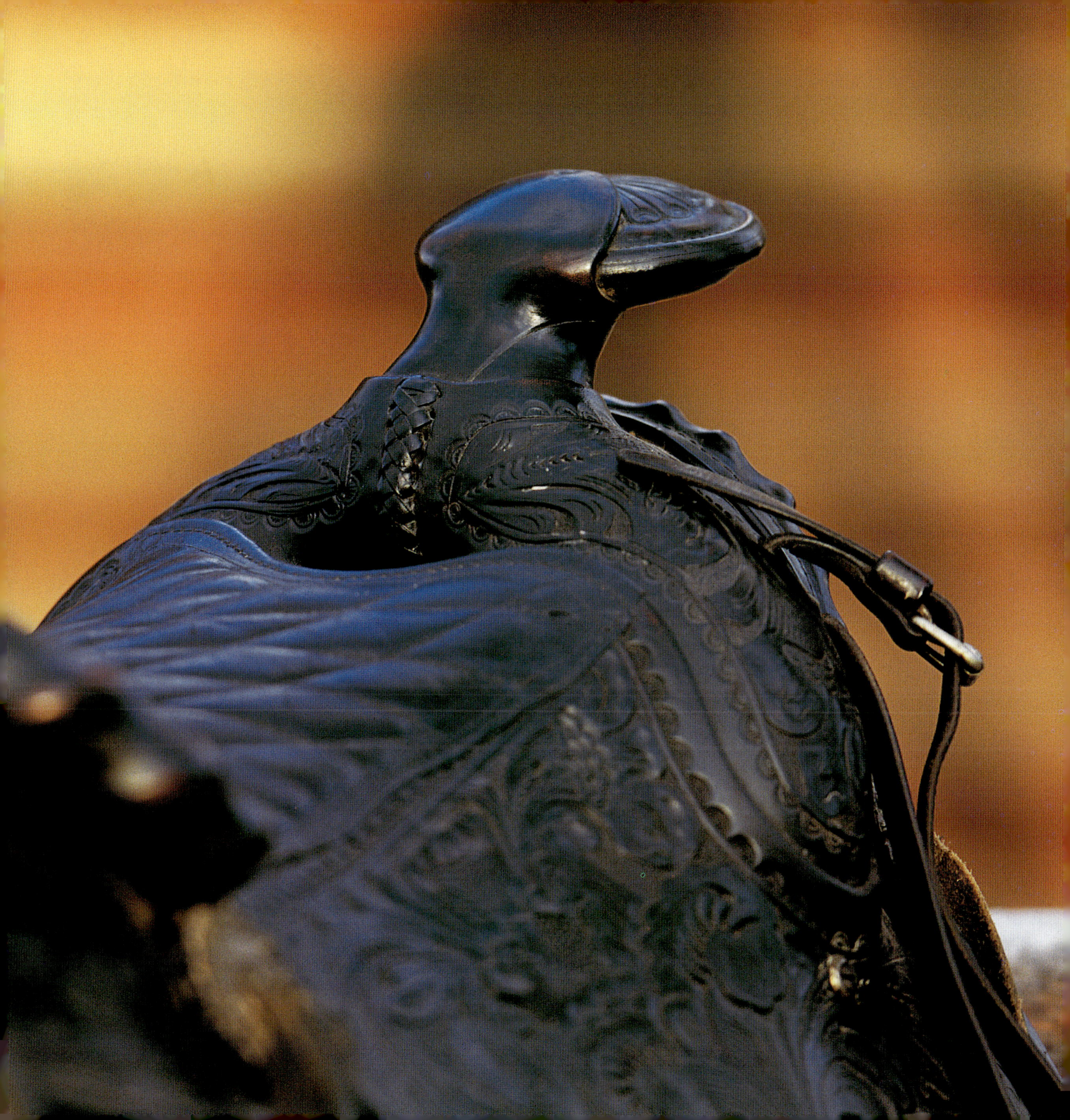

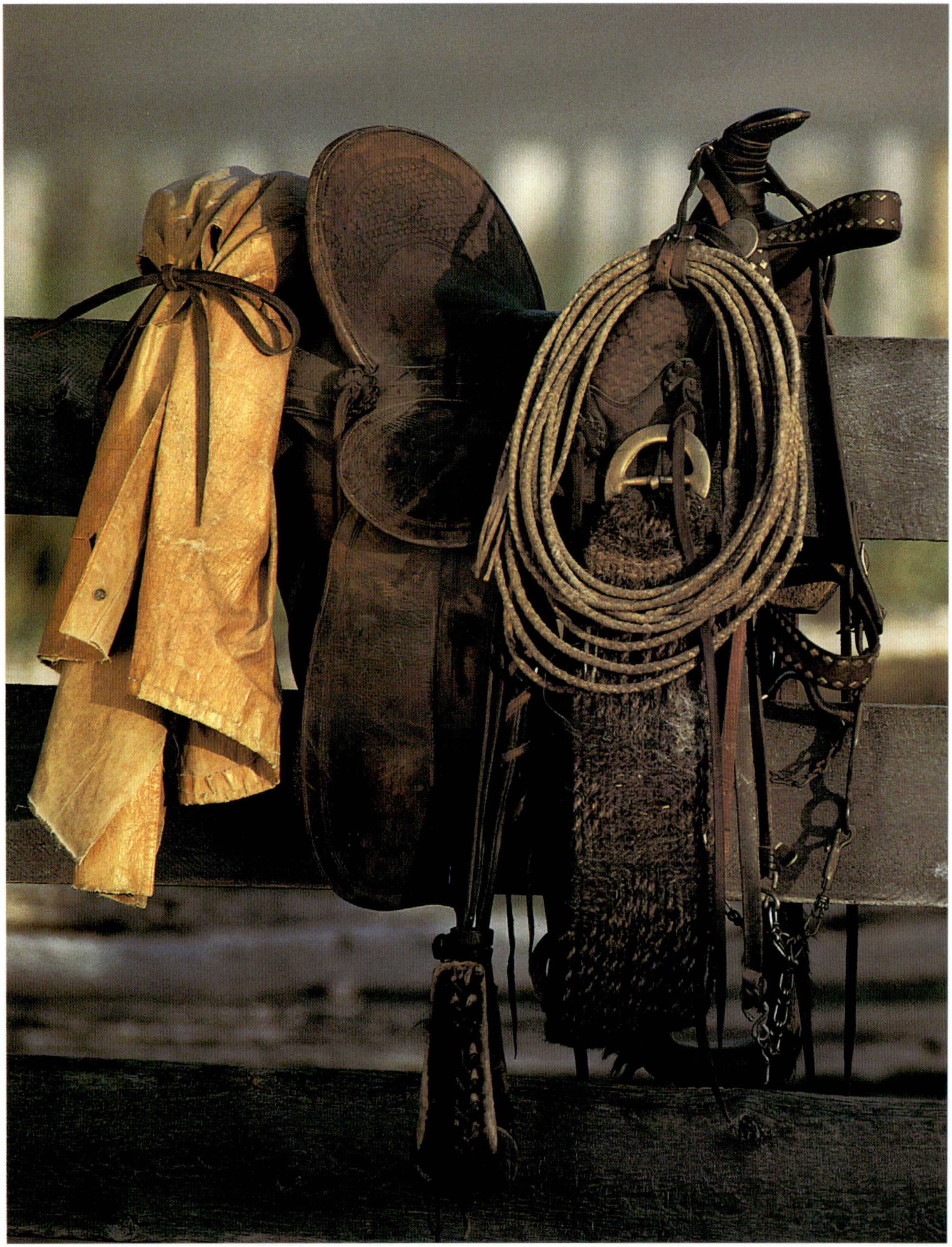

READY TO WORK—*1880s Sentinel Butte saddle with an original Fish slicker and hand-made rawhide reata as well as a horsehair cinch, Stoecklein Collection*

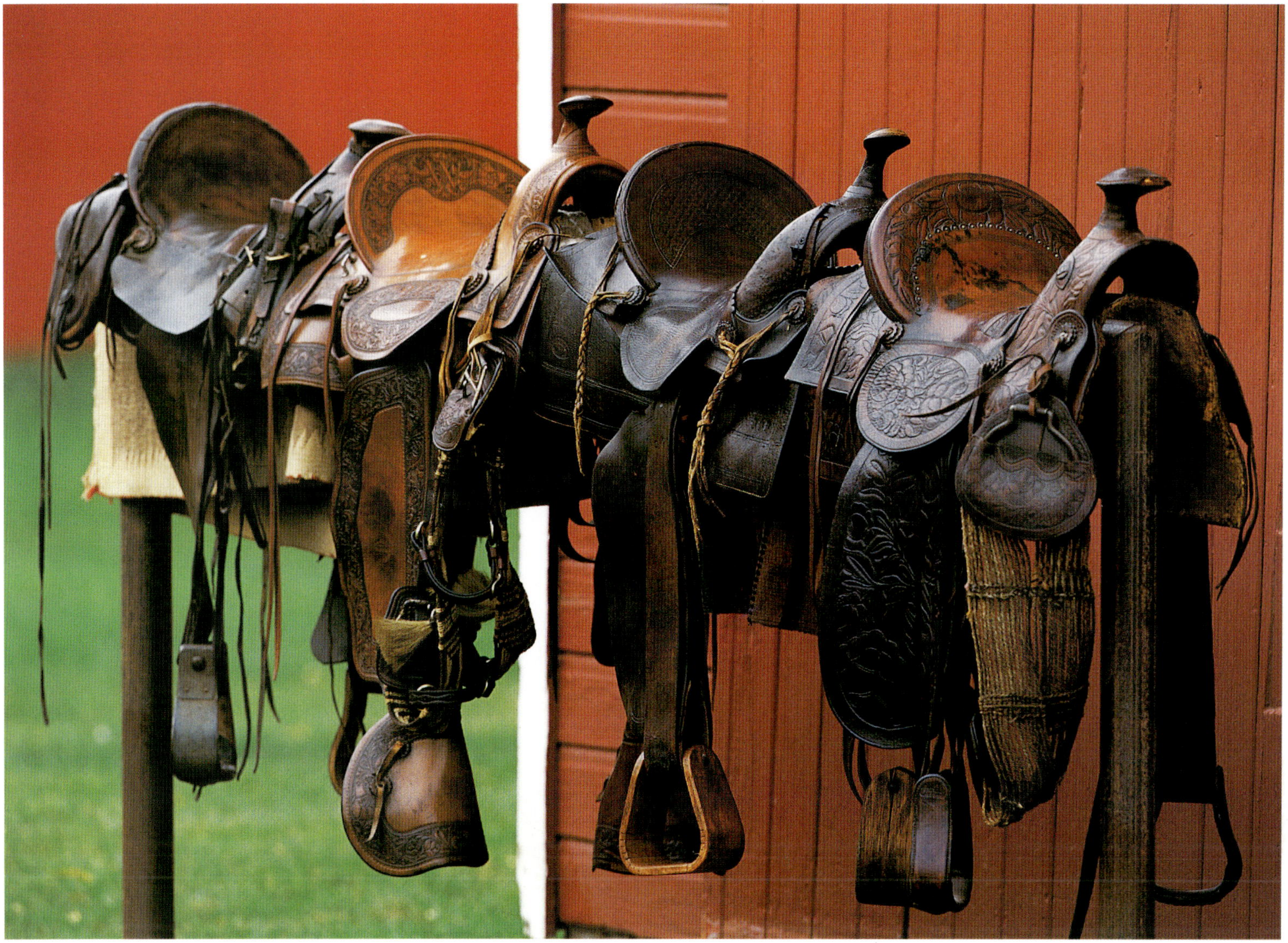

FOUR 1800S SADDLES FROM THE KING SADDLERY MUSEUM—*(left to right) Gordon Fitzhugh's Collins and Morrison saddle, Omaha, Nebraska, circa 1864; special order Main & Winchester saddle circa 1880s with border stamp, loop seat, and handmade double horsehair cinches; original Coggshall Miles City saddle, style #505 with single rig and crease wheel border; F.A. Meanea's most revered saddle model with Cheyenne roll and full floral carvings, 1882-3, Wyoming Territory*

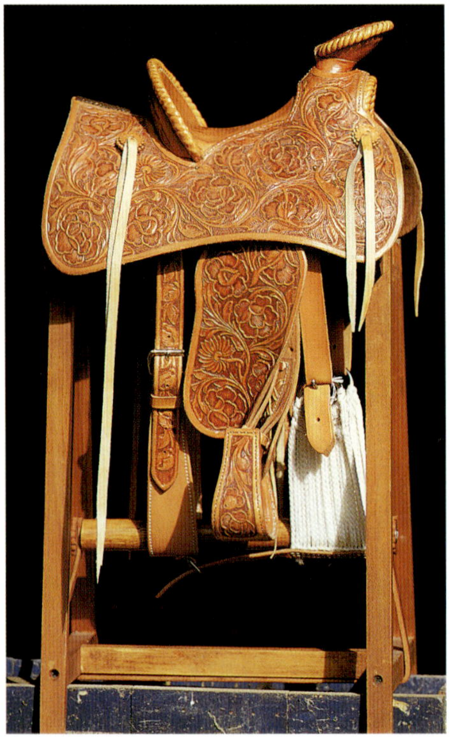

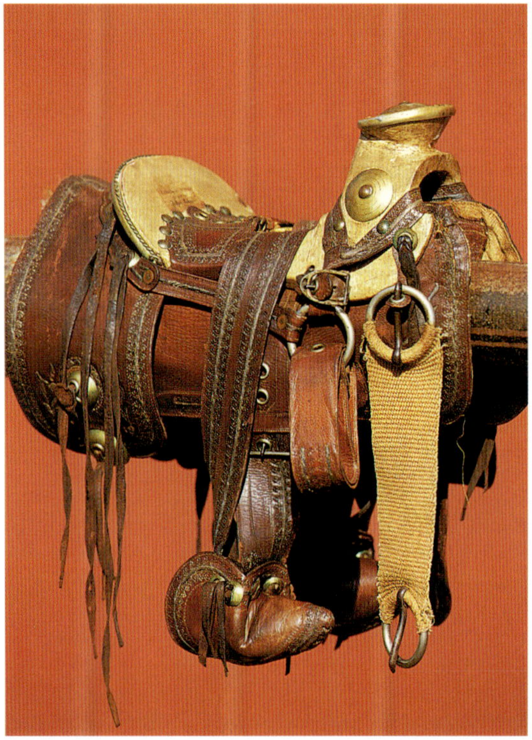

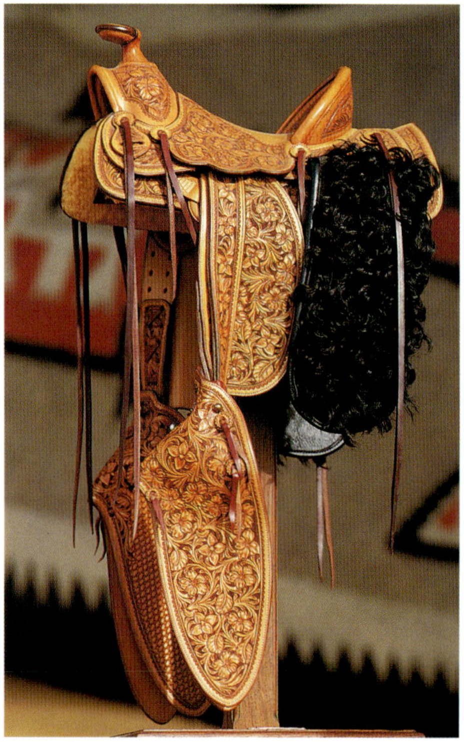

LLOYD DAVIS MINIATURE SADDLE, *fully flowered with rope edging on cantle, horn, and gullet*

OLD MEXICAN MINIATURE SADDLE *with exposed rawhide tree, mochila, tapaderos, and cactus fiber embroidery, pre-1900*

TAD MIZWA MINIATURE SADDLE, *replica of the 1760-80 vaquero style*

All from the King Saddlery Museum, Sheridan, Wyoming

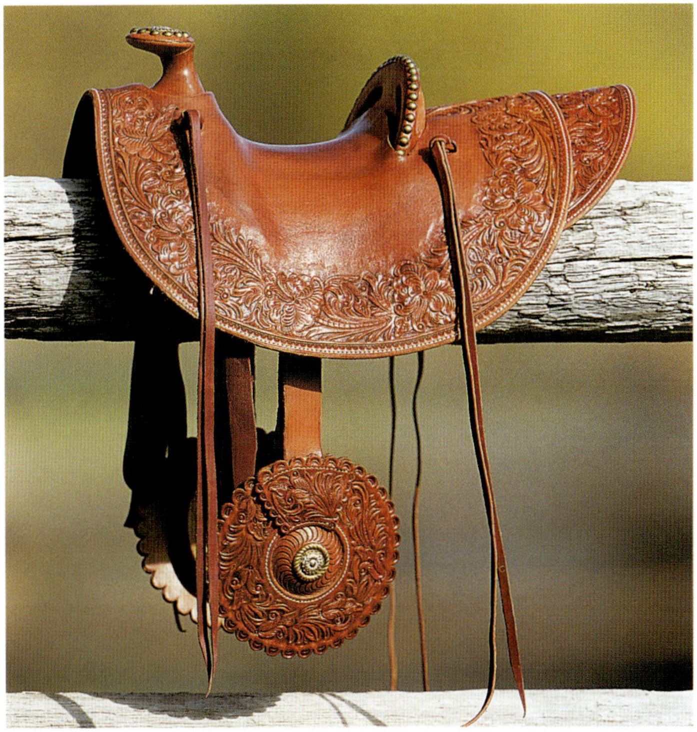

MINIATURE SADDLES *were originally salesman samples and later became objects of art and craftsmanship. As much work goes into one of these scale models as its full-size brother and its value is as much or greater.*

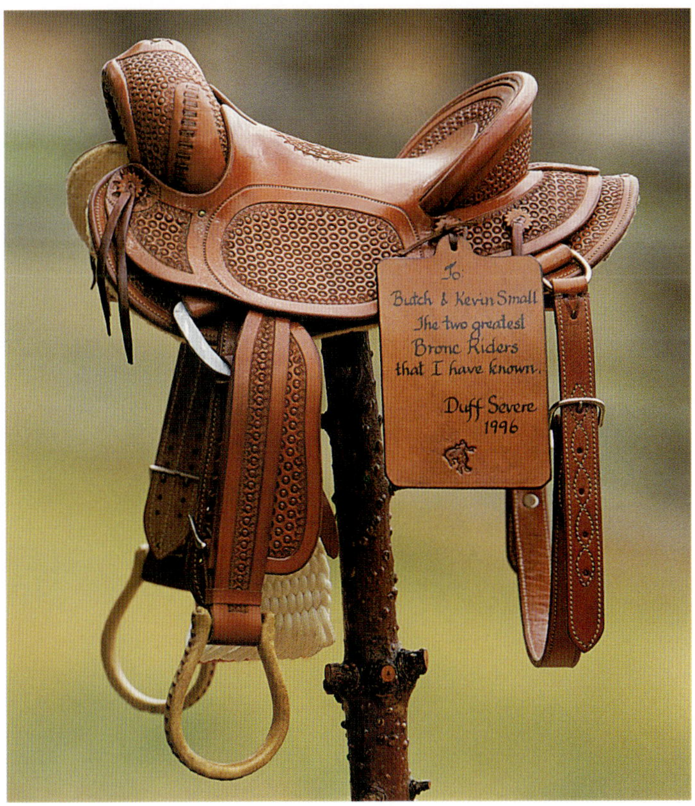

TAD MIZWA MINIATURE SADDLE, *Houston, Texas*

SEVERE BROTHERS MINIATURE SADDLE, *Pendleton, Oregon*

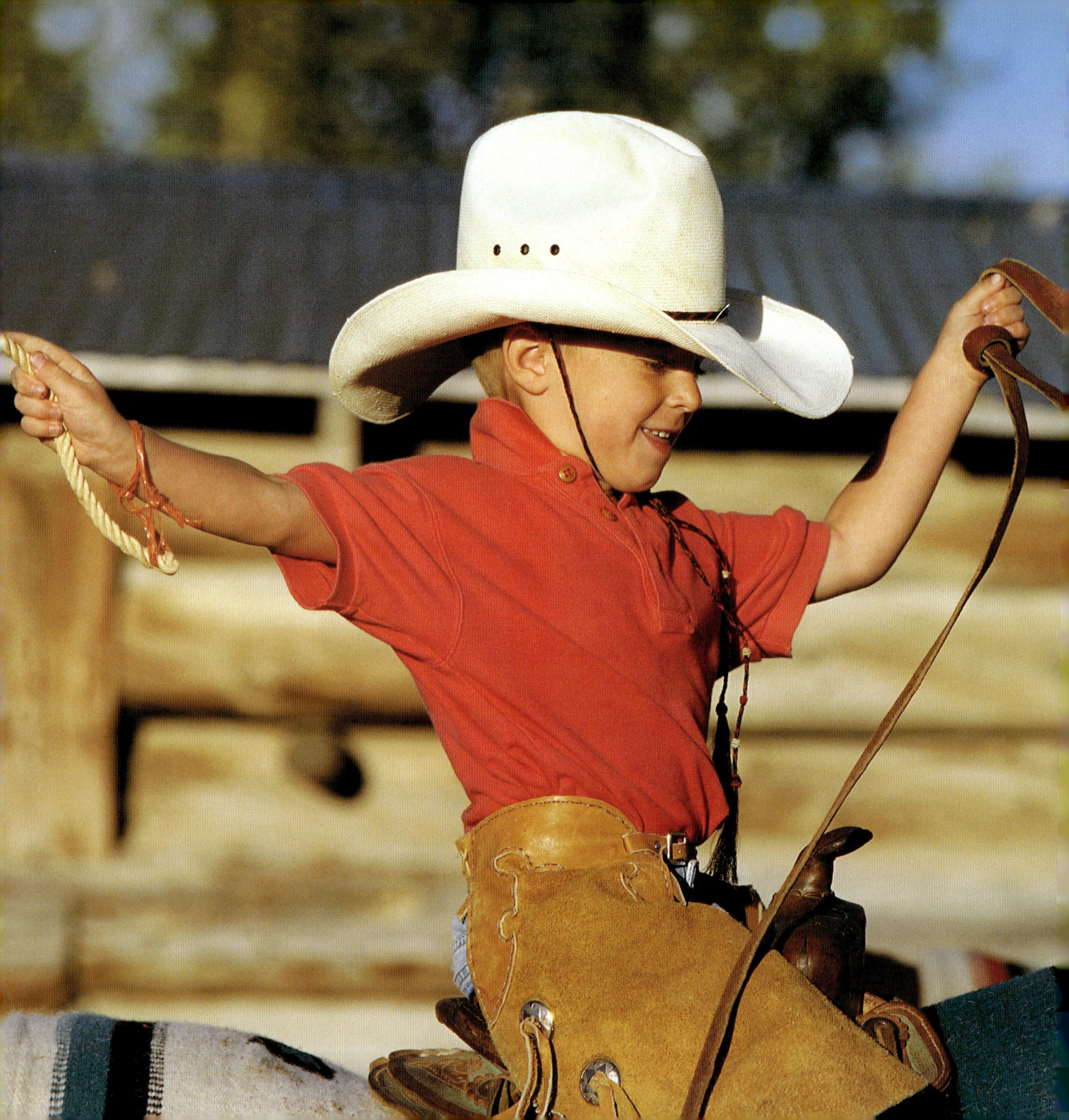

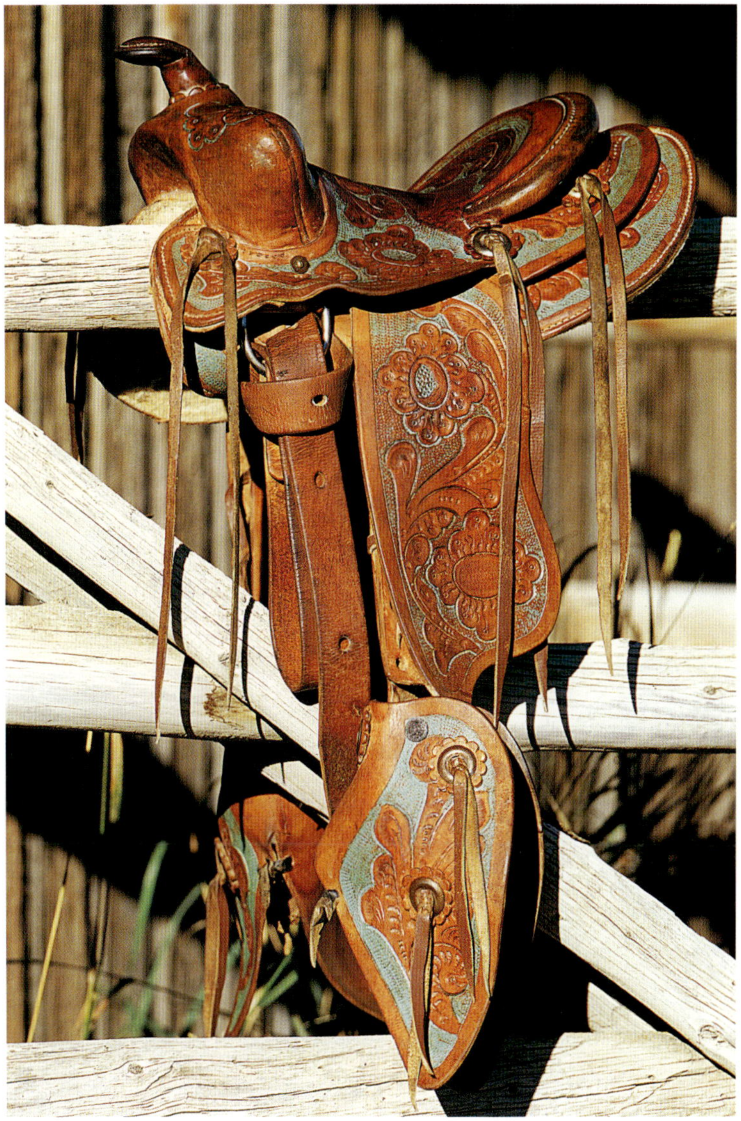

MEXICAN CHILDREN'S SADDLE, *circa 1914, Stoecklein Collection*

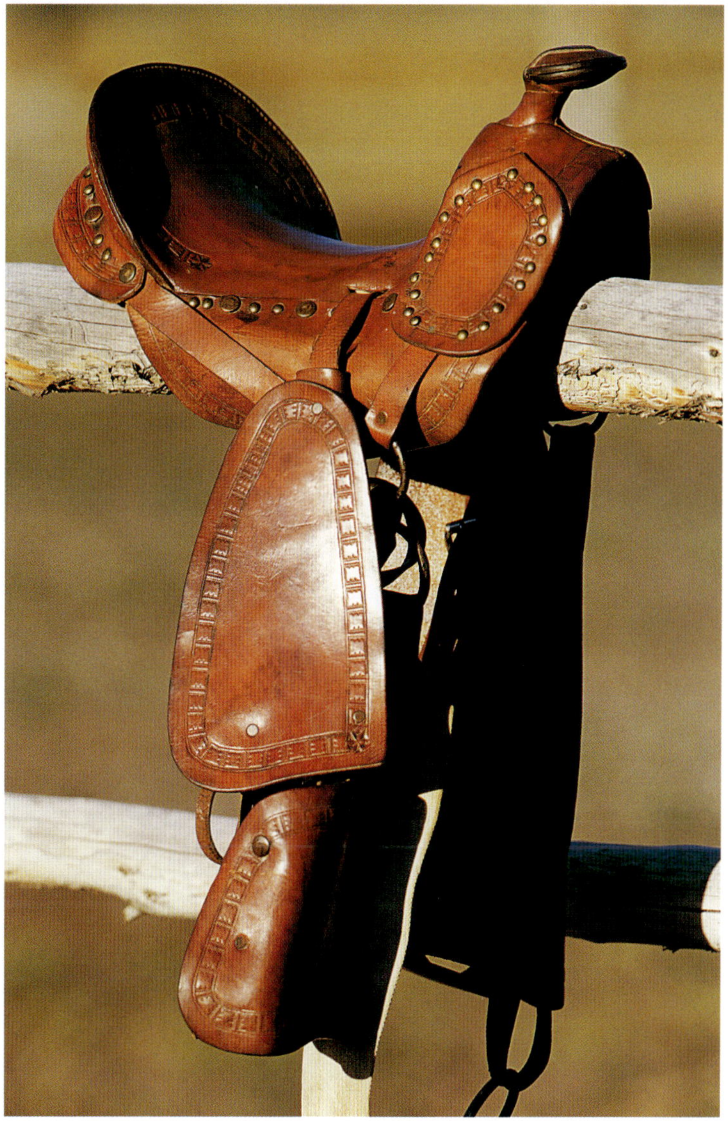

CHILDREN'S SADDLE, *maker unknown, early 1900s, Stoecklein Collection*

COLBY STOECKLEIN, *Mackay, Idaho*

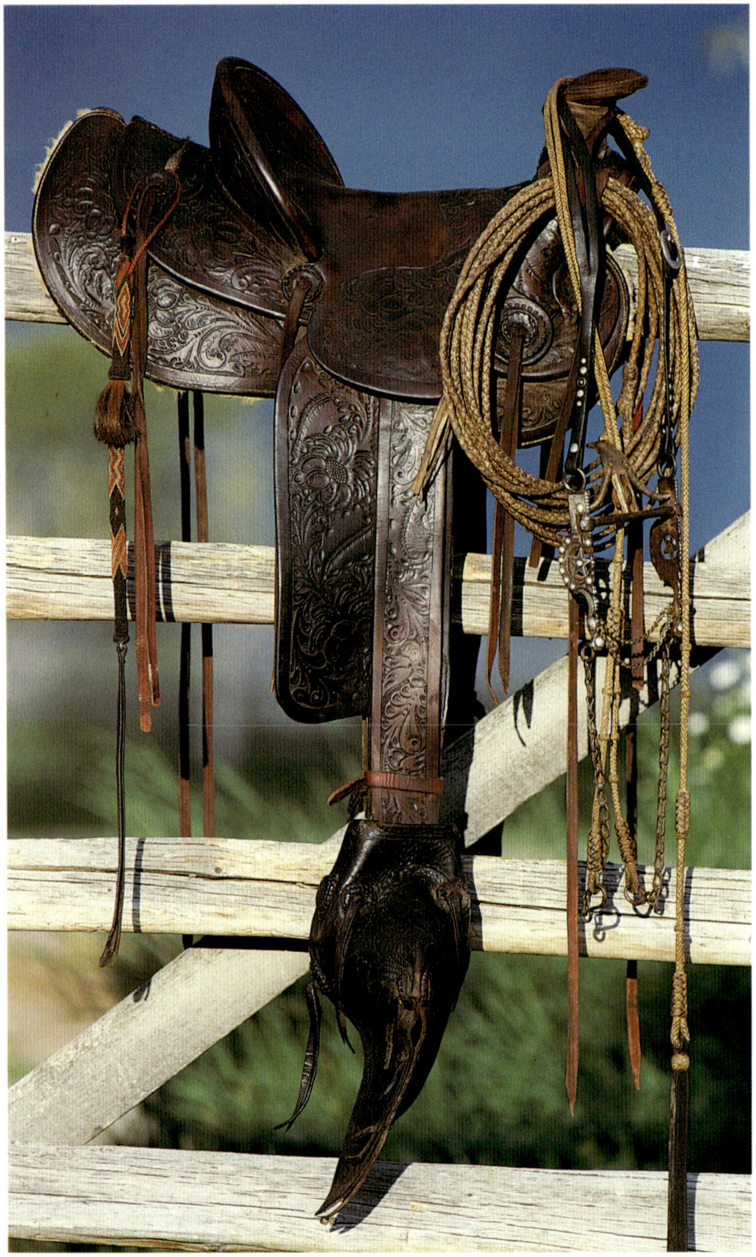

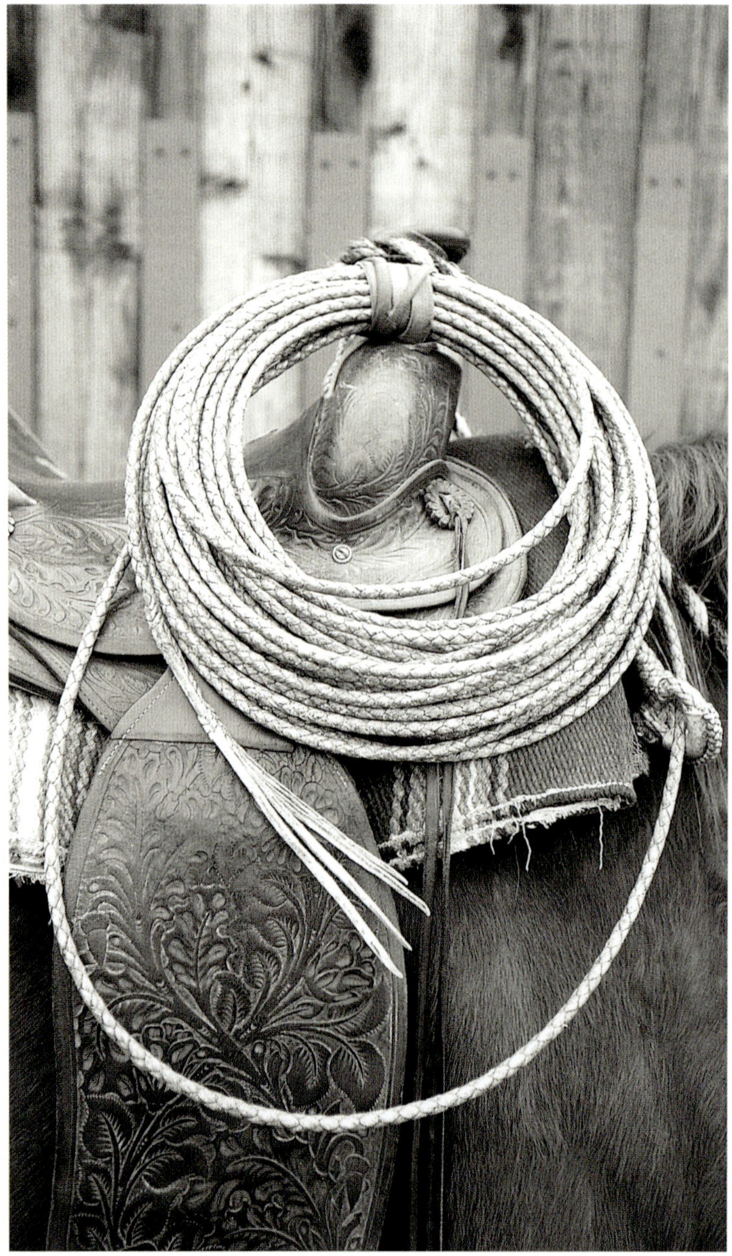

JOHN D. BUCKLEY VAQUERO SADDLE, *Monterey, California, circa 1920*

BILL CONGER SADDLE, *Los Angeles, California with handmade reata by Ernie Morris, Pleasanton, California*

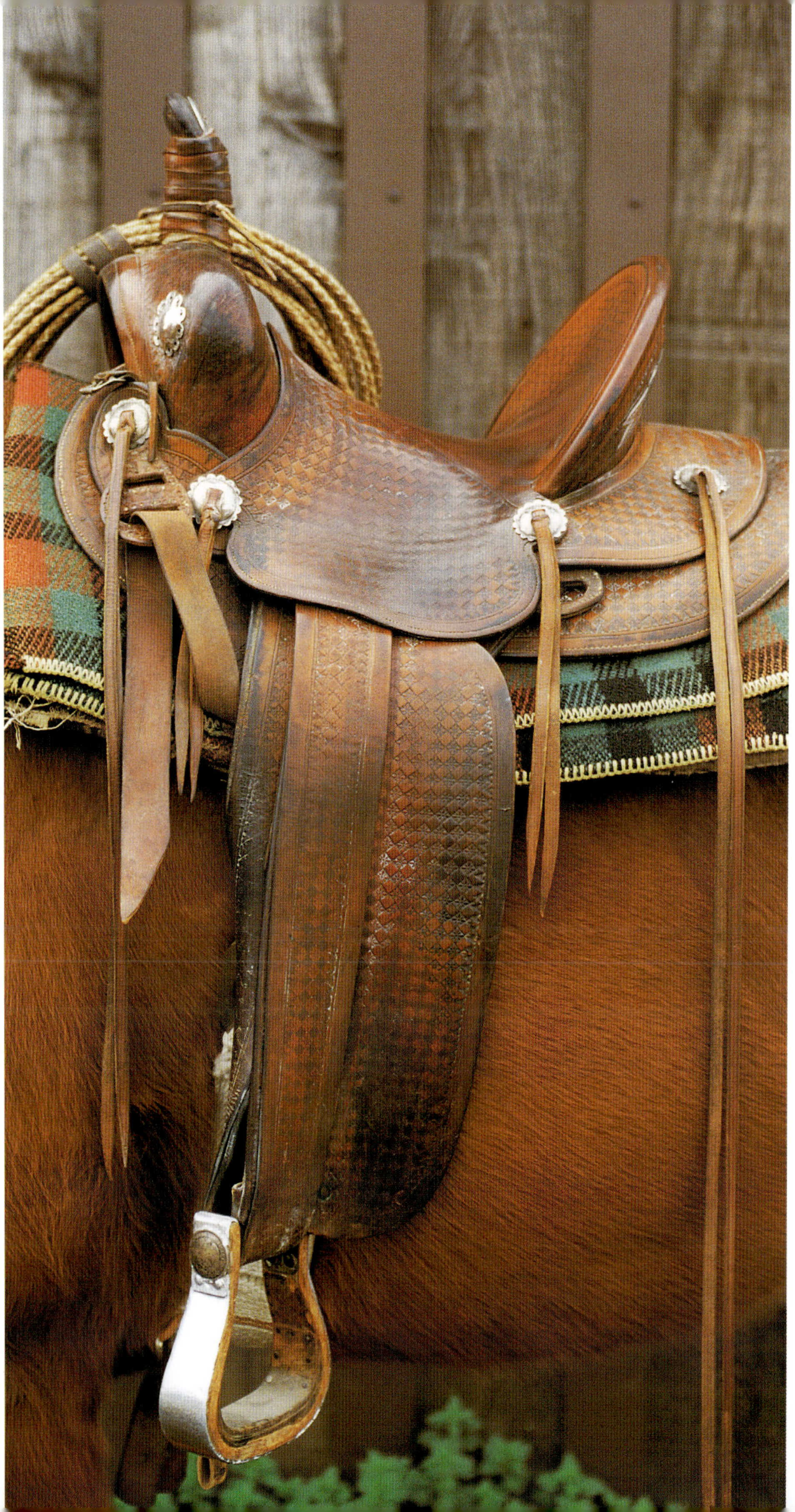

Jess Wilkinson *was a famous California vaquero. His grandson, Ernie Morris, is one of the last real California vaqueros—an artist and a true horseman.*

Jess Wilkinson Visalia saddle *with unique roping post, Visalia, California*

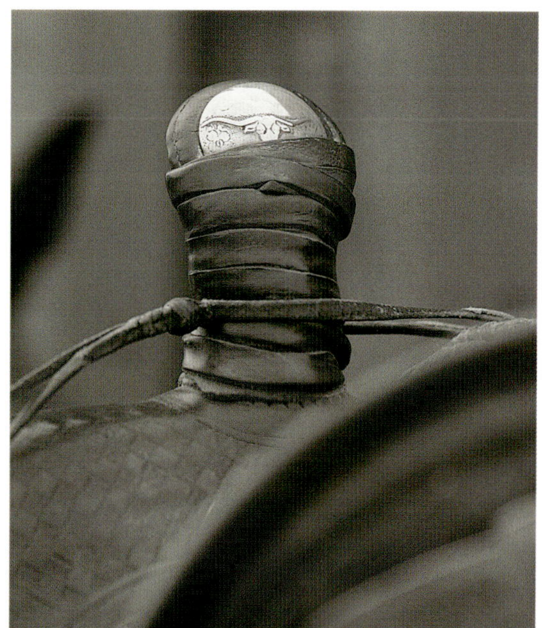

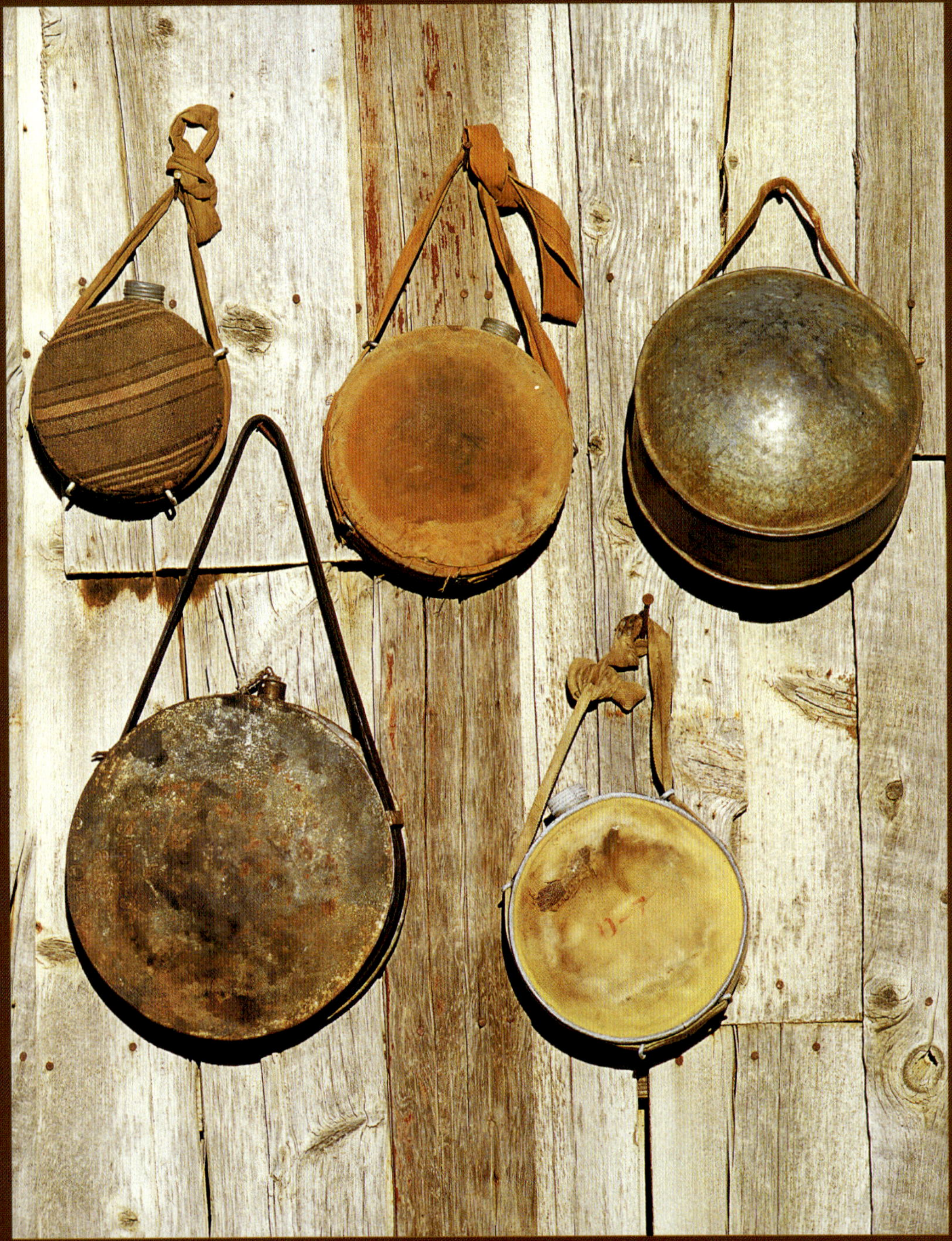

Canteens are a *big part of the West. Water is the all-important life-saving element on the hot and dusty trail rides. Today most canteens are made of plastic, making these relics of the old West more and more valuable to collectors.*

Canteens, *Stoecklein Collection*

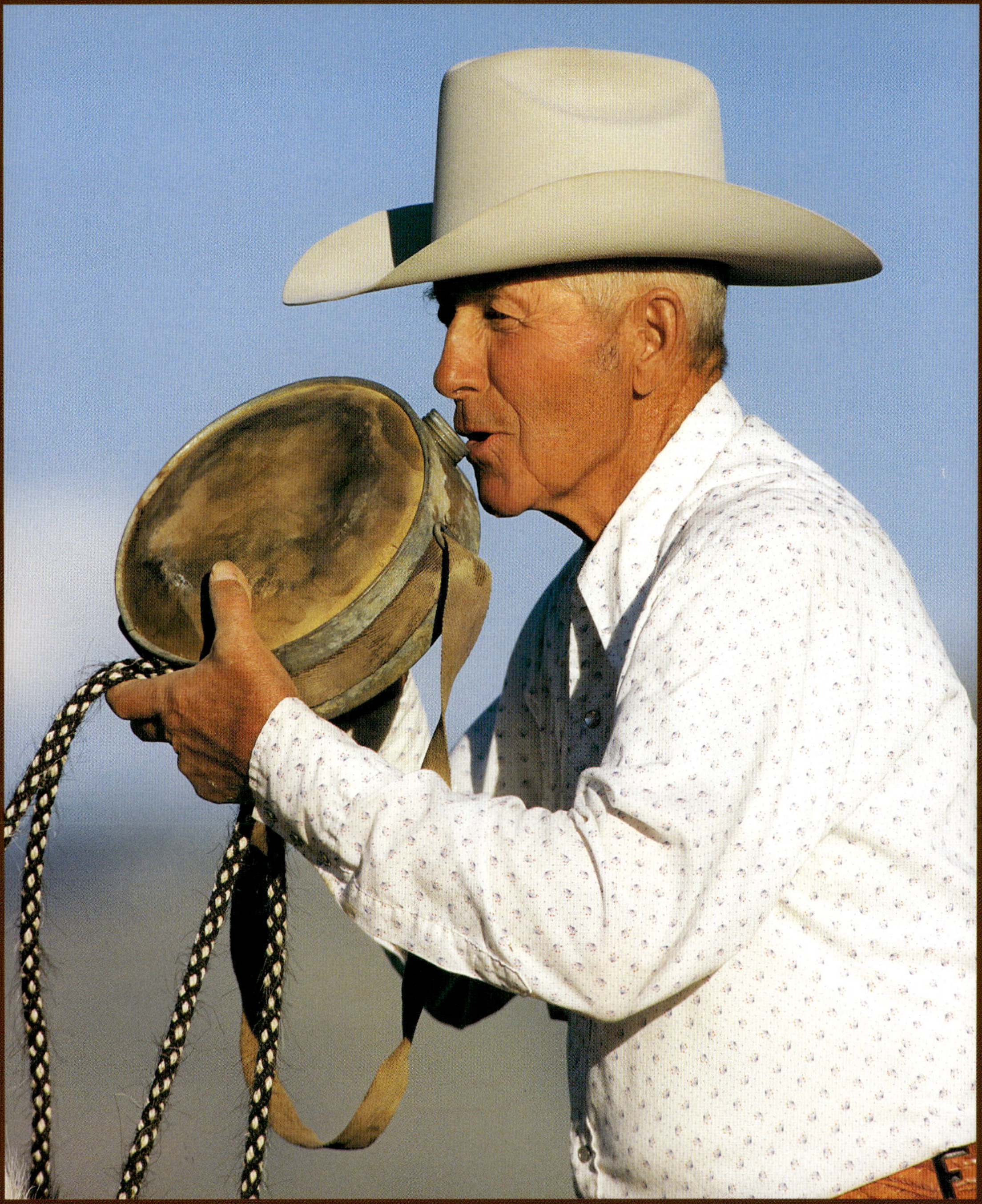

RAY SEAL TAKES A SIP *from an old canvas-covered metal canteen*

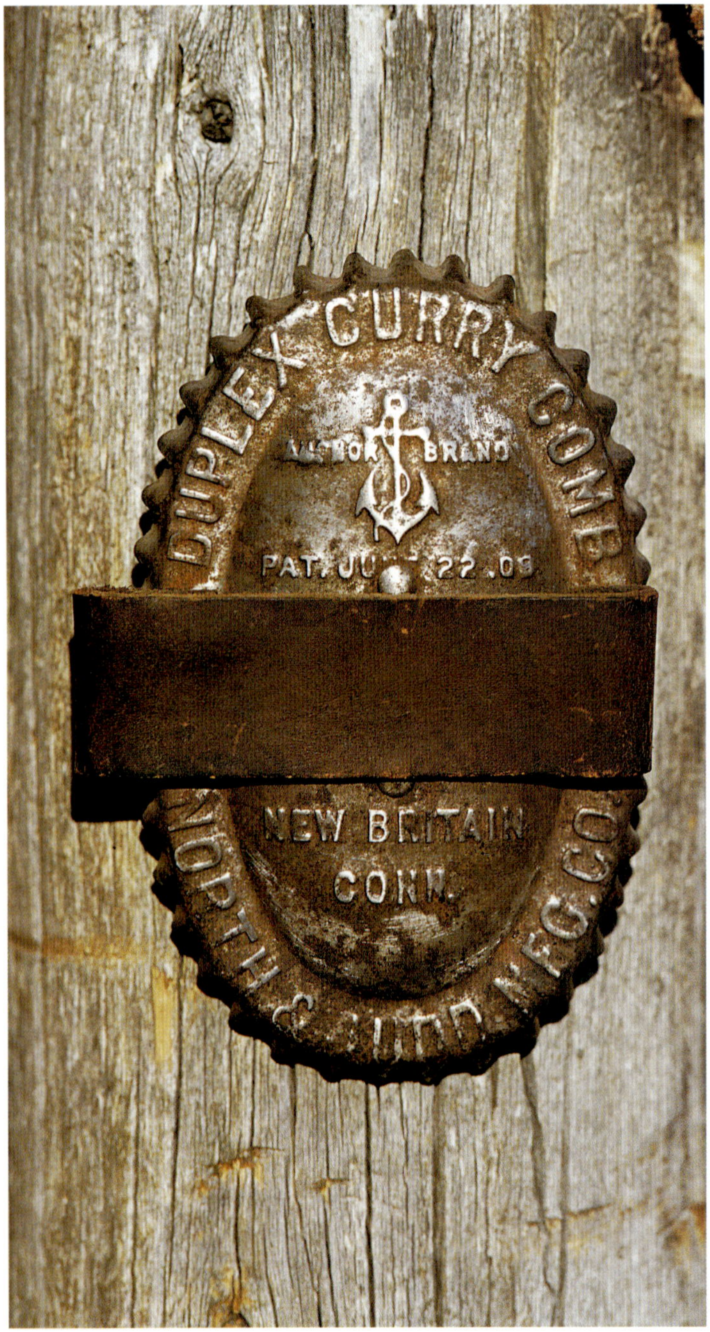
DUPLEX CURRY COMB
BRAND
NEW BRITAIN
CONN.

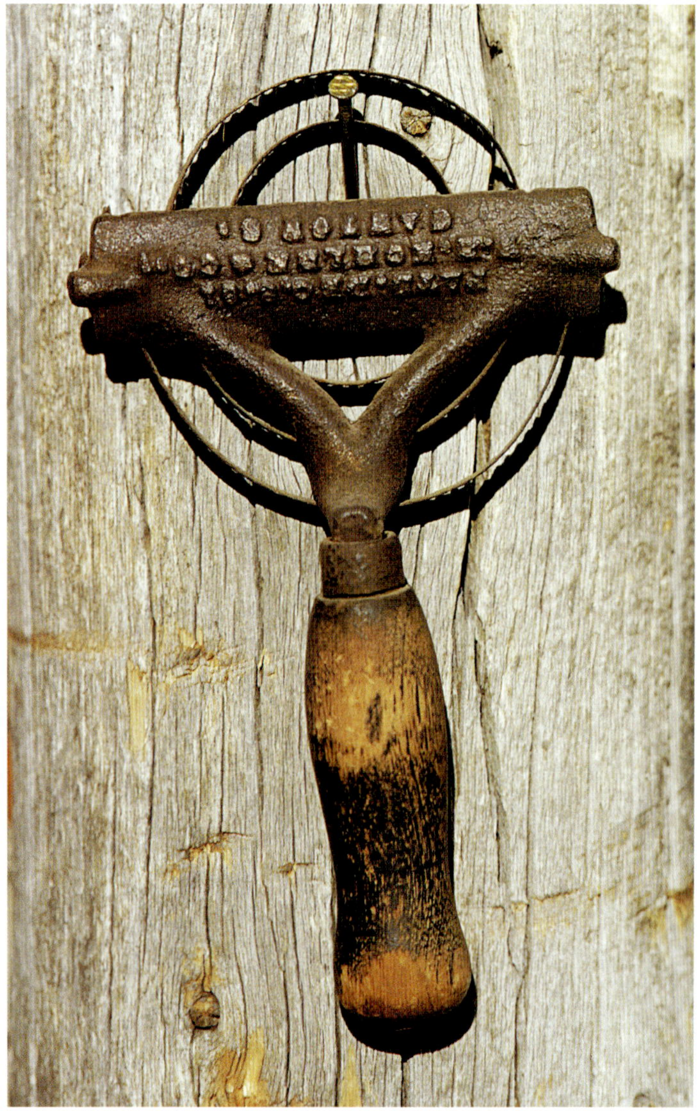

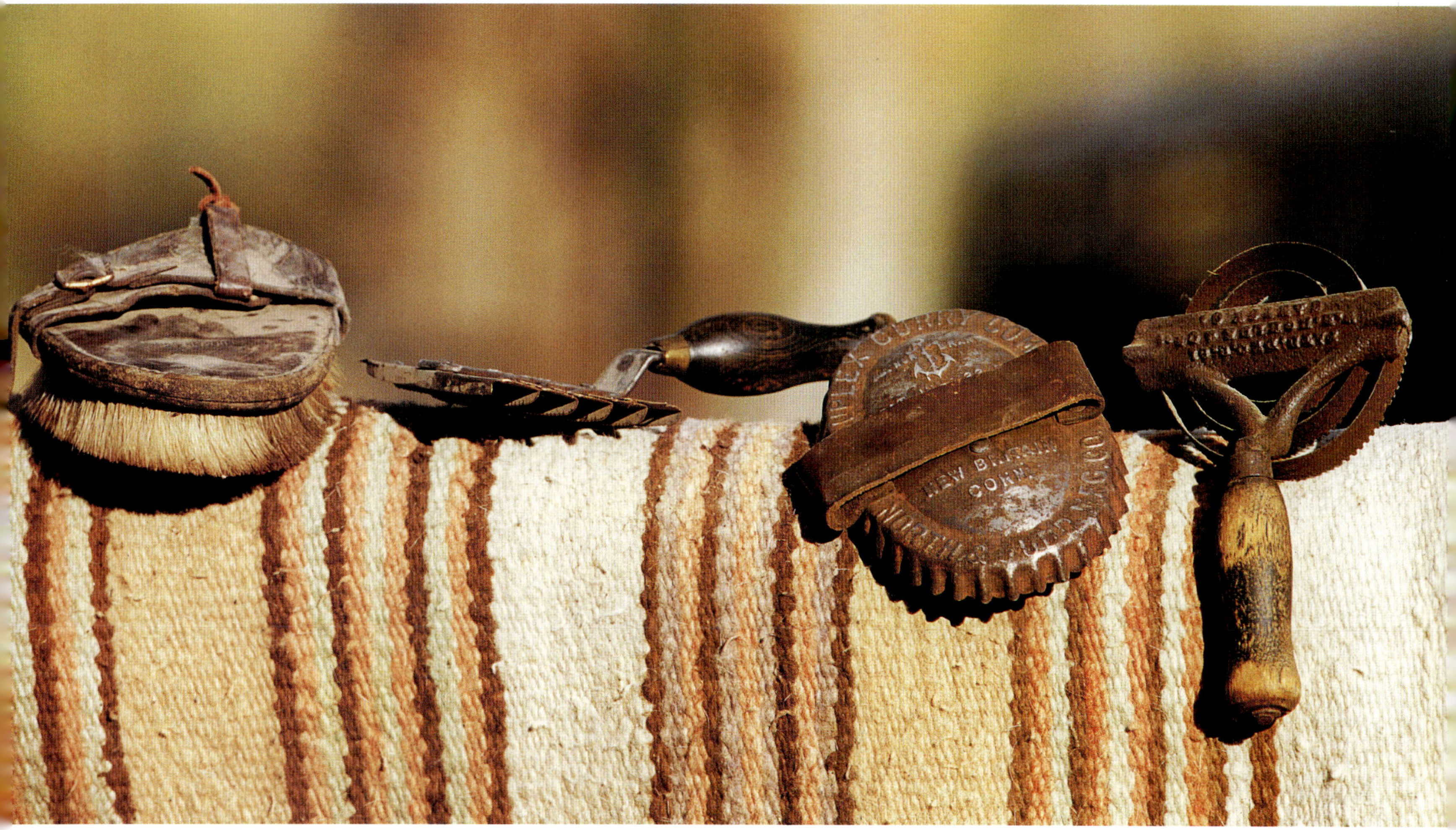

COMBS AND BRUSHES—*grooming and caring for a horse has always been very important. Some of the great saddle makers and bit and spur companies also made grooming tools such as curry combs and brushes.*

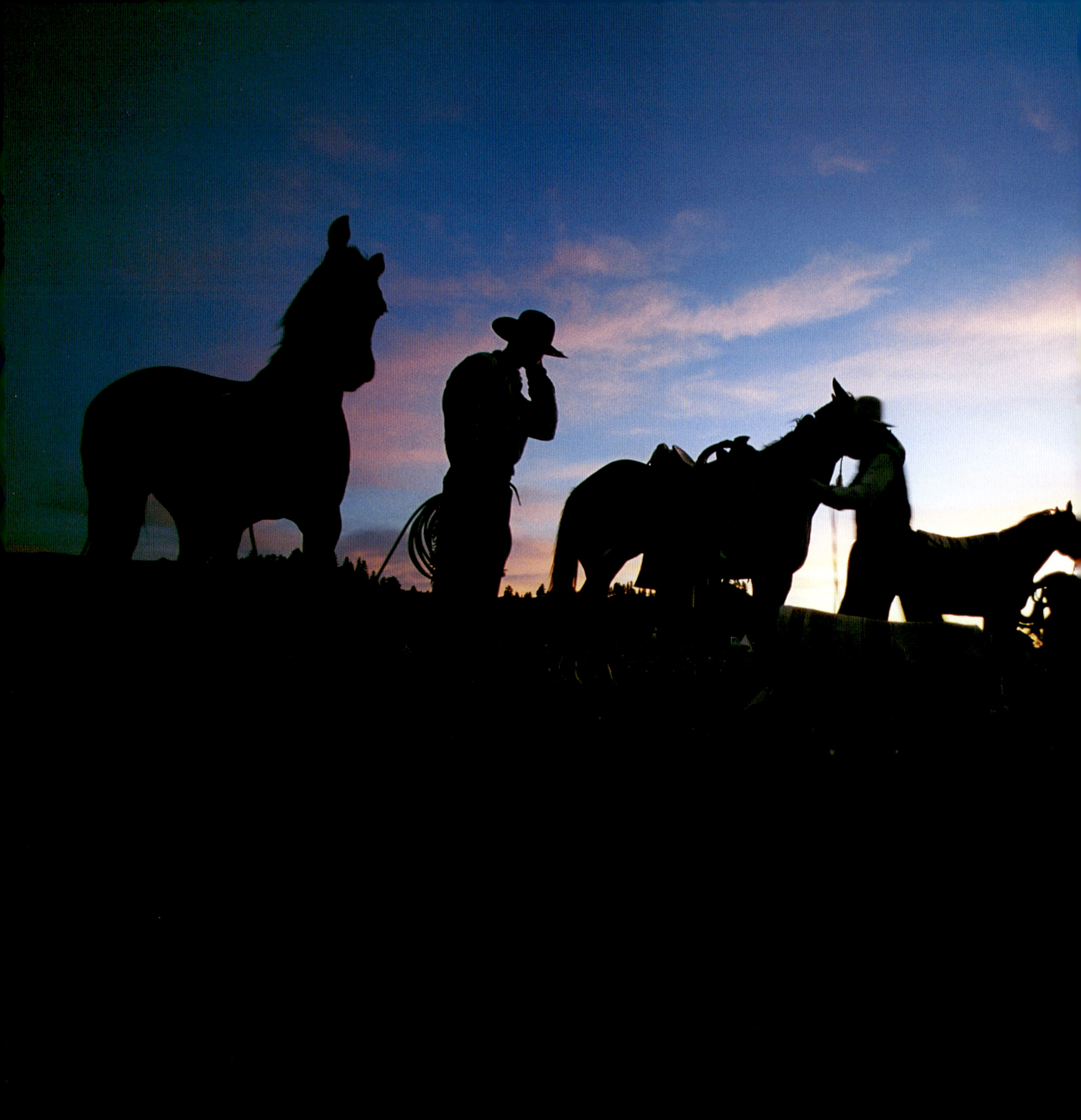

After World War II, *the cowboy returned to the range to find more jeeps and tractors and fewer saddle horses and horse work. It was the beginning of the end for the great ranches and a need for thousands of horses. Those cowboys who stayed and demanded to do things on horseback also started to change their gear and style of equipment. Gone were the big swells of the 1920s, '30s, and '40s. Along came the flat seat slick fork, or mild swell saddles. The makers of these saddles continued to develop new styles and new makers arrived to fill in the gaps. These men and their children have worked hard to keep the traditions of the West and of horsemanship alive.*

Time to saddle up, *sunrise, Padlock Ranch, Big Horn County, Montana*

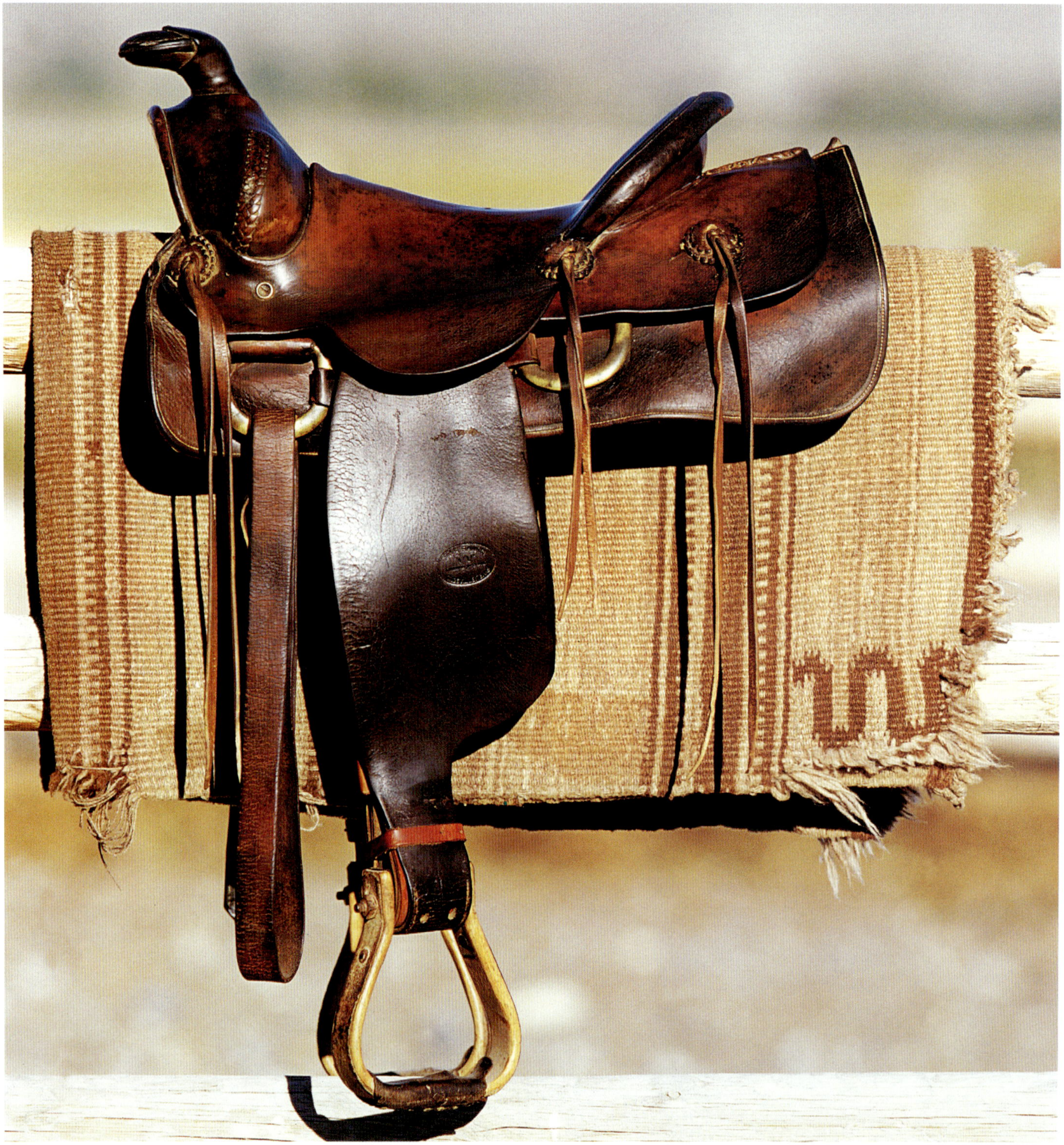

1950s SADDLE MADE BY THE KING RANCH SADDLE SHOP, *Kingsville, Texas with a very rare handmade saddle blanket, Stoecklein Collection*

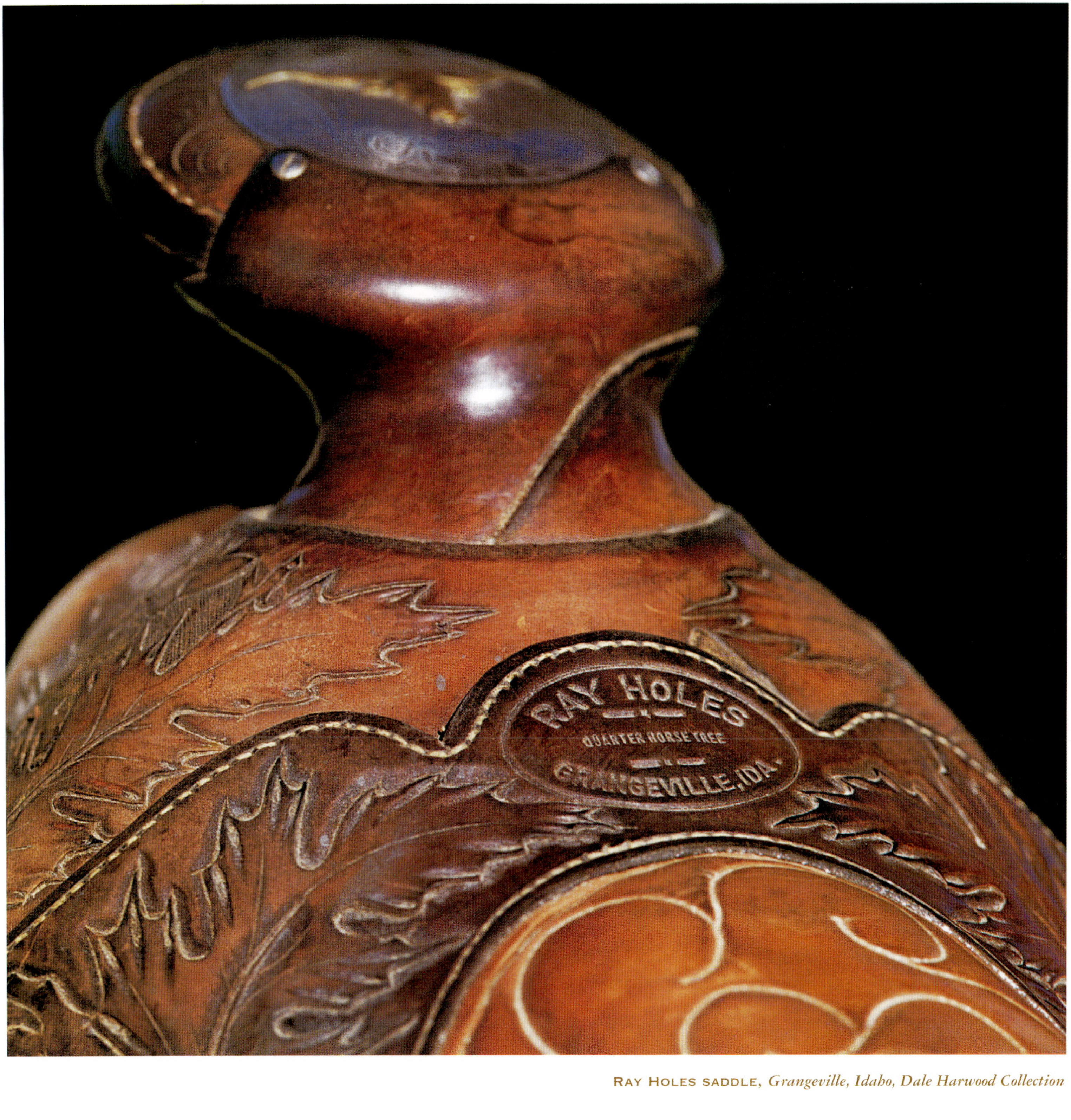

RAY HOLES SADDLE, *Grangeville, Idaho, Dale Harwood Collection*

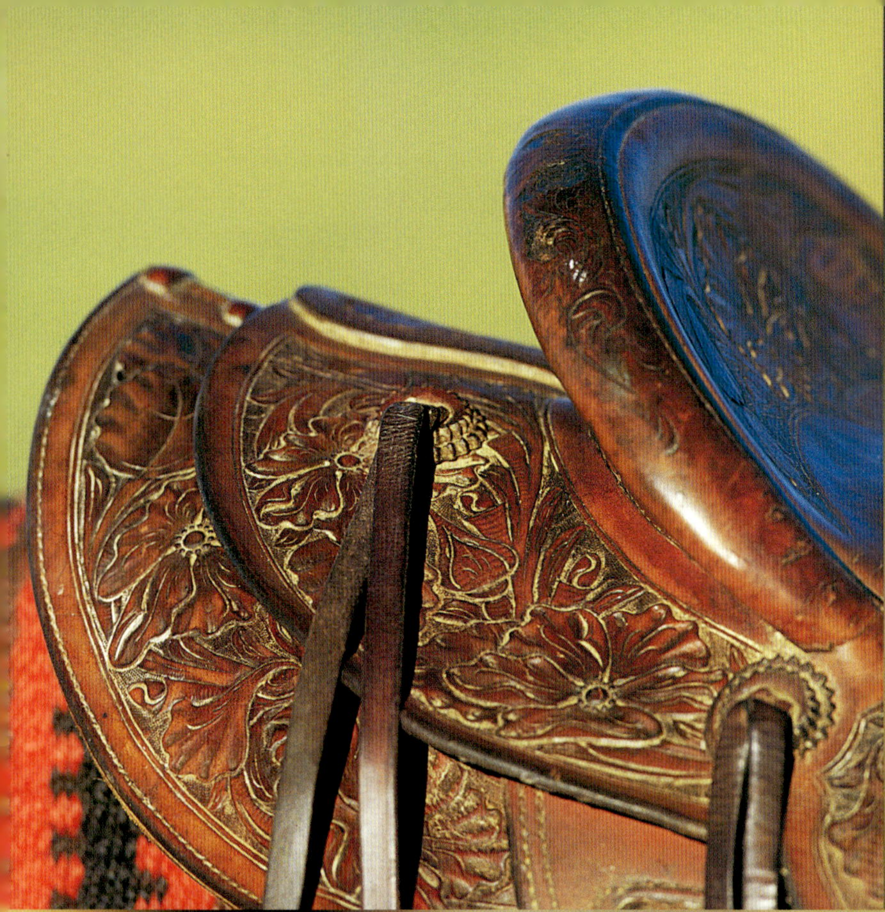

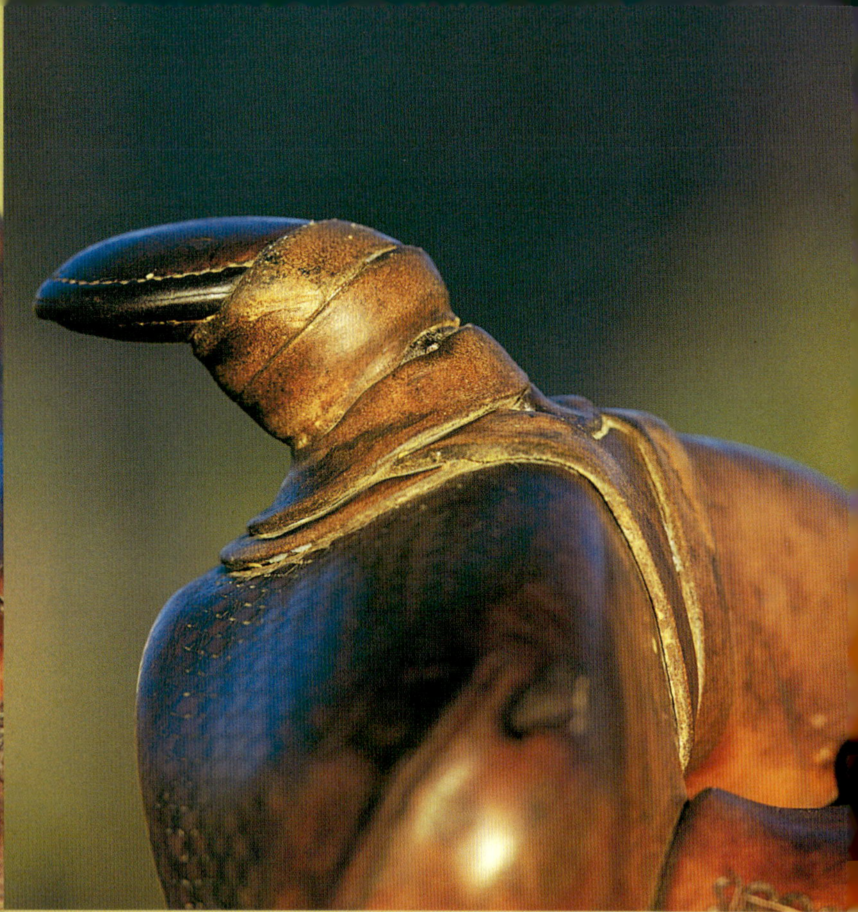

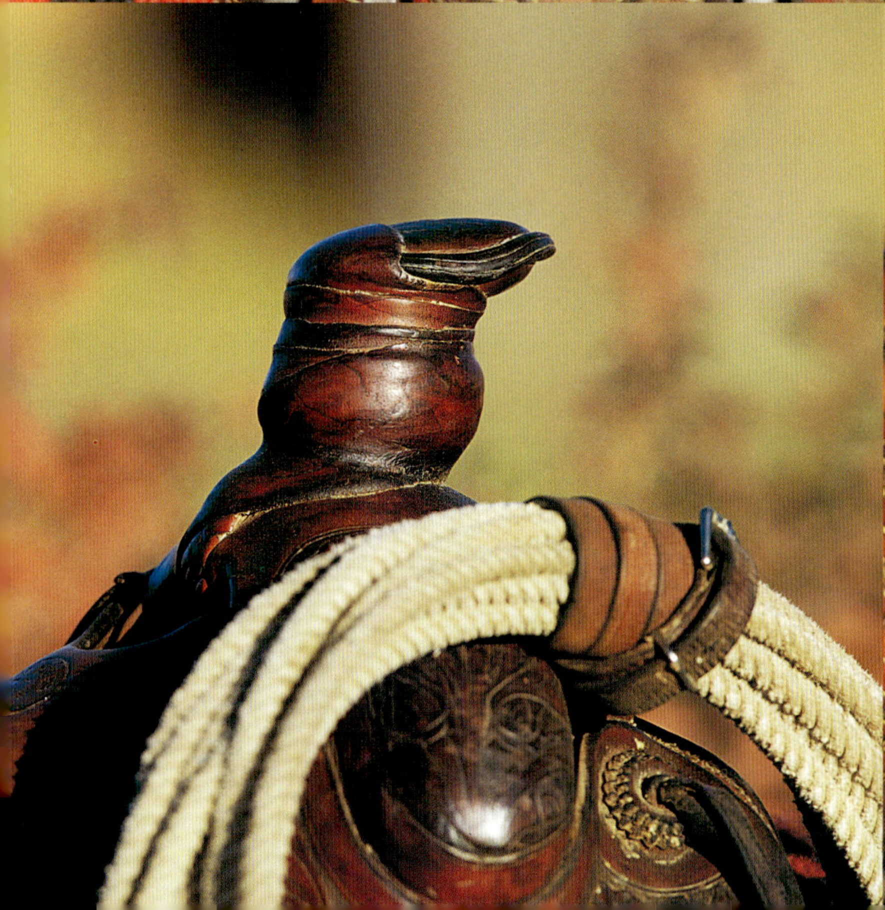

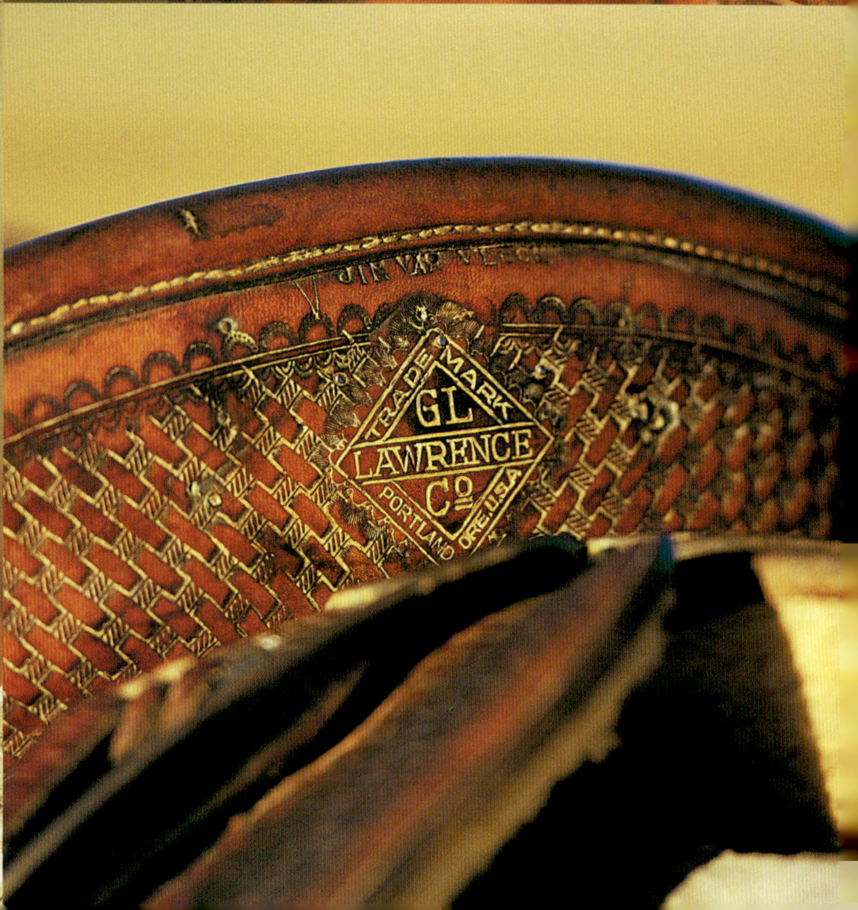
TRADE MARK
GL
LAWRENCE
Co
PORTLAND ORE. USA

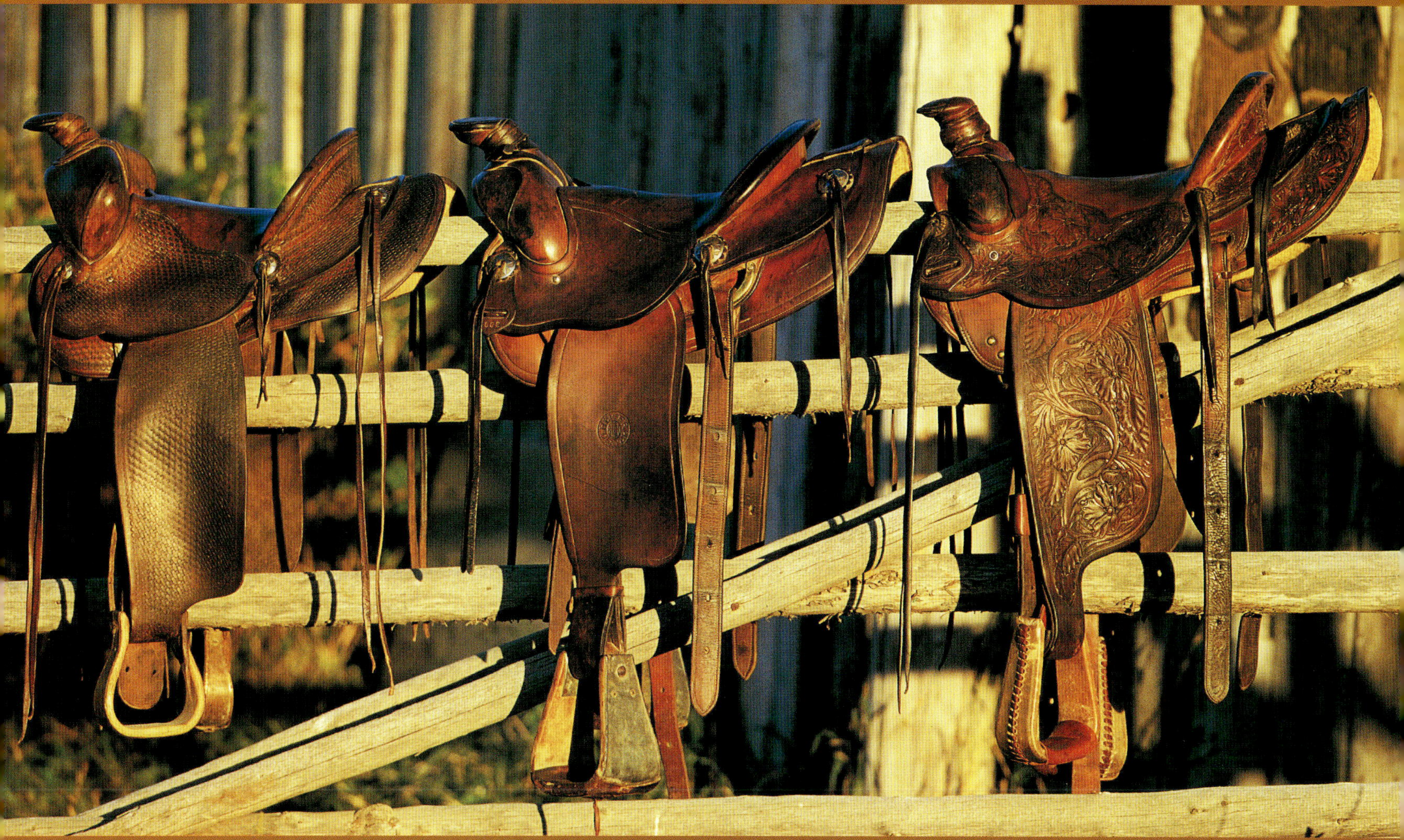

SADDLES MADE BY THREE OF THE BEST SADDLE MAKERS OF THE 20TH CENTURY—
Lawrence, Hyser, and Ray Holes, Stoecklein Collection

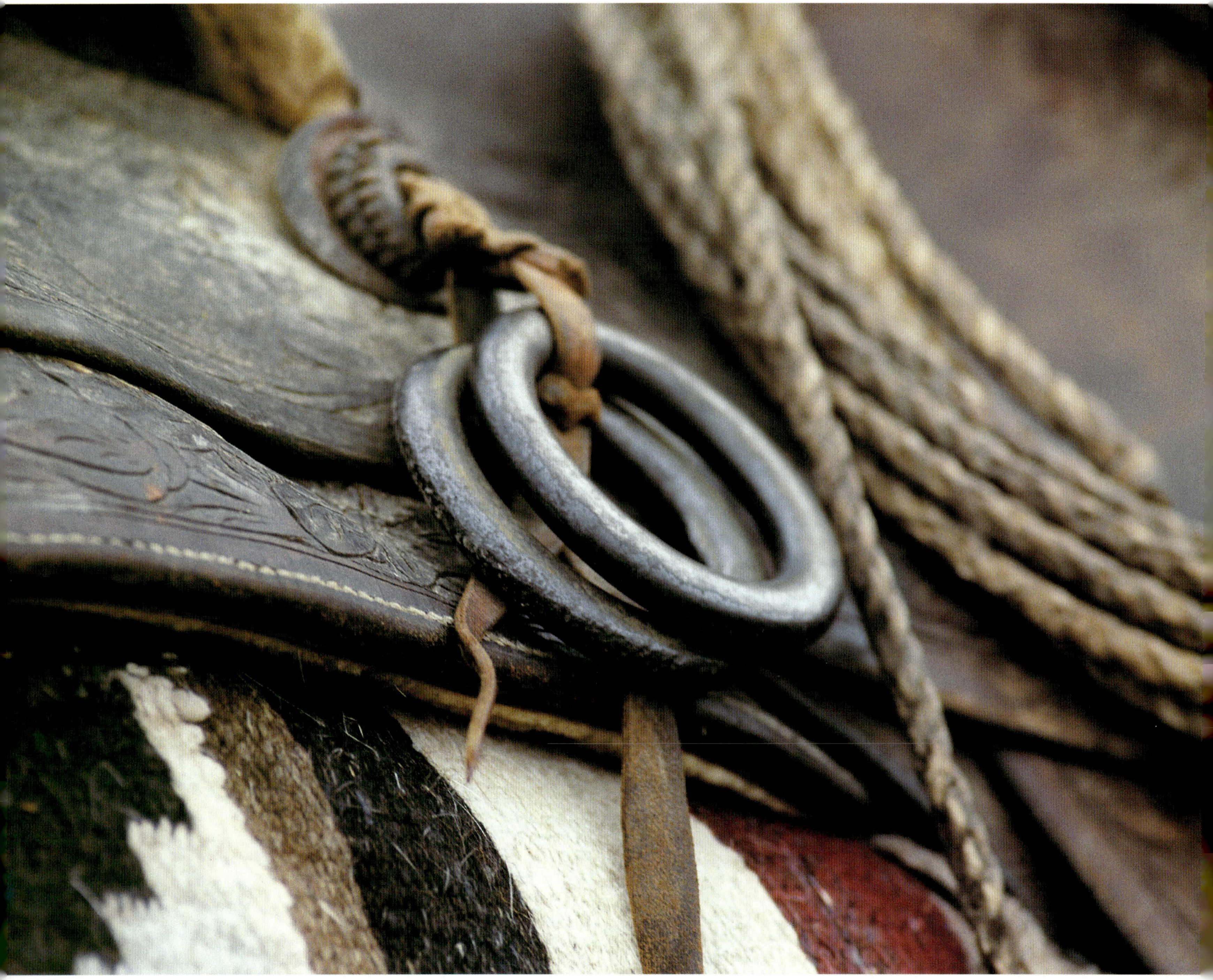

RUNNING IRONS—HAVING SADDLE RINGS TIED TO THE SADDLE *or carried in saddle bags is still against the law in many Western states. They can be used by a skilled rustler to alter a brand on freshly rustled cattle. These were on a cowboy's saddle in the Bruneau Desert of Idaho.*

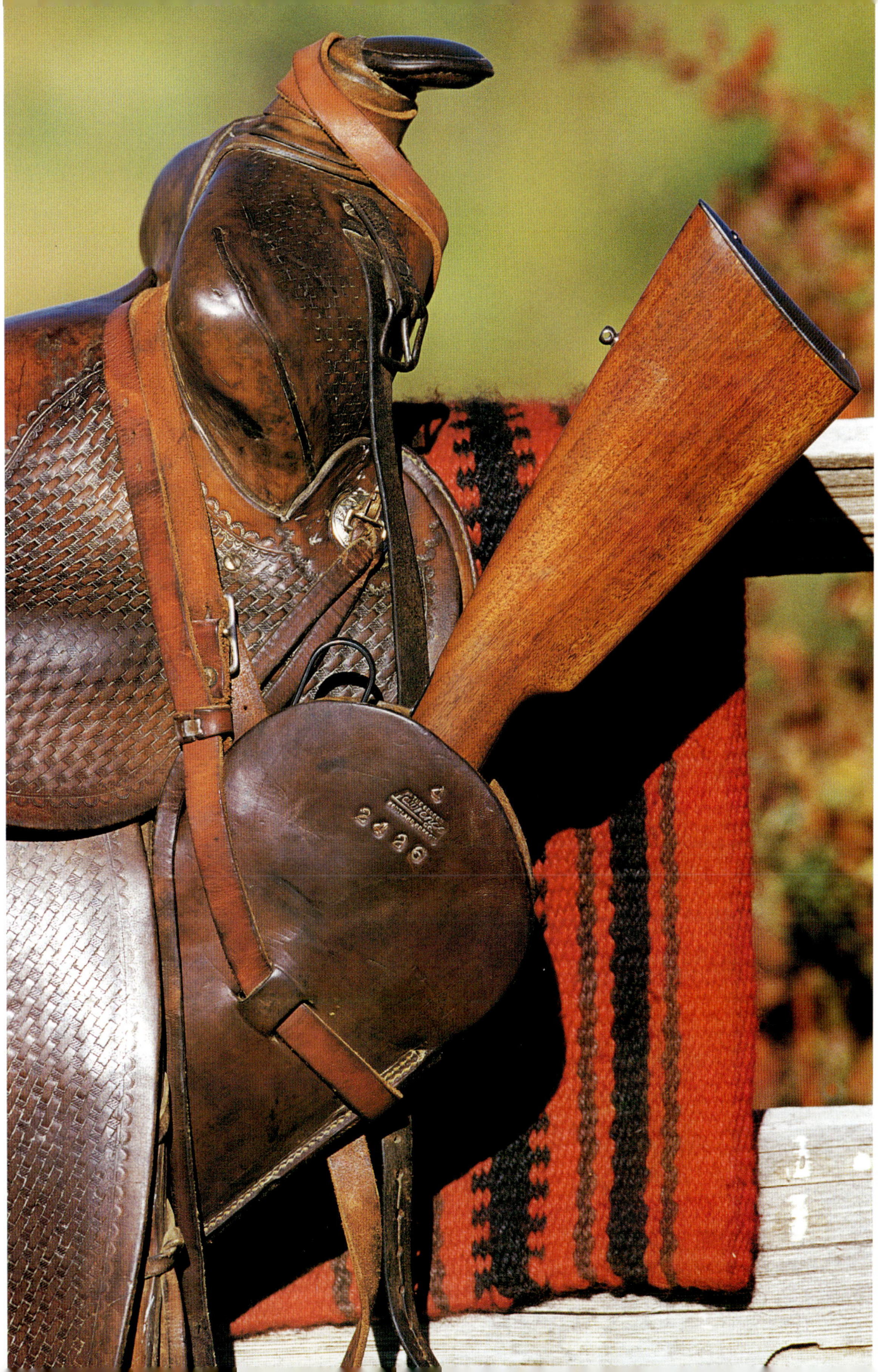

MOST SADDLE MAKERS *also made other products for horsemen such as scabbards. Some even made fishing creels and photo albums. This tradition continues today.*

G.L. LAWRENCE SCABBARD, *Stoecklein Collection*

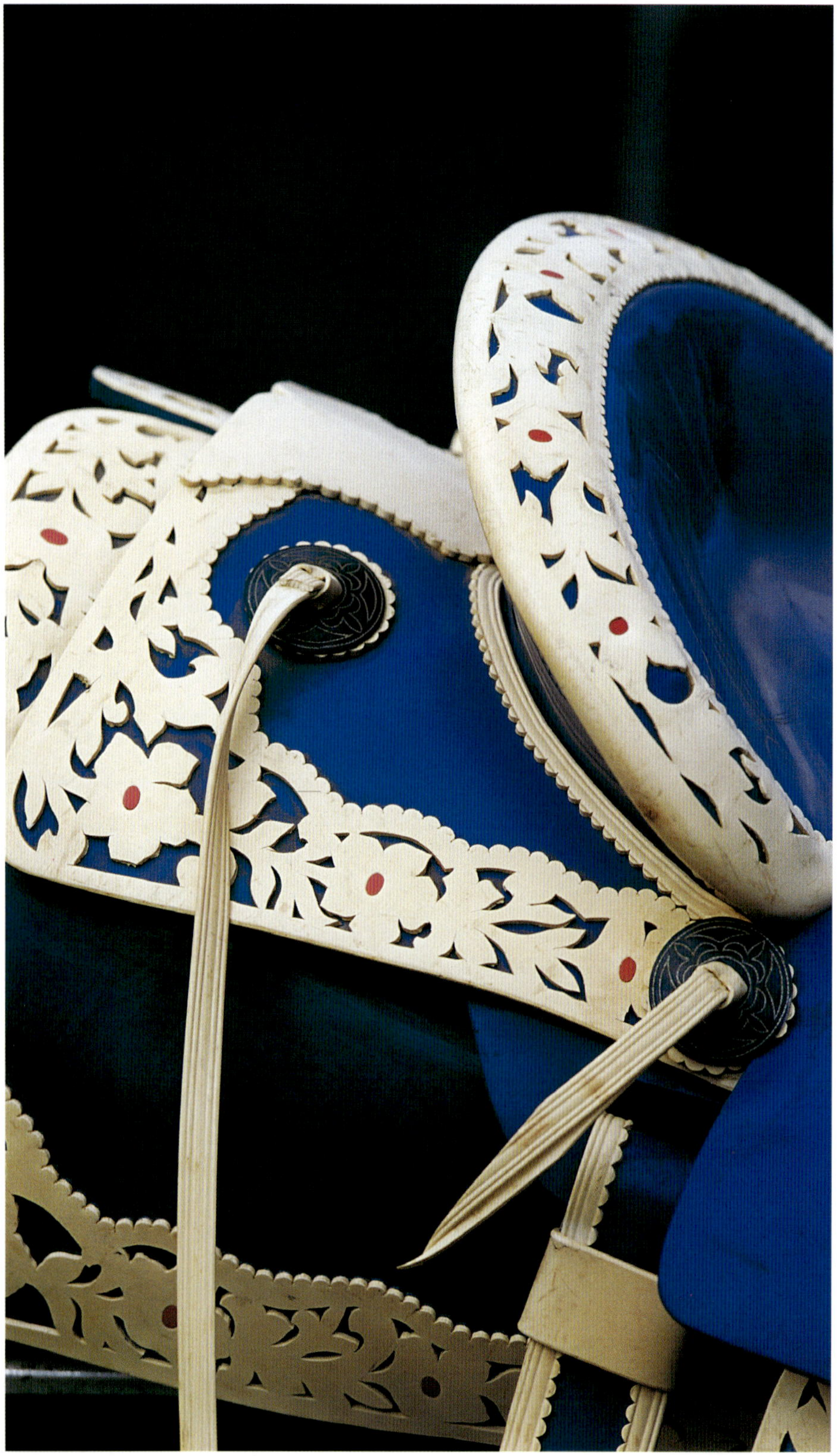

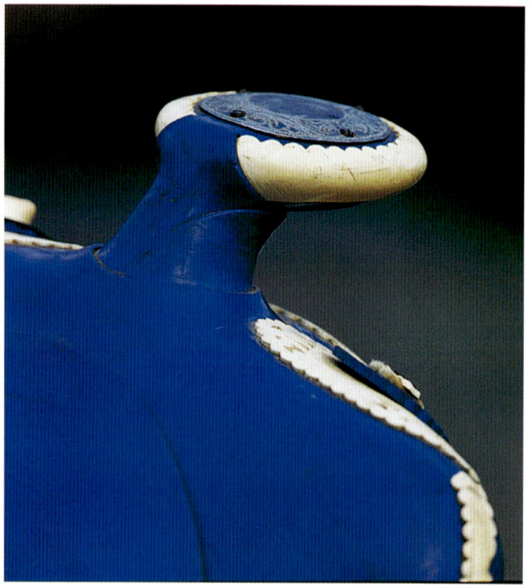

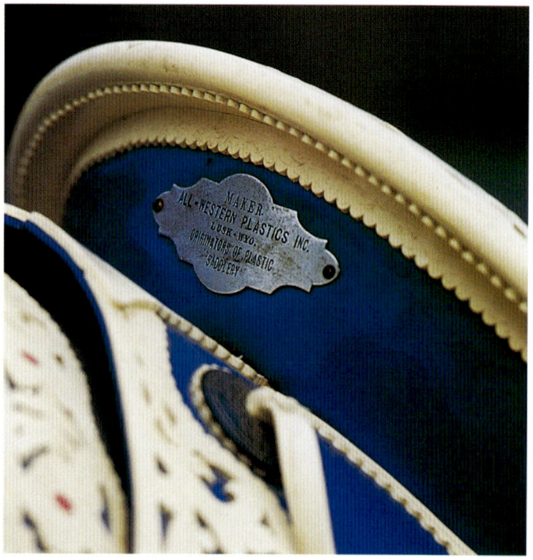

All-Western Pacific plastic saddle, *Lusk, Wyoming—this rare plastic saddle belongs to Scott Carter of the Flat Creek Saddlery in Jackson, Wyoming. Very few of these saddles were made and very few have survived.*

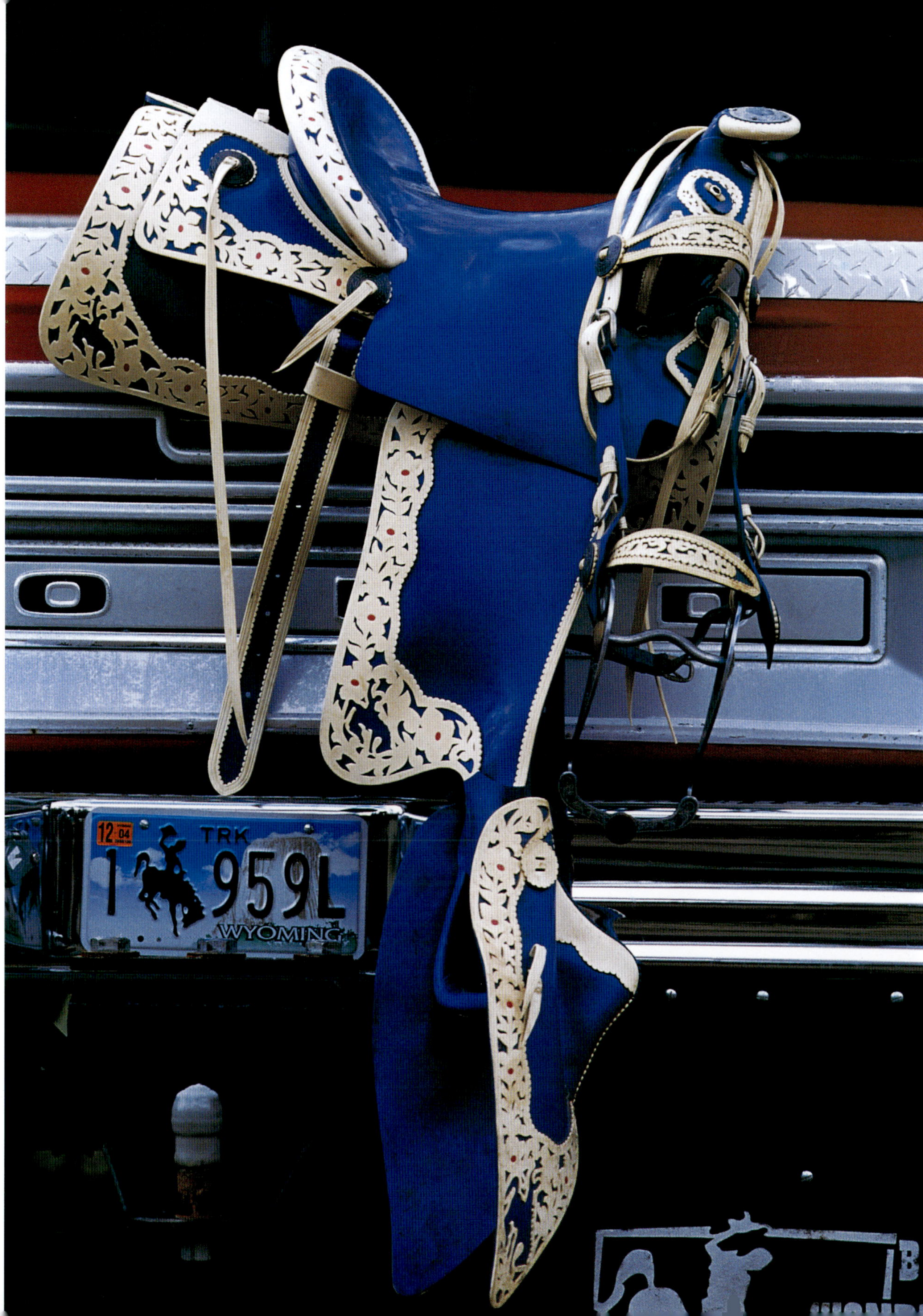
12 04
TRK
1 959L
WYOMING

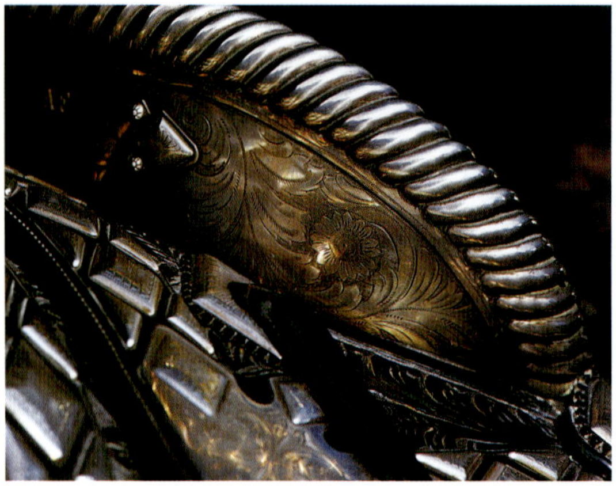

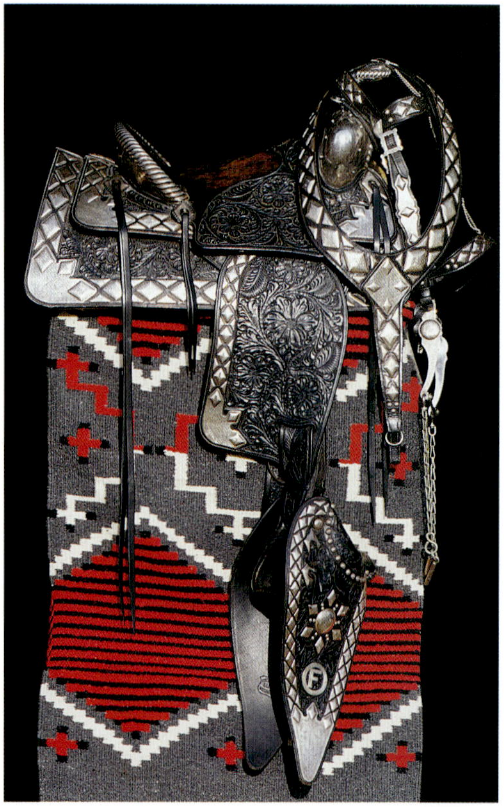

Silver saddles *are very collectible and valuable. The price can range from $10,000 to over $100,000.*

Bohlin silver mounted saddle *fully flowered with silver cantle, horn, swells, gullet, and tapaderos. Fully engraved single rig parade saddle with matching martingale and headstall, King Saddlery Museum, Sheridan, Wyoming*

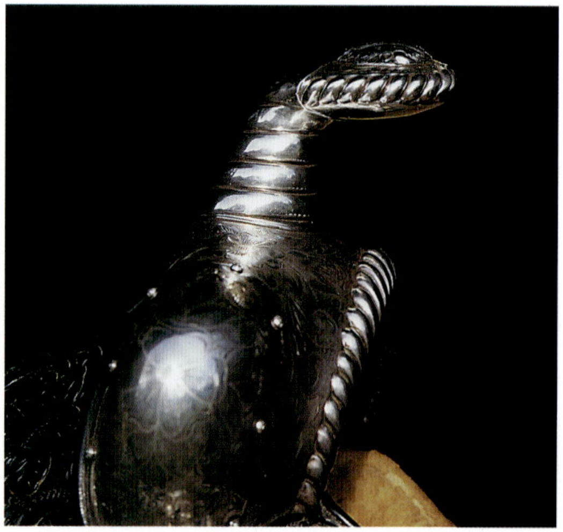

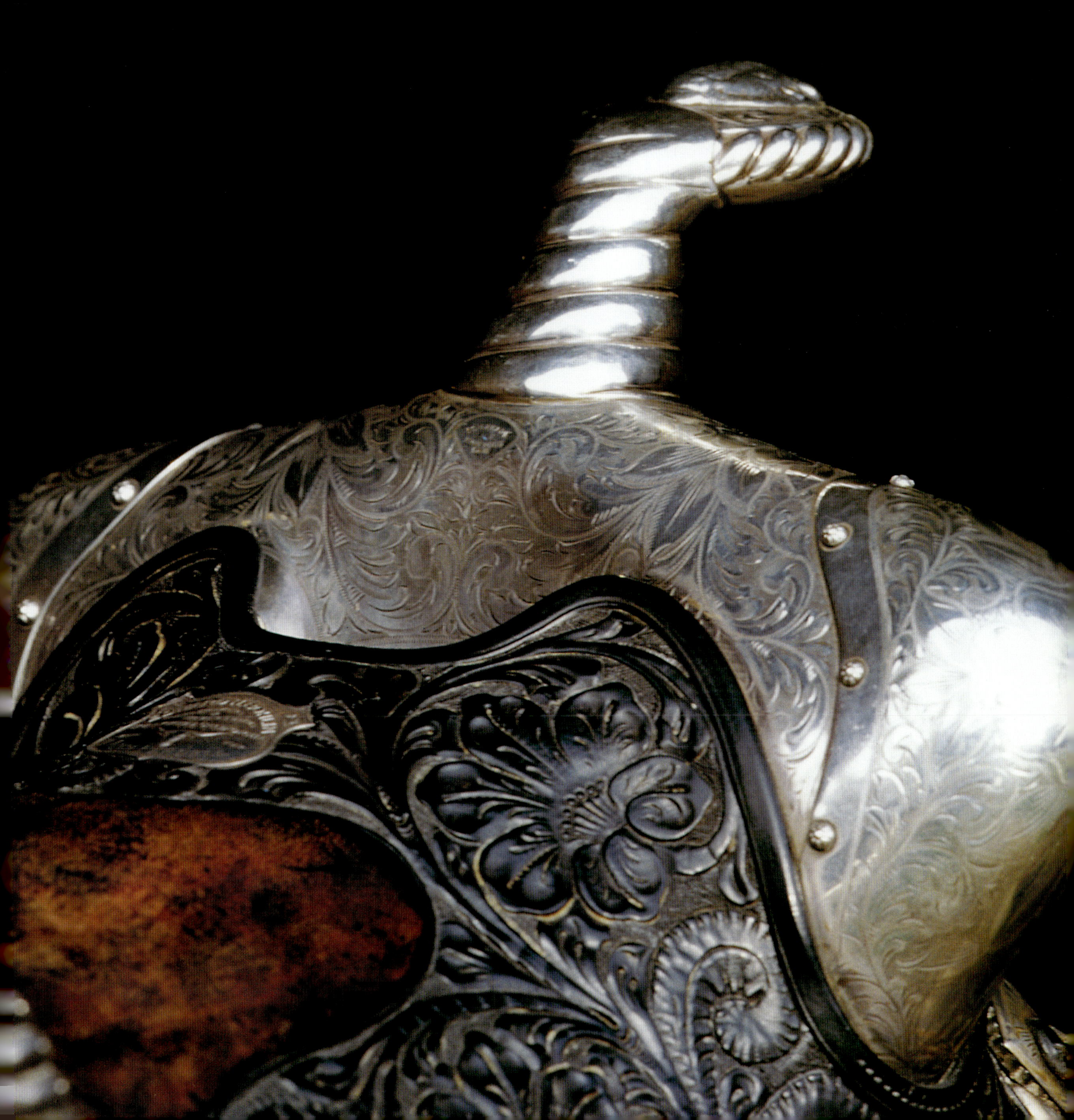

Rope hobbles

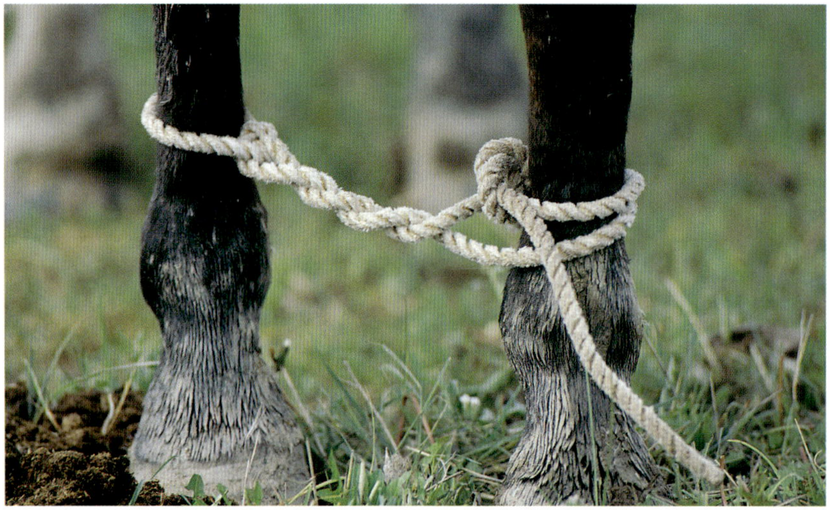

Hobbles,
Stoecklein Collection

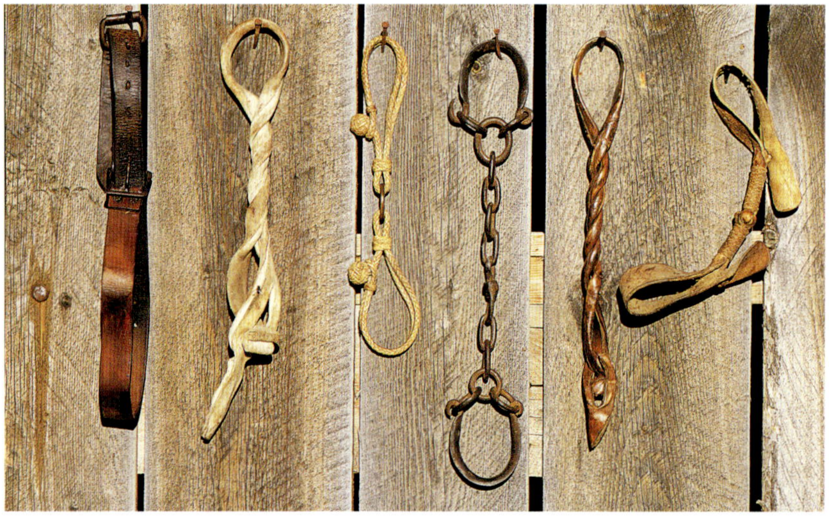

Store-bought Hobbles

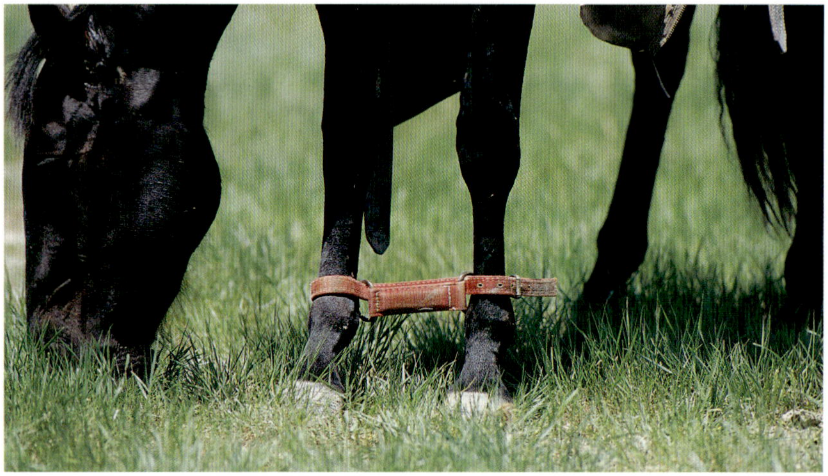

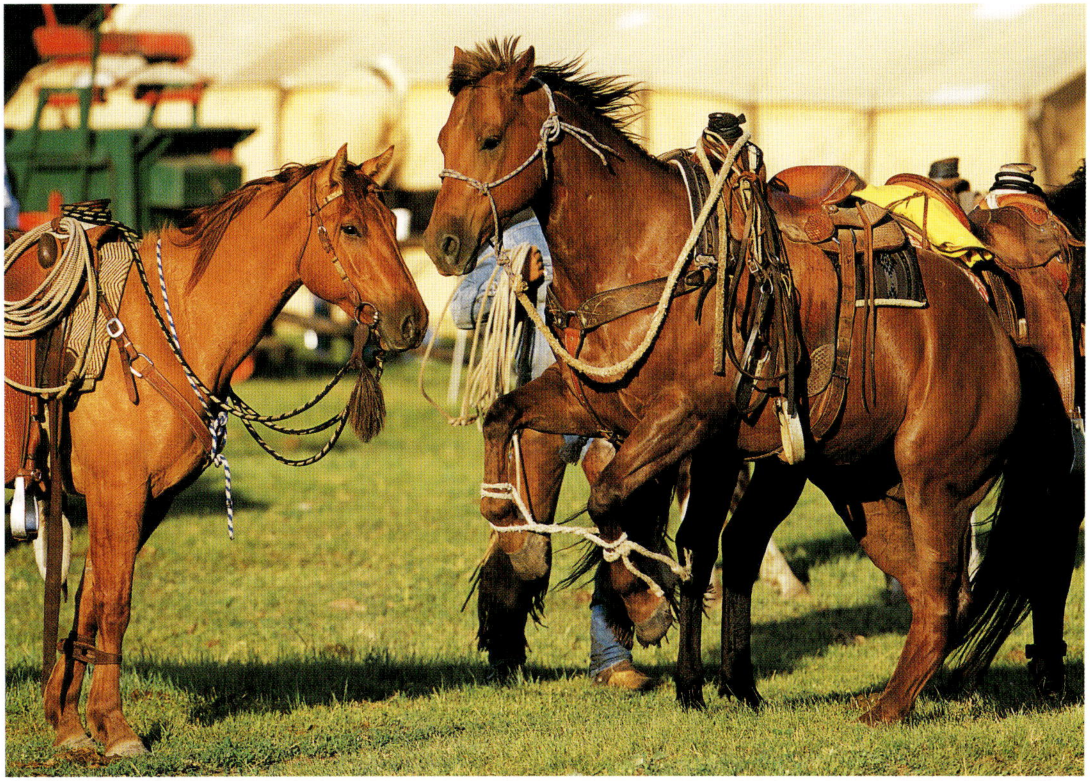

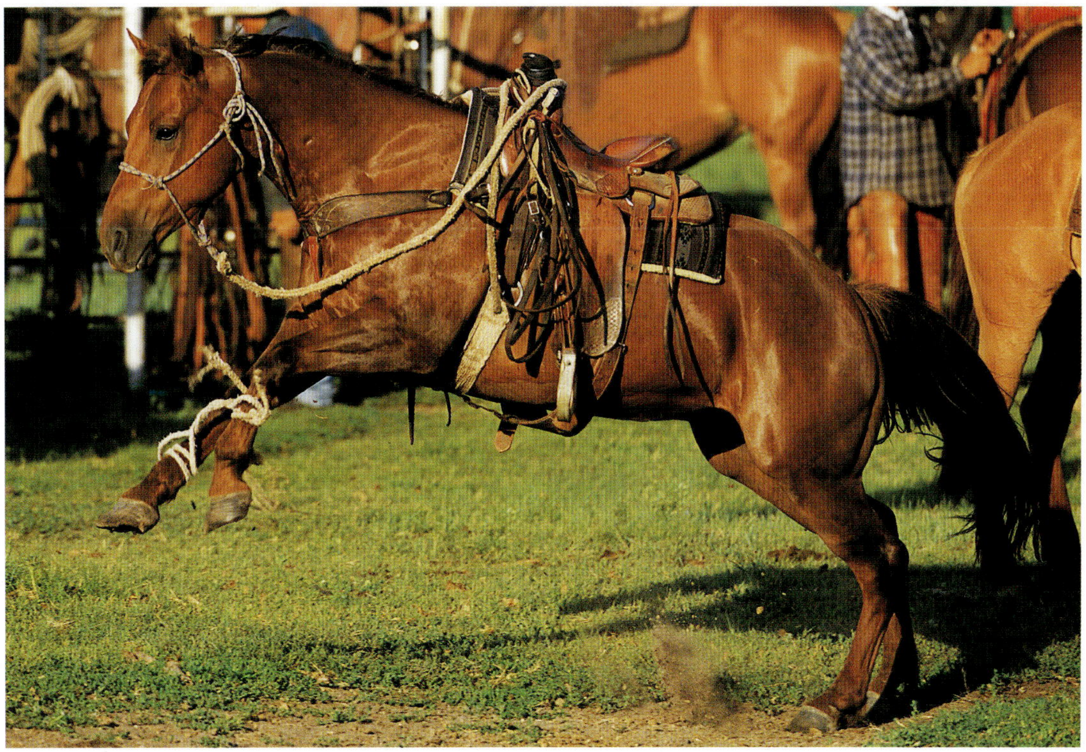

SOMETIMES THE FIRST HOBBLING CAN BE FUN TO WATCH, *Haythorn Land & Cattle Company, Arthur, Nebraska*

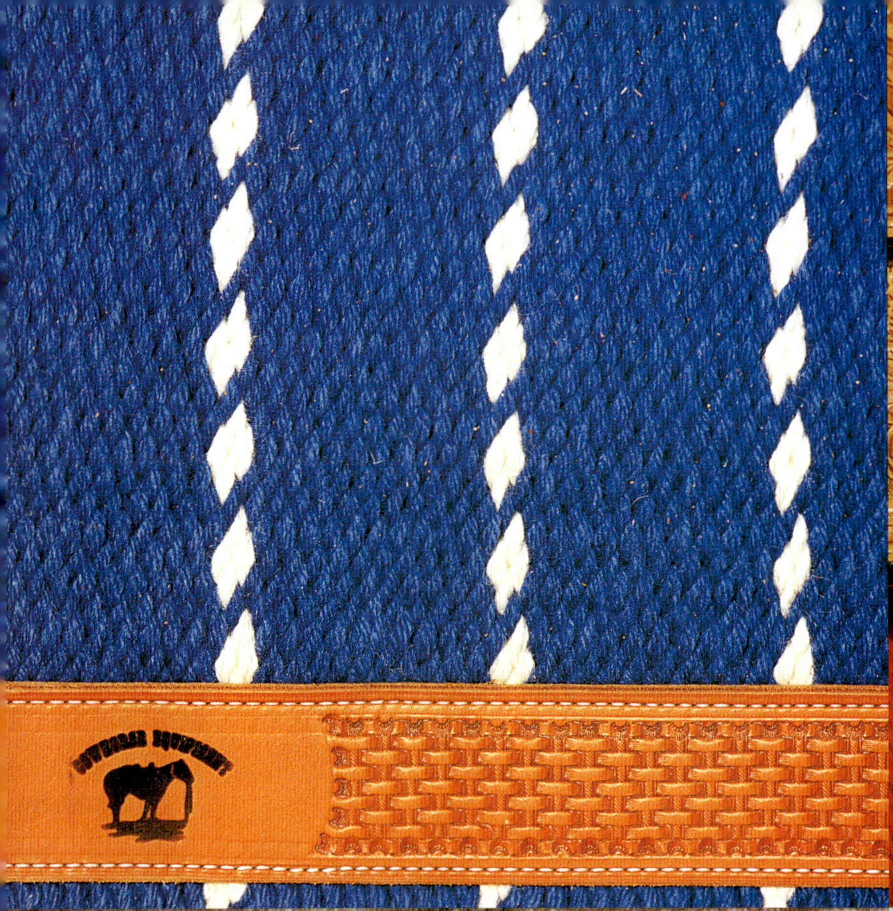
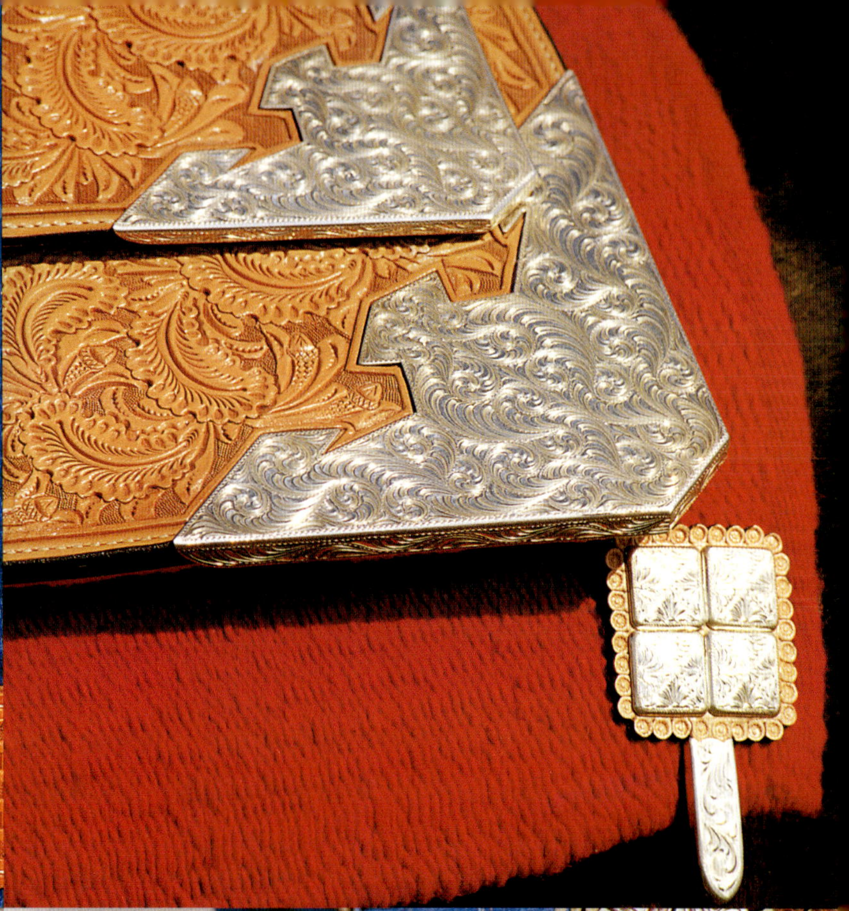
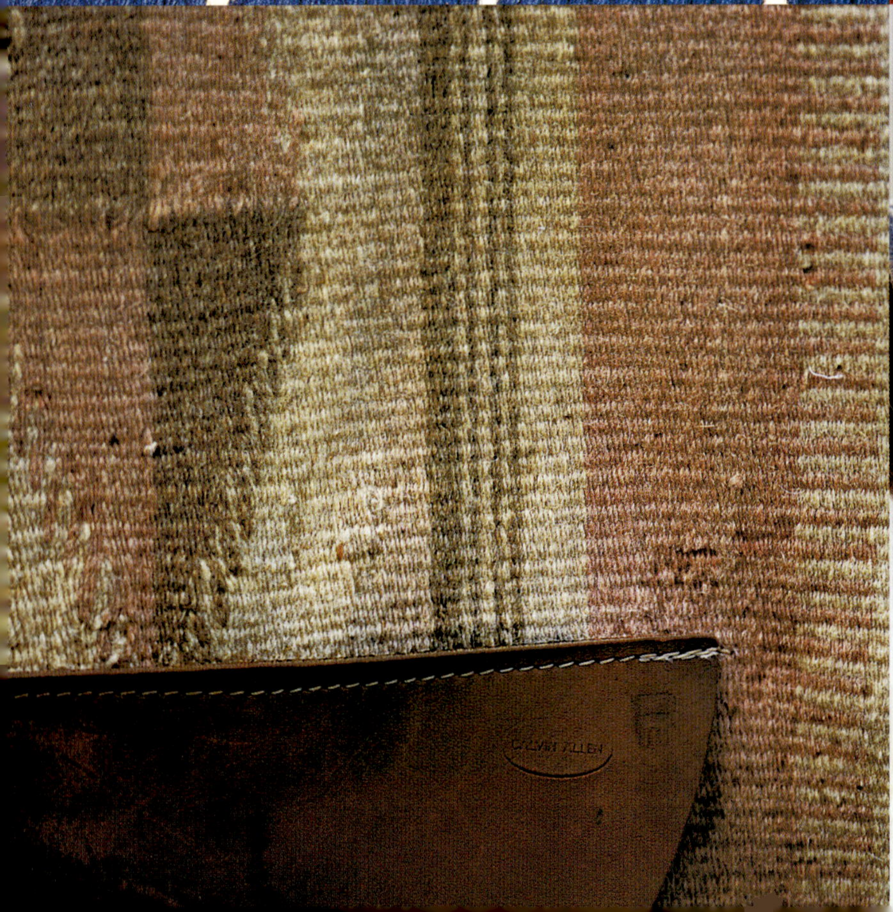
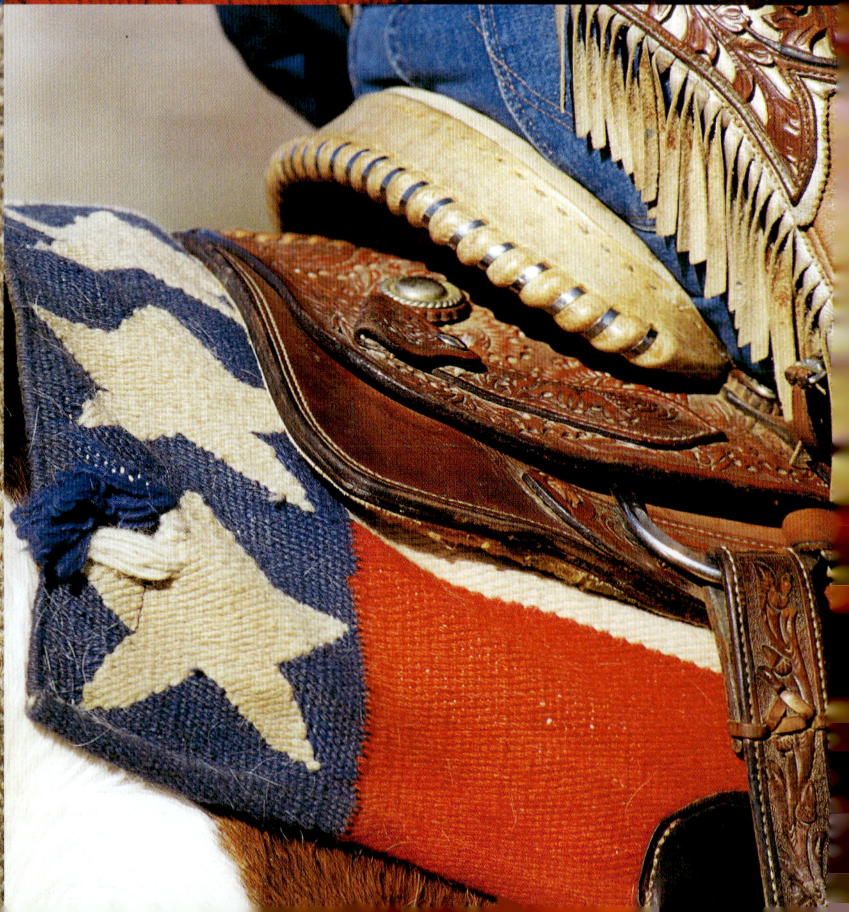

THE SADDLE PAD

is the first layer of protection between the saddle, the man, and his horse. It is one of the most important pieces of equipment. It helps to fit a saddle, keep the sweat away from the saddle, keep the horse aired and cool, provides extra cushion from the impact of the rider or the yank of a rope going tight. As much thought and innovation has gone into the saddle pad or blanket as any other piece of horse gear.

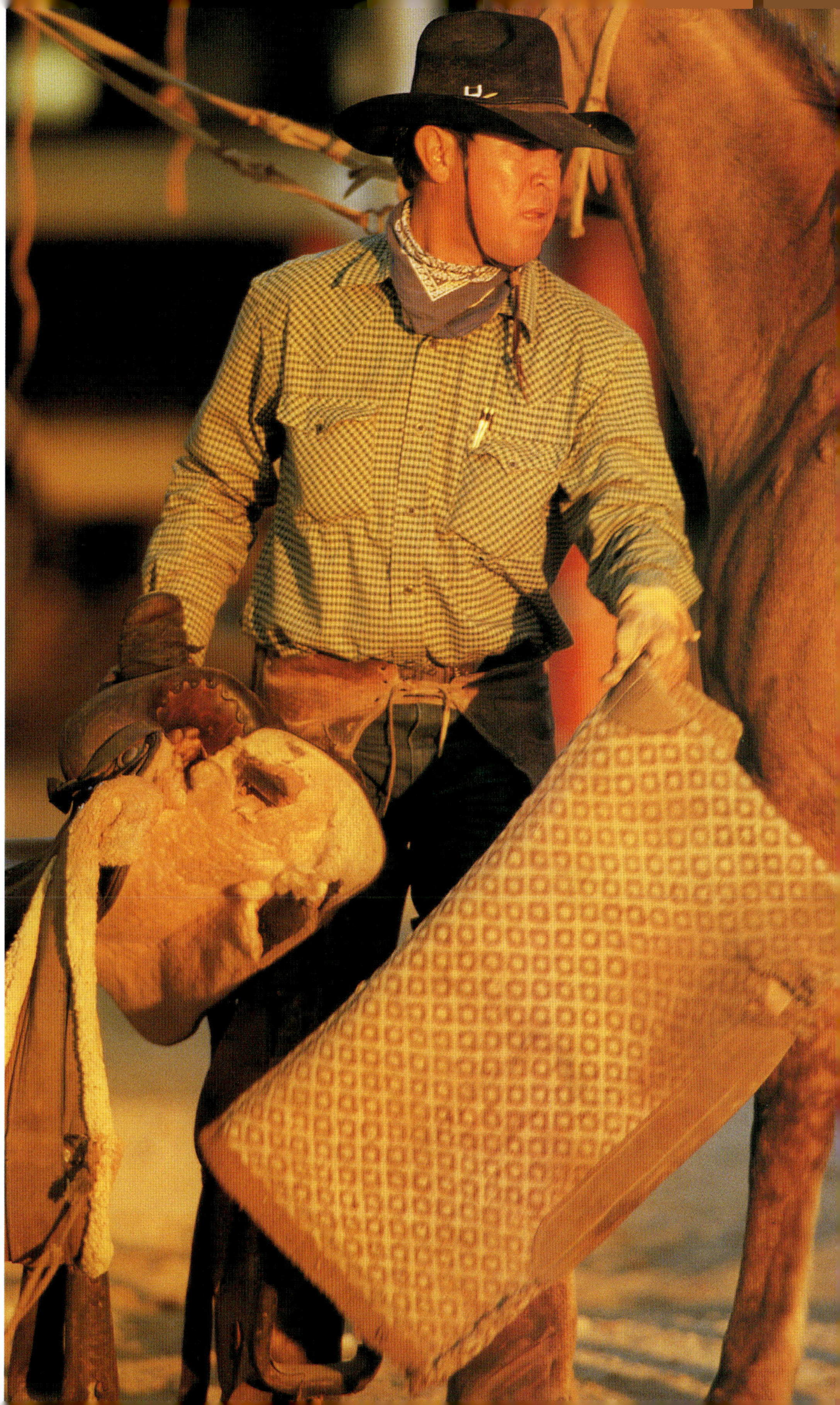

JUAN LUIS LONGORIA,
McAllen Ranch, Linn, Texas

A-Fork Saddles

There have been many different styles of saddletrees used in the last 150 years. Usually a change in style or design is made for functional reasons, sometimes for style, and almost never for art. The tree is the most important part of the saddle. It is what makes the saddle fit the horse and the rider.

The A-fork is one of the most popular saddletrees in use today for Western saddles. The slick fork design goes way back to old style California saddles but much innovation has made this tree fit for the bigger and wider Quarter Horses of today. It now has a bigger and stouter horn to accommodate the current roping styles.

The most popular of these tree styles is called the "Wade." The Wade tree is a modified fork that was originally designed to fit the maker's style and his horses. It was designed by legendary horseman Tom Dorrance and made famous by Ray Hunt. The most famous and sought-after of saddle makers is Dale Harwood of Shelley, Idaho. Dale Harwood has so many disciples and followers of his style and craft that he is often considered the father of the A-fork Wade tree revolution in Western saddles.

Today, Dale has a back-order list of 175 saddles. He is not currently taking any more orders. In order to get one of his saddles, a person must either find a used one to buy, which is close to impossible, or purchase the single saddle he makes each year for the Traditional Cowboy Arts Association (TCAA) Exhibition and Sale at the National Cowboy & Western Heritage Museum in Oklahoma City. Lastly, a person can try to get on the list for one of the few collector saddles that Dale makes each year.

Dale is a master artisan and a master saddle maker. He truly is a living legend.

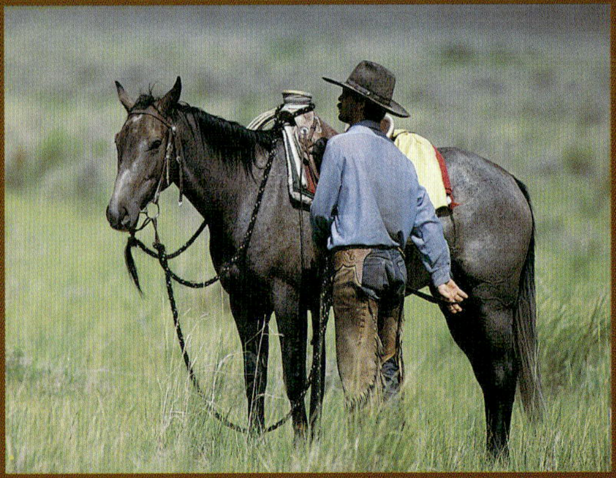

MARTIN BLACK,
Winecup Ranch, Nevada

RAYMOND JAYO *riding one of his prized Harwood saddles*

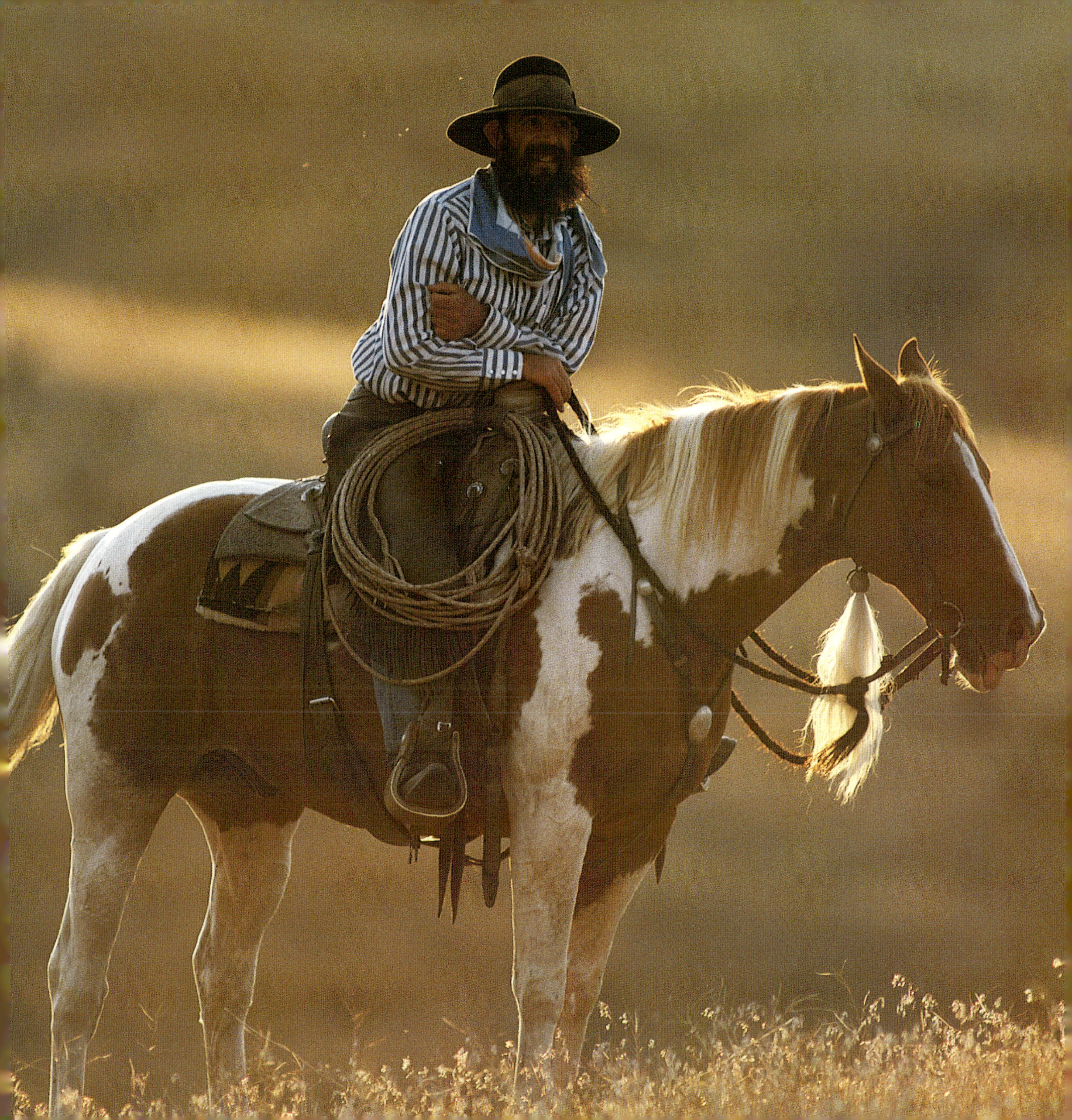

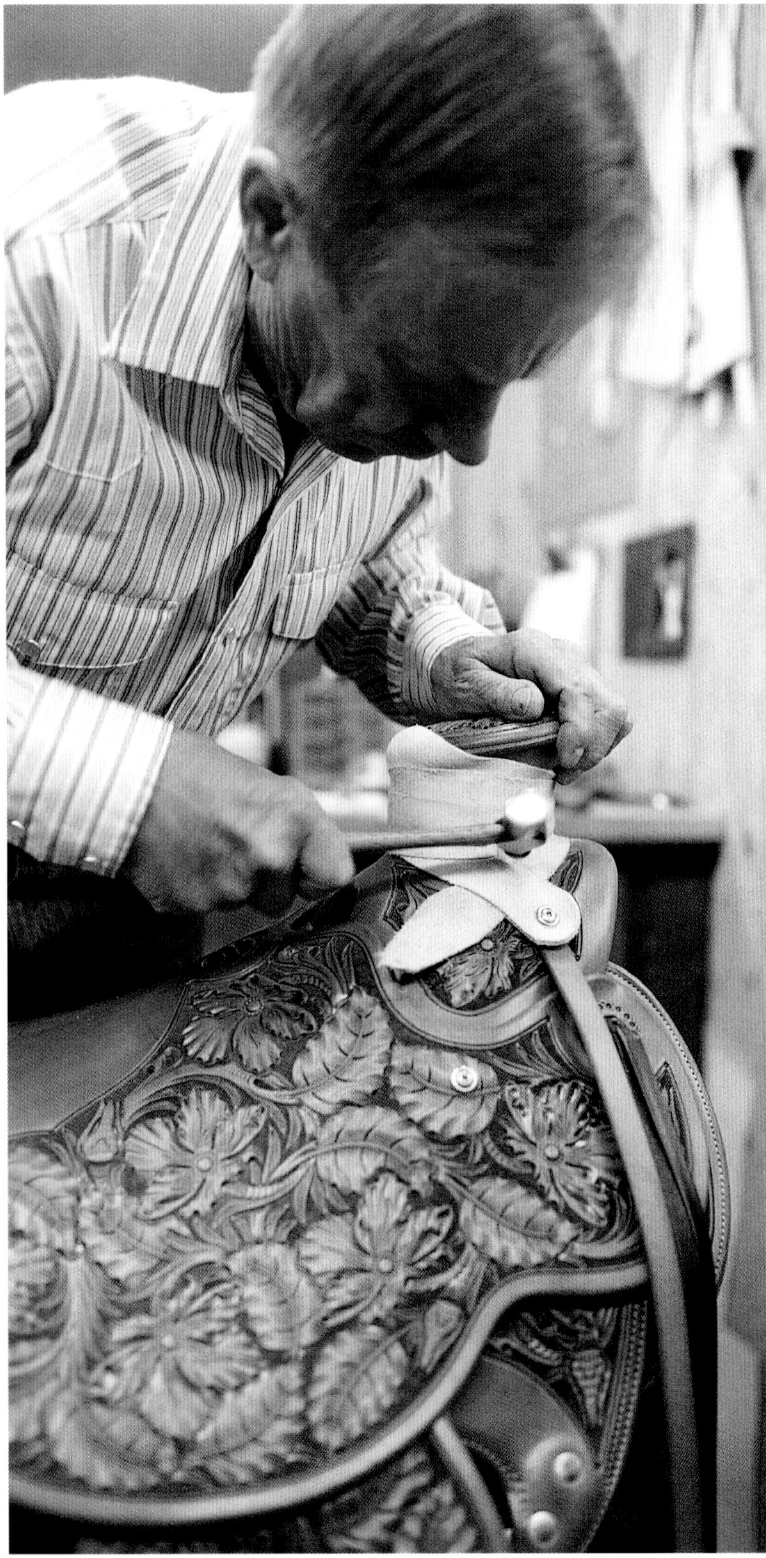
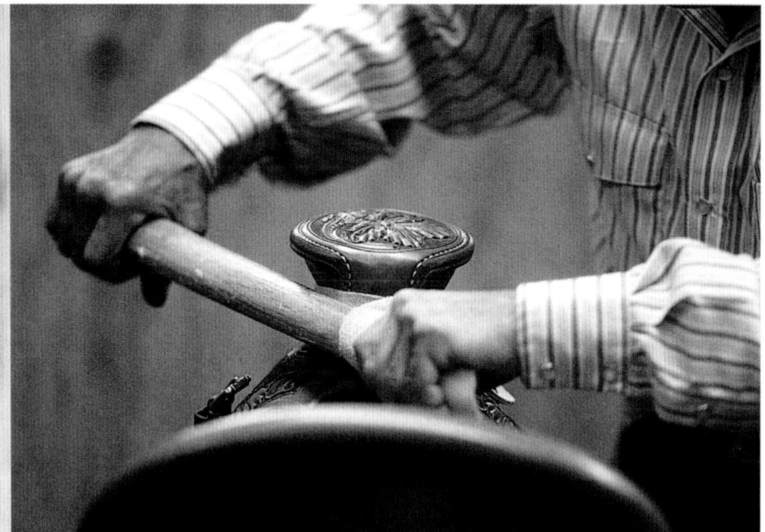
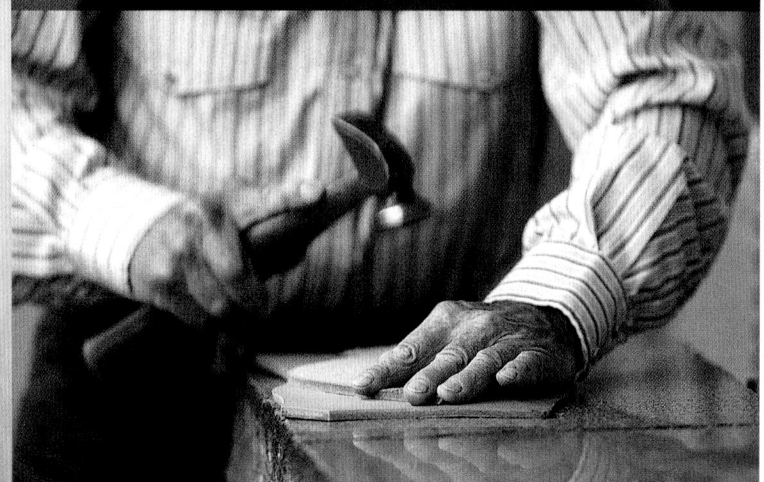
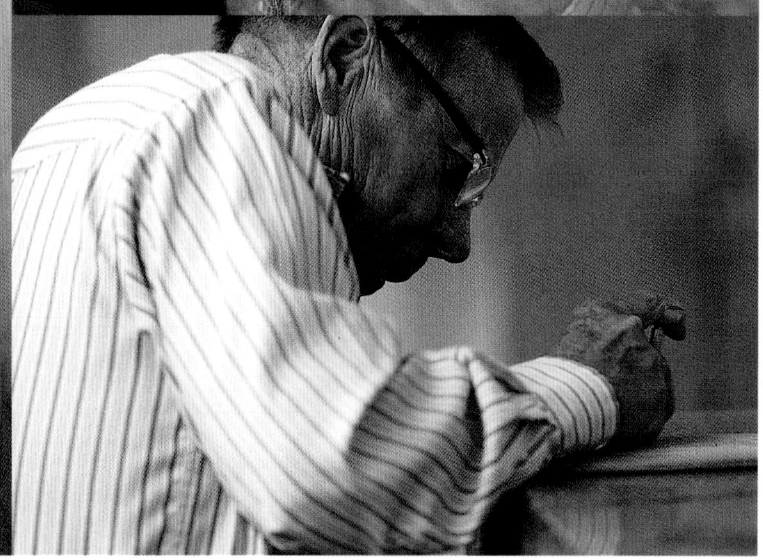

Dale Harwood

Dale Harwood is a legend and an icon in the cowboy and buckaroo world. He has been making saddles for 43 years yet he had no formal training. His saddles are bought by cowboys, performance horsemen, and collectors alike. Dale looks up to Ray Holes as a saddle maker and Bill Knight as a stamper. He is best known for his working saddles and makes most of his own trees. Dale is not taking any new orders currently and his waiting list is 10 to 12 years. Prices for Harwood custom saddles can range anywhere between $5,000 and $30,000. Dale's philosophy is to do the best he possibly can on each saddle and improve his product each time.

As a young man, Harwood learned the basics of his art in a shop in Soda Springs, Idaho. He worked hard at learning, and quickly gained a following. Trainers, pleasure riders, working cowboys, and ranchers became—and remained—the mainstays of his business. They depended upon his precision and perfection, and they were never disappointed in his product. During his period of apprenticeship, Harwood practiced listening to the masters and following in their steps. Those years proved to be the best possible foundation for the lifetime of acclaimed saddle making that was to follow. He opened a shop and retail business in 1961, which he maintained until 1982. At that time, he liquidated the business and moved his saddle and tree shop to his home outside Idaho Falls. His need for perfection continues. From start to finish, Harwood controls the quality of his saddles, processing his own rawhide, and making his own saddletrees.

His secret, perhaps, is that making saddles is all he ever wanted to do. He has followed a lifetime passion, and his commitment to the best possible work has added to his reputation as one of America's finest Western gear artisans. He has a passion for the history of his art, and he is determined to pass these lost techniques on to tomorrow's saddle makers. But for Harwood, it is more than just the creativity. Making saddles is about connecting with his Western heritage.

His work is in demand by horsemen around the world and his work has been exhibited at the Cowboy Poetry Gathering in Elko, Nevada, where he received Best of Show in 1997, and at Trappings of the West in Flagstaff, Arizona. Dale is a long-standing member of the Traditional Cowboy Arts Association (TCAA). (biography courtesy of the TCAA web site)

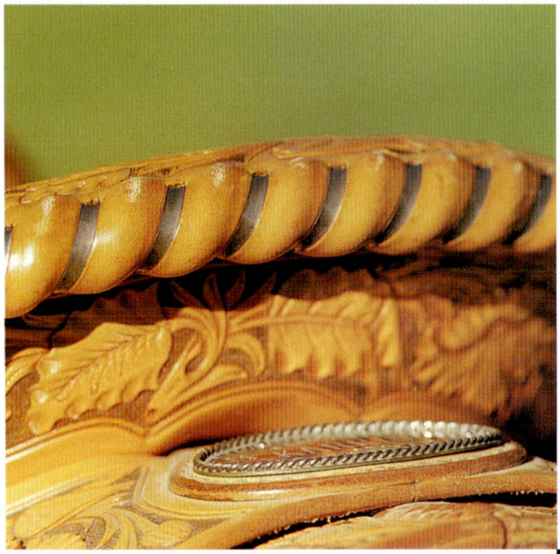

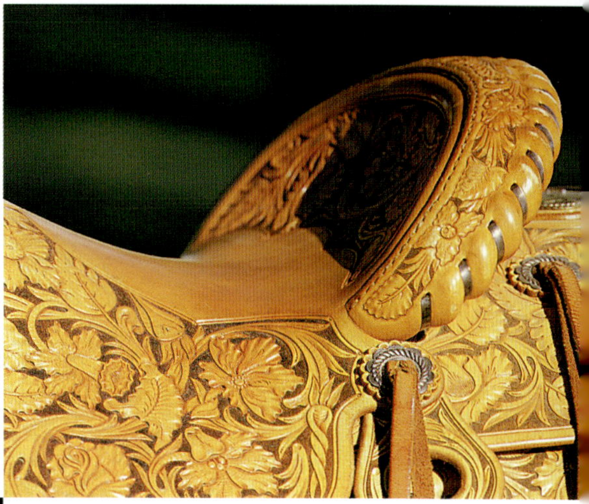

Dale Harwood saddle,
Shelley, Idaho

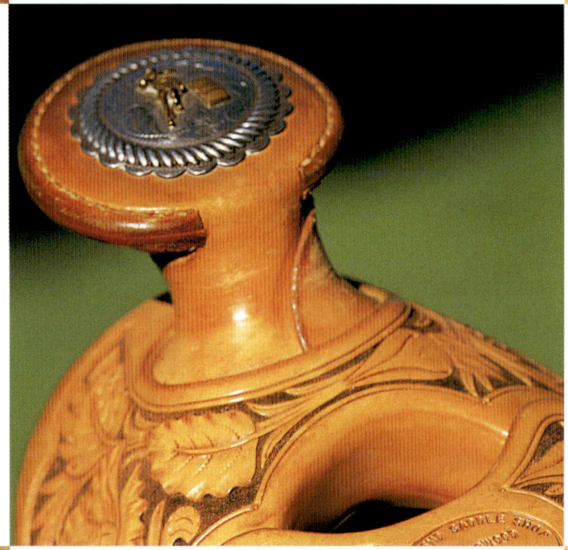

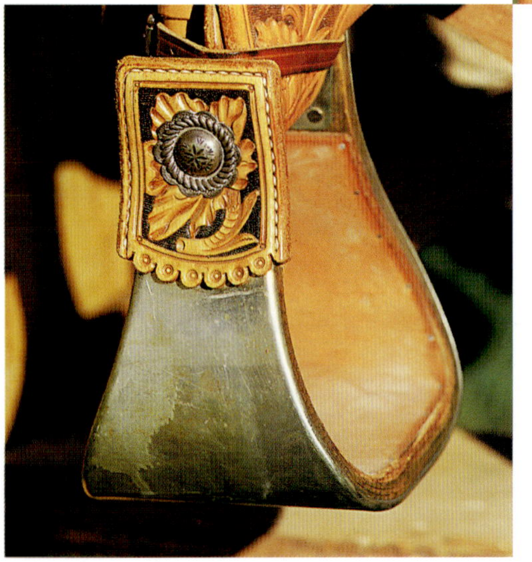

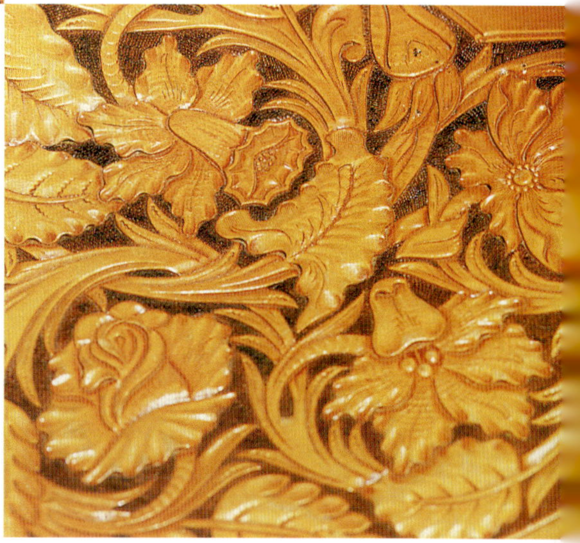

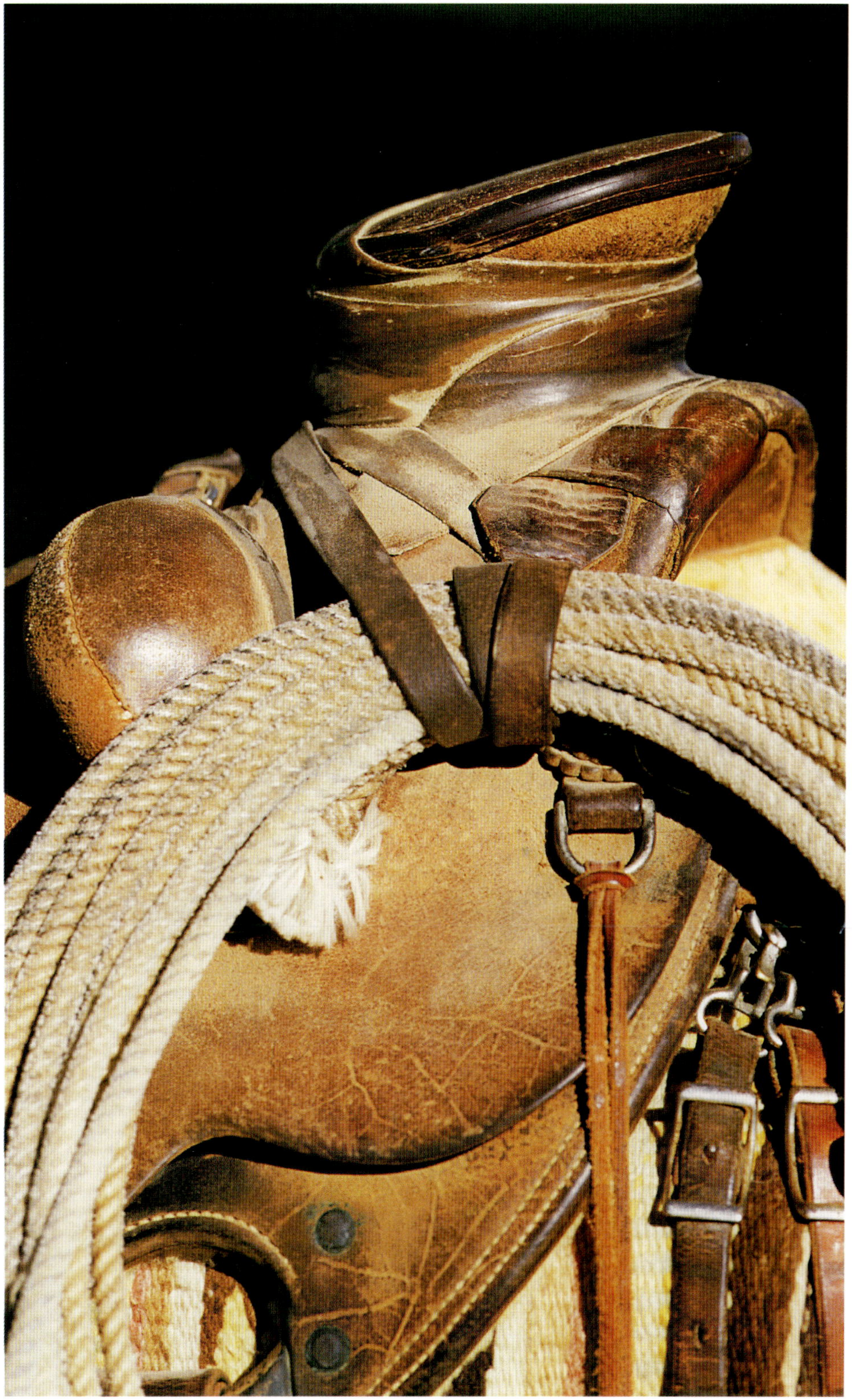

EARLY HARWOOD SADDLE
made on a Hamley tree

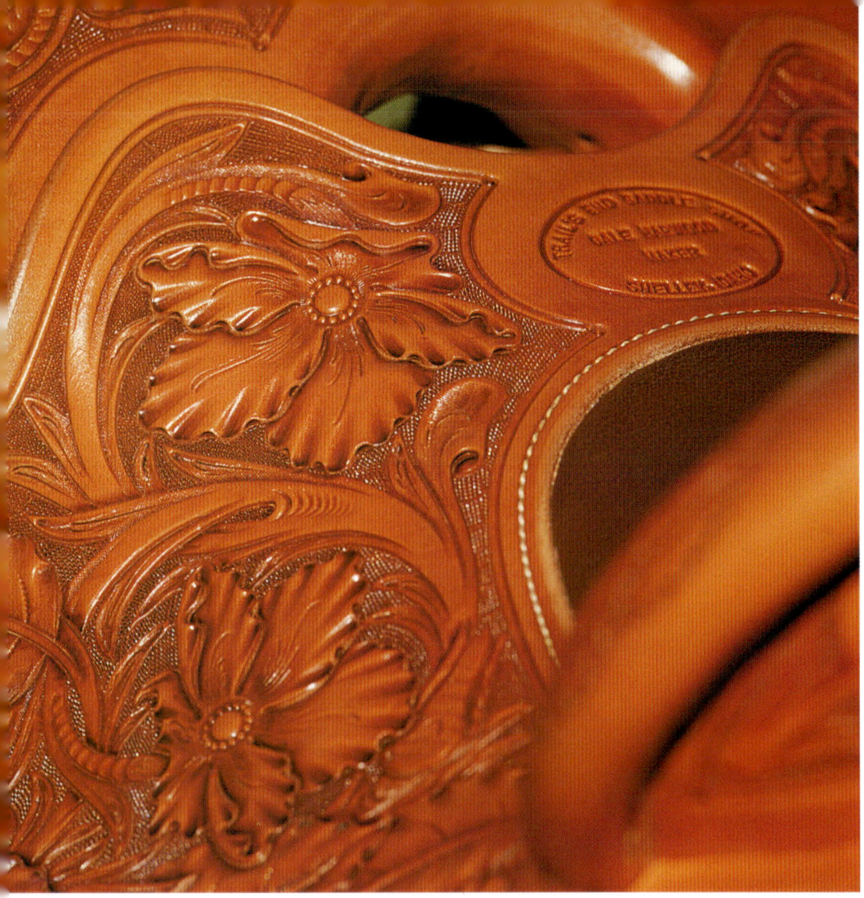
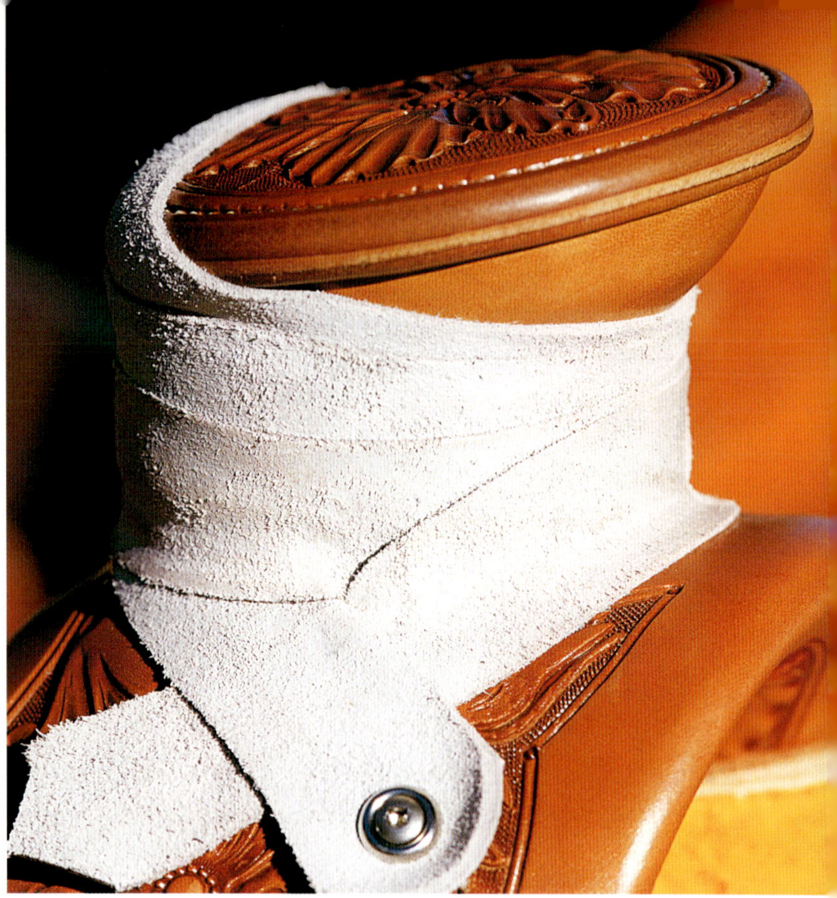
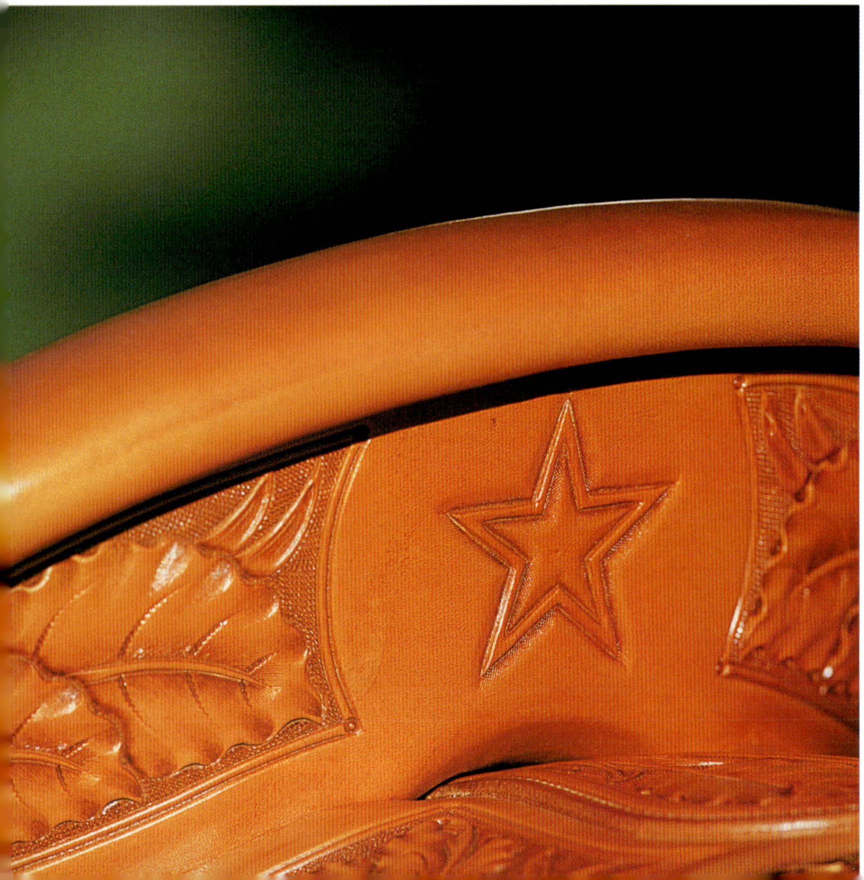
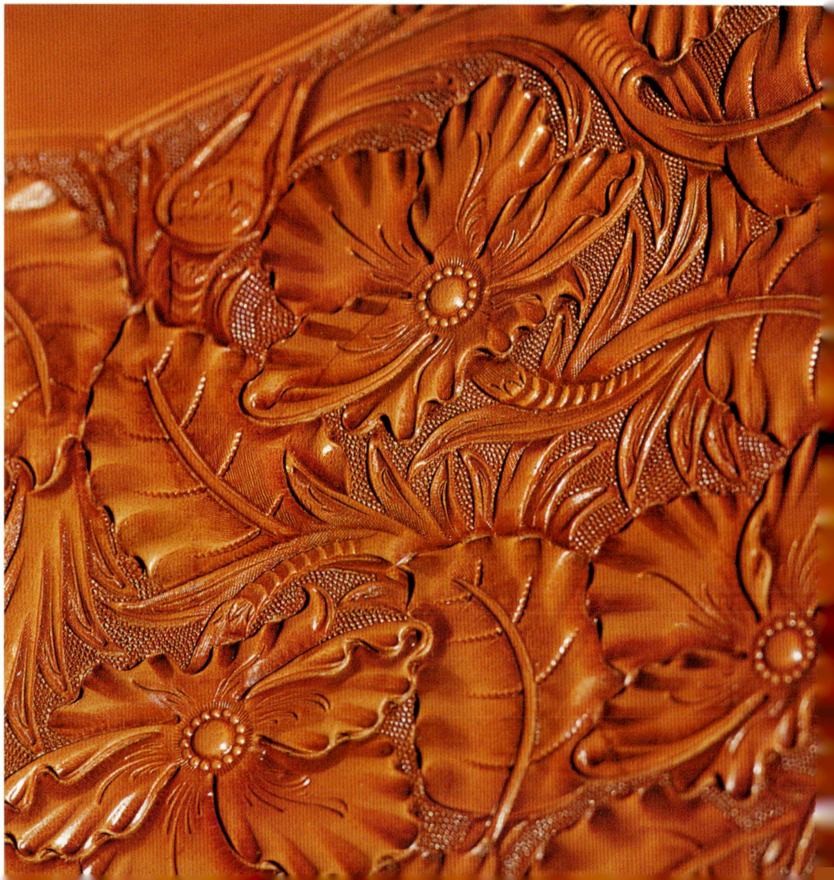

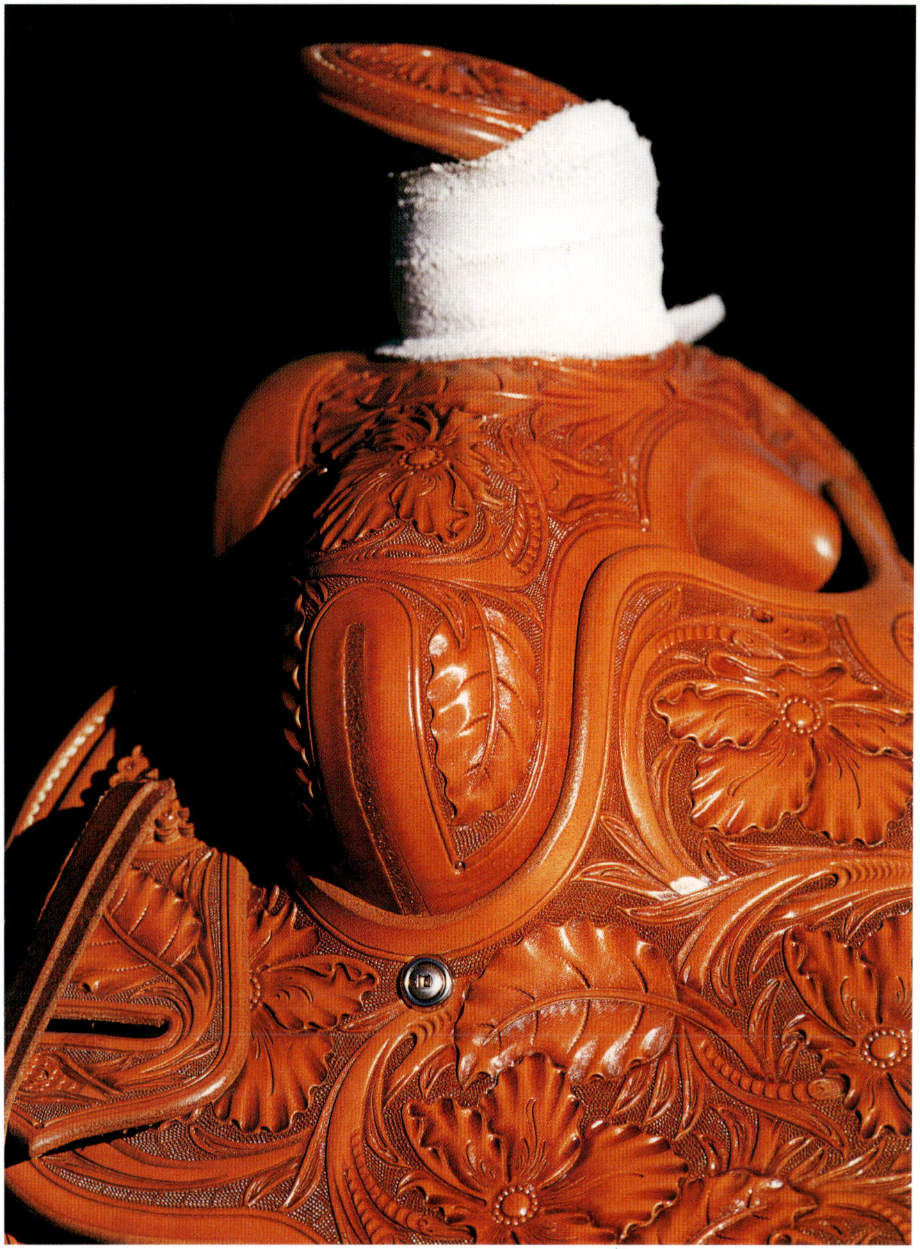

DALE HARWOOD SADDLE DETAILS, *Shelley, Idaho*

DALE HARWOOD *is not taking any more orders for custom saddles. He has taken orders for the next ten years—the only other way to get one of his saddles is to look on eBay—they are some of the most sought-after saddles, coveted by collectors and horseman around the world.*

Don King

No book on Western saddles would be complete without Don King. Don King started crafting saddles off and on in 1946 and steadily in 1963 and he is now retired. Don always had an interest in leather stamping and the art of saddle making. He learned the craft of stamping by hanging around saddle shops. He apprenticed under Rudy Mudra in Sheridan, Wyoming. Rudy had a reputation for being one of the finest carvers and saddle makers in the Sheridan area. In 1947, King opened his own saddle shop in a garage but soon decided that he preferred to break horses for a living. In 1961, the business opened in the back of a sporting goods store in Sheridan as a supplier of quality cowboy equipment. King made saddles for cowboys, performance horsemen, and collectors but he is best known for his roping and working saddles. Don has since left the business to his sons and has retired to his shop where he continues to refine his art, making his own stamping tools to create his intricate designs. The lasting legacy of Don King is not only his own art but also his introduction of countless others to the art of leather carving and his contribution to those whose styles have been influenced by him. (biography courtesy of Travel-to-Wyoming.com)

Don King saddle detail, *King's Saddlery, Sheridan, Wyoming*

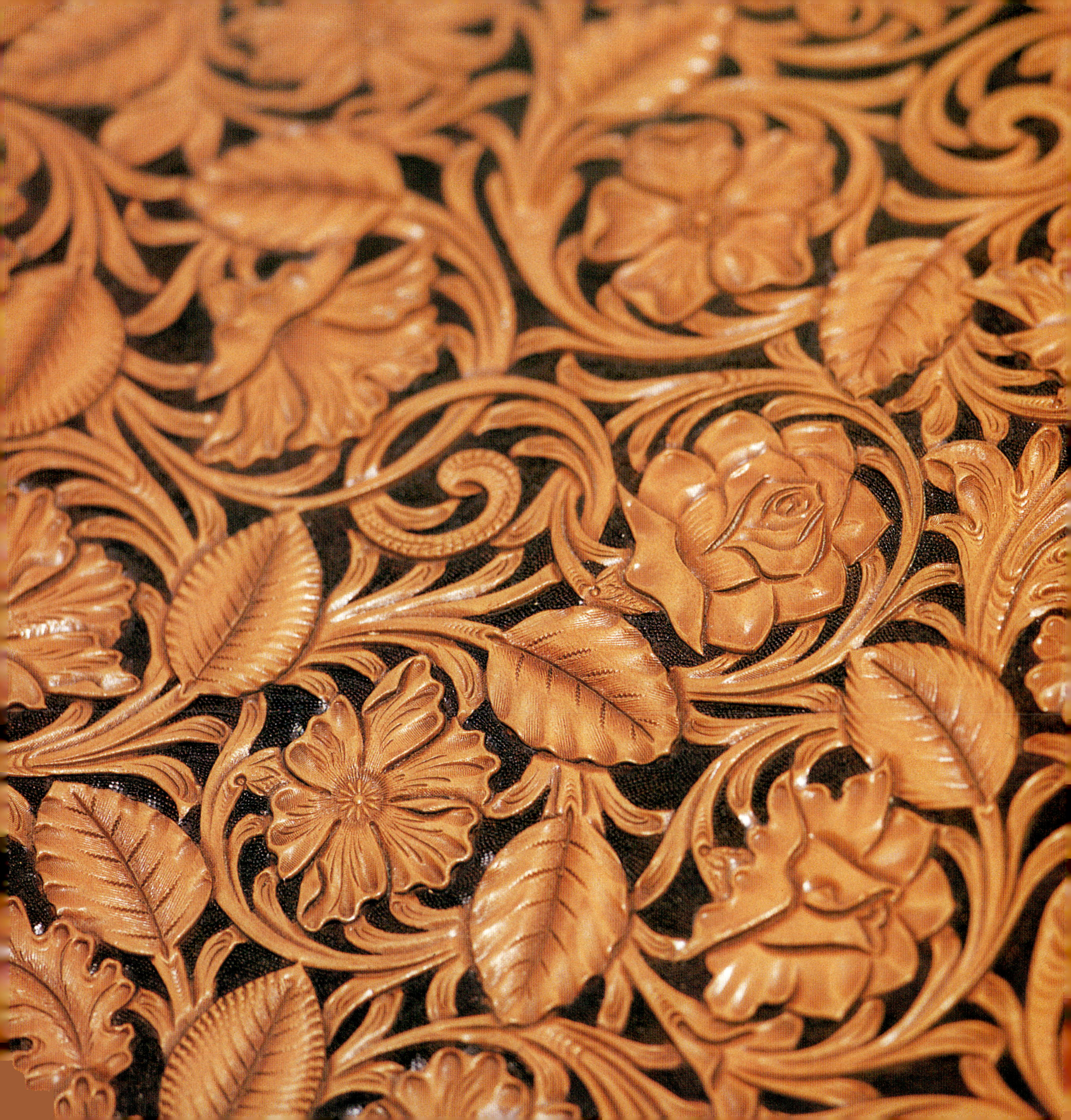

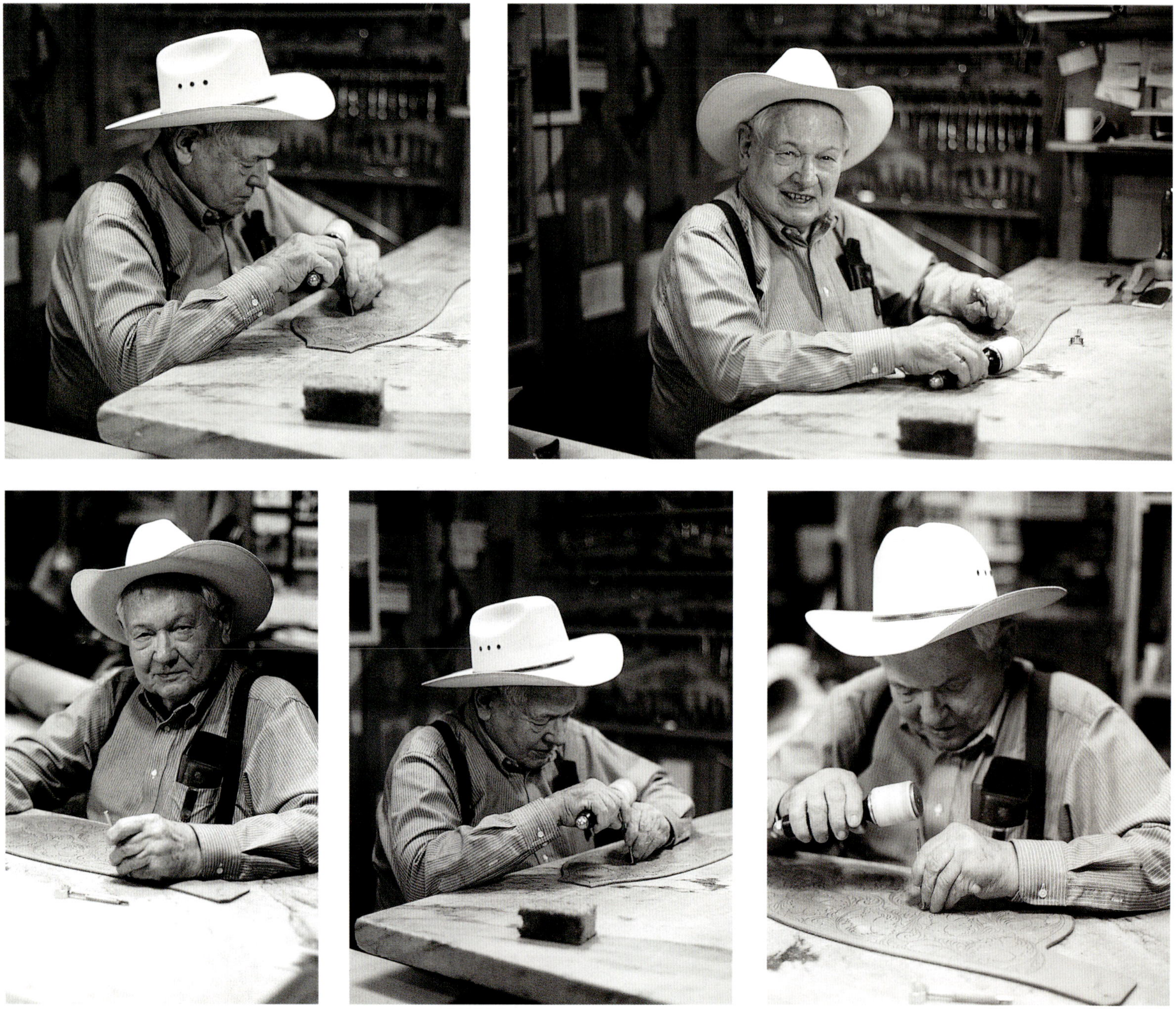

Don King at work *in his shop at King's Saddlery, Sheridan, Wyoming*

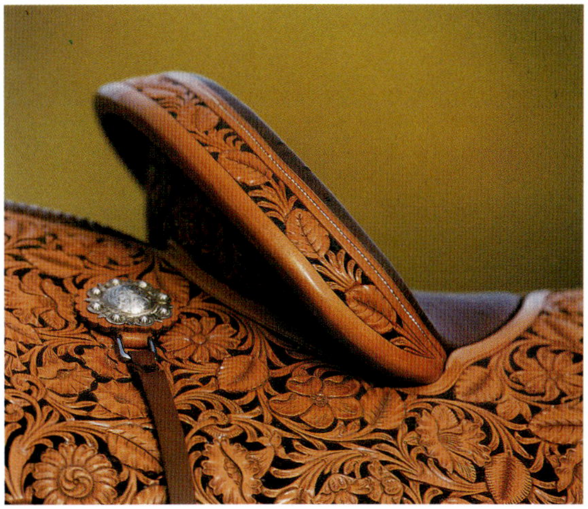

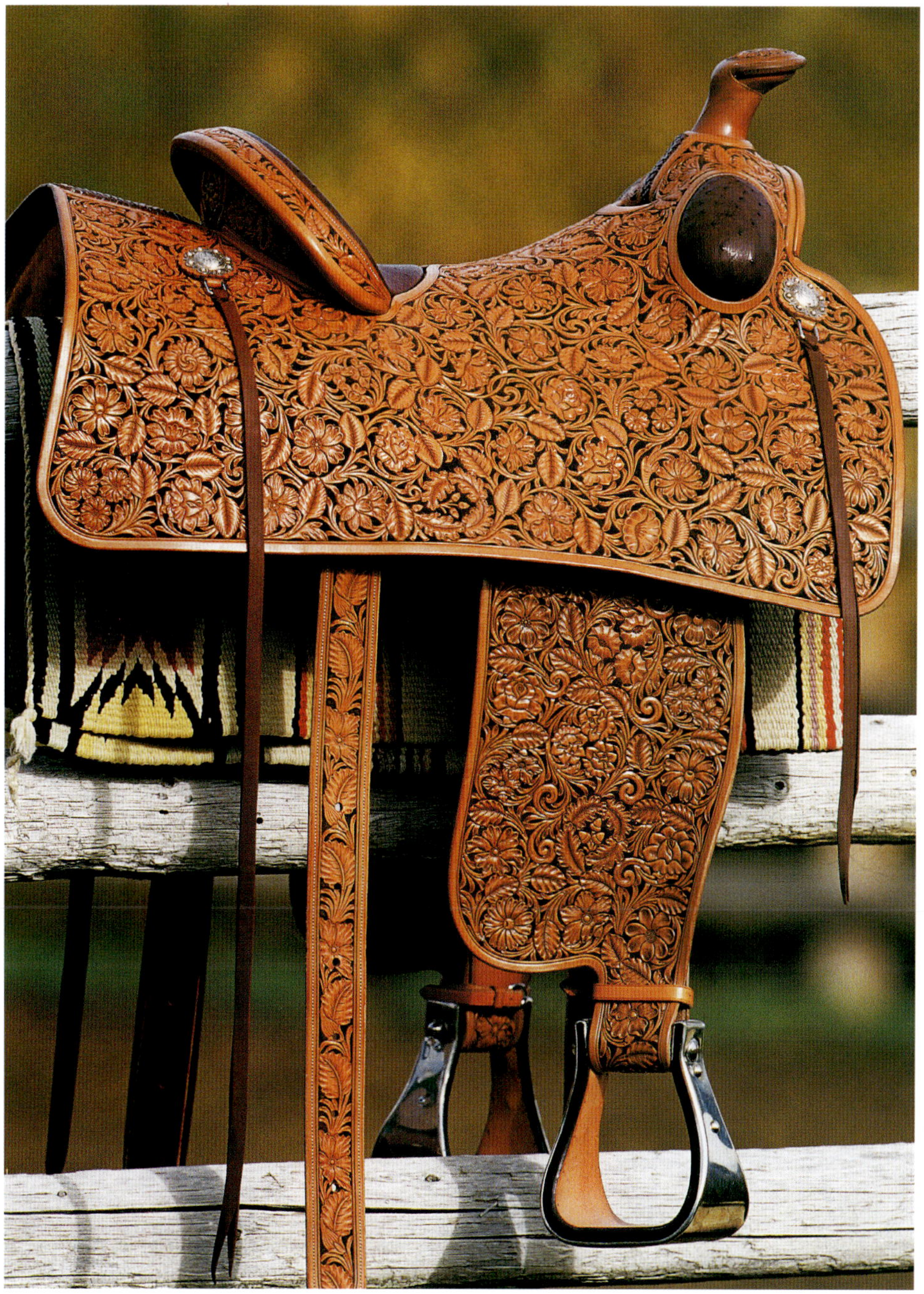

Don King saddle, *fully flowered Mother Hubbard with ostrich skin seat and swells, made for the TCAA of the Cowboy Hall of Fame in Oklahoma City, Oklahoma*

CHAS WELDON

In 1976, Chas Weldon began making saddles and he has been going strong for 28 years. He was hired as an apprentice to Chuck Harris at the Connolly Saddlery in Billings, Montana where he learned the proper professional methods of repair, strap, and saddle building. According to Chas, his client list includes a wide range of types—cowpunchers, soccer moms with horses, fancy movie stars, and best friends. His mentor was the man who taught him the trade, Chuck Harris. Chas is best known for his working saddles, made with an emphasis on a polished finish. The most typical tree of his era is the "Wade style." Chas also altered it and came up with the "Brannaman tree" which was very popular in the 1990s. Saddles made by Chas usually take a year for completion; he does not take orders for a longer wait period than one year. As Chas says, saddles should be as good inside as they are outside. He believes in doing his best on every aspect of the piece and recommends knowing good saddletrees and using them. The finish work on a saddle is very important—Chas thinks you should do every bit of work on a saddle as if Don King or Dale Harwood was looking over your shoulder.

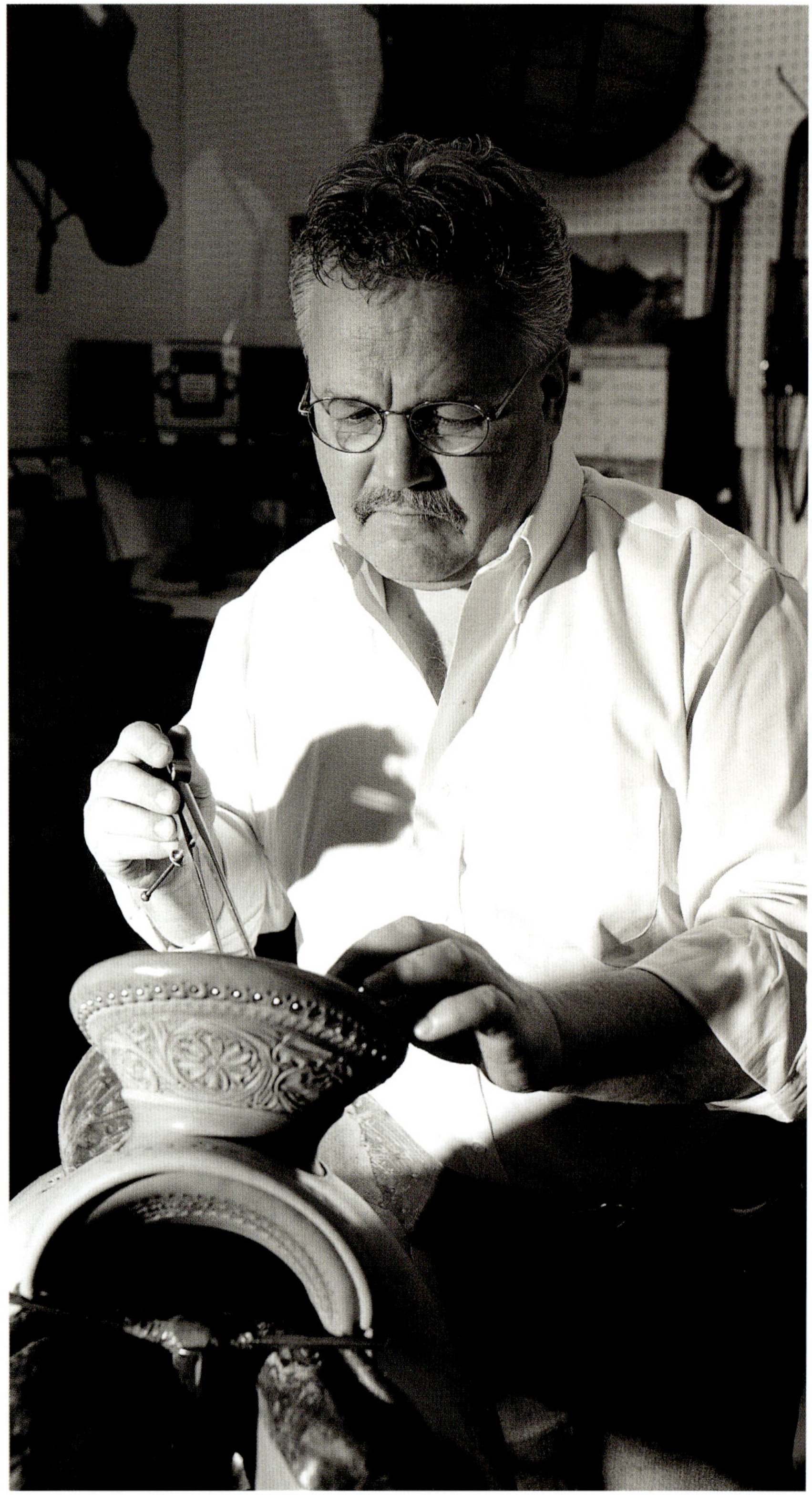

SADDLEMAKER CHAS WELDON,
Billings, Montana

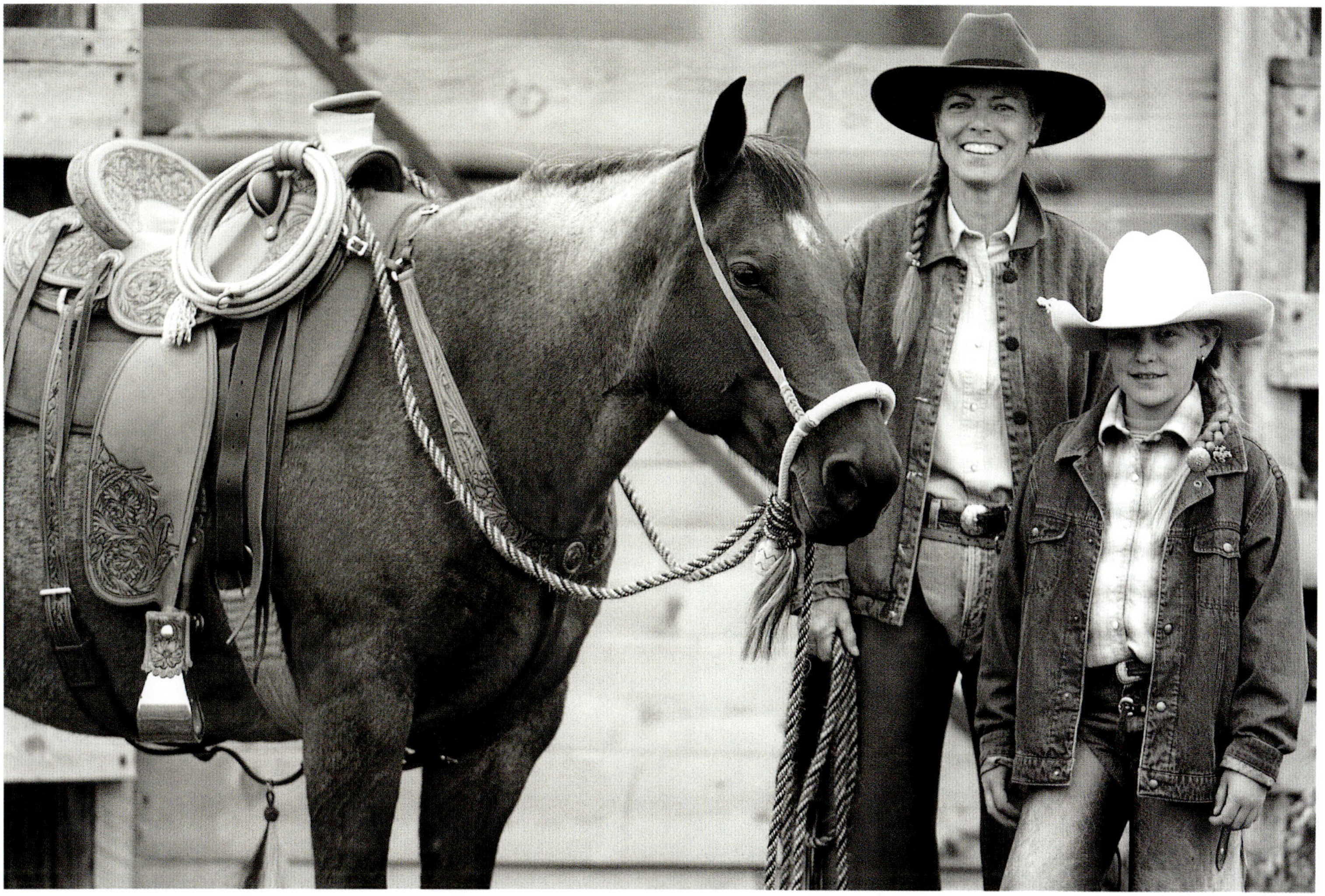

MARY BRANNAMAN AND HER DAUGHTER, REATA *with her new Weldon saddle*

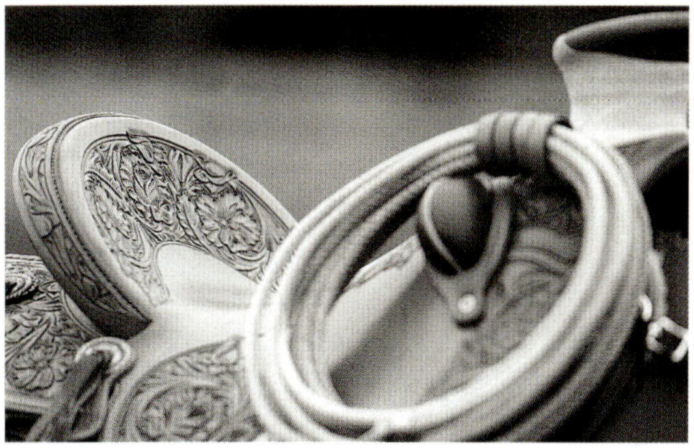

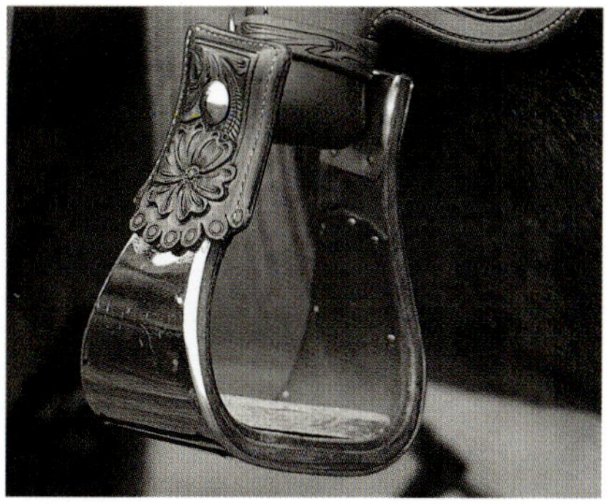

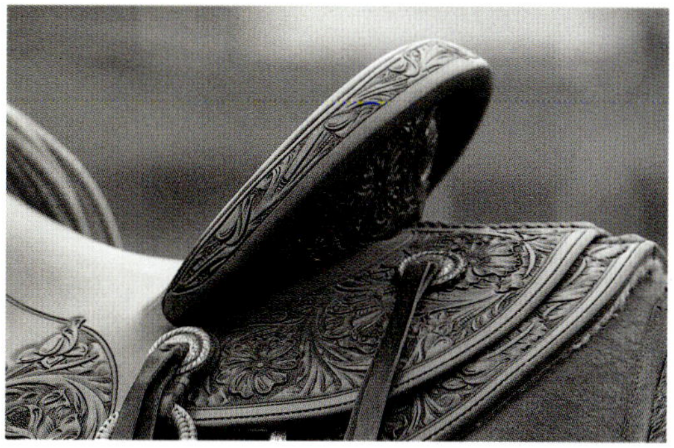

DON BUTLER

Don Butler started making saddles in 1972 and opened his own shop in 1976. He traded a winter's worth of stamp work for instruction on how to put a saddle together. Don started out making saddles mainly for working cowboys but lately has tipped towards a wider range of clients. Bob Douglas was the person who showed Don how to make a saddle and he also admired the work of Lloyd Davis, Don King, Chester Hape, and Bill Gardner. Don is best known for his working saddles that he crafts with Wade, Will James, and Improved Association trees. Prices for Don's saddles start at $3,600 and go up from there and he does have a waiting list. Don's goal in the saddle making business has been to build a saddle that fits the horse and the cowboy perfectly. He has always wanted his finished product to be pleasing to the eye along with being functional.

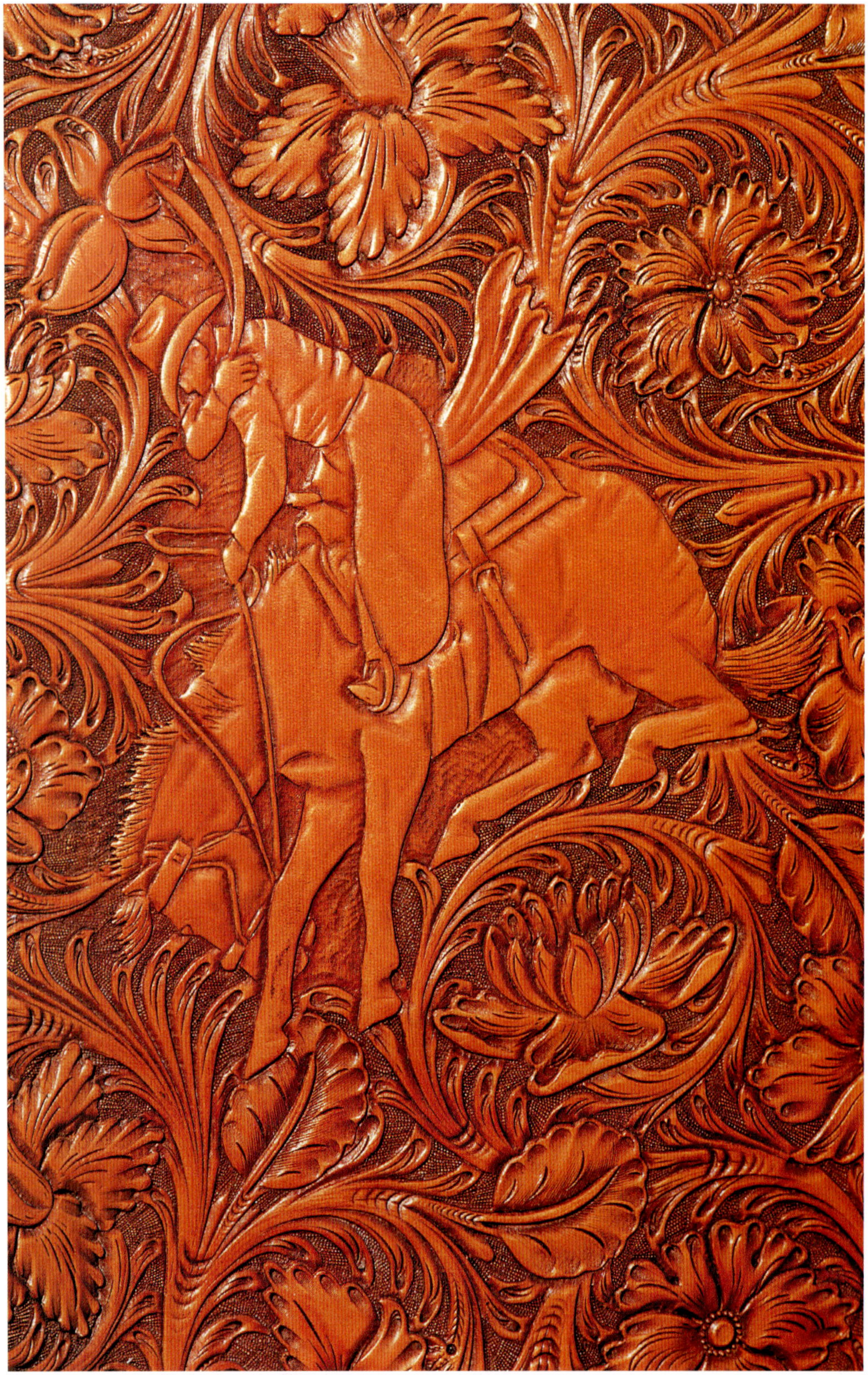

DON BUTLER SADDLE, *Custom Cowboy Shop, Sheridan, Wyoming*

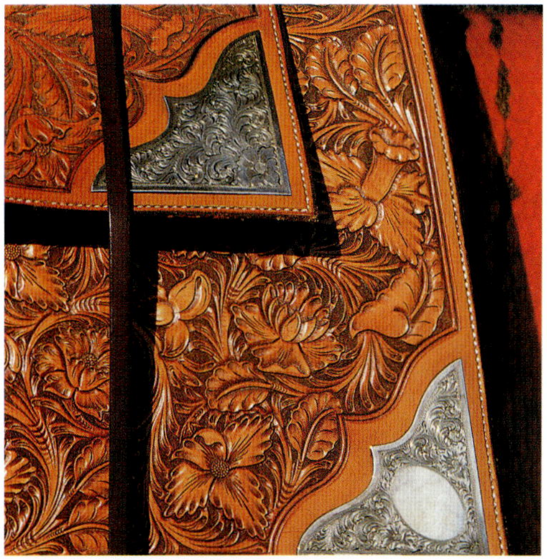

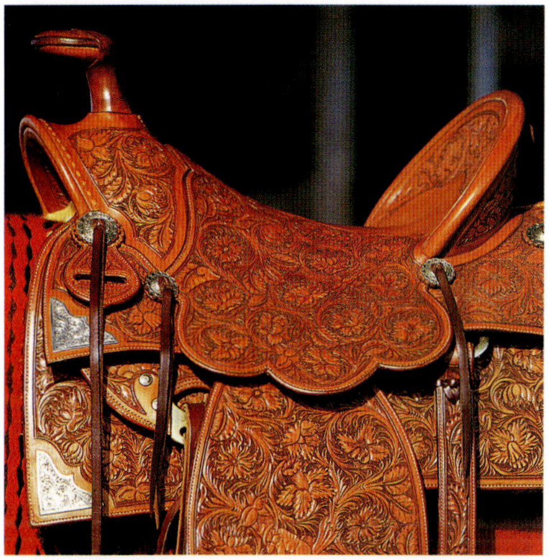

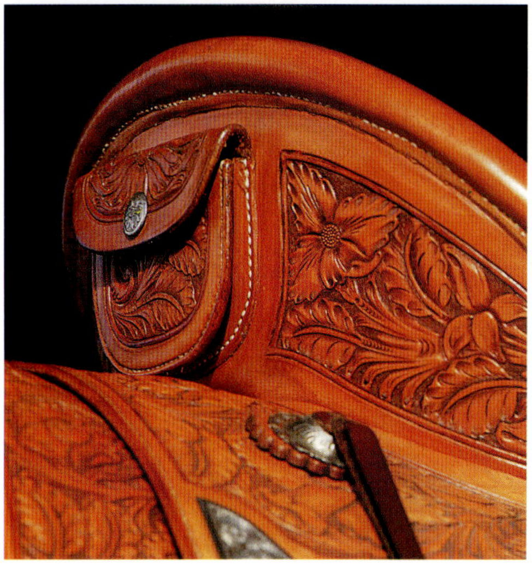

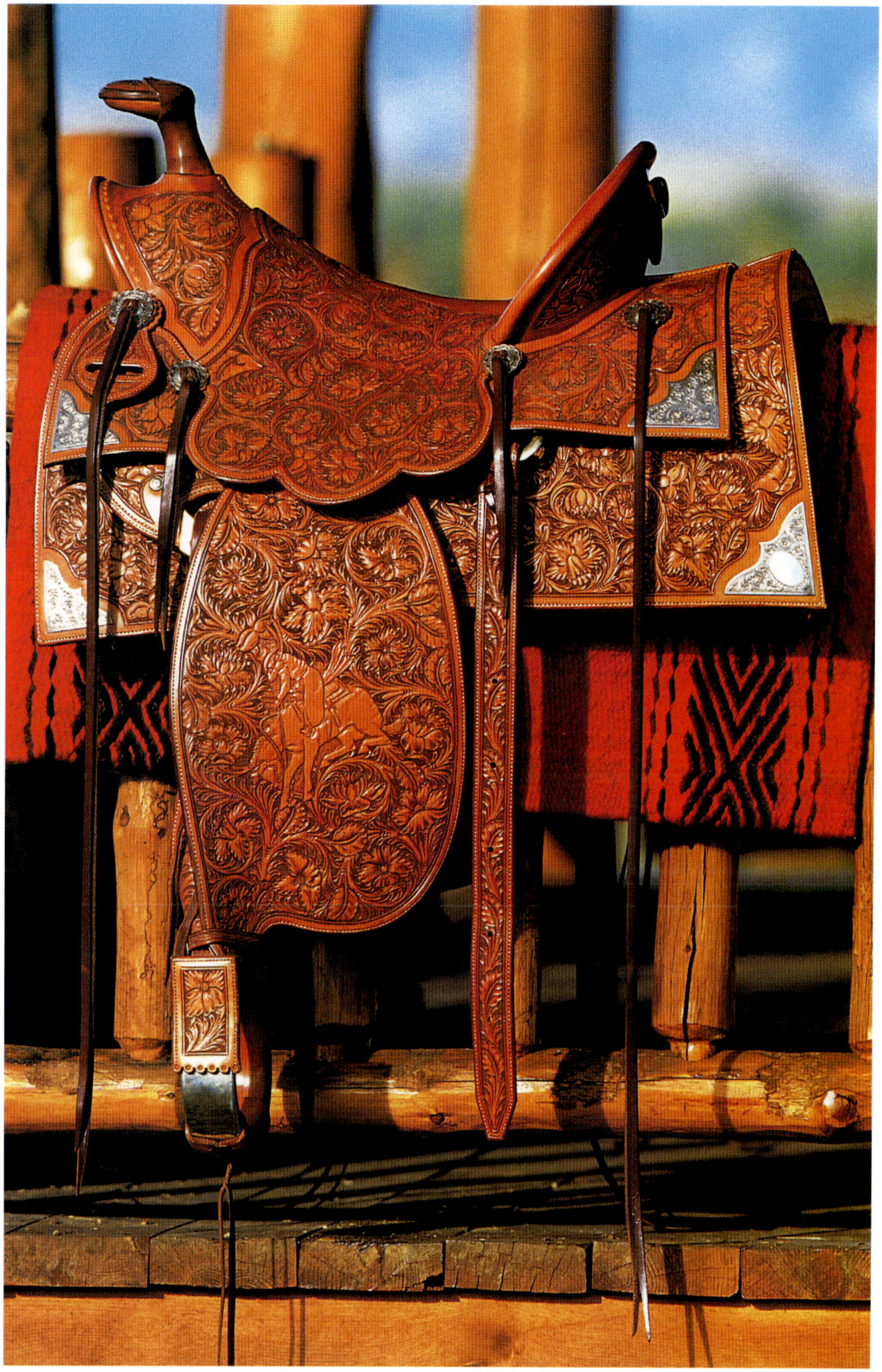

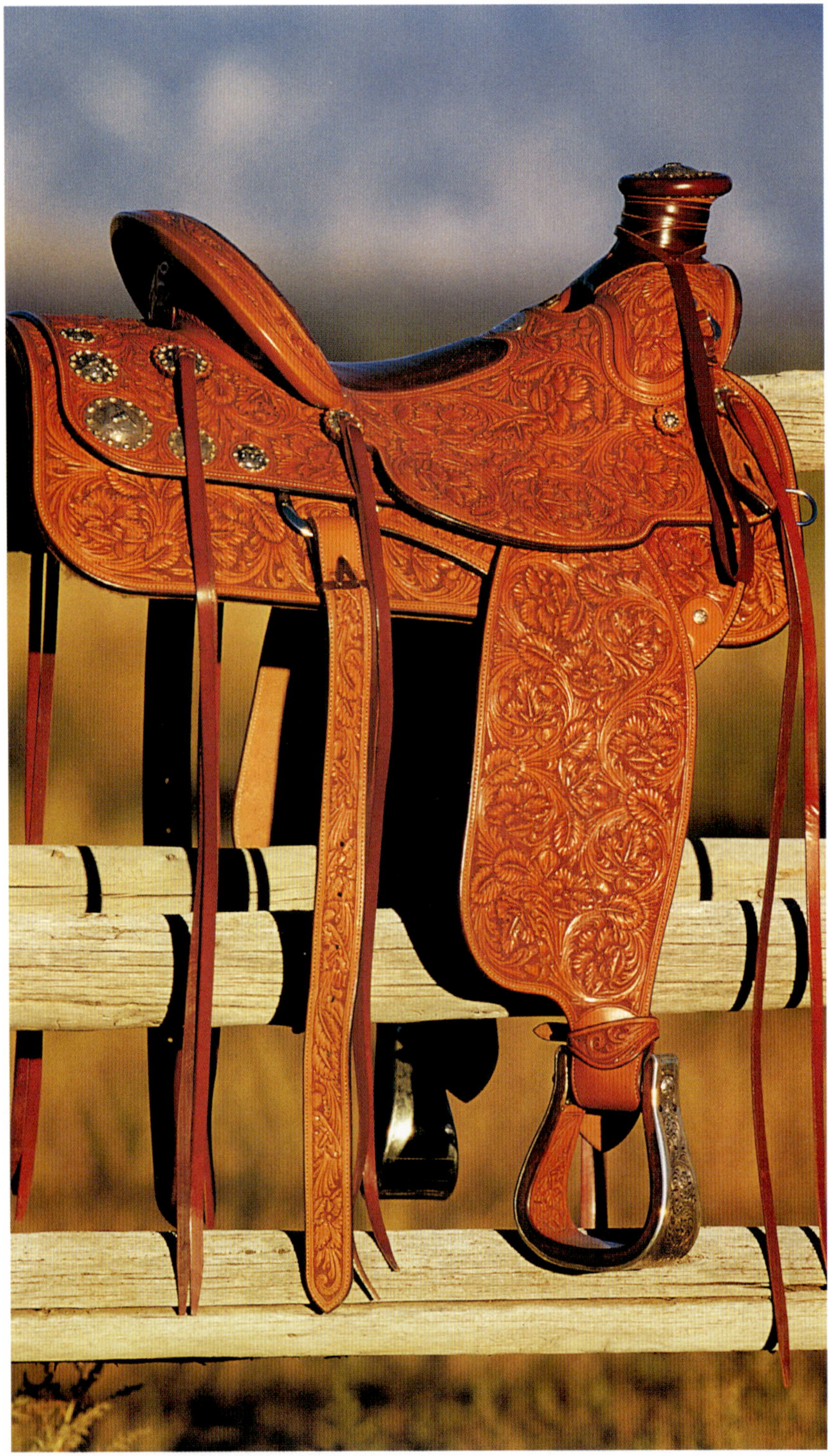

J.M. CAPRIOLA SADDLE, *Elko, Nevada*

J.M. CAPRIOLA

J.M Capriola Company has been in the saddle business since 1929. J.M Capriola started making saddles at the turn of the century and ranched for 20 years before opening his own shop. The store sells saddles to cowboys, ranchers, movie stars and presidents, but the people who make up the largest portion of their clientele are the customers who make a living on horseback. Because the shop is located in Nevada, the working saddles with slick forks are usually the most popular. Capriola uses wood and rawhide trees made by Keith Gertch. The shop makes about 30 saddles per year and the wait time is typically about 16 months. The normal base price for a Capriola saddle is $2,700. The Capriola slogan is "to make the best and repair the rest." They use the best saddletrees, the best leather, and the best craftsmen. They are very proud of their products and their customers are proud to have Capriola saddles and hope that they will one day be valuable heirlooms.

J.M. CAPRIOLA *75th anniversary saddle details*

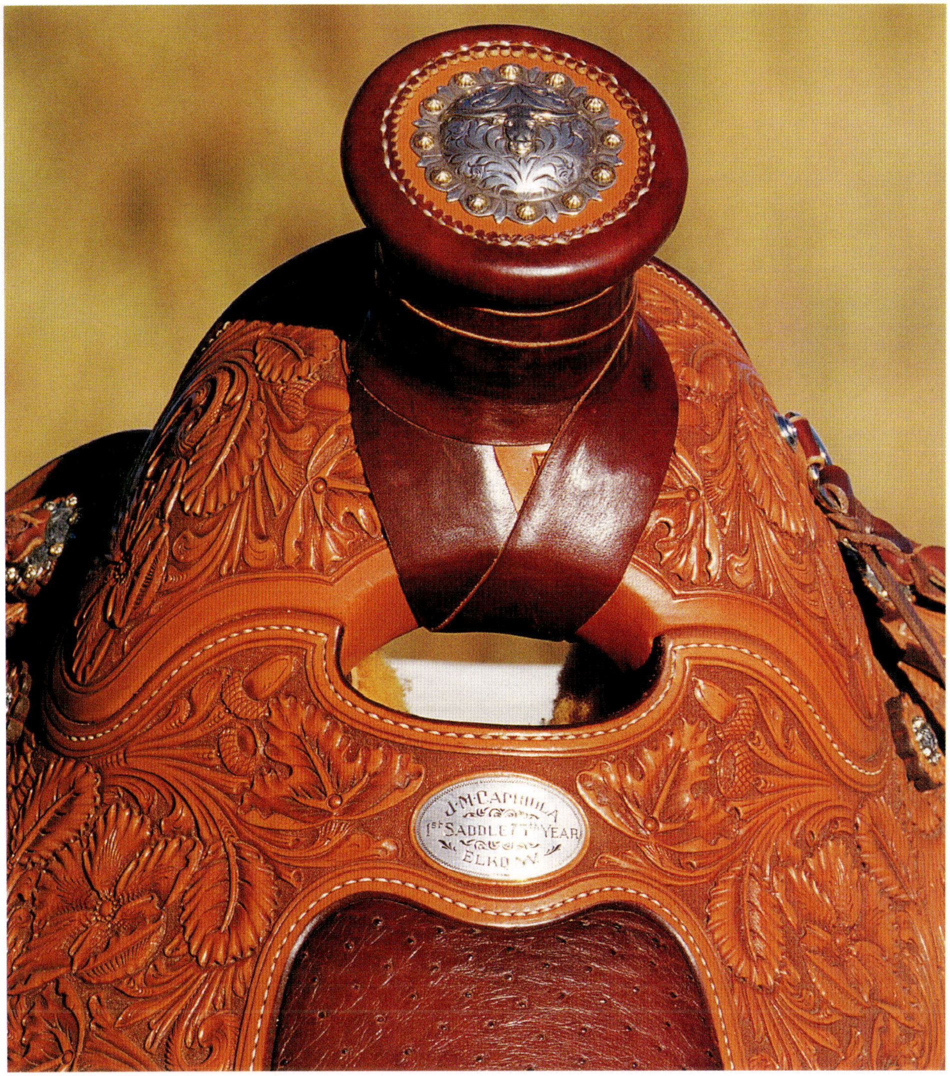

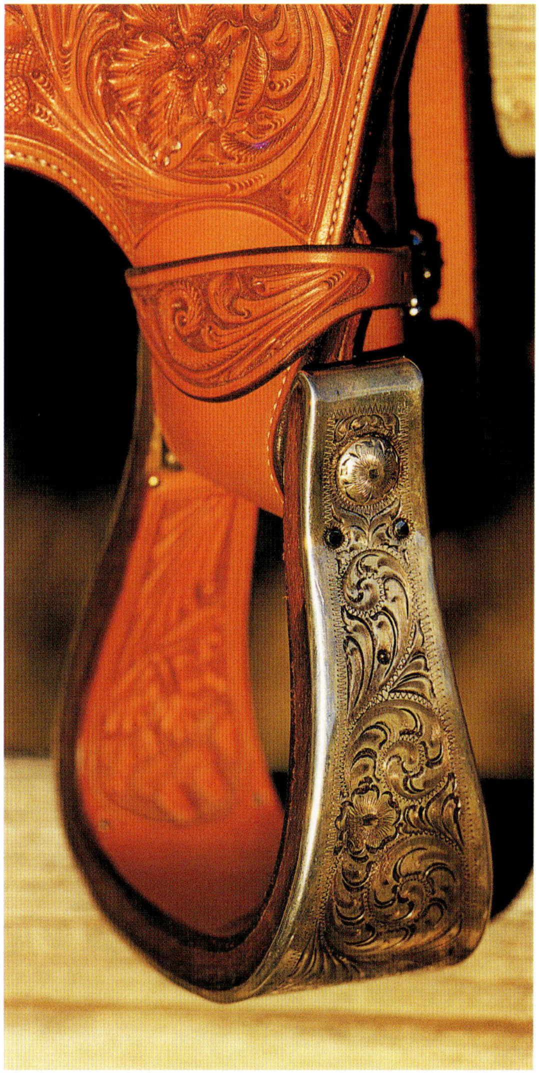

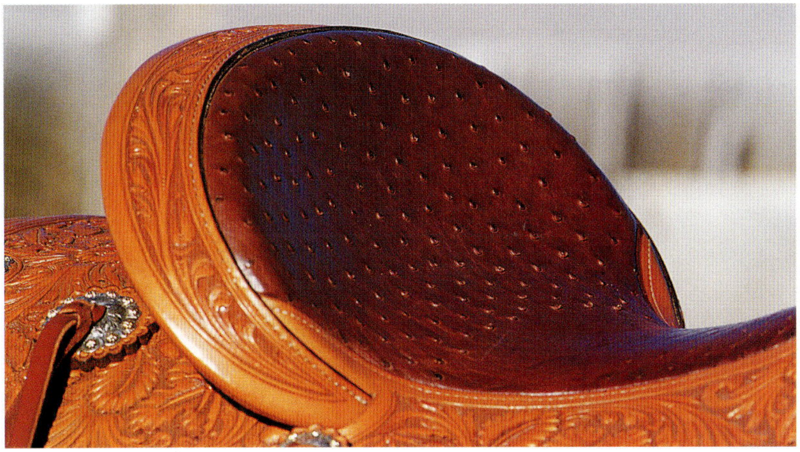

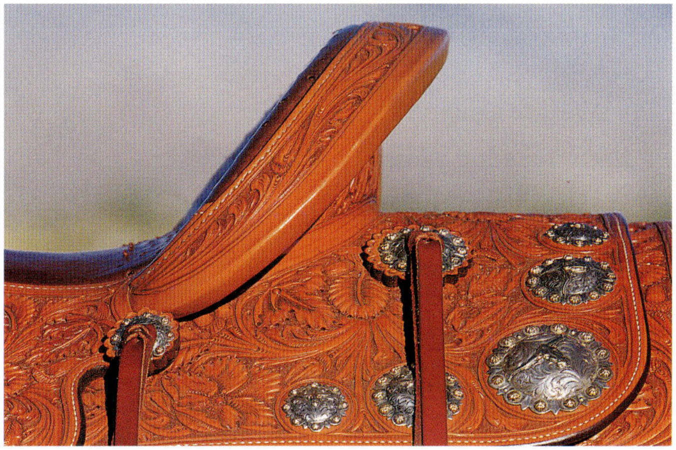

NANCY HOGGAN

Nancy Hoggan started making saddles 17 years ago and learned the trade from master saddle maker, Dale Harwood, who helped her build her very first saddle. Nancy learned from his advice over the years. Most of Nancy's customers are working cowboys—rodeo pick-up men, ranchers, day work cowboys—who make a living on horseback. She credits Dale Harwood with having the most impact and input into her own saddle making. She also admires the work of Don King and Ray Holes. Most of Nancy's saddles are working saddles, built to fit a horse well and hold up under hard use. She uses slick fork, shovel cantle saddletrees and lots of Ray Hunt trees with small wood post horns. Sometimes she uses small swell fork trees, such as Lewis or Lew Allen Ropers. Orders for Nancy's saddles are usually about 18 months out and the prices hover around $3,000. Nancy says that saddle making is a daily challenge to produce a product that fits the horse and pleases the rider. The saddle should fit its purpose and be built to last. She enjoys the creative aspect of saddle making and she constantly strives to improve her workmanship and knowledge. Her heroes are the craftsmen whose work she admires and the cowboys whose horsemanship she admires. Nancy's goal is to learn something from everyone she meets.

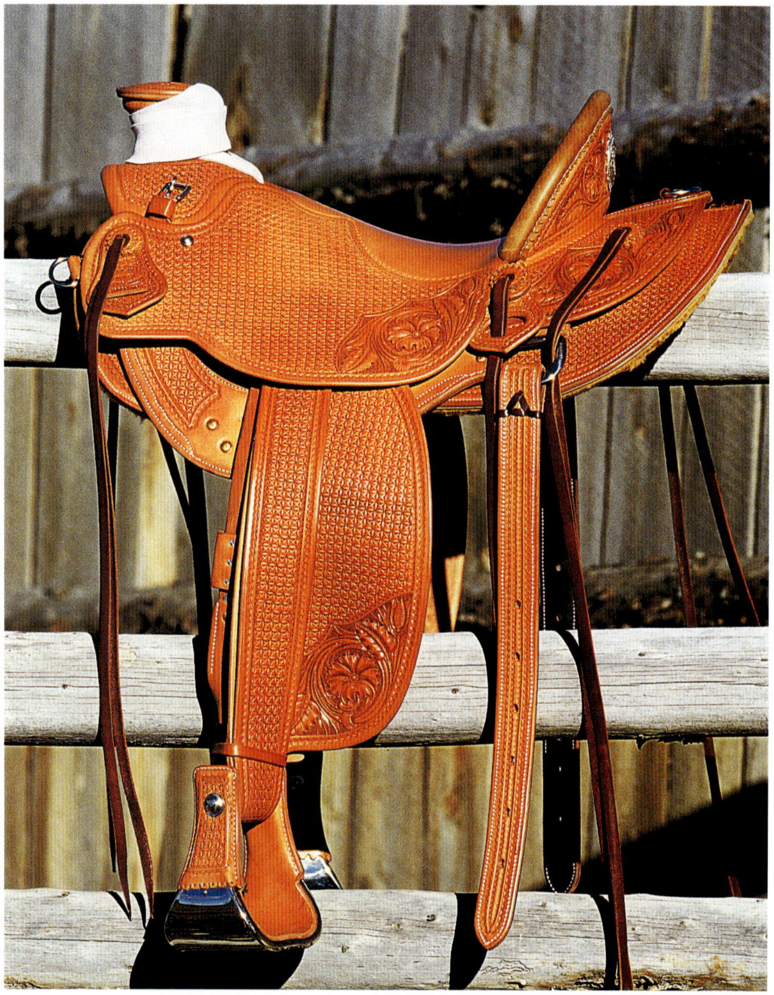

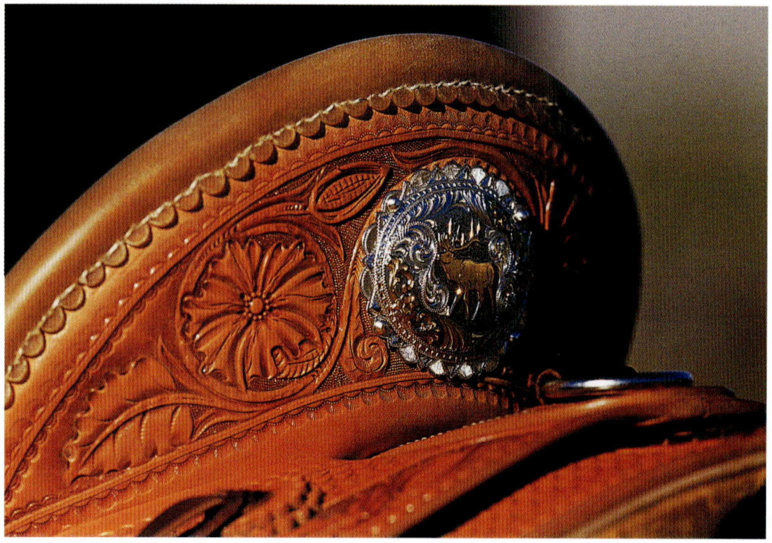

NANCY HOGGAN SADDLE, *Hoggan Custom Leather, Gooding, Idaho*

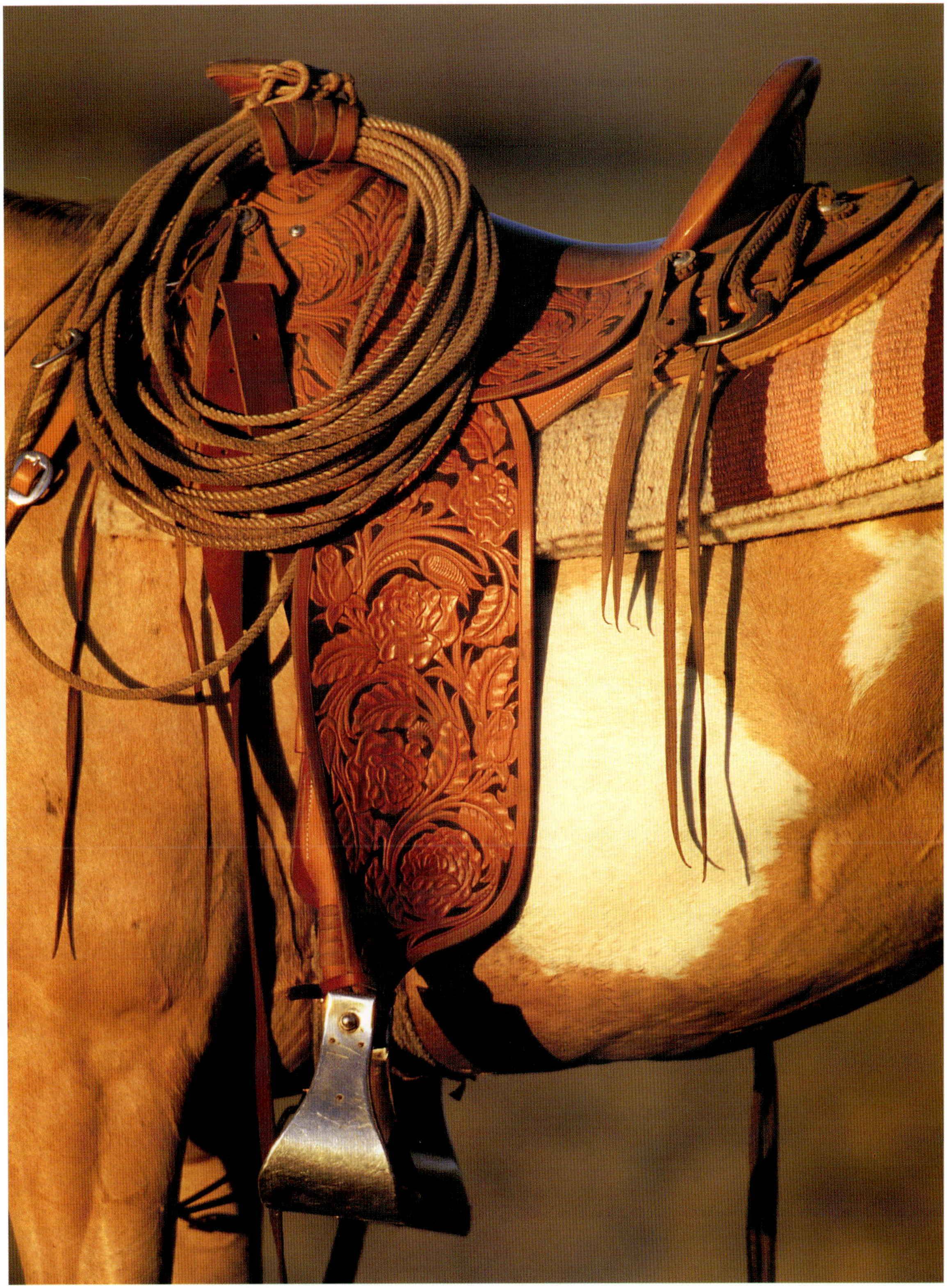

CURT PATE'S LEFT-HANDED SADDLE *made by Nancy Hoggan*

Marc Brogger

Marc Brogger has been in the saddle making business since 1981. He served a three-year apprenticeship under Jim Lathrope and he makes saddles mostly for cowboys and performance horsemen. He admires Jim Lathrope, Dale Harwood, and Ray Holes. Marc uses 75% slick fork trees and 25% swell fork trees in his work and is best known for his working saddles. The waiting list for a Brogger saddle is a couple of years and the saddles typically sell for $3,000 to $5,000. Marc feels that a saddle is no less than a functional piece of art and that its function is essential. A saddle that doesn't fit the horse or the rider correctly is not much of a saddle at all. Marc uses only the finest materials he can get his hands on and places a lot of emphasis on simplicity. He works hard to produce consistent, tight saddles with smooth lines. He stresses that it is only through the support of his family and friends and other great saddle makers that he has been able to achieve the level of expertise he has.

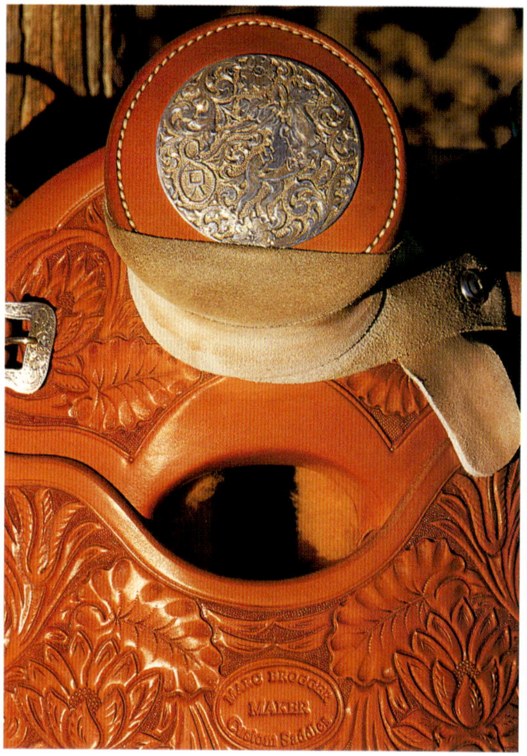

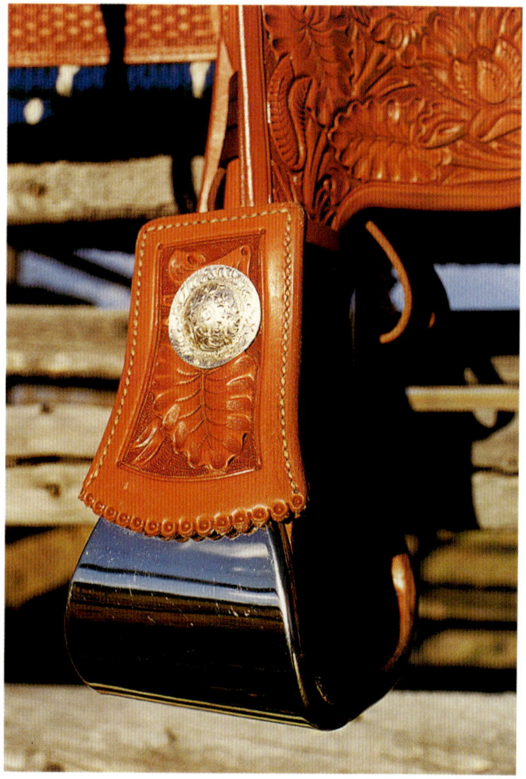

MARC BROGGER SADDLE, *Three Forks, Montana*

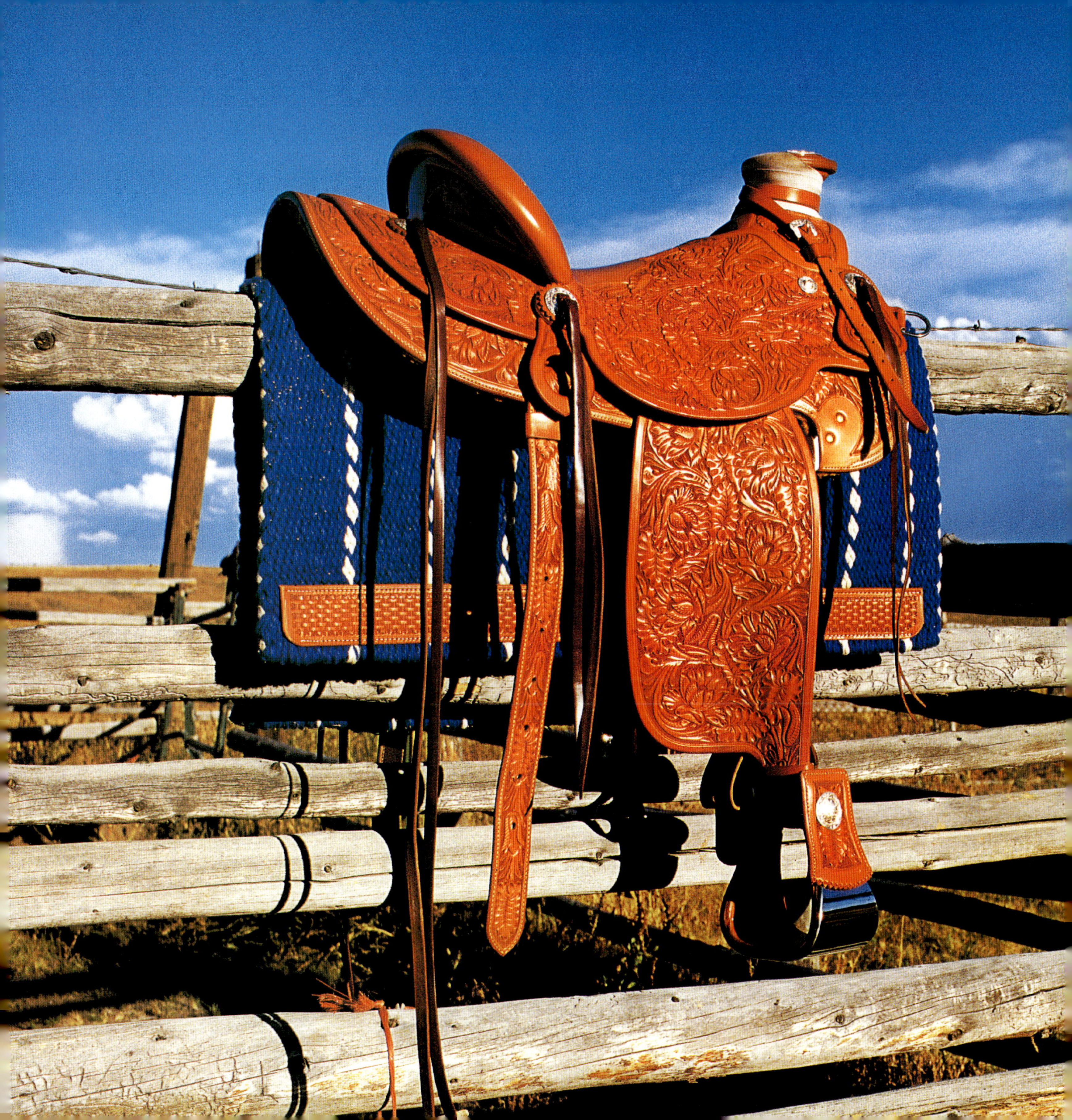

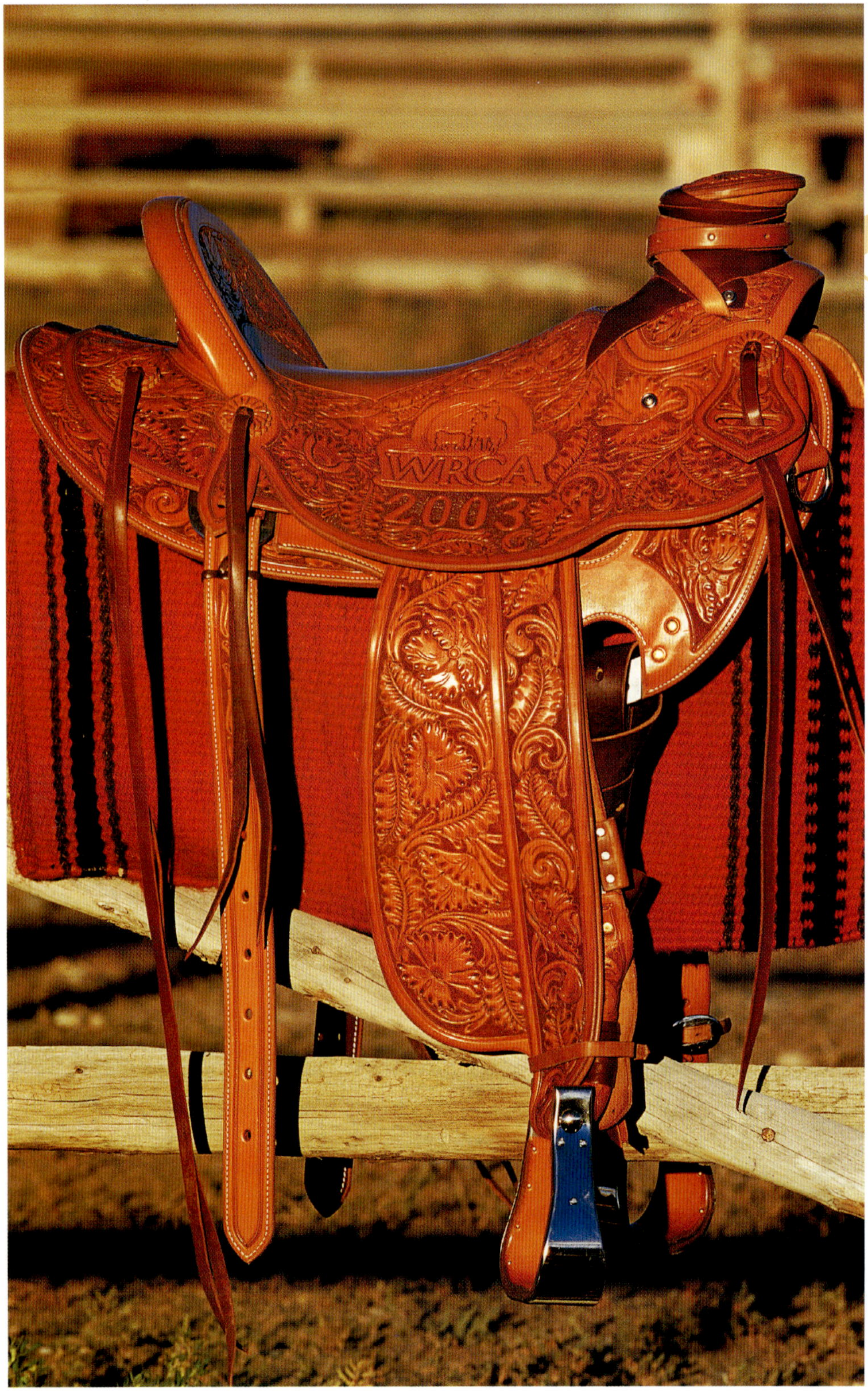

Scott Brown

Scott and his wife Becky grew up in the Texas panhandle. After Scott built saddles in Amarillo and the cowtown district of Fort Worth, they moved to Elko, Nevada where he built saddles and cowboyed for the next 15 years. Scott was impressed by the craftsmanship in the Northwest, and refined his technique believing that his saddles, although utilitarian items, should be aesthetically pleasing. In 1993, Scott and Becky and their two sons moved to Alpine, in the Big Bend region of west Texas where Scott built saddles for Big Bend Saddlery in Alpine. He recently moved to Salt Lake City with his family. (biography courtesy of Claggett/Rey Gallery, Vail, Colorado)

Scott Brown Big Bend WRCA trophy saddle *made for the 2003 World Championship, Alpine, Texas*

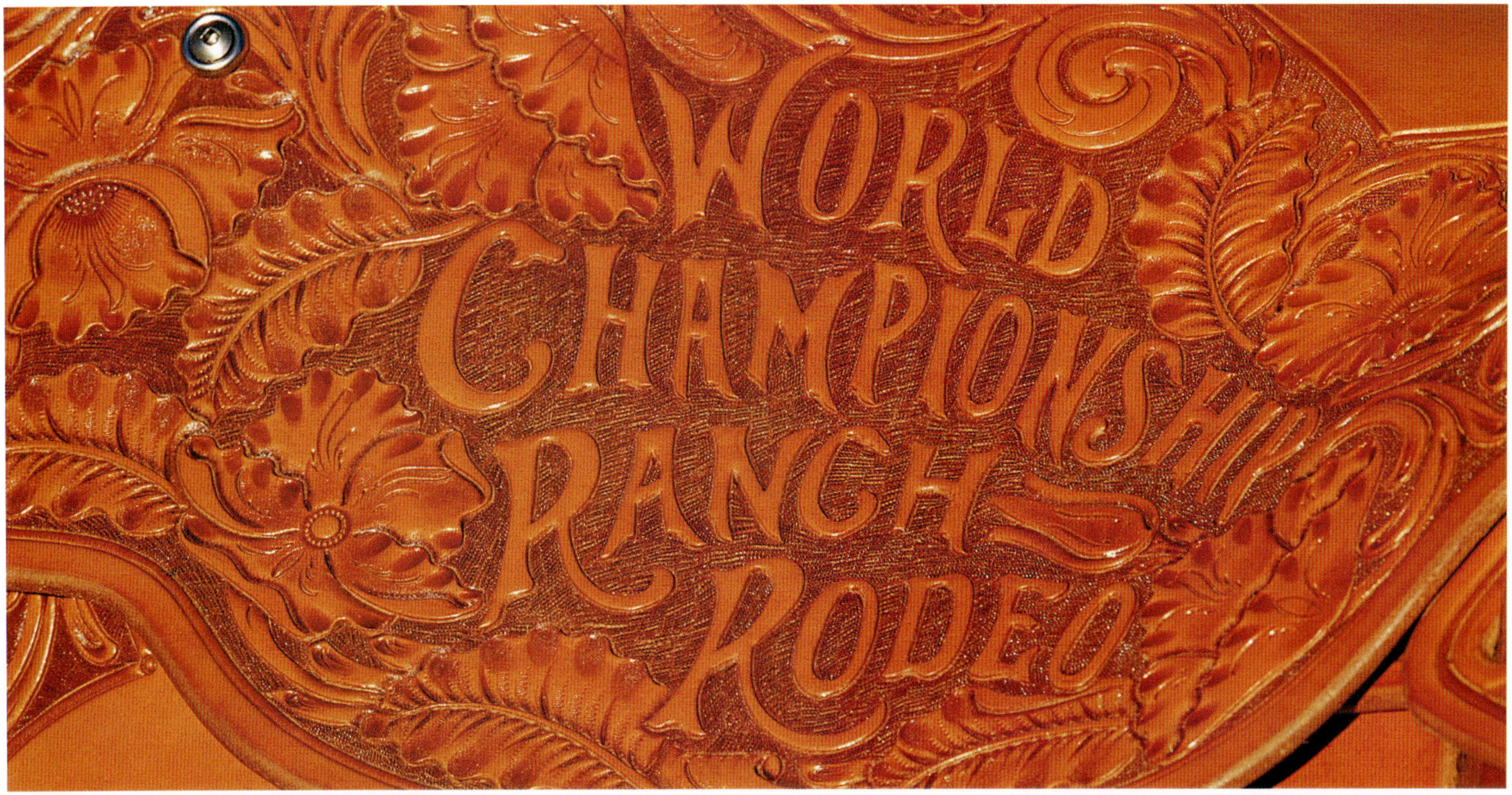
WORLD
CHAMPIONSHI
RANCH
RODEO

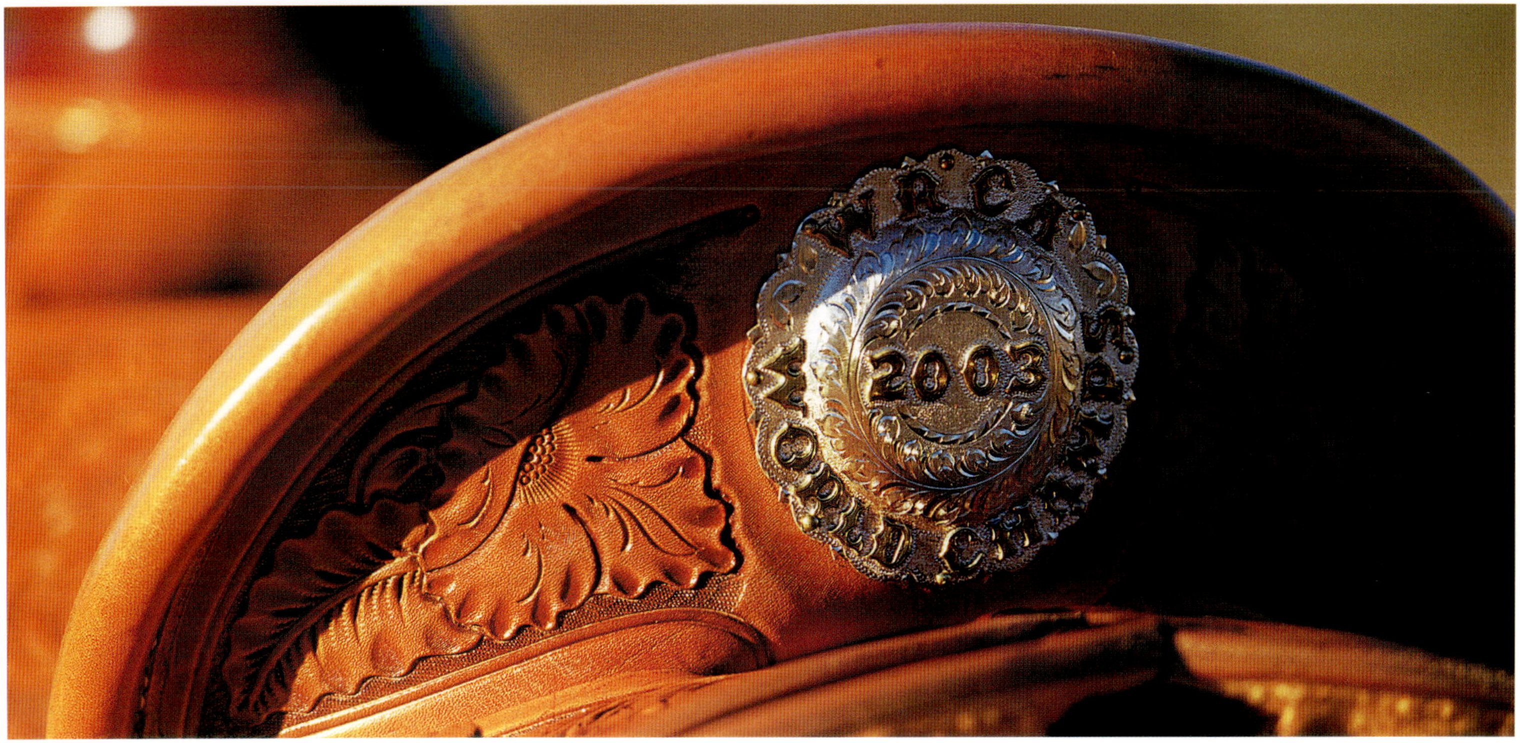
W.R.C.A.
2003

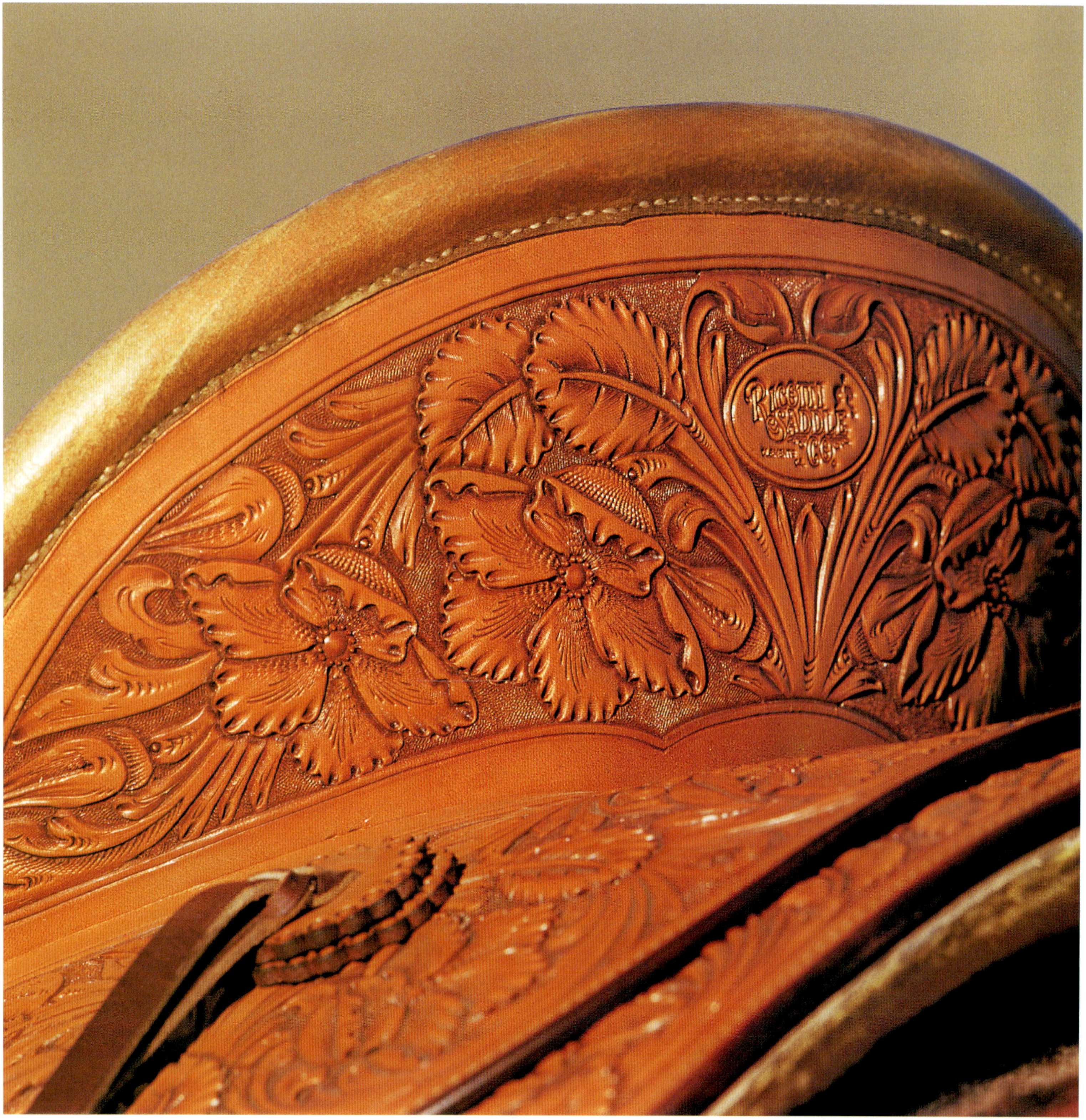
RICOTTI SADDLE CO.

Rick Ricotti

Rick Ricotti was born and raised in Hollister, California, and graduated from Cal Poly, San Luis Obispo in 1966. Through the years, Rick had been drawn to saddle making as a hobby. As the years passed, his hobby grew into an obsession. Around this time, Rick became acquainted with Vic Vasquez, foremost a silversmith and a saddle maker. Rick says that Vasquez was good to him in every way when it came to the craft and knowing about the tools. As the years passed and his hobby grew, Rick decided to move with his wife, Susan, to Jackson and dedicate himself to saddle making full time. Rick continued to learn, by trial and error, how to make saddles, breast collars, headstalls, and other leather items. He started to make a reputation for himself and continued to meet people involved with horses and cattle. Around this time, he received a call from Jack Sparrowk, a commercial cattleman who lives near Clements, who told him about a business that was for sale in Clements. It was 1987 when Ricotti Saddle Company was founded and Rick moved from his one-man shop in Jackson to the heart of Clements on Highway 88. Ricotti Saddle Company is a Western store and saddle-making shop. Rick is happiest sitting on the other side of the swinging door in the workshop, creating the beautiful saddles, briefcases, and belts that adorn the walls and racks of the other side. Rick says he thinks it is important for a person to feel comfortable when working and if they don't, it will show up in their work. A Ricotti saddle is "one of a kind." A new pattern is made for each one and never reused. Because of the time-intensive process, production is limited. They build around 30 saddles a year and keep 60 to 65 saddles on order all the time. Orders come to Ricotti's from Canada, Switzerland, Germany, and from across the United States. Most of their advertising is by word of mouth. Ricotti's also does a lot of repair work and has a mobile tack unit that goes to 26 shows throughout the year. It is just as important to Rick that somebody is satisfied with a custom order as somebody is with a repair. Ricotti's has made award saddles for the National Reined Cow Horse Association's (NRCHA) Snaffle Bit Futurity and many of the association's year-end champions. They have also made award saddles for the Reno Championship Snaffle Bit Futurity. Also on the list every year are the trophy saddles for the Grand National at the Cow Palace in San Francisco, California. (biography courtesy of Cascade Horseman, June 2001 issue, "Dreams Come True: Ricotti Saddle Company," Andra Campbell)

Rick Ricotti saddle, *Clements, California*

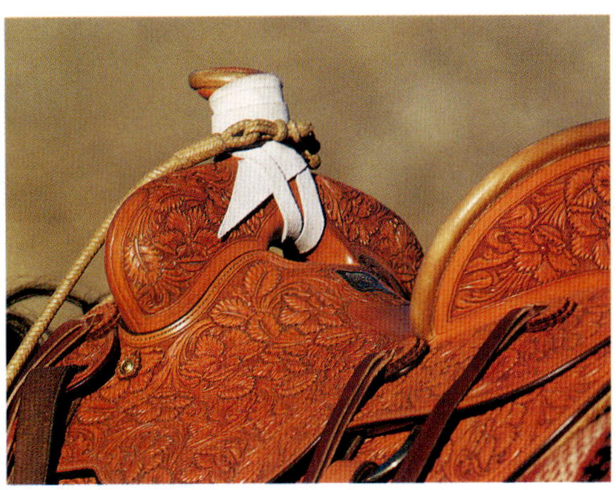

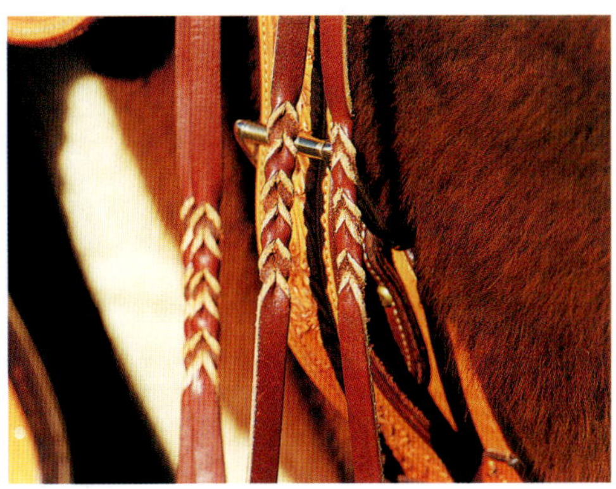

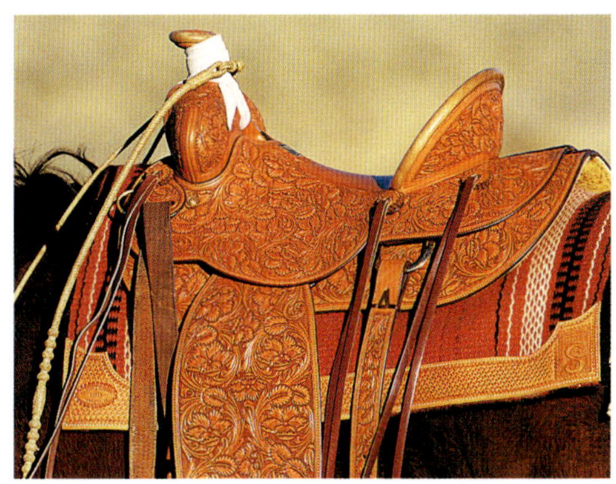

McCall Saddle Company

McCall saddles are handcrafted in the heart of the West for the working cowboy. It is the closest a cowboy can get to a custom-made saddle, without the custom cost. Over 45 years of combined experience in saddle design, construction and customer satisfaction—along with a real knowledge of cowboy needs—goes into each McCall saddle. The saddle makers begin with a handmade rawhide covered tree, uniquely designed and built just for them. Each tree has a solid, long-grain lodgepole pine bar and cantle, with a laminated fork. The woods are then bullhide covered, deer-rawhide laced and nailed—no staples are used. All skirts are lined with genuine bark-tanned wool. In striving to fit the horse with a good tree and the rider with a good seat, McCall also recognizes the need to make custom options available. Stirrups are available in several different styles. McCall has over 20 separate hand tooling patterns or combinations. Each saddle is tooled by one individual according to the customer's specifications. The skilled saddle makers and toolers know their business and are proud of their work. Inspired by the traditions of our Western heritage, McCall Saddle Company is pleased to offer our line of quality saddles designed and built in the heart of the West to meet the needs of today's working cowboy.

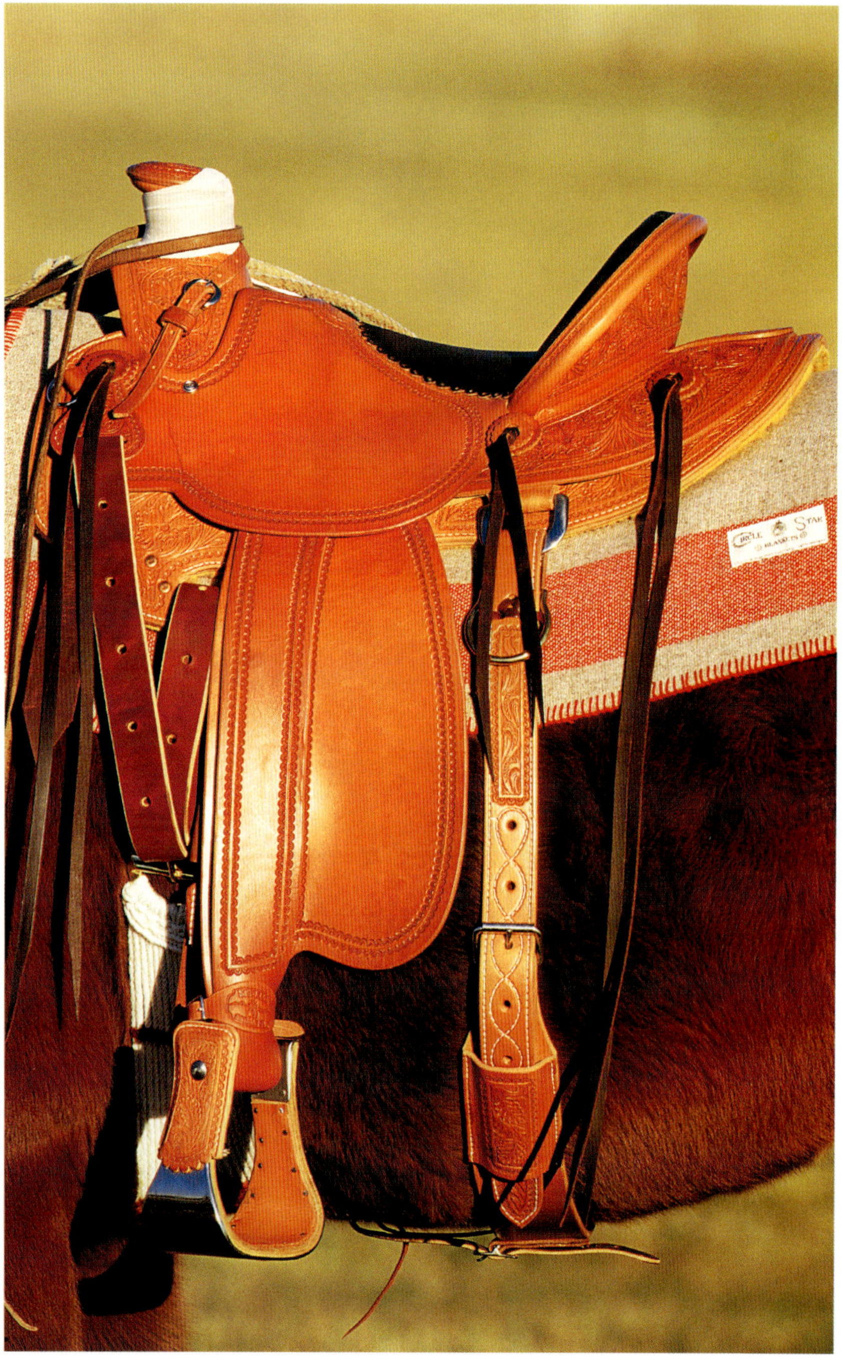

LADY WADE® SADDLE WITH A 3/4 PATCH SEAT,
made by McCall Saddle Company,
Brighton Feed and Saddlery, Brighton, Colorado

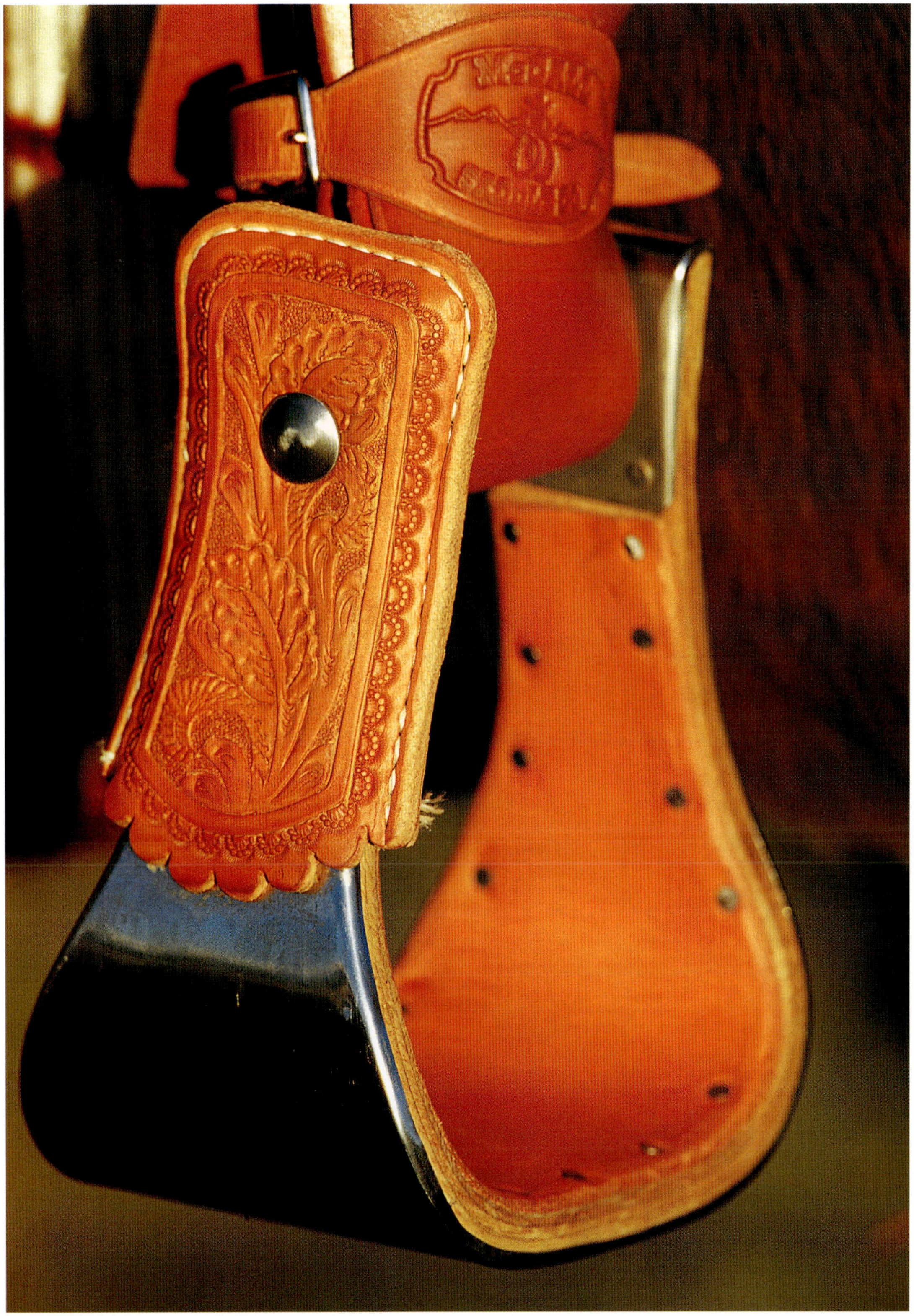

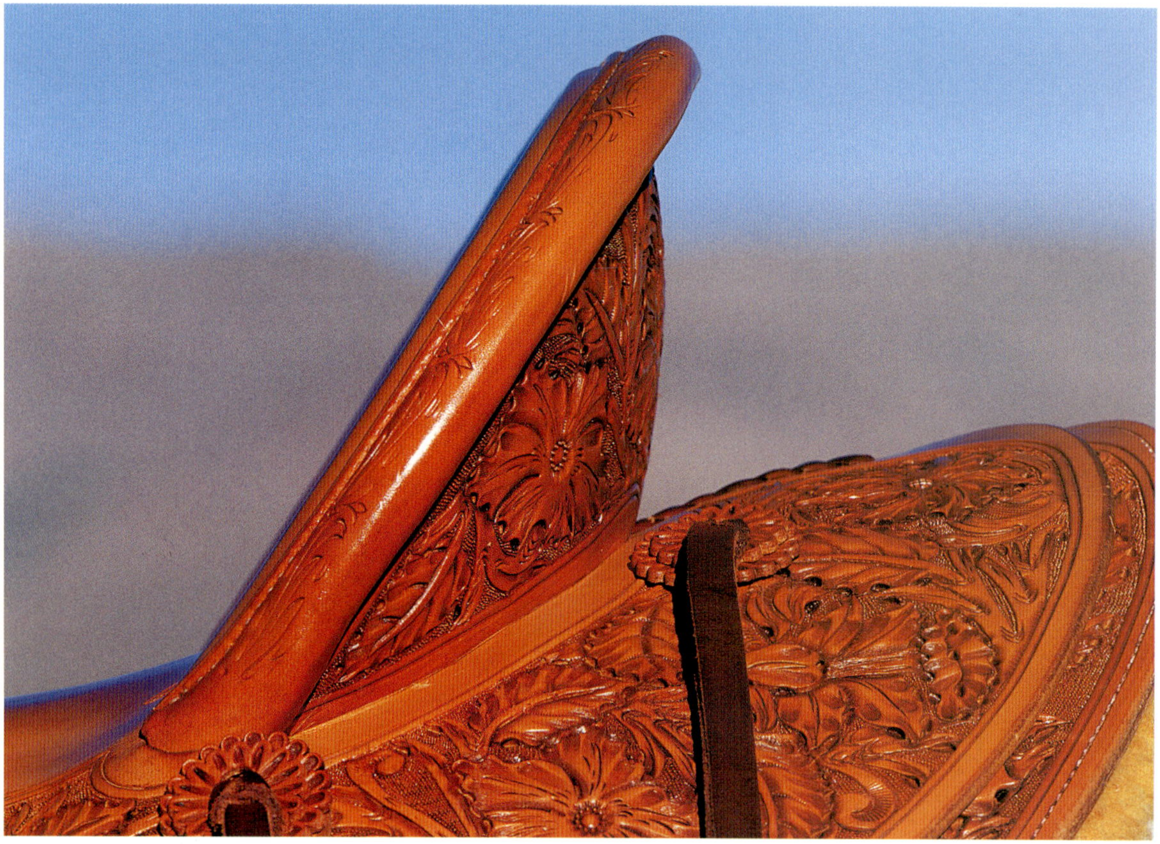

Bob Severe saddle, *Burley, Idaho*

Bob Severe

Bob Severe has been making saddles for 36 years and he is completely self-taught. His customers are mainly cowboys but he also has made saddles for performance horsemen and collectors and is best known for his working and roping saddles. Duff Severe and Dale Harwood are the craftsmen he looks up to the most in his trade. He typically uses Wade 1940 and 1956 saddletrees. The base price for a Severe saddle is around $2,600 and there is about a one-year waiting list to receive one. At Severe, they make the best saddles they can using the best materials available. They do not believe in using imported leather and take no short cuts in quality for the saddletrees or the saddle itself. They do the best they can on each saddle and take a great deal of pride in their products.

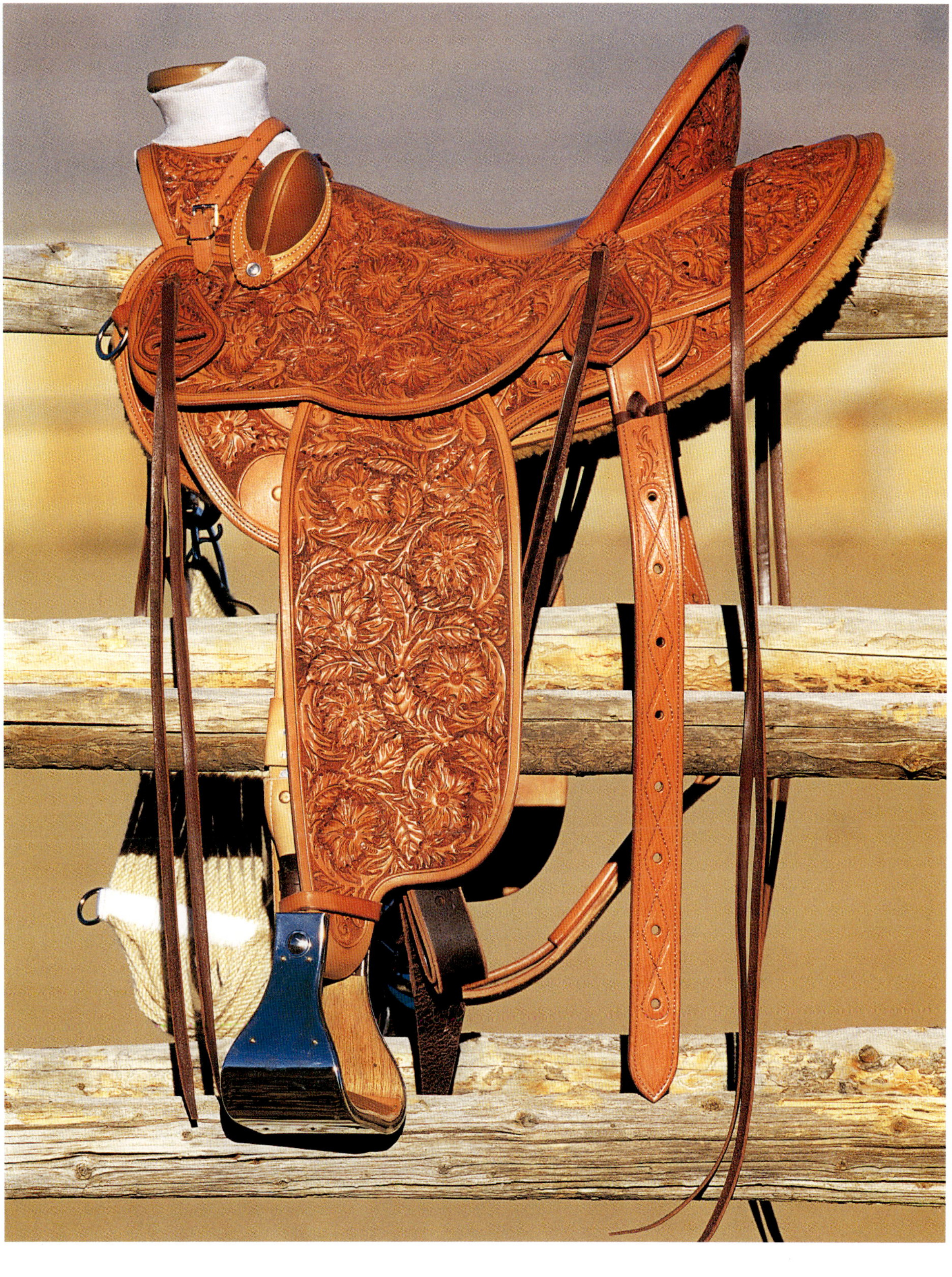

Western Performance Saddles

It all started with a basic Western saddle for riding and herding cattle. As cowboys and cowgirls started to have more and more free time to rodeo or ride cutting, reining, or cow horses, the requirements for their tack changed. Today there are saddles specially designed for every event from cutting to team roping, barrel racing, steer wrestling, and so on. These performance saddles can range in price anywhere from $2,000 to $30,000. Saddles are given as prizes at most events. The trophy saddle collections of great horsemen and women can sometimes fill an entire train car. A trophy saddle is a highly prized possession for any horseman. The selection of performance saddles in this book is a very small sampling of what is available, but it offers an understanding of what is necessary for each equine event.

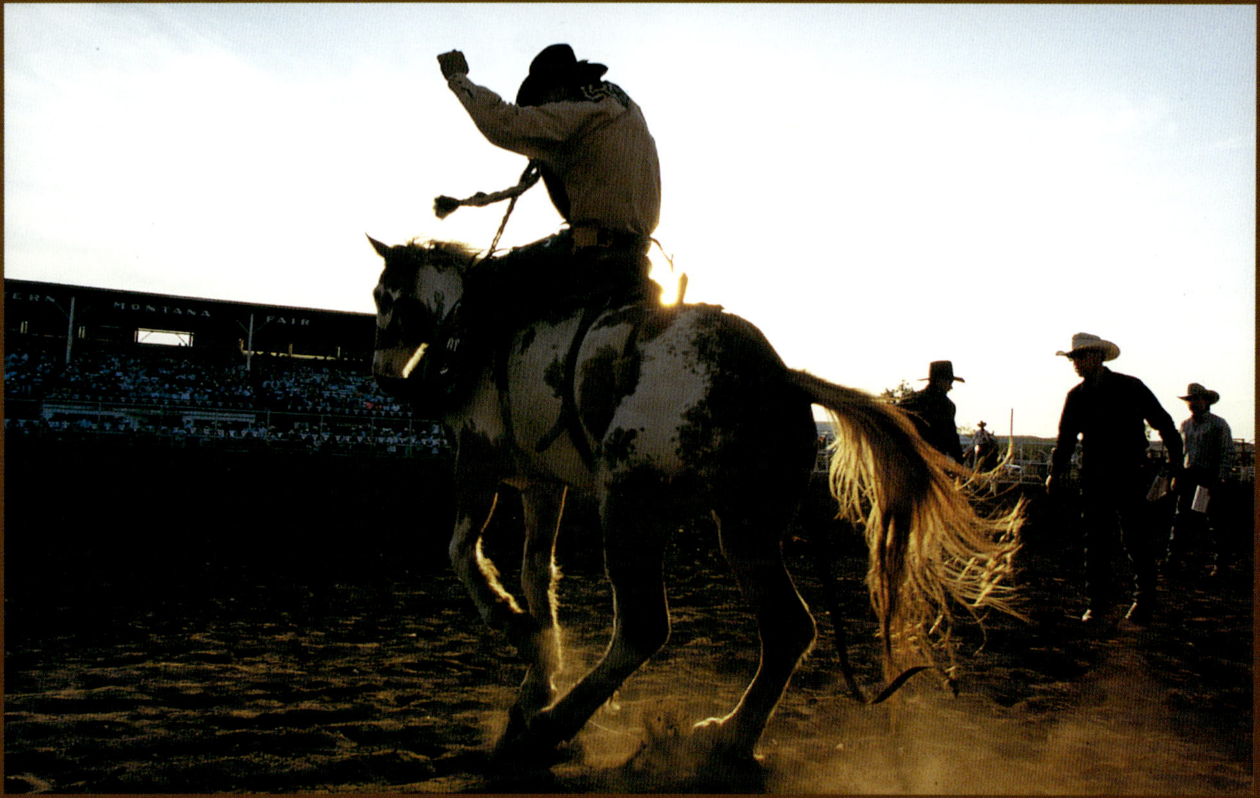

Miles City Bucking Horse Sale, *Miles City, Montana*

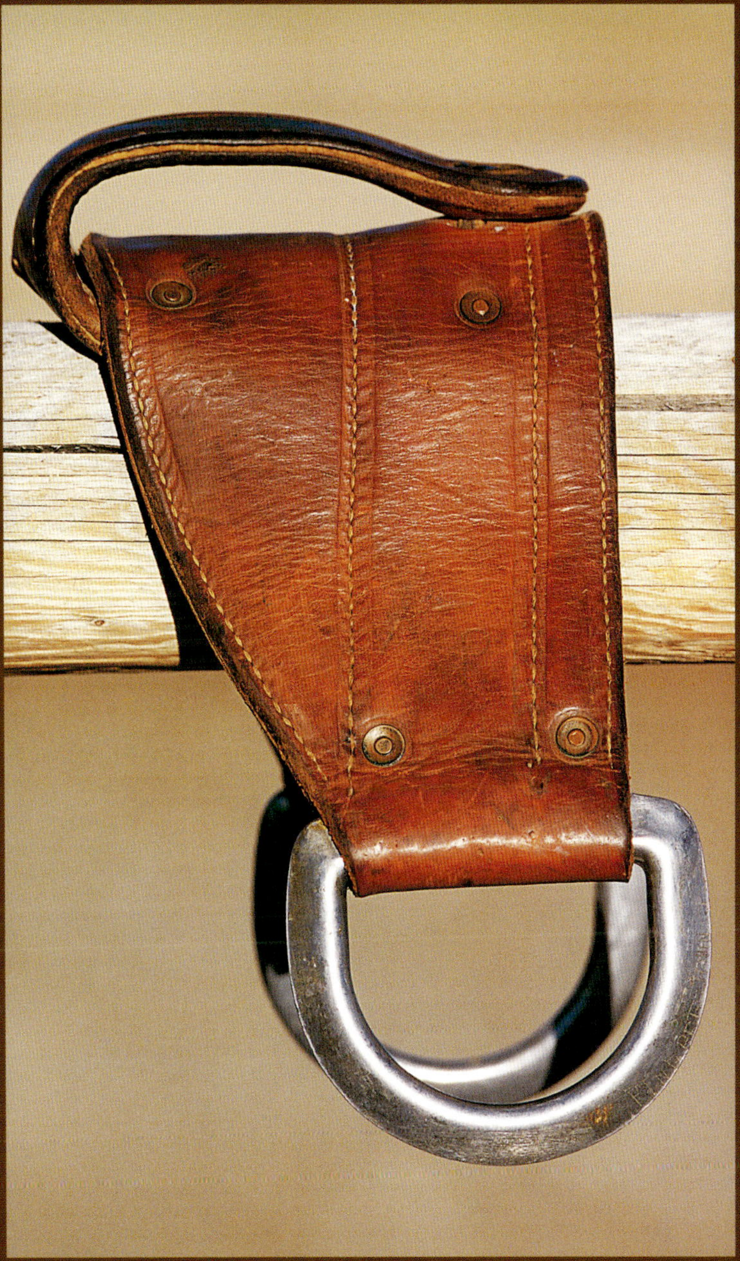

ANTIQUE BAREBACK RIGGING, *Stoecklein Collection*

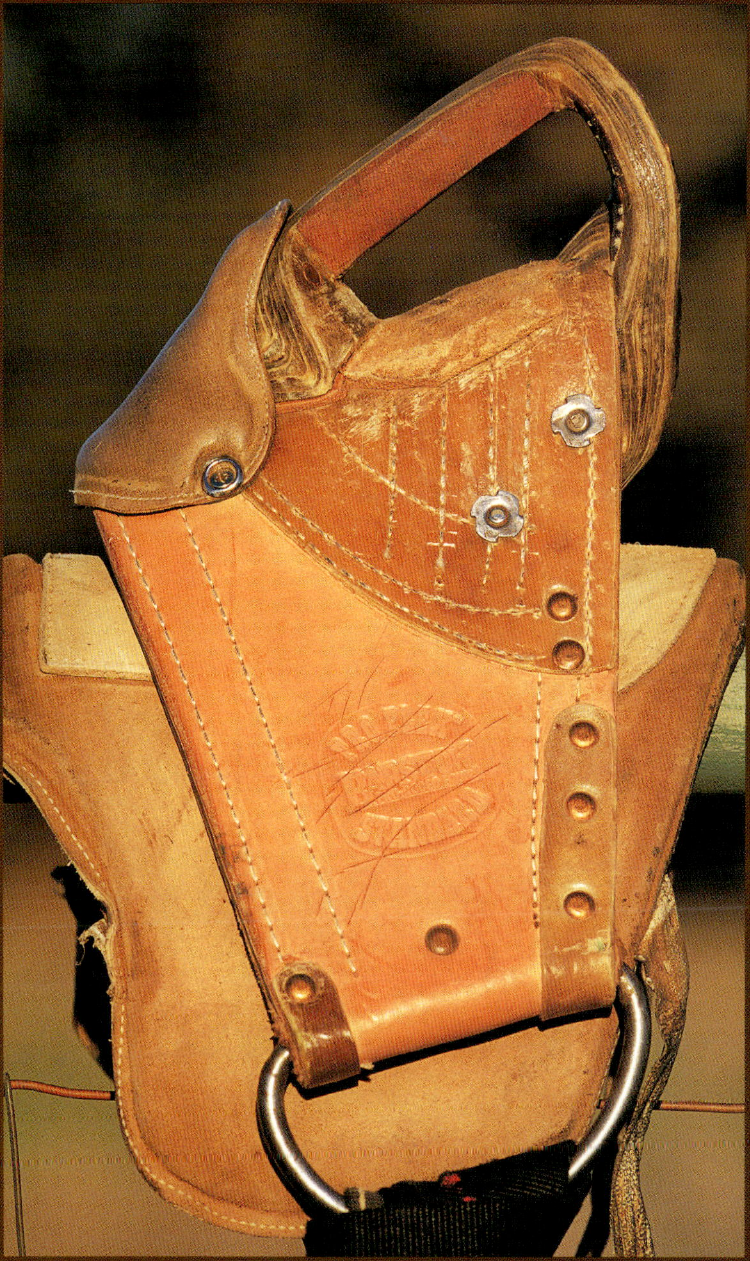

TY MURRAY'S BAREBACK RIGGING—*In 1998, Ty won his seventh All-Around Cowboy title, an all-time world record in the sport of rodeo.*

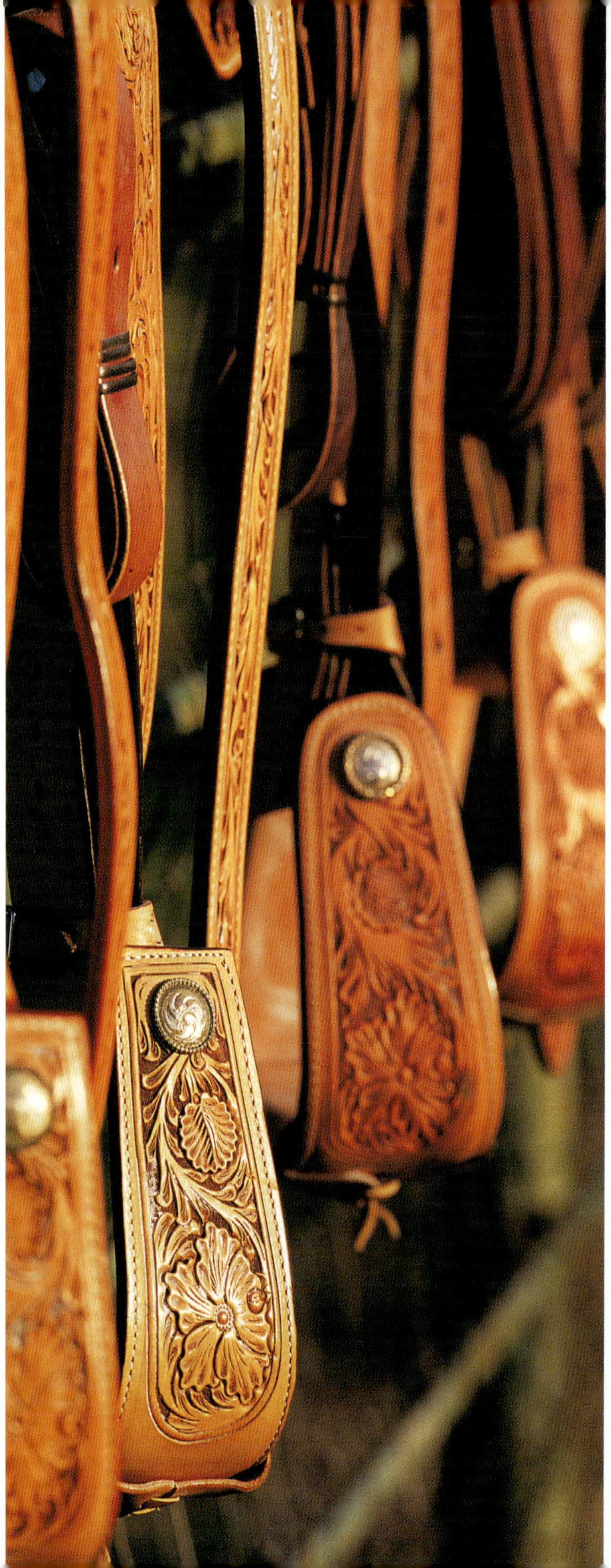
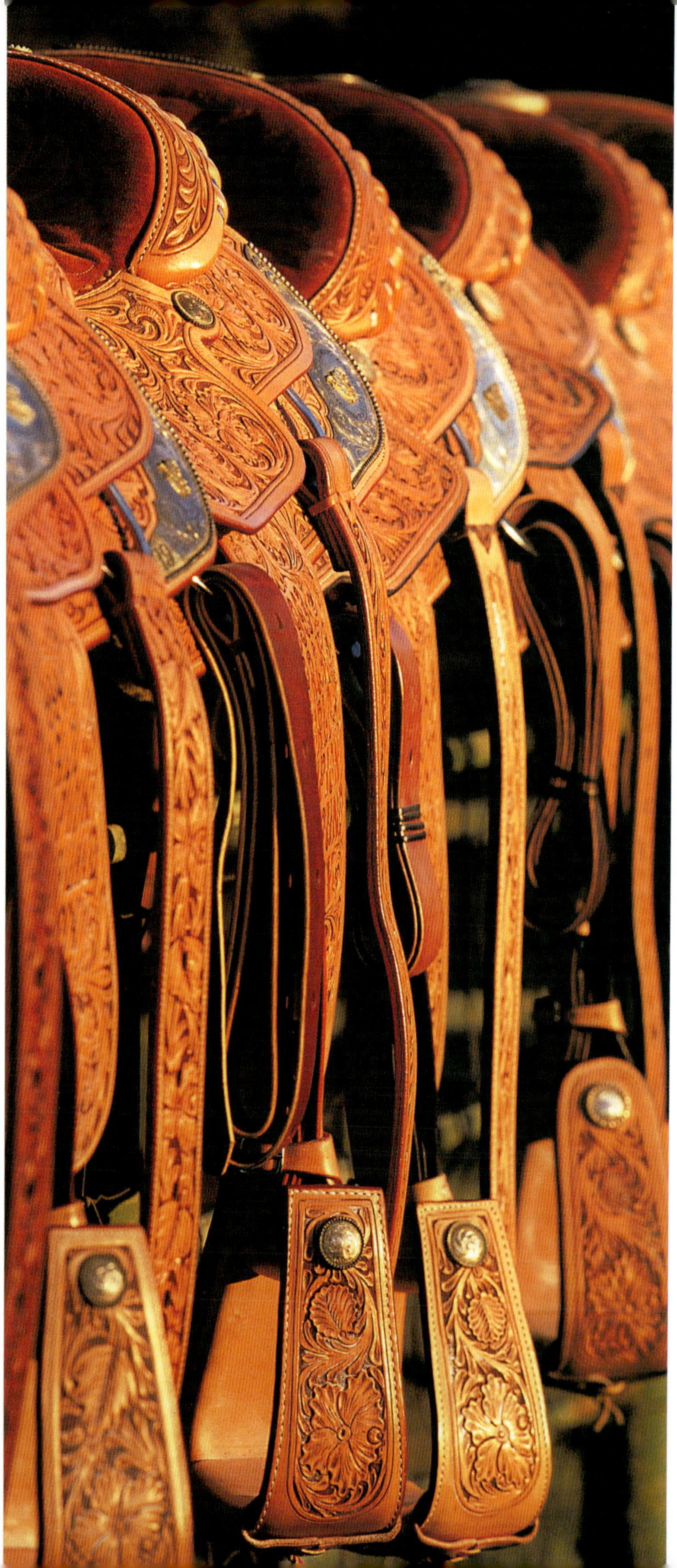

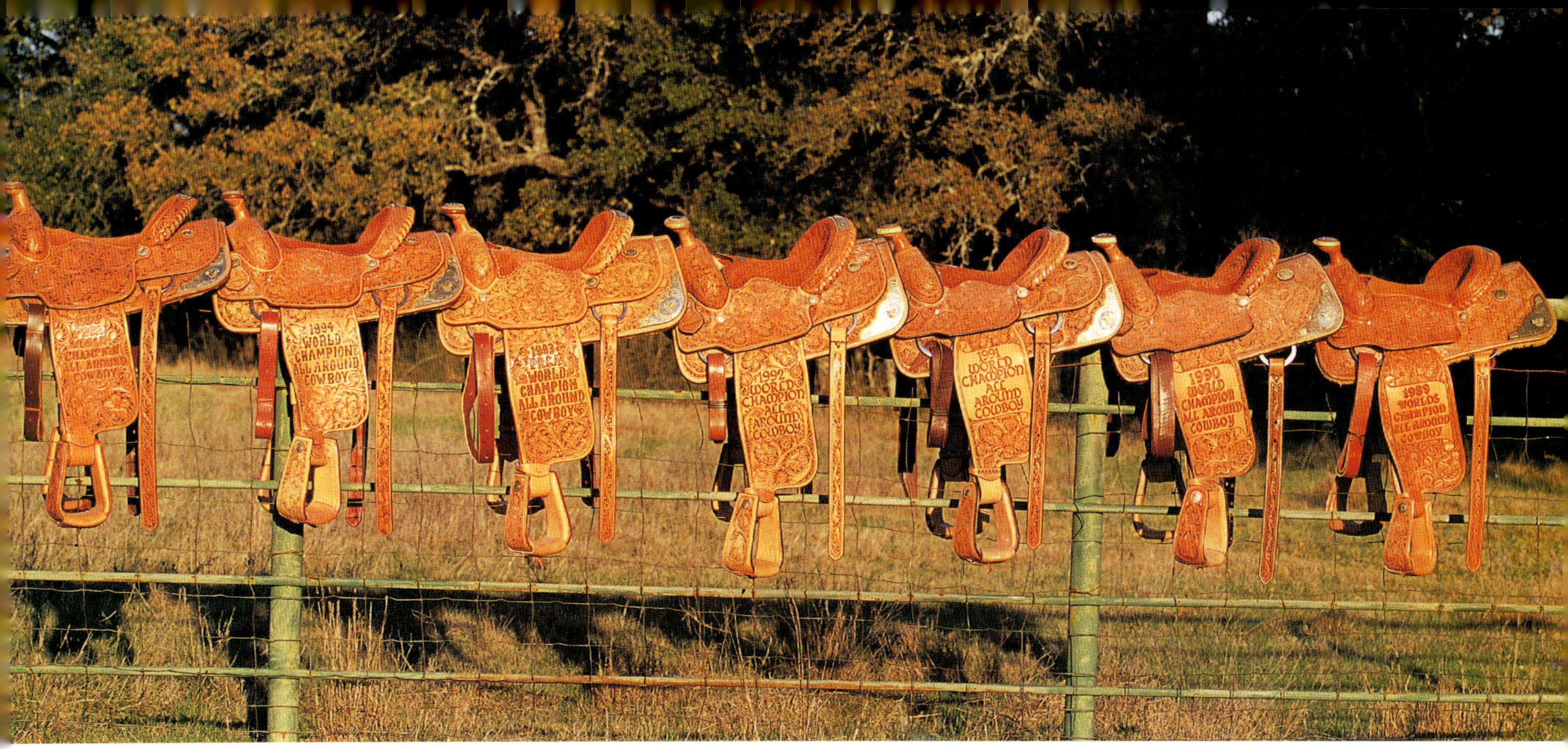

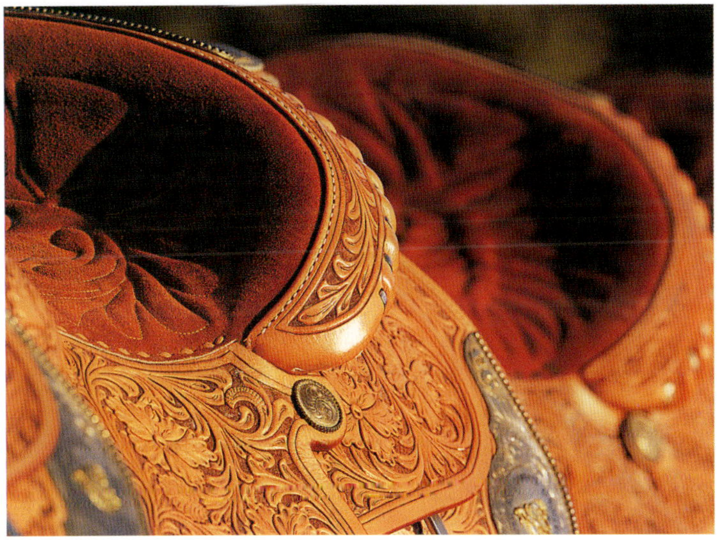

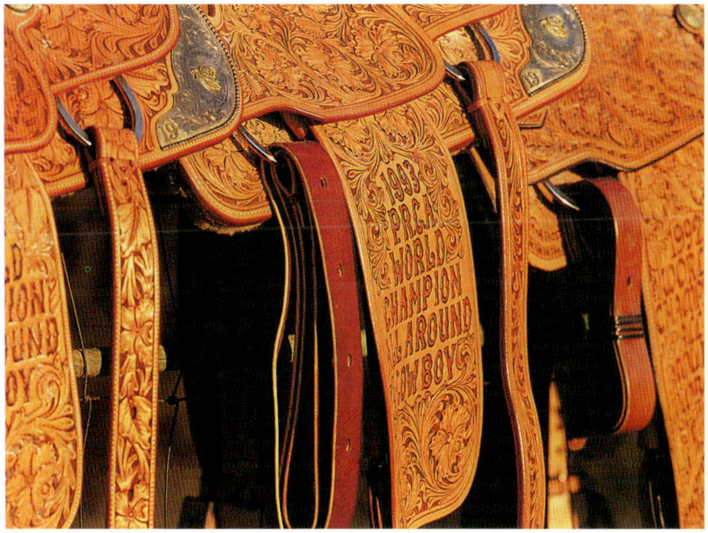

TY MURRAY'S COLLECTION OF WORLD CHAMPIONSHIP TROPHY SADDLES.
Ty's combined PBR and PRCA earnings to date are nearly $3 million.
He is the most accomplished rodeo athlete in the sport's 100-year history.

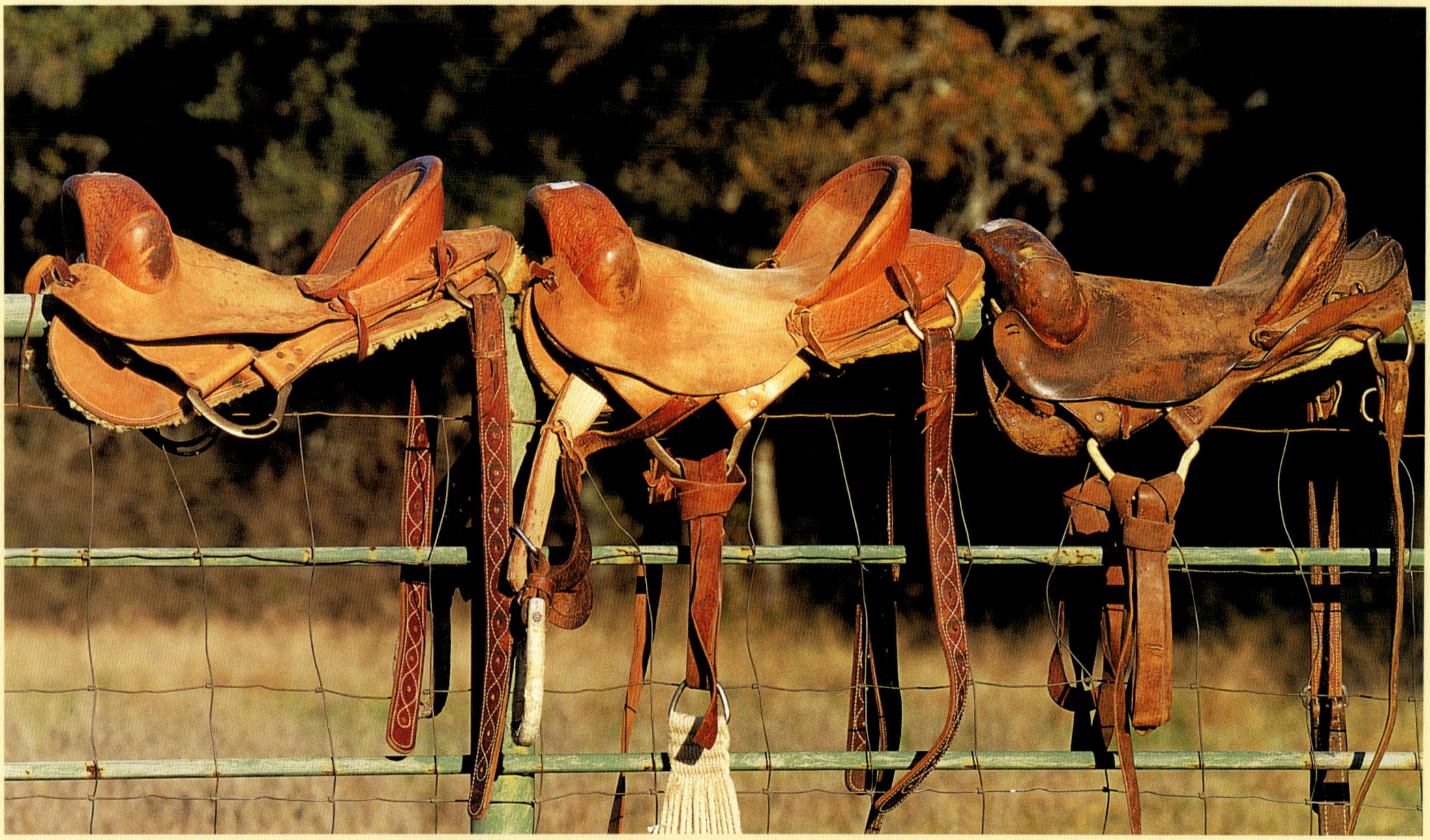

TY MURRAY'S SADDLEBRONC SADDLES

BUTCH SMALL RODE THIS SEVERE BROTHERS BUCKING SADDLE *while qualifying for 13 National Finals Rodeos. His earnings were close to a million dollars with this saddle.*

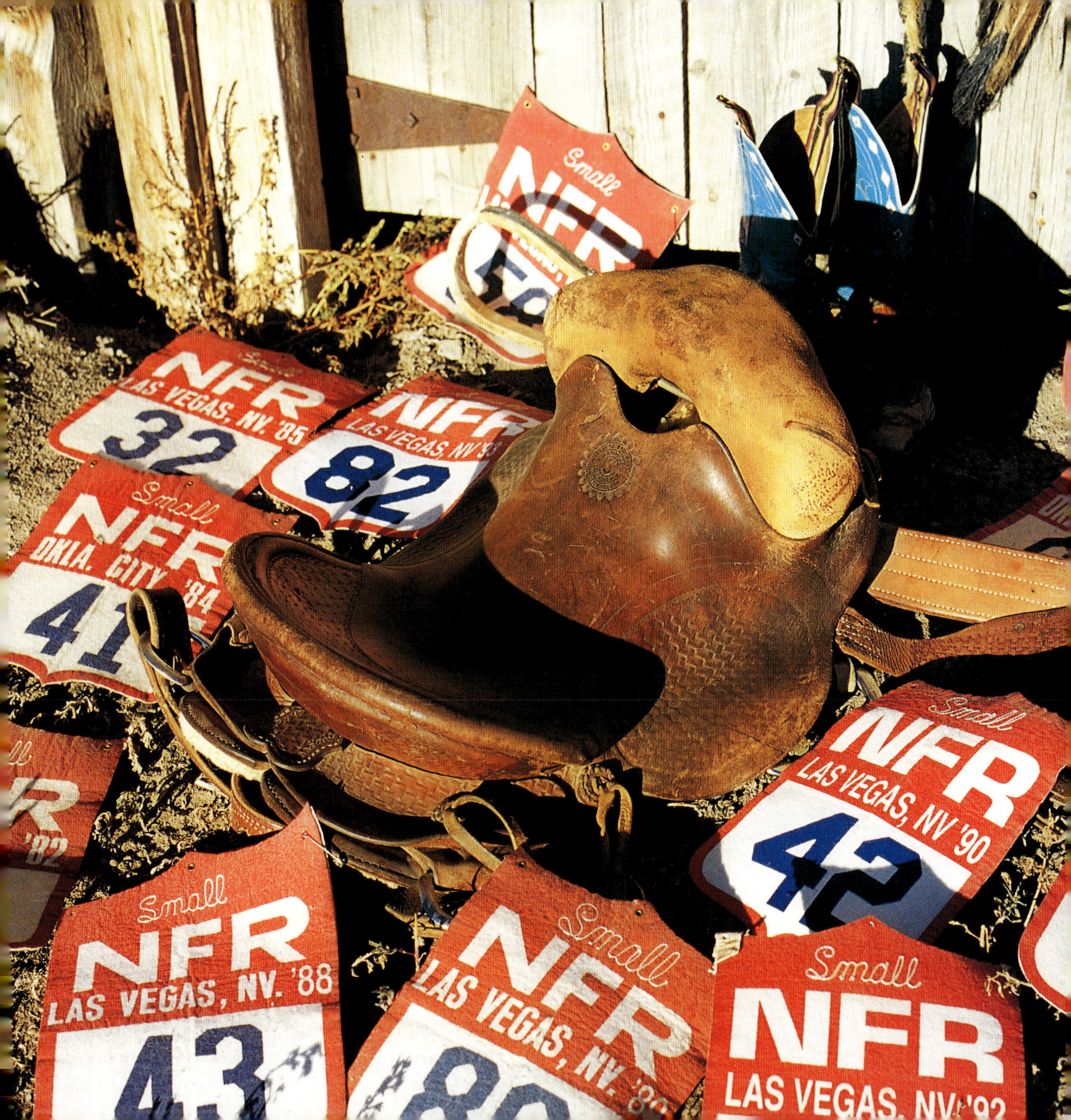
Small
NFR
Small
NFR
LAS VEGAS, NV. '85
32
NFR
LAS VEGAS, NV '93
82
Small
NFR
OKLA. CITY '84
41
Small
NFR
LAS VEGAS, NV '90
42
Small
NFR
LAS VEGAS, NV. '88
43
Small
NFR
LAS VEGAS, NV.
Small
NFR
LAS VEGAS

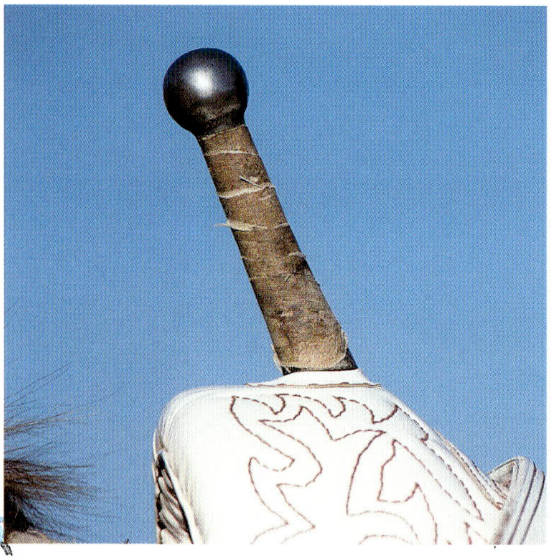

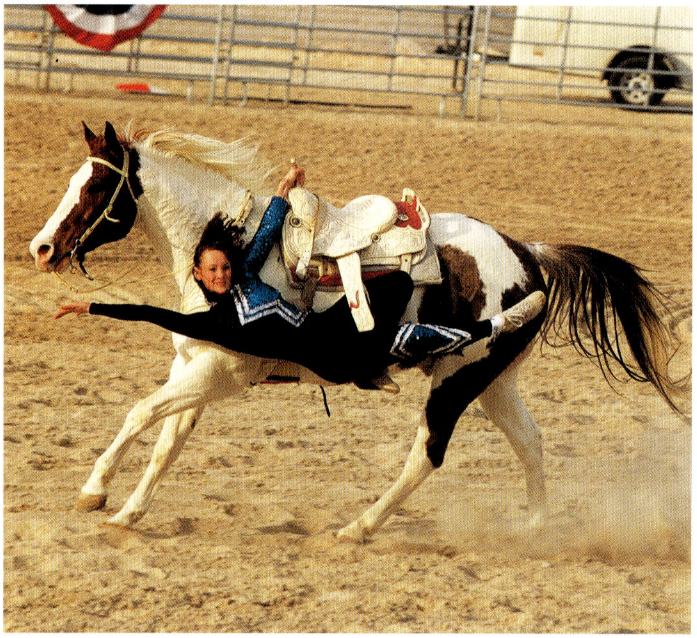

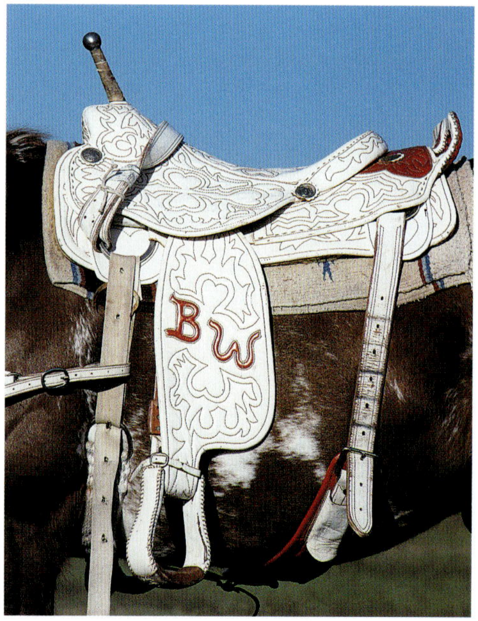

BREE WORTHINGTON AND HER TRICK SADDLE,
Weatherford, Texas

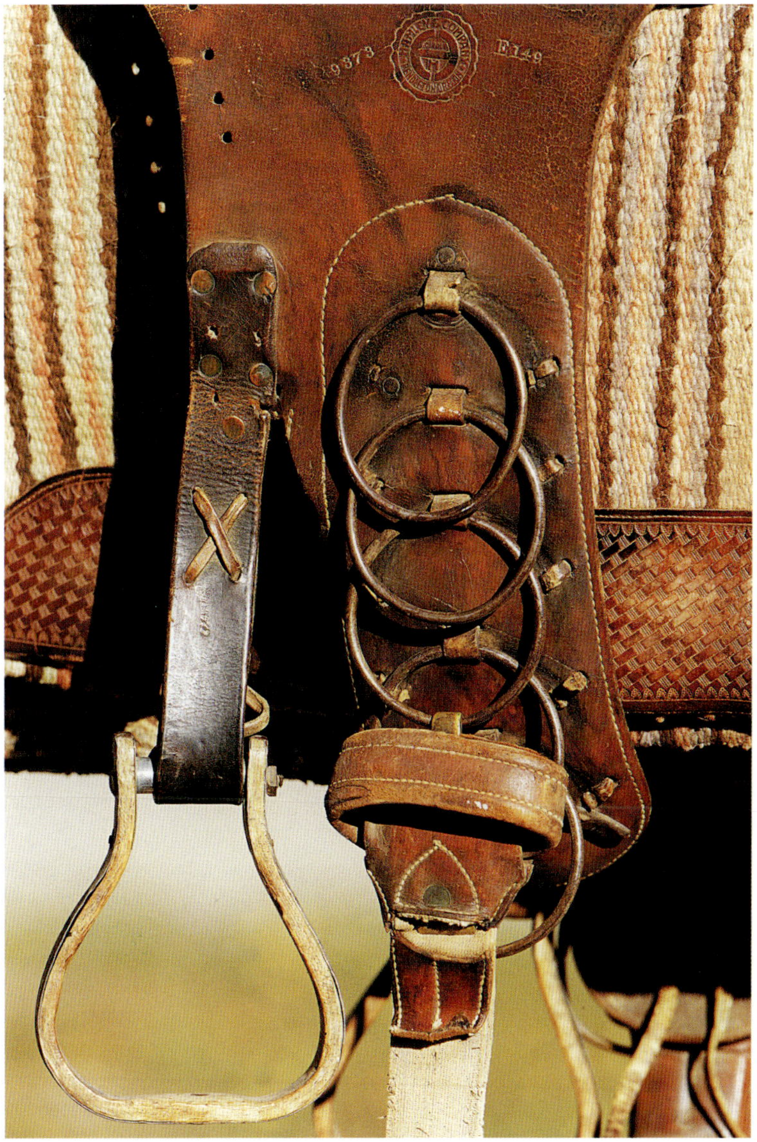

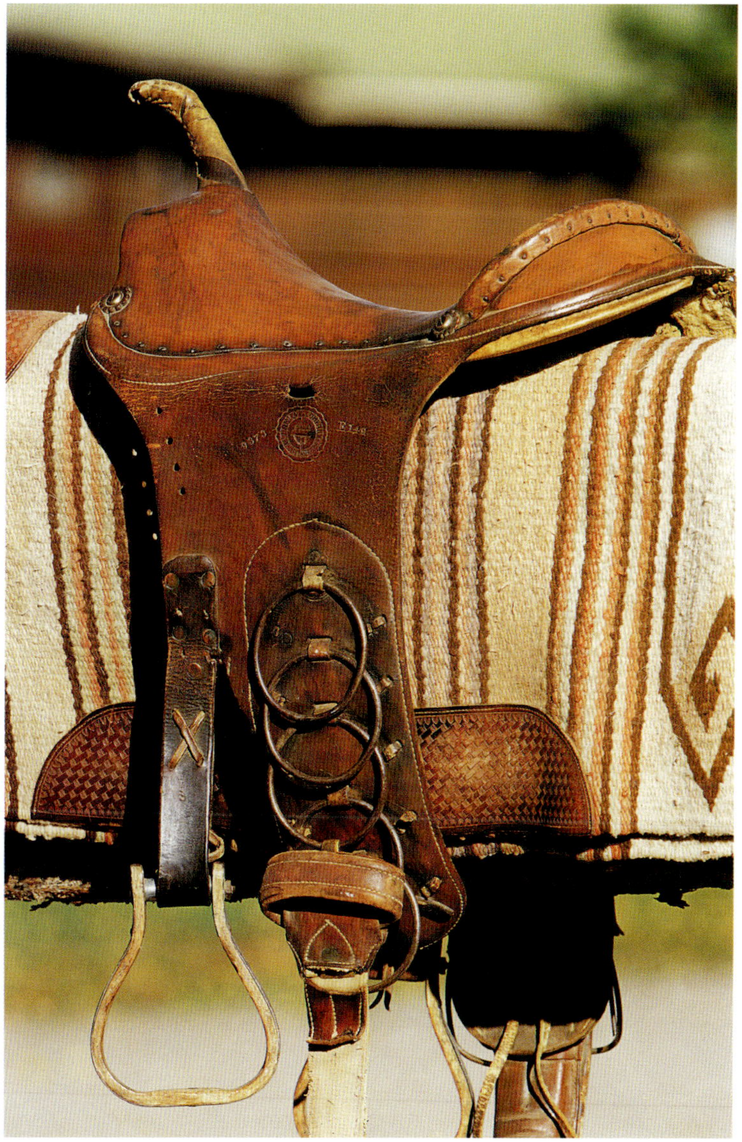

HAMLEY RELAY SADDLE—*relay races and trick riding were a big part of most rodeos. Very few rodeos today feature these great events. Flat Creek Saddlery Collection*

Steer Wrestling Saddles

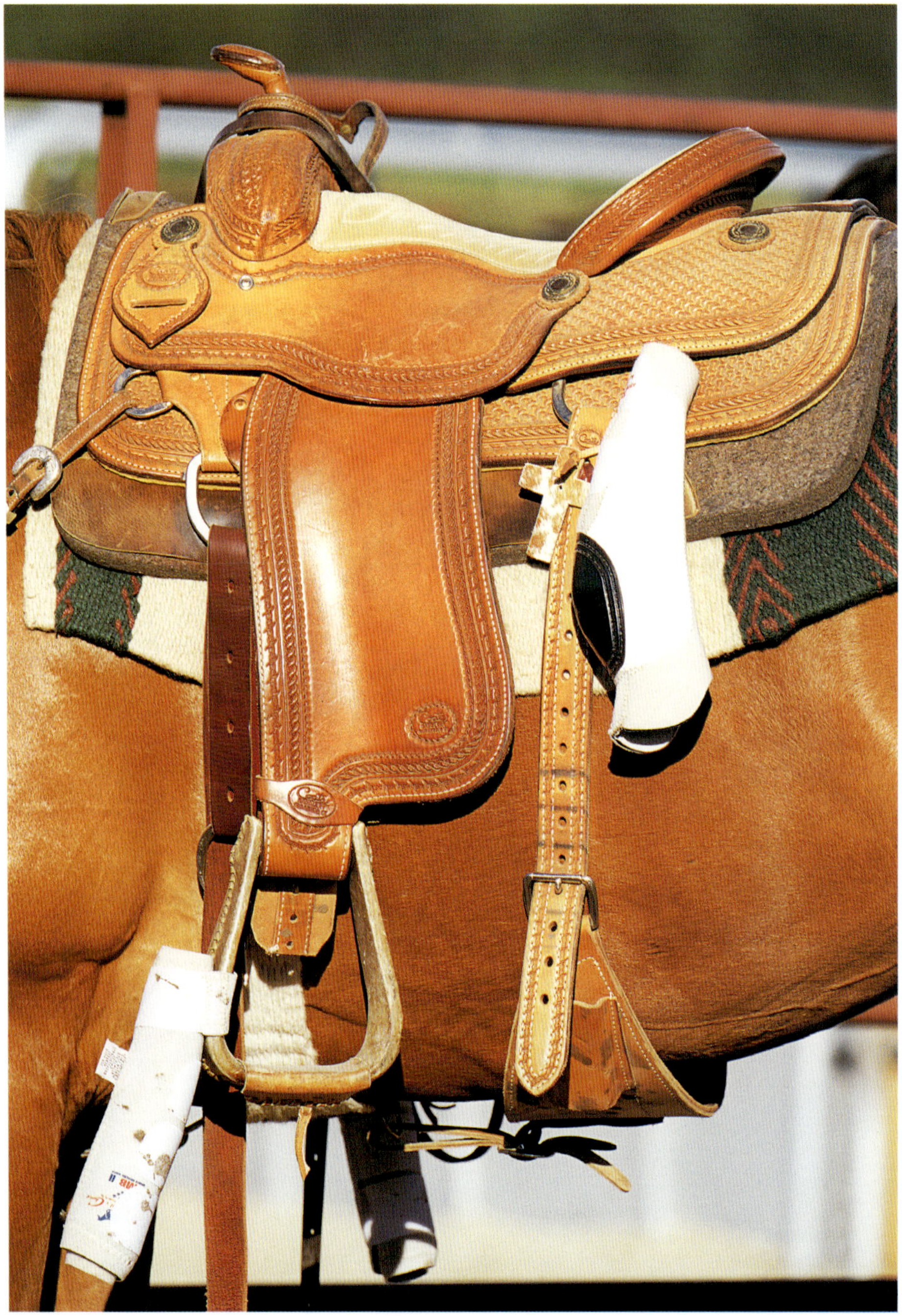

Steer wrestling saddle,
Larry Coats Saddlery,
San Angelo, Texas

For Rod Lyman, *champion steer wrestler, the most important thing about his saddle is the fit. According to him, even if the horse is the best in the business, if it has a sore back, the horse will not be able to do its best. Rod believes that a good saddle should be an extension of the horse's back.*

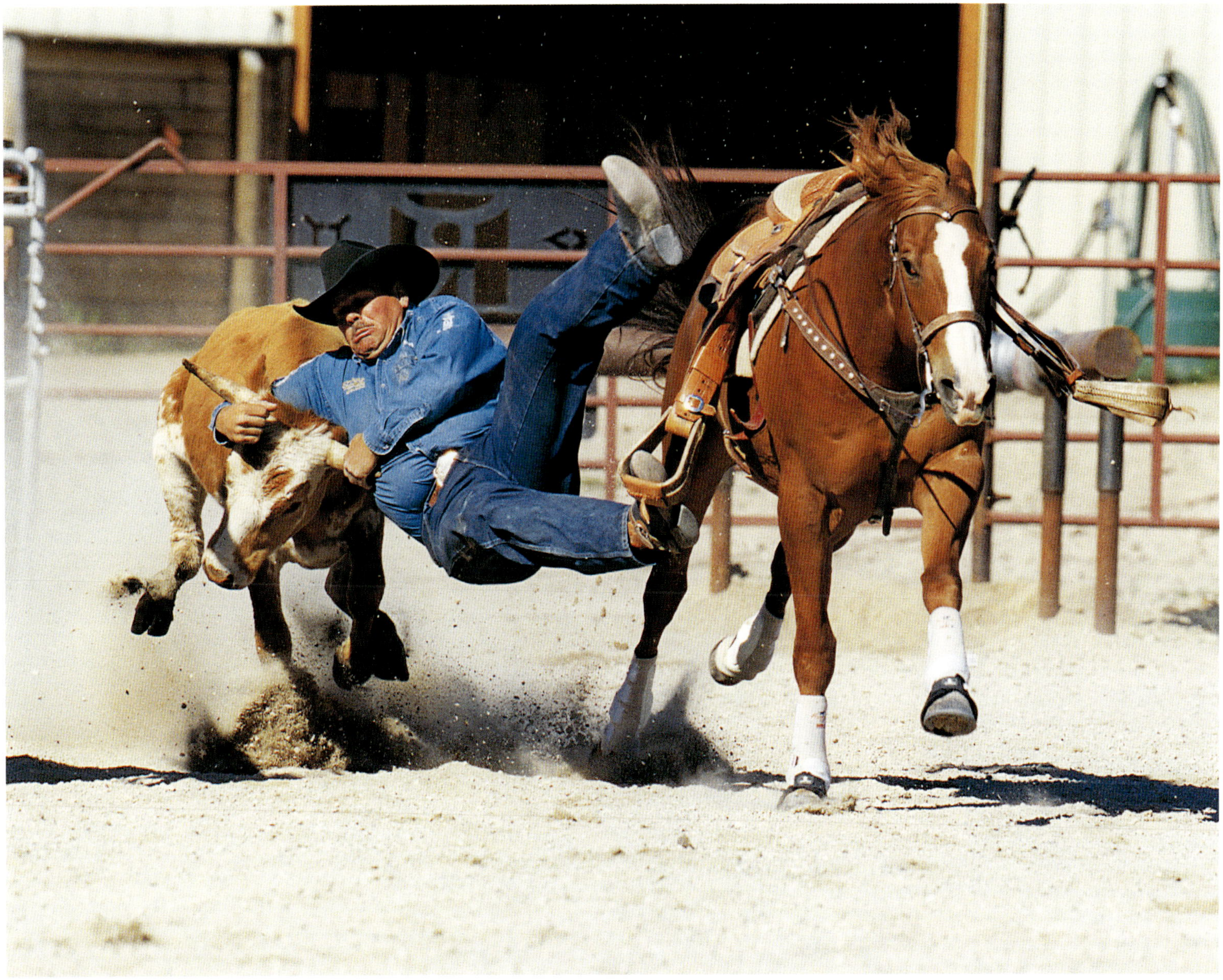

Rod Lyman, champion steer wrestler, *Victor, Montana*

Barrel Racing Saddles

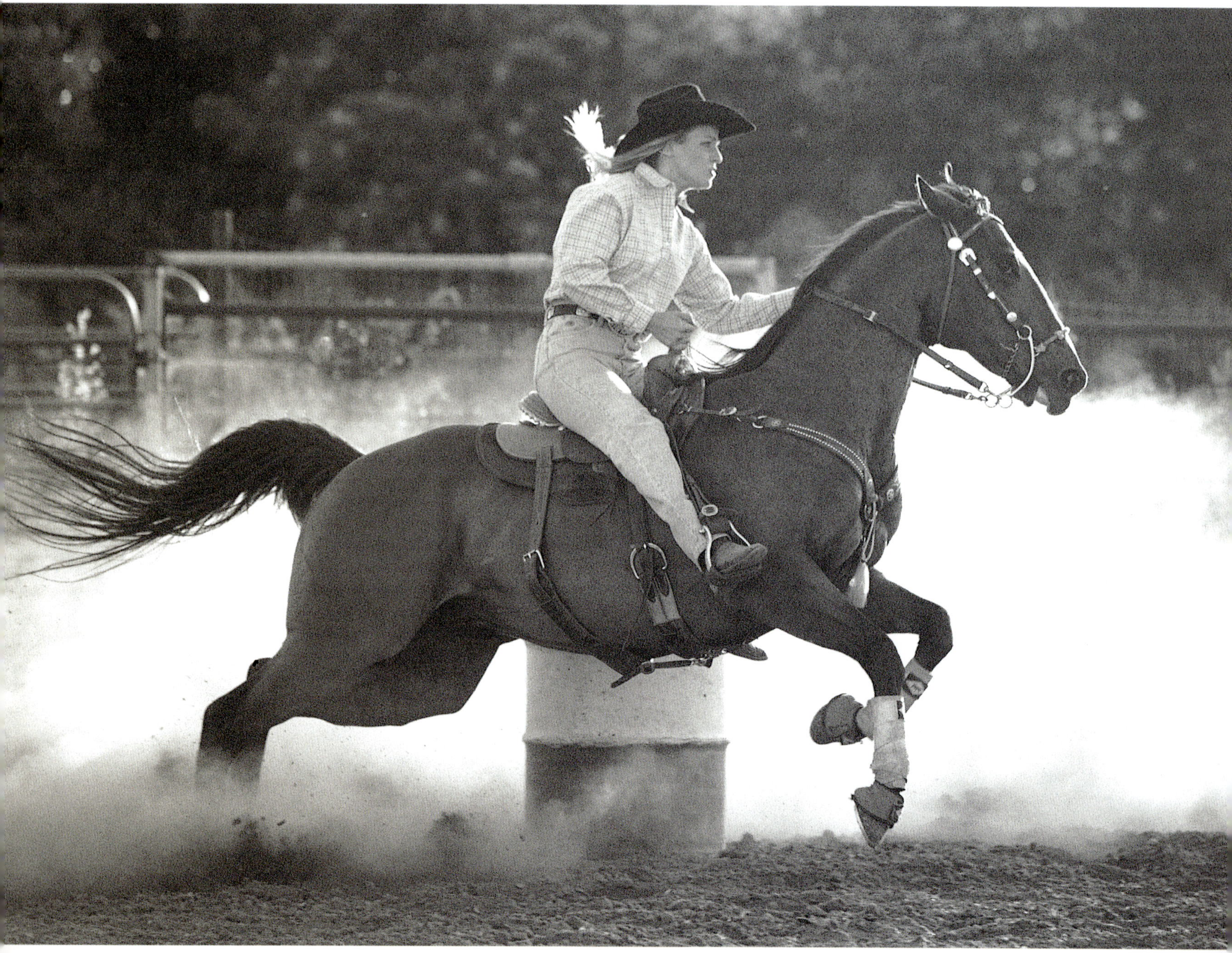

Danyelle Campbell, *barrel racing, Washington, Utah*

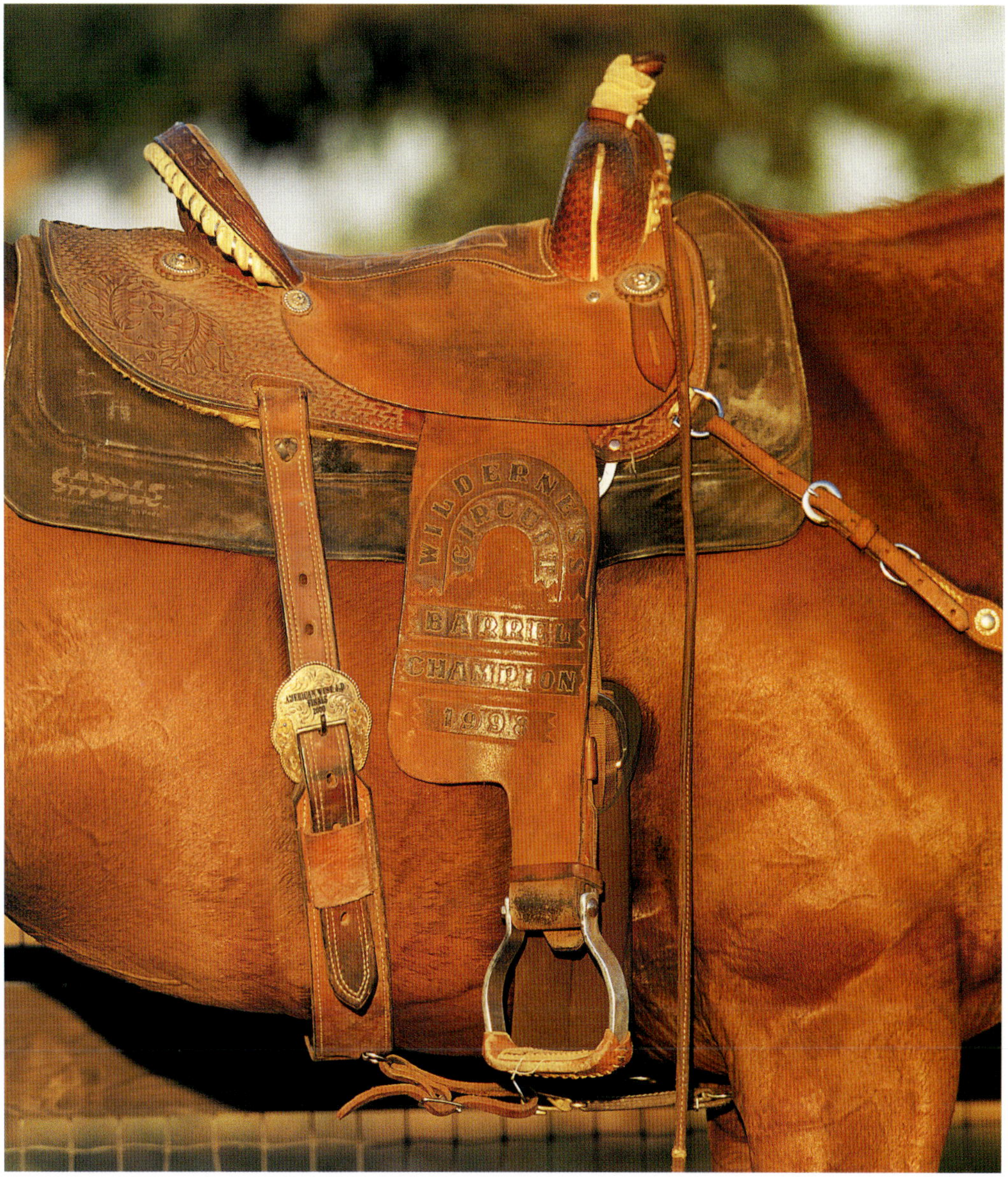

DANYELLE CAMPBELL'S TROPHY SADDLE

DANYELLE CAMPBELL OWNS EIGHT SADDLES *that she uses on a daily basis and more that she has won in barrel racing competitions. The features she looks for in her saddles include rough-out seat jockeys and a classy look. She likes a saddle to fit her horses well, and she likes her fenders to be directly underneath her. Danyelle's favorite saddle is one made by Larry Coats. She says that she loves the way she feels in it and that it sits her perfectly on all of her horses.*

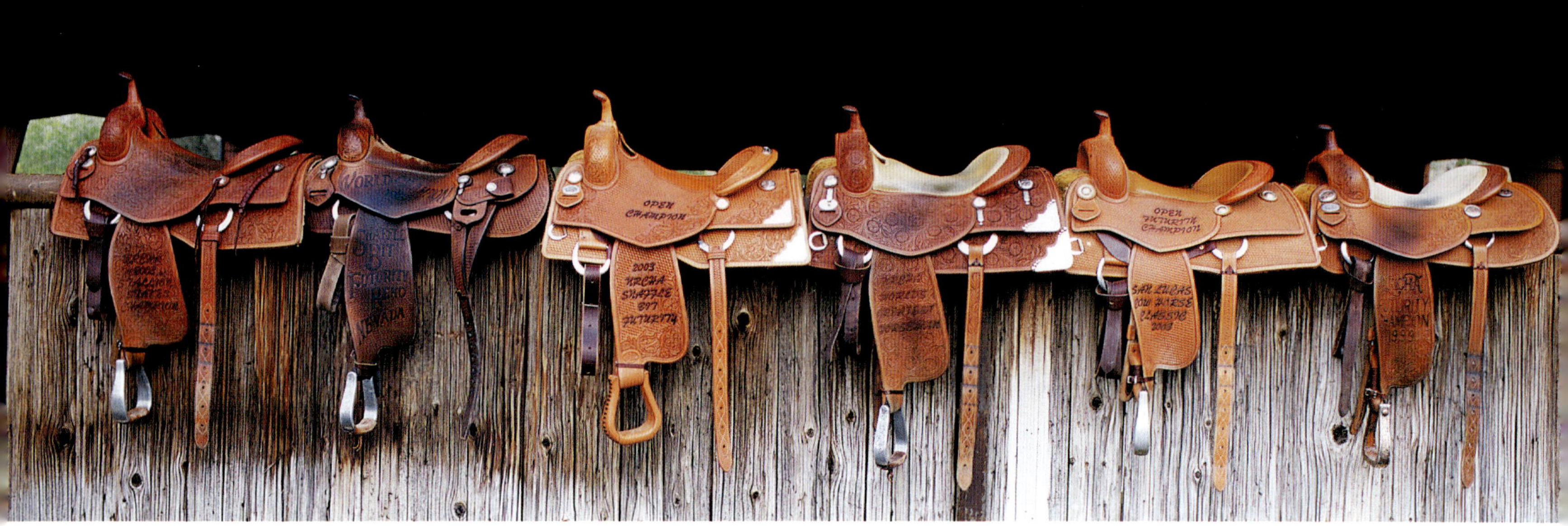

BOB AVILA'S SADDLE COLLECTION

BOB AVILA OWNS MORE THAN 50 SADDLES, *most with custom silver and engravings from significant wins from his career, including World's Greatest Horseman and Snaffle Bit Futurity Champion. Bob looks for certain qualities and features in the saddles he uses, including comfort, freedom of leg movement, durability, and quality. The most important thing in a saddle to him is the way it looks and feels. He thinks a good saddle should fit a horse comfortably and closely.*

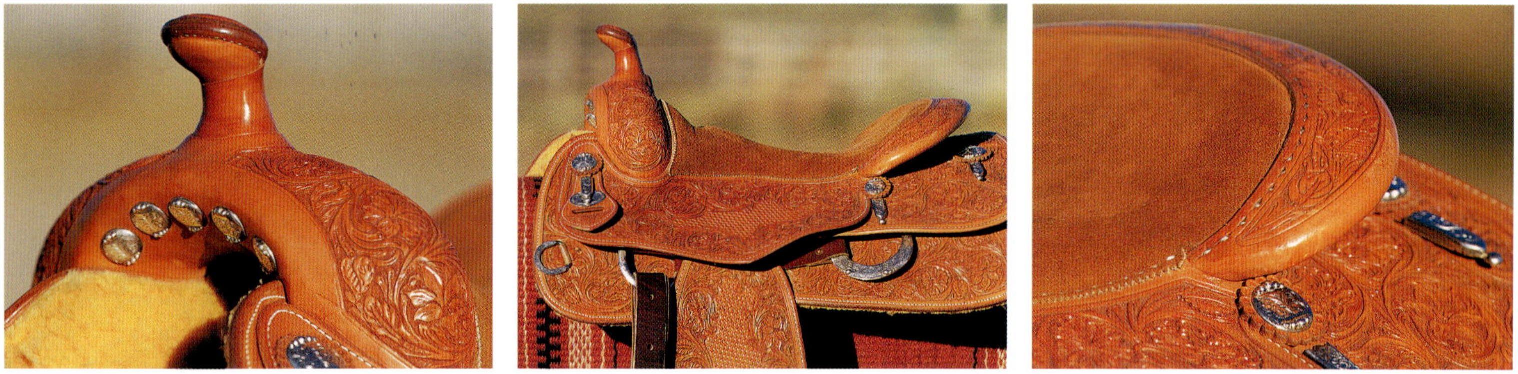

BOB AVILA REINER SADDLE *made by Bob's Custom Saddles, Phoenix, Arizona with Paradise Valley and small basket stamp tooling and silver conchos, tips and rear dees done in the teardrop style*

BOB AVILA, *Temecula, California*

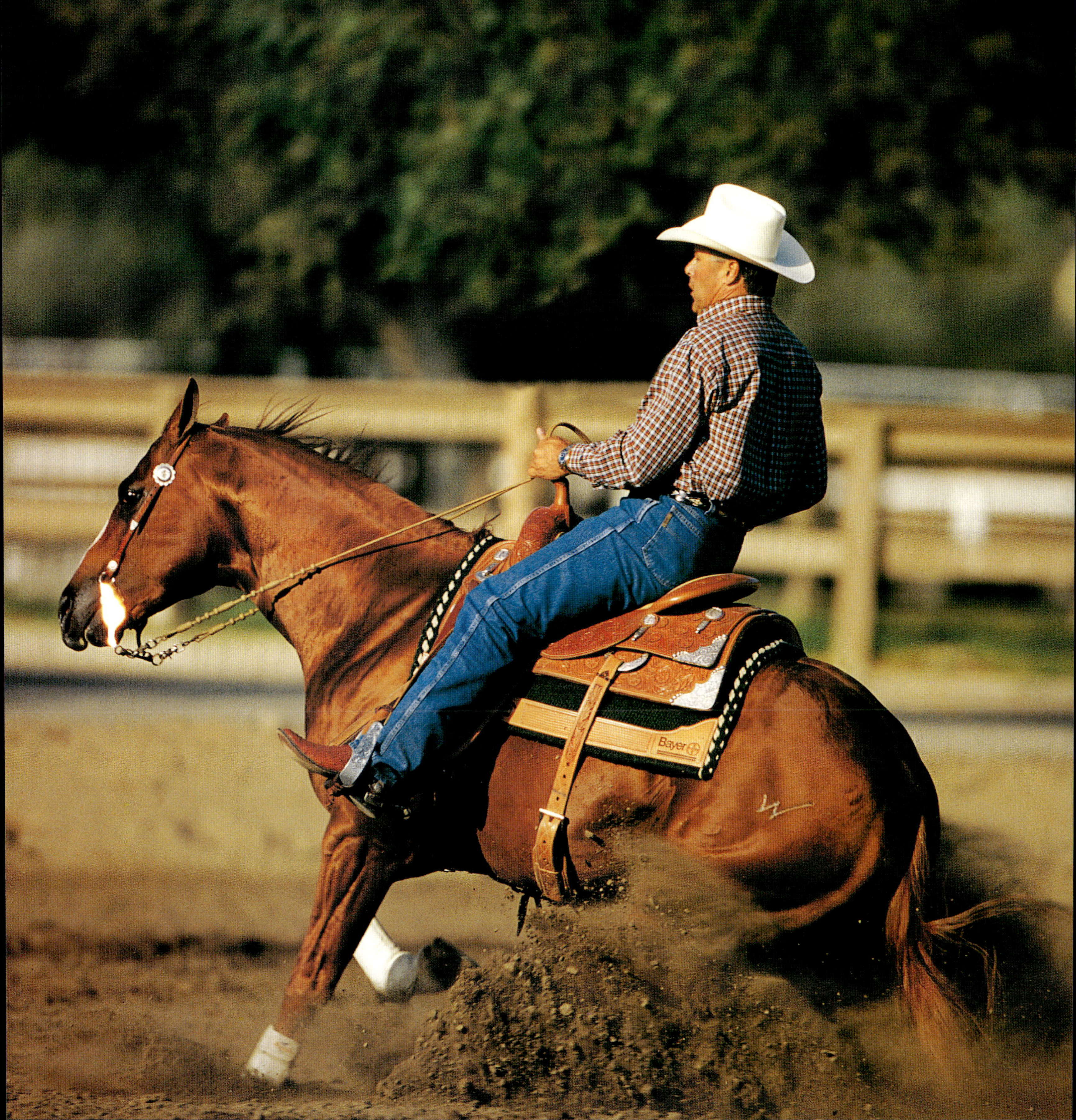
Bayer

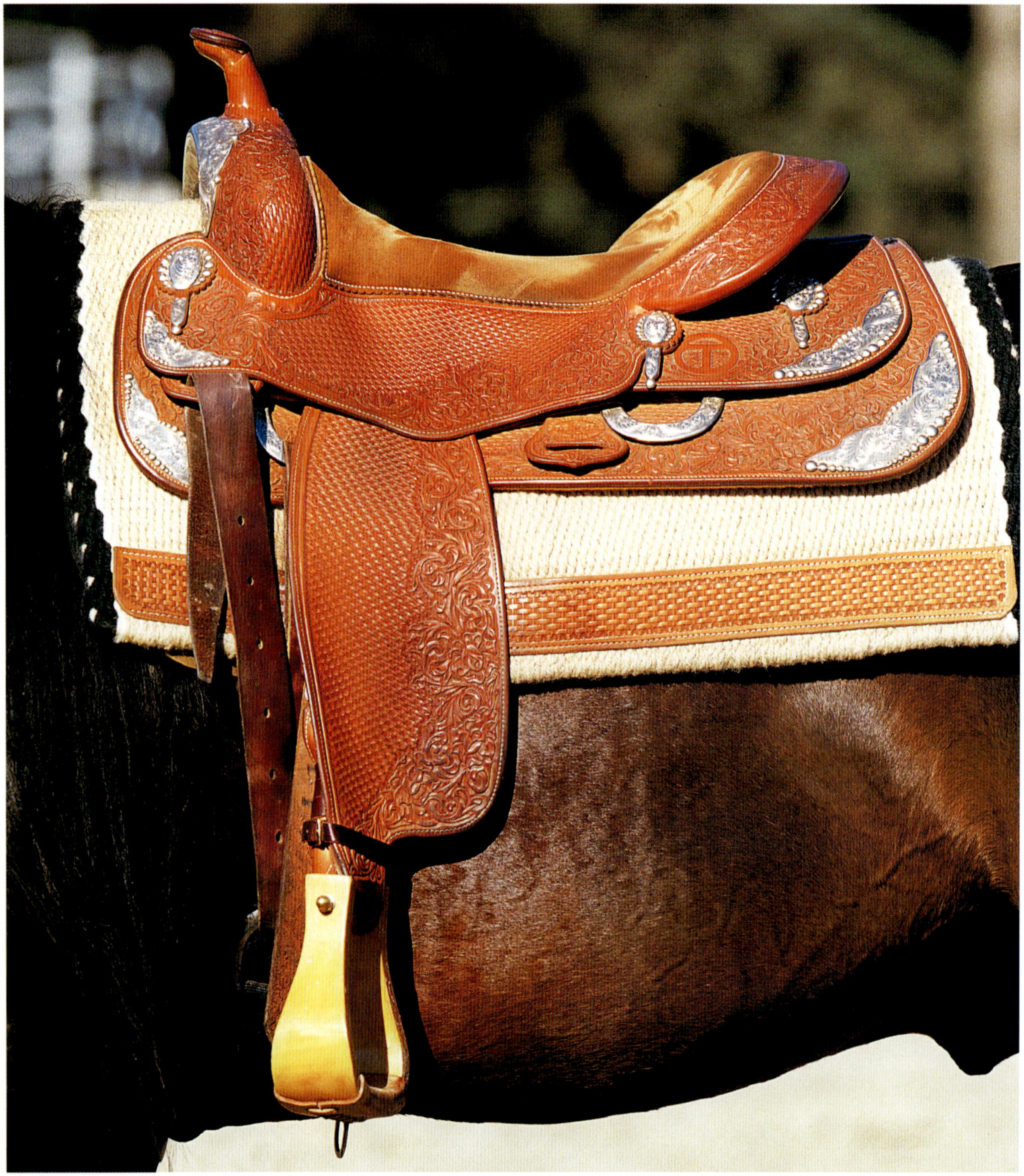

Donn Leson saddle *made for reining and cowhorse work for Toscani Quarter Horses, Casale Marittimo, Italy*

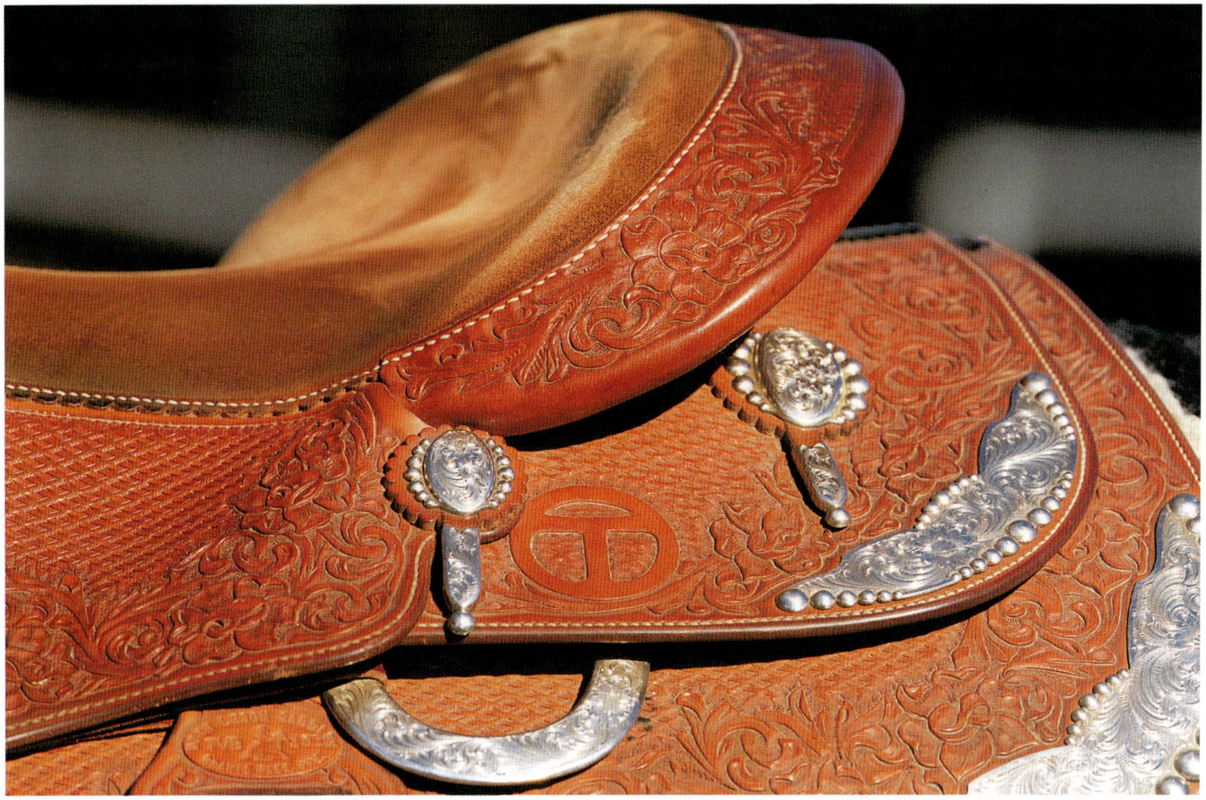

DONN LESON

Donn Leson grew up in the high desert ranch country of Eastern Oregon, where his parents owned a saddle and harness shop. He spent his summer vacations in the saddle, learning practical horsemanship skills from the last of a dying breed of cowboy. He began working with leather in his parents' shop at the age of 10. In 1966, Donn opened his own saddleshop. He primarily made saddles for the rodeo and working cowboy who needed a saddle that could be ridden all day without soring either the cowboy or the horse. He eventually specialized in saddles for the professional trainer and serious horse show enthusiast. Originally, Donn focused on making cowhorse and cutting horse saddles as well as pleasure horse saddles that combined unparalleled beauty and performance. Later, he introduced a close-contact reining horse saddle which, since 1993, has dominated NRHA events and redefined the way reining saddles are made today. Leson Saddles has been fortunate to build saddles for the most knowledgeable and successful trainers in the industry. Their customer list is impressive. More than 50 major championships have been won on Leson saddles including 30 AQHA World Championships in the last decade, the NRCHA Snaffle Bit Futurity and the NCHA Futurity and Superstakes, and four NRHA Open Futurity Championships and two Reserve Championships in only six years.

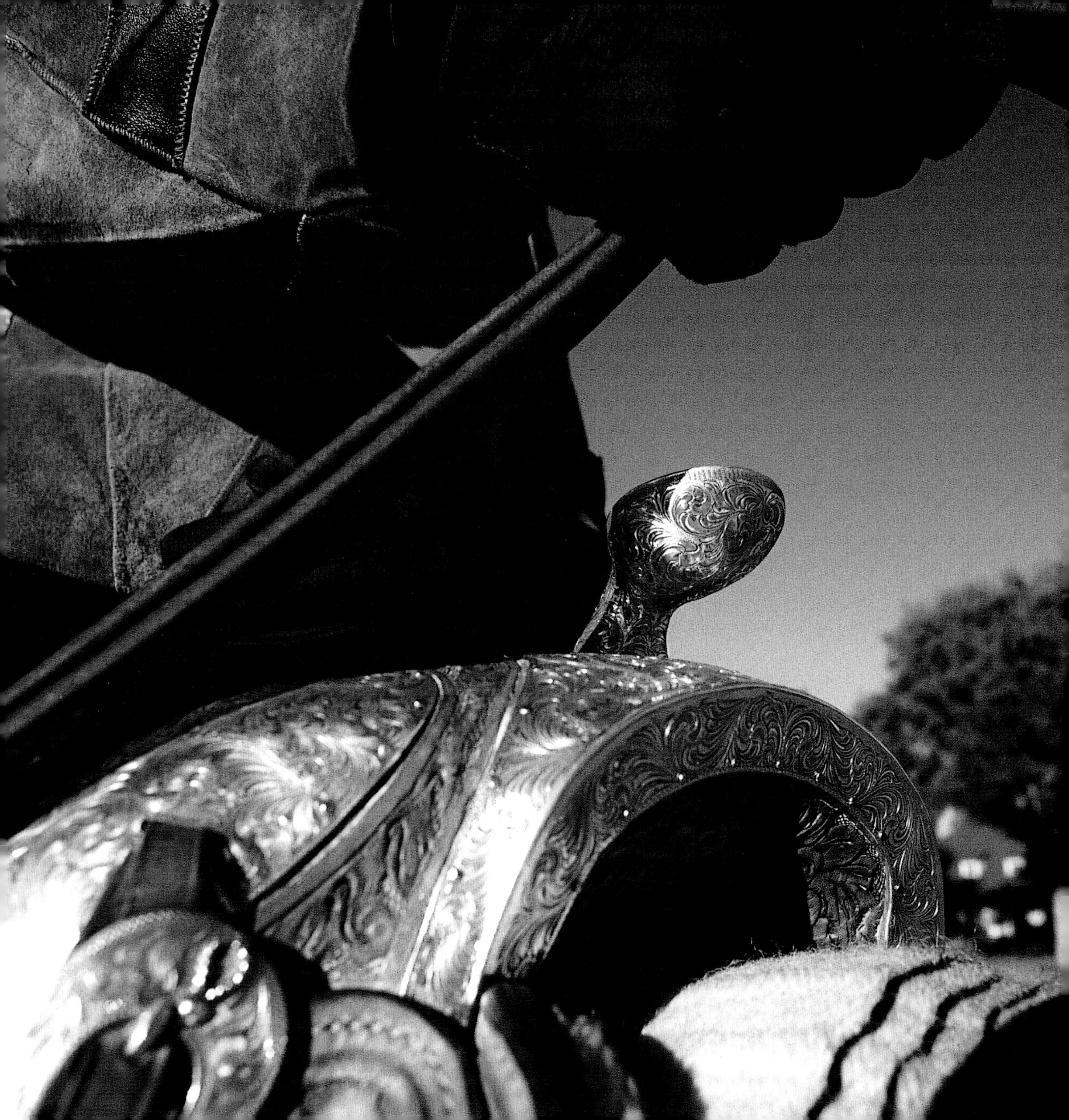

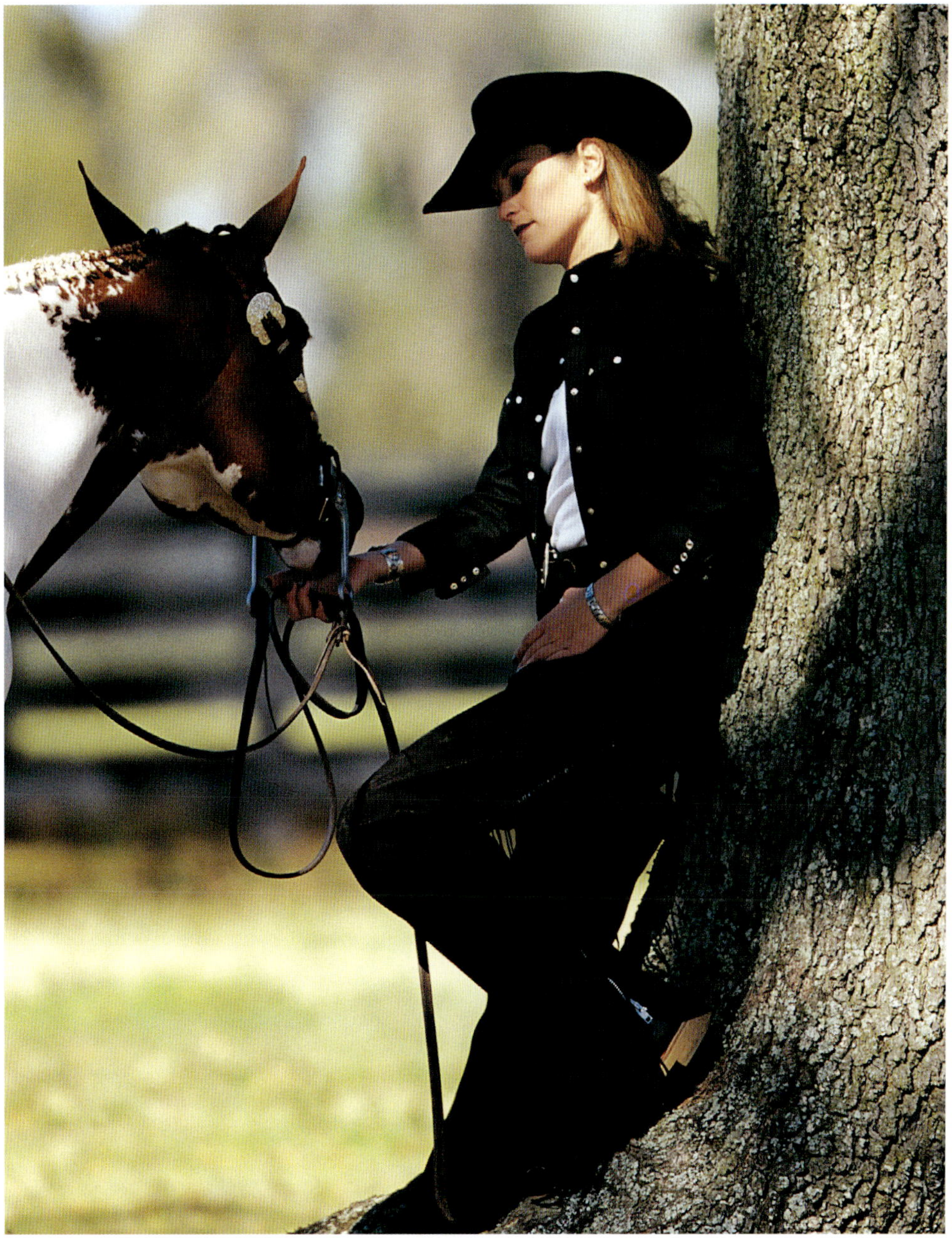

BROOKE BERG, *Ocala, Florida*

ALL-AROUND WESTERN PLEASURE SHOW SADDLE *with genuine silver accents owned by Lynn Palm of Ocala, Florida made by Harris Leather and Silverworks, State Road, North Carolina*

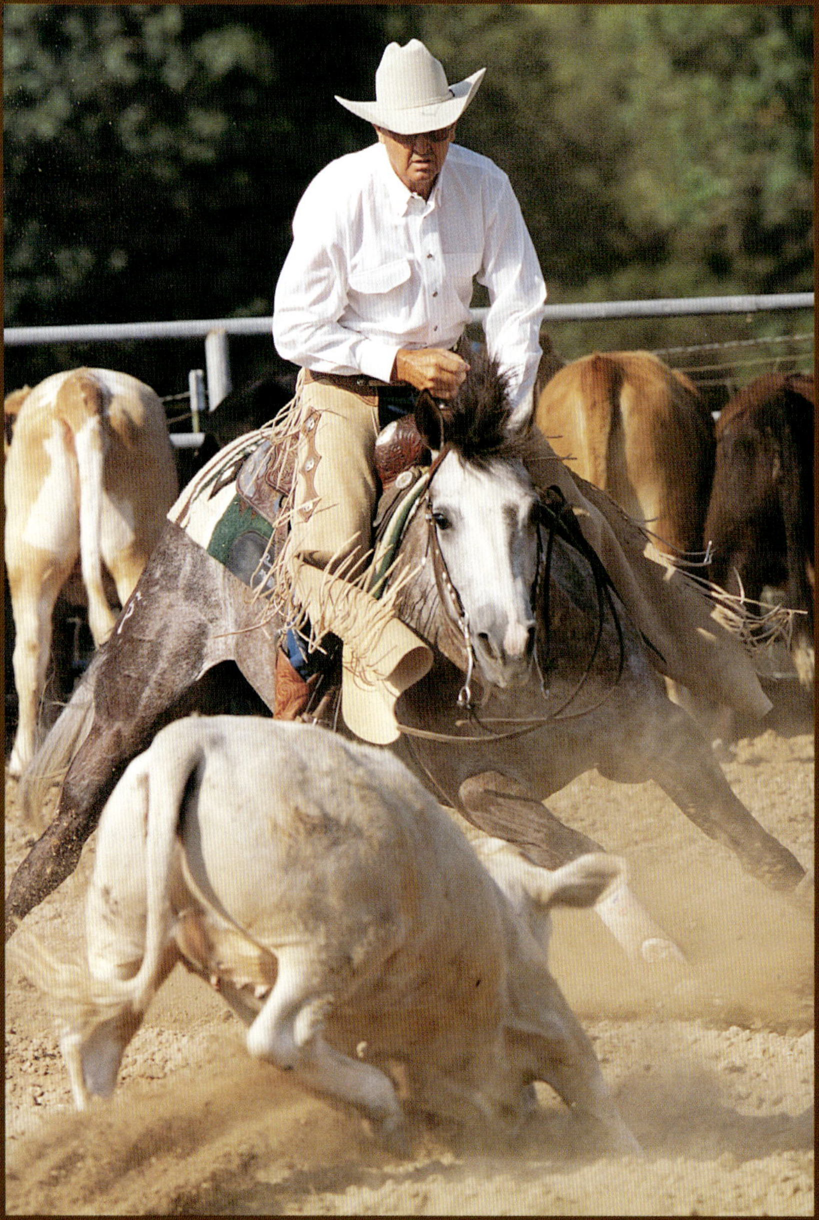

LEON HARRELL *cutting on his grey mare, Annie, Kerrville, Texas*

LEON HARRELL IS ONE OF THE MOST SUCCESSFUL CUTTING HORSE TRAINERS *in the world. He has been cutting since 1964 and he is a legend. He probably owns saddles by almost every saddle maker and he did a lot of work in the early 1970s with Donn Leson to develop saddles specifically for cutting. One feature that stood out in these saddles was the cut-up skirt, which allowed a rider to hold his legs closer to the horse and provided for more feel, flexibility, and fluidity with the animal. For the past year, Leon has been working closely with Sean Ryon to develop an even better cutting saddle. Leon thinks it is the best saddle out there and fits a horse perfectly. He says it simplifies the sport by about 25 percent. The most important aspects of a cutting saddle to him are the comfort and the feel. He feels that Sean Ryon's leather and workmanship is top-shelf. His Ryon saddle is slightly narrower than others and it is built up a little, not perfectly flat. This allows him enough room to flow and flex with his horse, which is very important in the sport of cutting.*

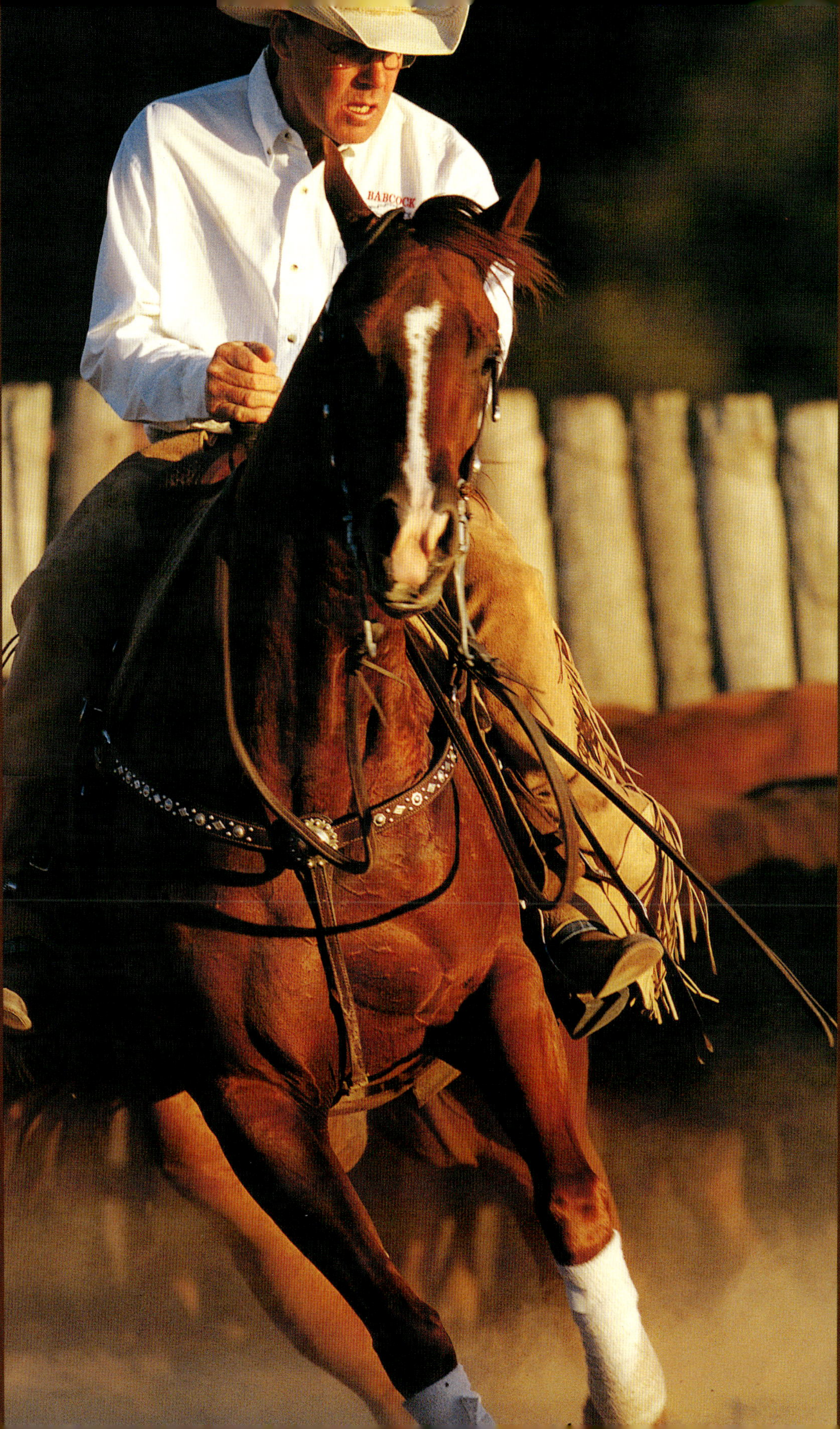

RON RALLS
Gainesville, Texas

SEAN RYON

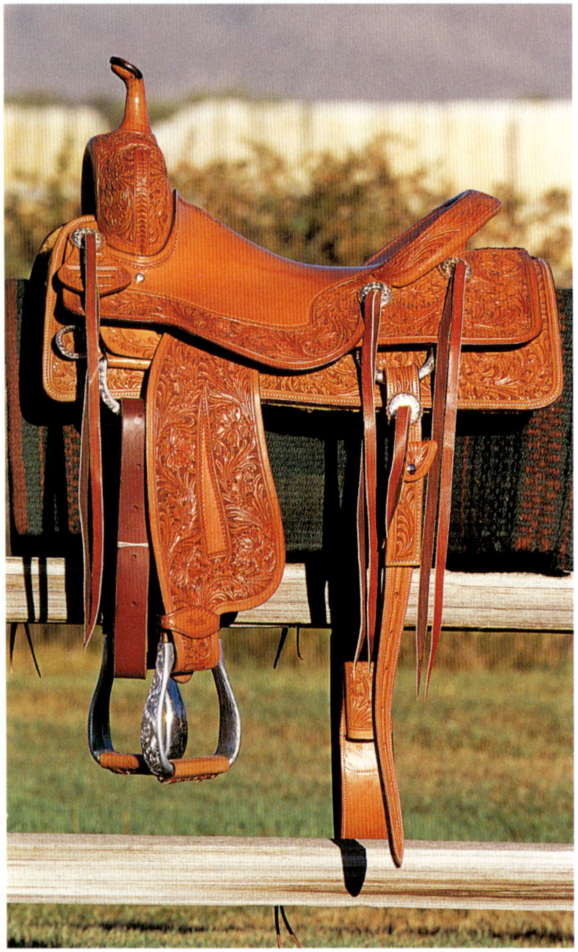

Family tradition and Western wear continue to flourish in the Stockyards of Fort Worth, Texas. Sean Ryon is the proprietor of the Sean Ryon Western Store. With his sons, Kevin, Mathieu, and Michael, he carries on a tradition that would make Great Grandfather Windy Ryon proud. The original Ryon Family Store opened in 1944 in the Livestock Exchange Building in the Stockyards, and began by supplying tack to local ranchers. Today, Sean Ryon caters to the Western horse enthusiasts and showmen across the country as well as abroad. Sean spends about a third of his time traveling to horse shows across the country, offering his full collection of Western wear and supplies. Sean is active in the Western performance events as well, competing in NCHA and NRHA events. So not only is he educated about the collection of products he sells, but he is also passionate about the industry to which he caters. As such, Sean Ryon Saddle Shop is a sponsor of many regional and national events. Go to any major horse show around the country or the world, and you will see some of the top professionals in the industry riding a Sean Ryon saddle. World caliber reining, cutting, and cowhorse pros such as Jim Watts, Robert Rust, Leon Harrell, Freddie McGee, Terry Thompson, Matt Gaines, and Rock Heddlund all ride Sean Ryon saddles. When a major title is on the line, these trainers know that the craftsmanship, fit, and style of a Sean Ryon saddle are going to put them at the top of their game. (biography courtesy of Sean Ryon Saddlery web site)

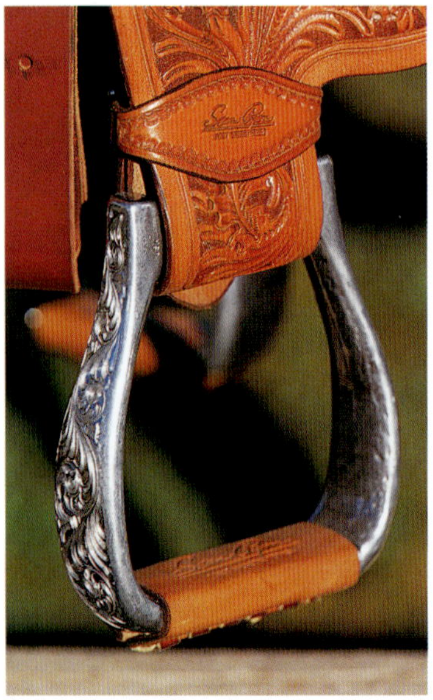

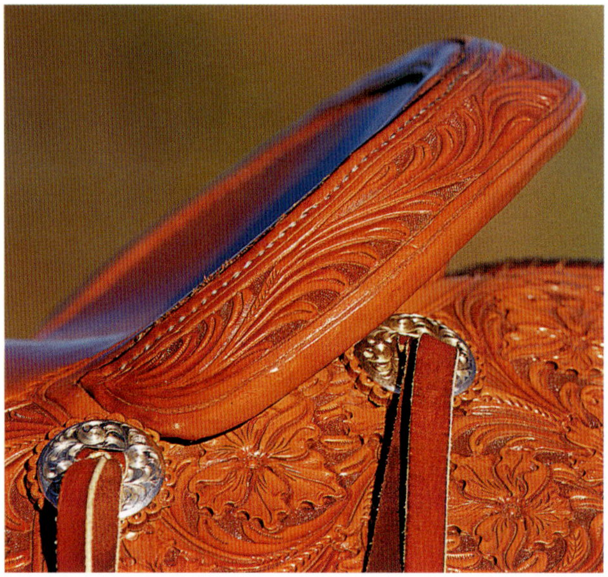

SEAN RYON SADDLE, *Fort Worth, Texas*

M.L. Leddy

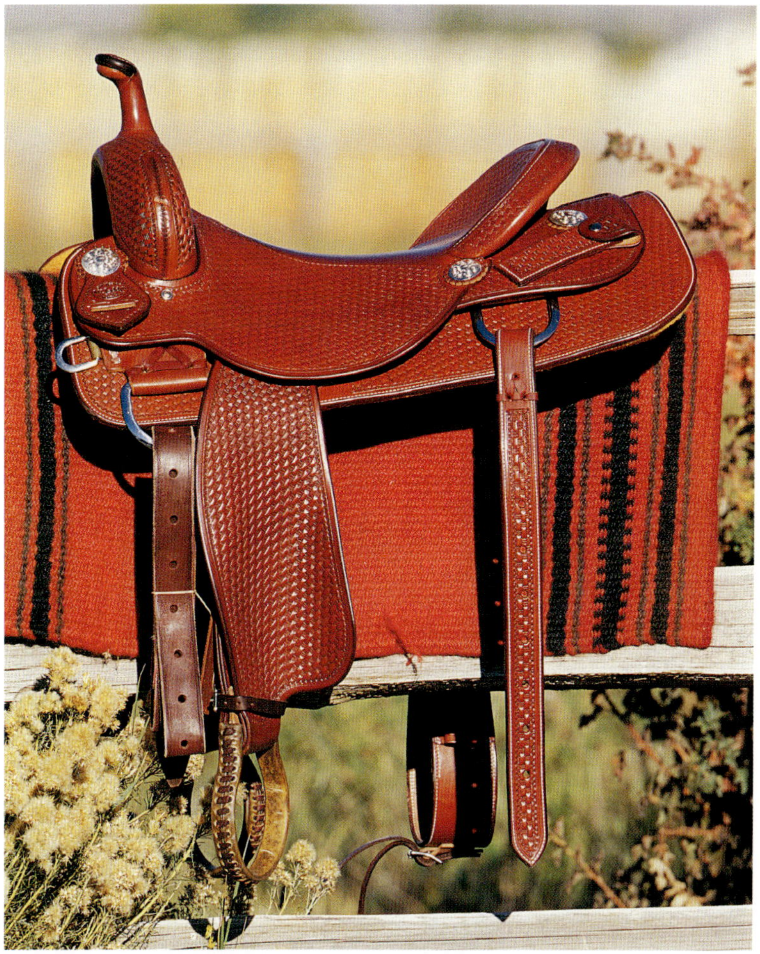

In 1918, M.L. Leddy left the family cotton farm near the San Saba River and began repairing boots and saddles for a local saddlery. As work was slow, he decided to make a pair of boots, which caught the eye of a local rancher. The customer liked the fit and the quality so well that he returned for another pair. Mr. Leddy bought the saddlery in 1922, and with the help of five brothers, started a legend and tradition of fine boot and saddle making. The business began to grow, and moved to San Angelo, Texas, in 1936. In 1941 an additional location was established in the historical Fort Worth Stockyards. From these locations, M.L. Leddy's continues to carry on the same tradition the family started in 1922. Leddy's is now in the fourth generation of family ownership, and continues to be proud of its heritage. Each custom-made boot and saddle is completely handmade from start to finish using the finest materials available, by craftsmen who, through years of experience, are truly experts in their field. Leddy boots, saddles, hats, and tack have been the choice of presidents, kings, celebrities, ranchers, businessmen, and professional horsemen all over the world. To this very day M.L. Leddy's is synonymous with quality, and remains one of the oldest, most respected names in handmade boots and saddles in Texas. (history courtesy of M.L. Leddy's web site)

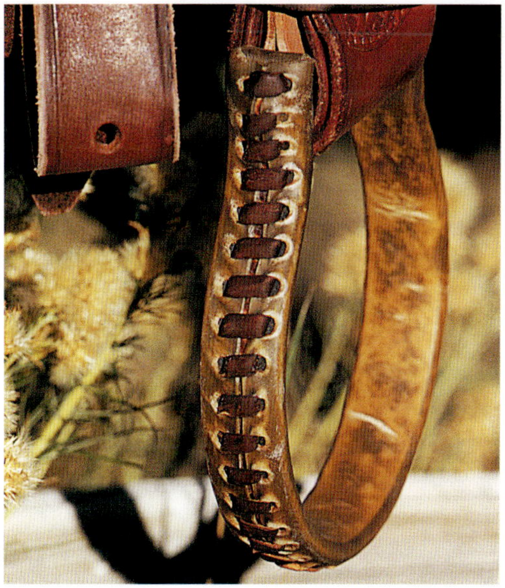

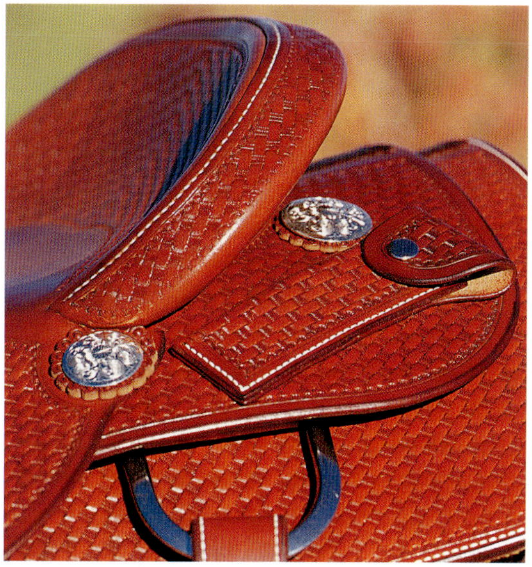

M.L. LEDDY SADDLE, *Fort Worth, Texas*

LARRY COATS

Larry Coats has been handcrafting fine saddles for 28 years and he learned the trade at the TSTI in Amarillo, Texas. He was raised on a farm in Juniata, Nebraska and he started his own saddle shop, Coats Saddlery, in 1991. The shop now turns out over 500 saddles per year. Larry makes saddles for cowboys, performance horsemen, and collectors and he most admires the work of saddle maker Bob Marrs. Customers have to wait about three months for a Coats saddle and Larry is best known for cutting, working, roping, and barrel racing saddles. The average price for one if his saddles is around $2,600. Larry thinks that a good fit for the horse and rider, along with a saddle's overall appearance, is most important.

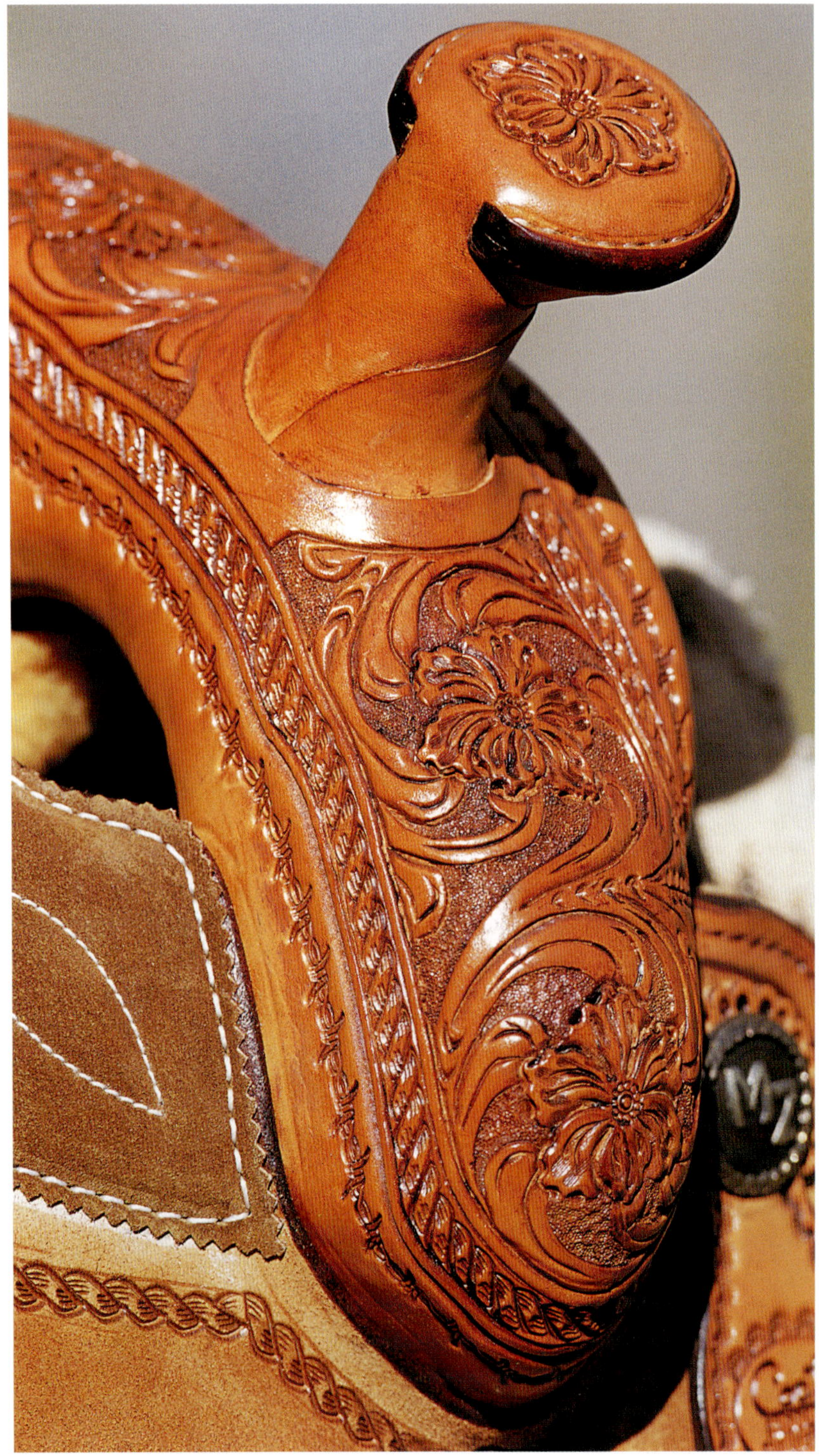

LARRY COATS SADDLE, *San Angelo, Texas*

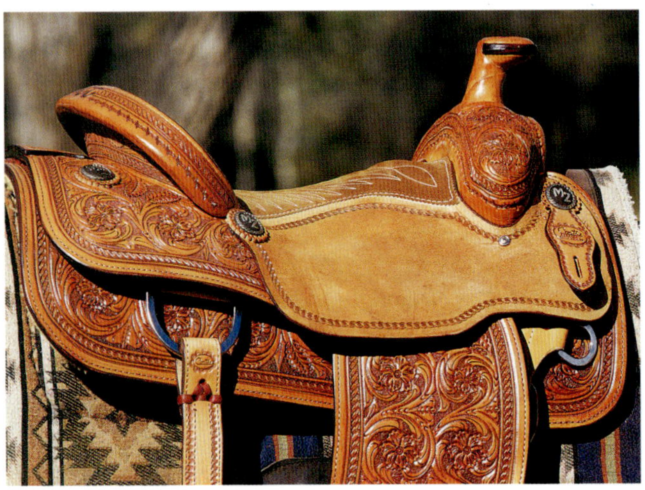

Crates Leather Company

Crates Leather Company was founded in 1981 and the Crates family has been in the saddle making business for over 60 years. The shop currently produces about 100 saddles per week. They make large numbers of saddles sold through their catalogs and field salesmen to retail shops in the United States as well as abroad. Crates is known in the industry for "arena products"—gear for rodeo performers, pro and non-pro, as well as reiners and working cowboys. They are also popular in the pleasure and trail riding disciplines. They use both rawhide-covered saddletrees and Equi-Fit trees for their saddles. The most popular ones are team roping and all-around styles. The time frame for the production of a Crates saddle is about three to four months. They make over 200 saddle models and types and are considered a "production shop" rather than a "custom saddlemaker." At Crates, form follows function. Style is, and always will be, very important. They want the final product to fit the horse and rider precisely for the particular discipline involved, whether it is working, roping, show, barrel racing, or anything else.

Crates Leather Company saddle, *Chattanooga, Tennessee*

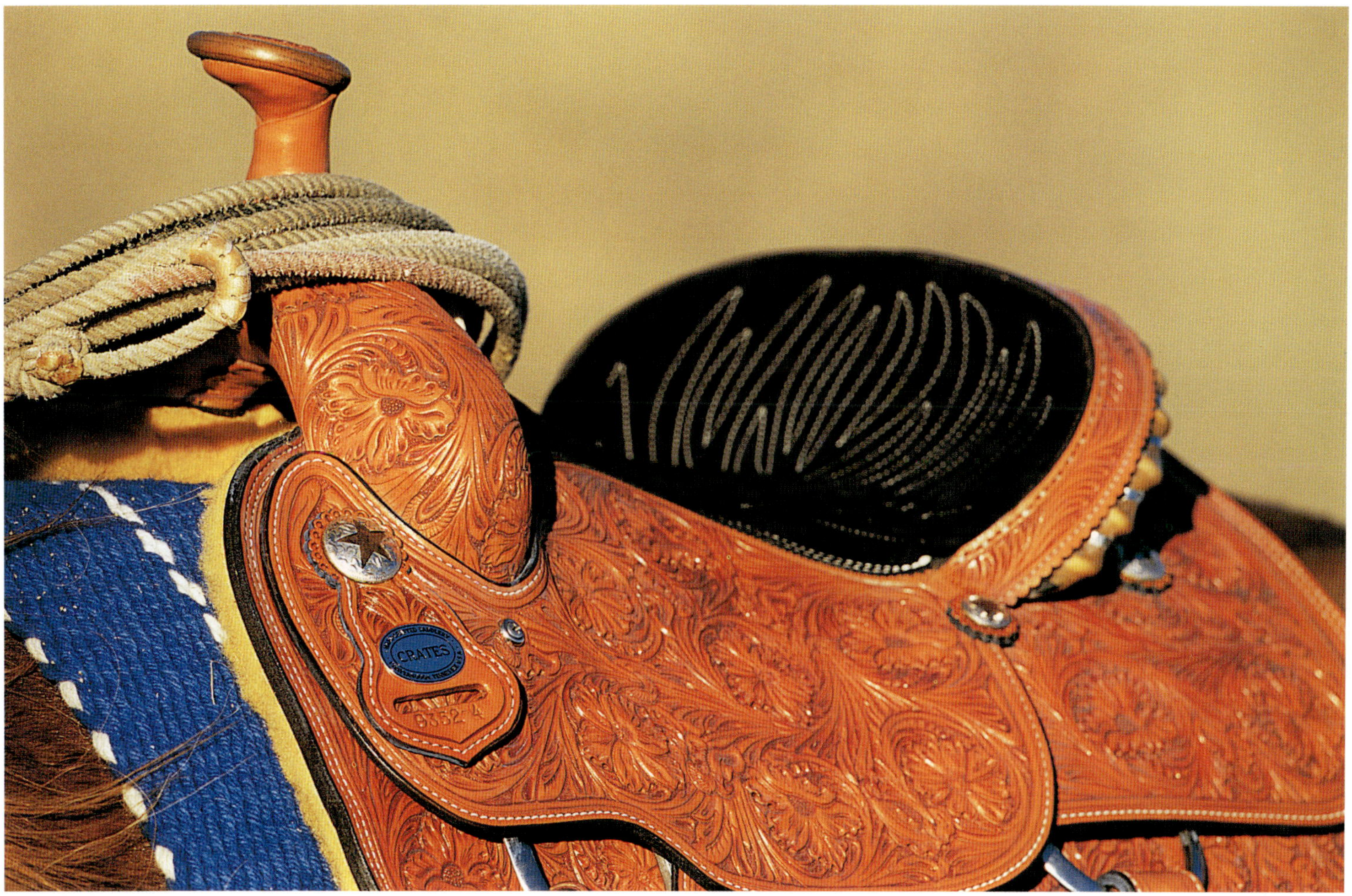

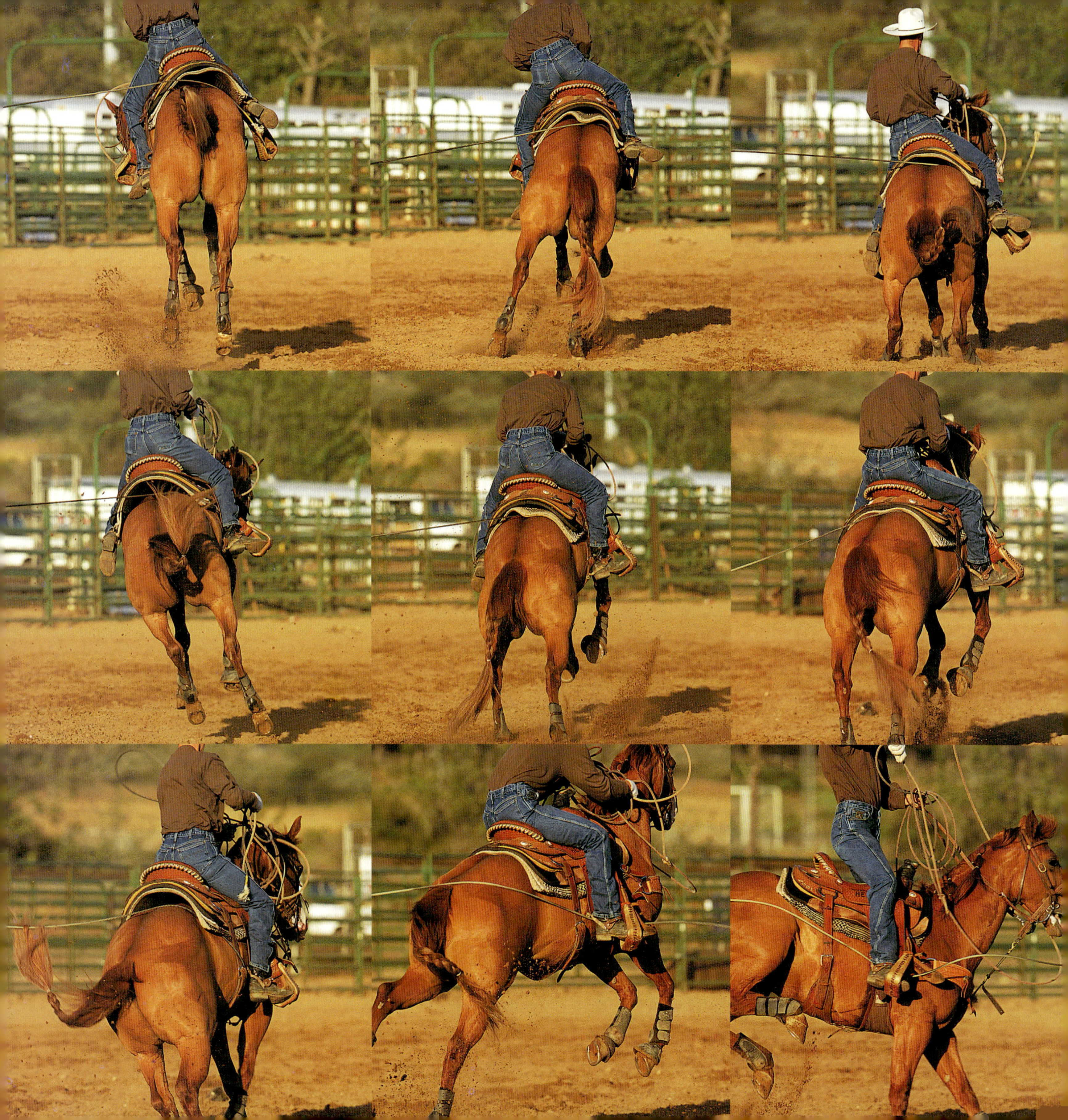

MARK GOMES, *Estancia Ranch, Paso Robles, California*

IF YOU GET YOUR ROPE IN THE WRONG PLACE YOU ARE IN FOR QUITE A RIDE. *Cal Poly Rodeo Team, San Luis Obispo, California*

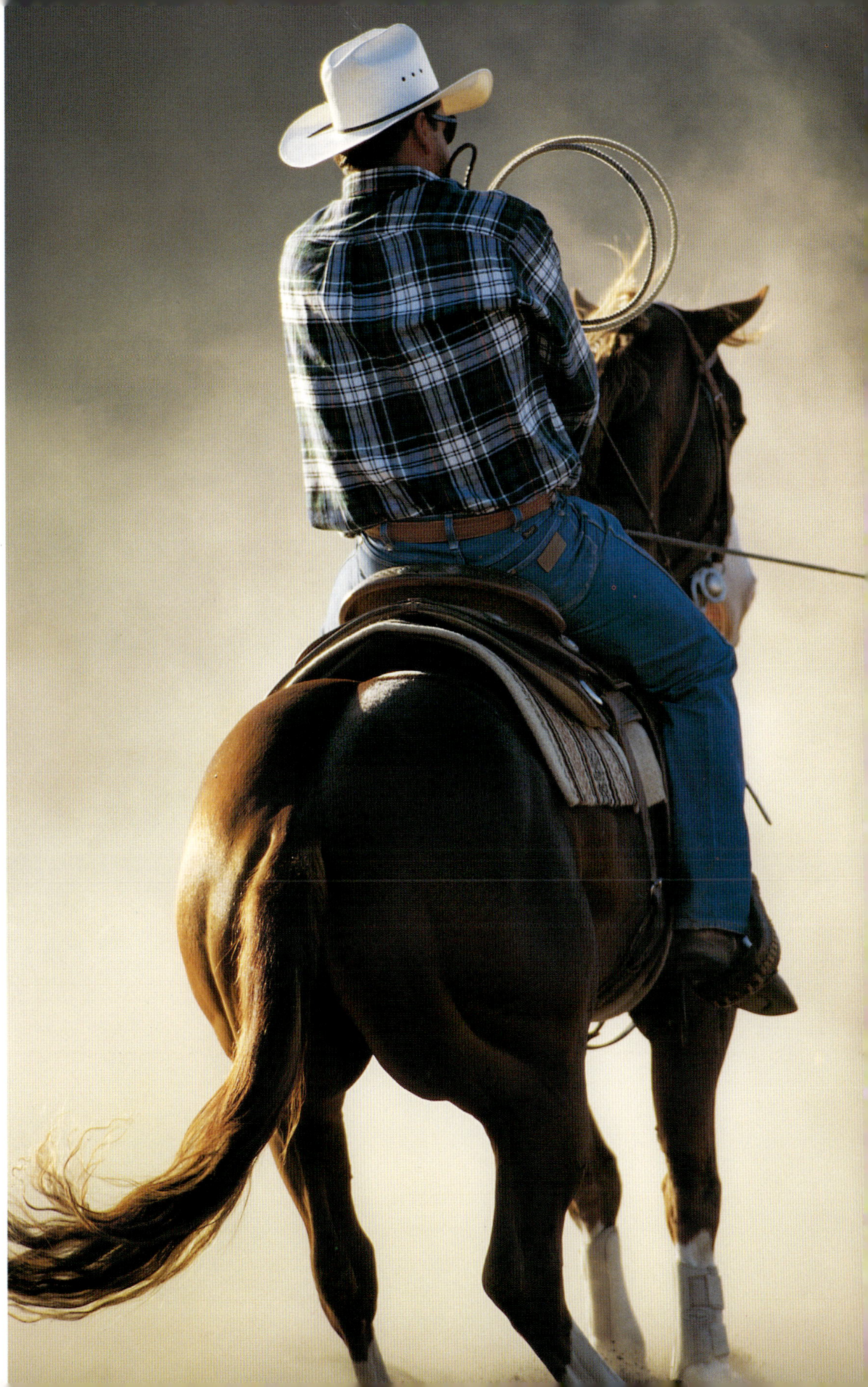

Pack Saddles

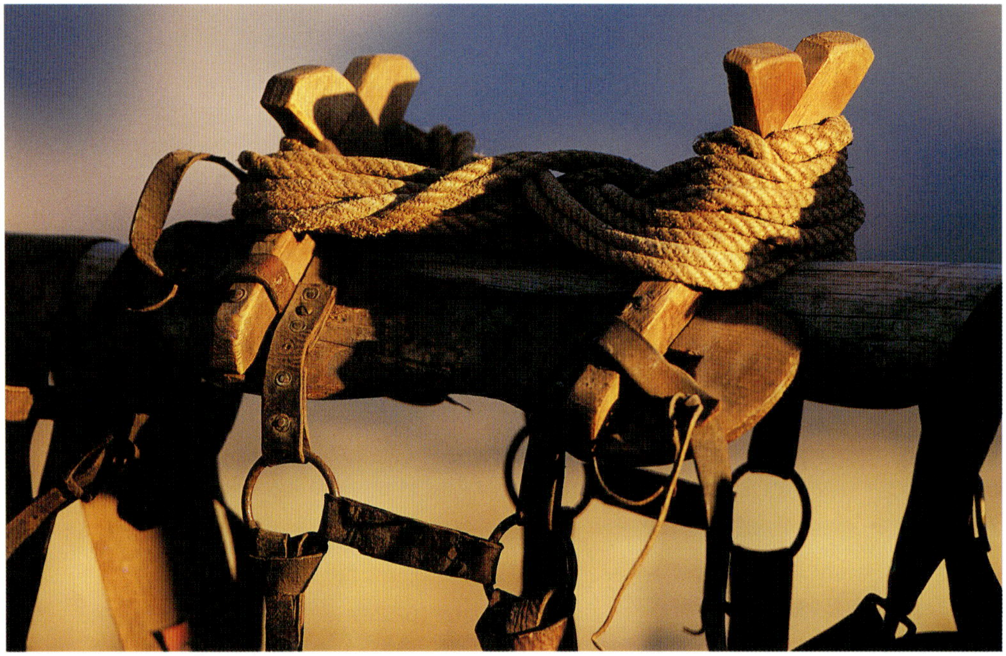

Cross buck pack saddle

Decker pack saddle

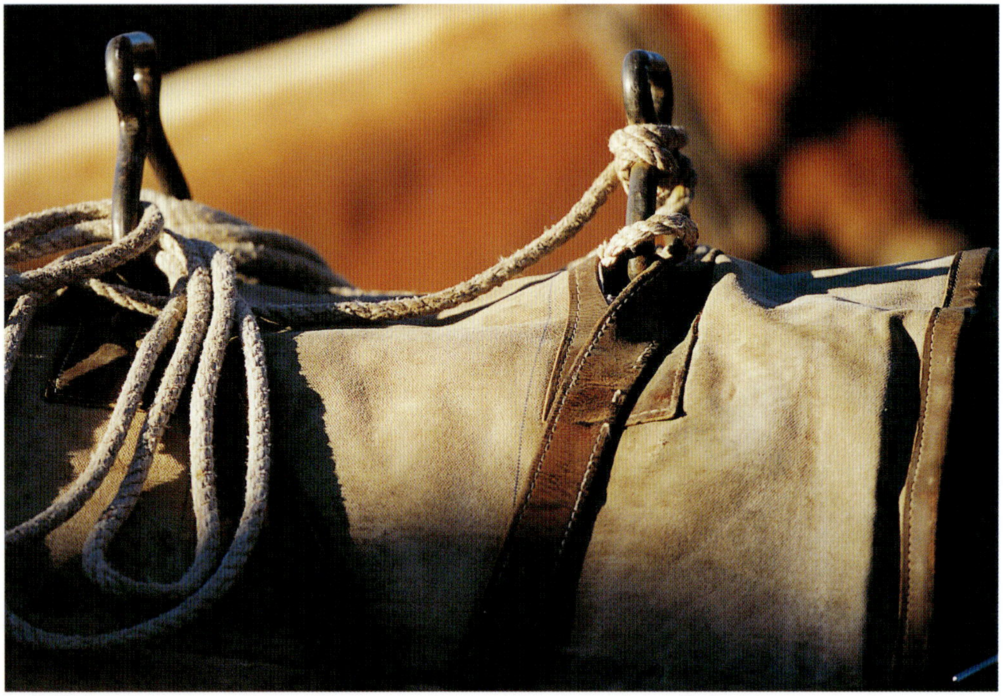

Fred Reyes packing salt in the Santa Barbara Mountains, *Walking R Ranch, Maricopa, California*

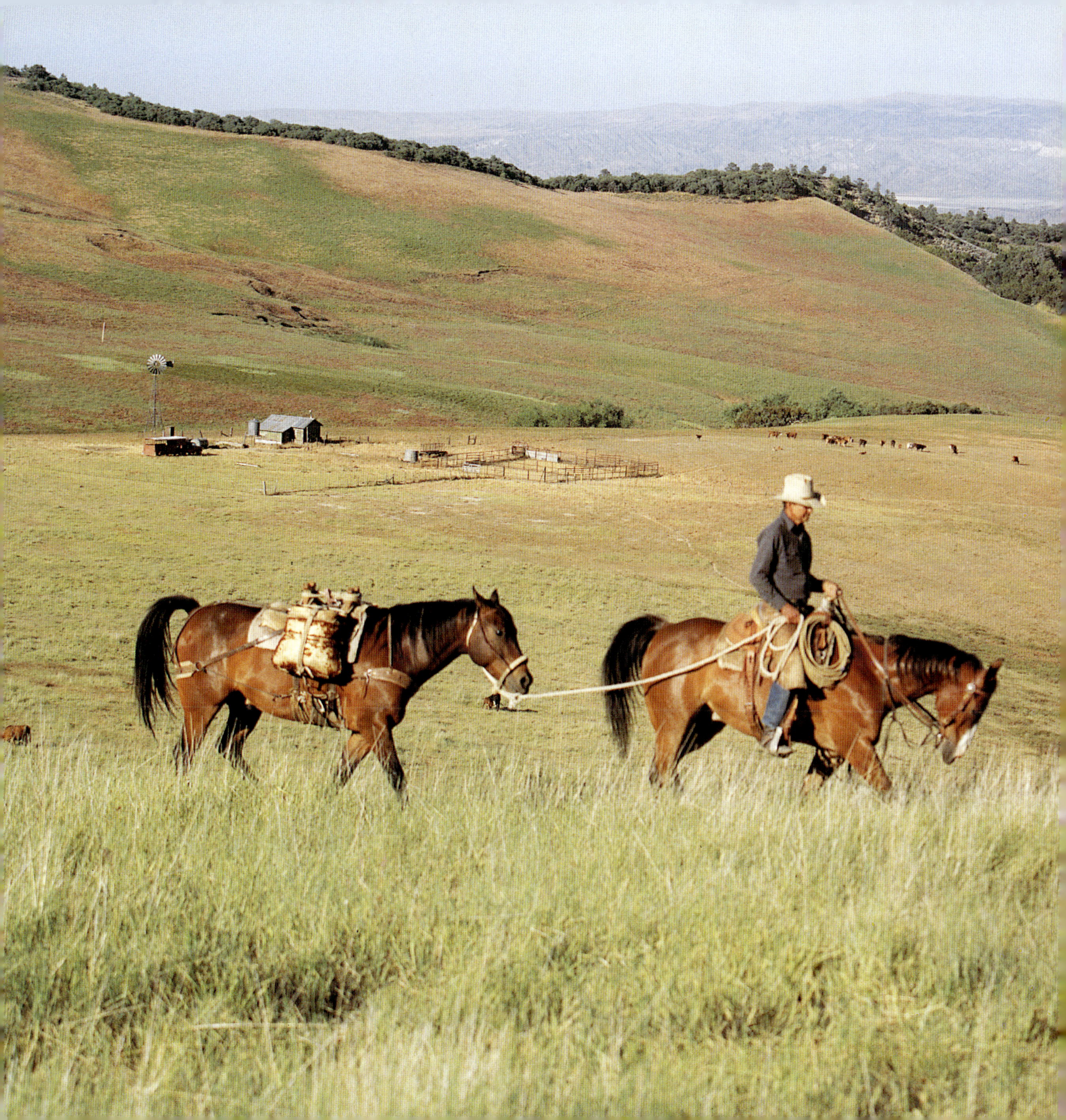

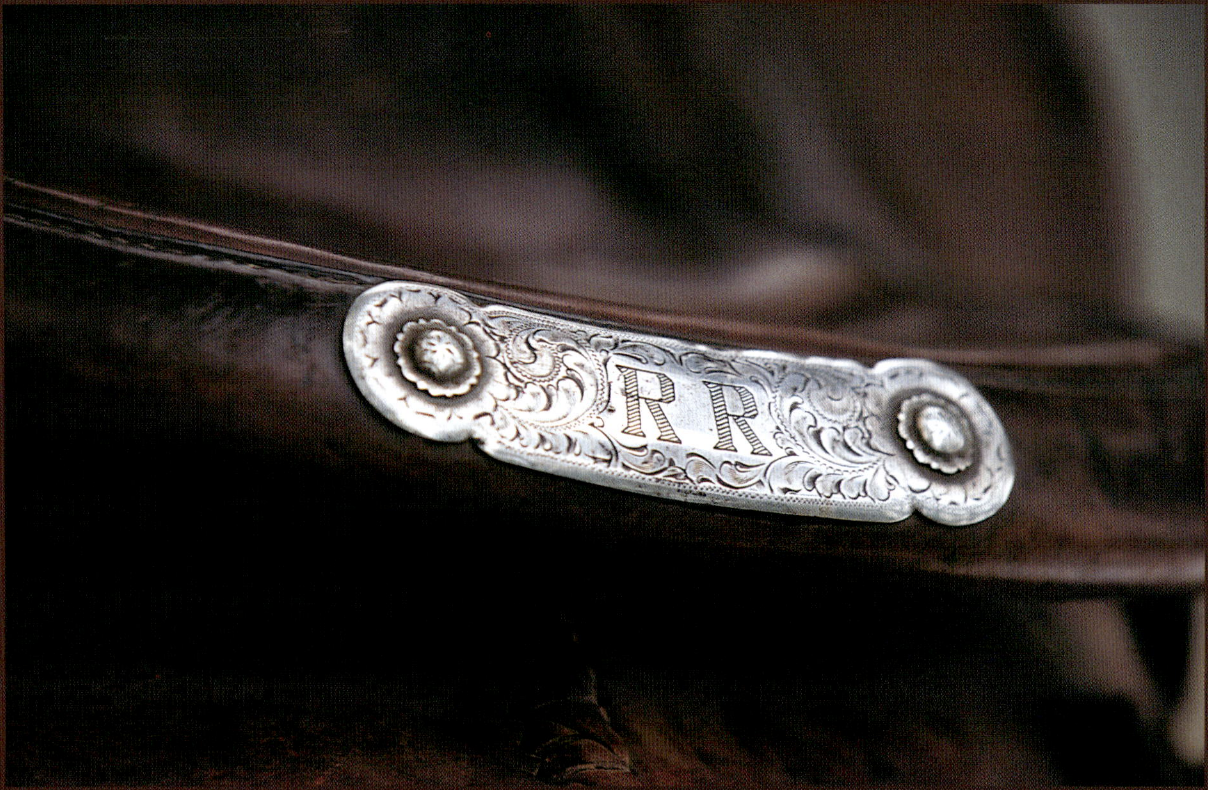

This saddle was a gift to President Ronald Reagan *from the King Ranch. Today it resides in Los Olivos, California with Doug Herthel, the President's veterinarian and Sergeant Murphy, the President's last riding horse.*

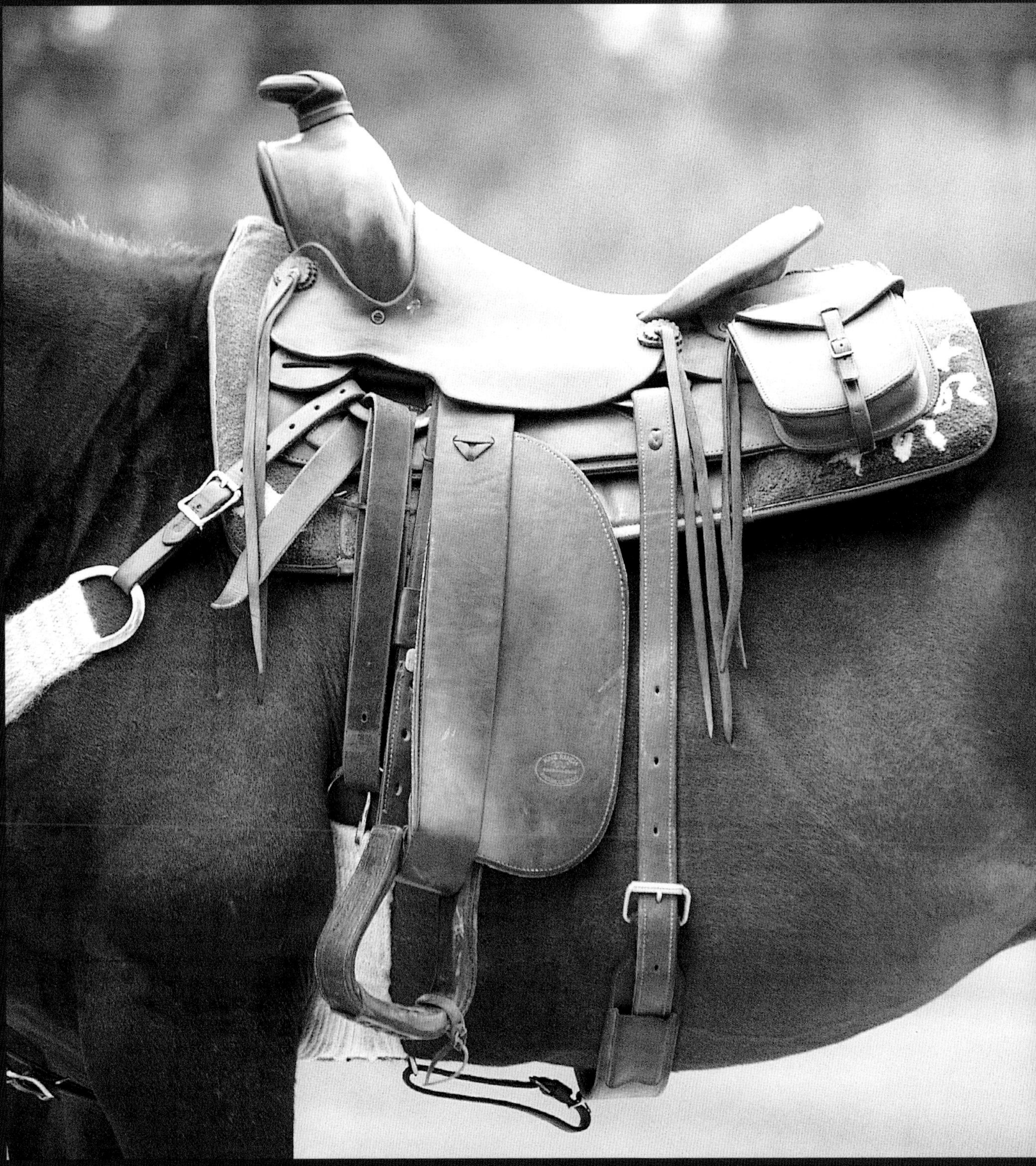

Saddle Company Directory

(All information courtesy of the book "Old Cowboy Saddles & Spurs," 7th Edition, by Gretchen and Mike Graham, Ruxton's Trading Post, published by Old West Trading Company, copyright 2003)

All Western Pacific
In Lusk, Wyoming. Owned by Tom C. Neilson & William Vandergriff. They made 60 all-plastic saddles in 1946-47.

Big Bend Saddlery
PO Box 38 • Alpine, TX 79831
800-634-4502
Contemporary saddle shop owned by Gary Dunshee.

Ed Bohlin
Edward H. Bohlin was born in Sweden in 1895 and came to America before WWI. He was a working cowboy in Montana and Wyoming. One of the ranches he worked on was owned by the famous Buffalo Bill Cody. While in between jobs, he opened his first leather shop in Cody, Wyoming. He later opened a leather shop in Hollywood, California. Around 1923, he expanded his business to include saddles, spurs, and fast-draw holsters. Bohlin was known as the saddle maker to the stars. Tom Mix and Gene Autry were among his friends and customers. He was a real artist and craftsman. Bohlin died in 1980. The Edward H. Bohlin Company is still in business today.

Marc Brogger
4333 Madison Road • Three Forks, MT 59752
Marc Brogger once worked for Nancy Peterson at the Three Forks Saddlery in Montana.

Don Butler
Custom Cowboy Shop • 350 North Main Street
Sheridan, WY 82801
307-672-7733
Don Butler was born in Billings, Montana in 1946. Don learned saddle making from Bob Douglas and how to carve leather from Lloyd Davis and Don King. He started making saddles on his own in the early 1970s.

J.M. Capriola
500 Commercial Street • Elko, NV 89801
775-738-5816
Joe Capriola made saddles for G.S. Garcia in Elko, Nevada. Joe opened his own shop in 1929. He died in 1947. The company is still in business today.

Clark Saddlery Company
John Clark started his saddlery in Portland, Oregon in 1878. John died around 1923 and his family continued until 1927. Clark's Bucking Roll was patented in 1901.

Coats Saddlery
6910 Treece Road • San Angelo, TX 76905
325-651-5080
Contemporary—Larry Coats learned saddle making in Amarillo in 1976. He worked for R.D. Mork, Texas Saddlery, Piland Saddlery and was a partner with Anderburg in Clarendon, Texas. He has his own shop in San Angelo, Texas.

Charles Coggshall
Charles E. Coggshall of Miles City, Montana bought the Hugh Moran Shop in 1895. In 1897 he went into a partnership with Al Furstnow that only lasted a few years. The Miles City Saddlery was formed by Bert Coleman as president, Charles E. Coggshall as a silent vice president, Clem Kathmann as superintendent, and Frank J. Jelinek as secretary-treasurer in 1909. They incorporated and then changed their stamp to read "The Miles City Saddlery, Makers of the Original Coggshall Saddles." The Three-Quarter-Rigged Montana Saddle originated in Miles City.

Crates Leather Company
515 North Holtzclaw Avenue • Chattanooga, TN 37404
423-622-7503
Dan Crates, contemporary shop.

Ernst-Buckley Saddlery
John P. Buckley and Otto Ernst opened the Ernst-Buckley Saddlery in Sheridan, Wyoming in 1902. In 1907 Ernst bought Buckley's share of the business. Buckley moved to Lander, Wyoming in 1907 and then to Monterey, California sometime before 1922 where he owned and operated the Monterey Saddlery, 1930s-1940.

R.T. Frazier
Robert Thompson Frazier was born in 1850. He worked for Peter Becker in Colorado Springs, Colorado before moving to Pueblo, Colorado in 1880. Around the mid-1880s he went into a partnership with S.C. Gallup. In 1892 they legally formed the S.C. Gallup and Frazier Saddlery that lasted until 1898. When G& F split up, Gallup continued to use their trademark steer. Frazier's trademark became the phrase "Builder of the Famous Pueblo Saddle." Frazier was a brilliant businessman who used mail order catalogs and advertising to make the Pueblo Saddle famous. The Frazier Saddlery employed over 50 saddle makers at a time. In 1917 he was the largest producer of stock saddles in the US. R.T. Frazier amassed a considerable fortune from the saddlery, real estate development and other enterprises. The Frazier home is on the National List of Historic Places. R.T. Frazier died in 1931. His widow Kitty ran the saddlery until it was closed in 1958. She died in 1959.

Al Furstnow

Albert F. Furstnow established the Al Furstnow Saddlery Company of Miles City, Montana in 1884. One year later he bought the Goettlich Saddlery and in December of 1894 he went into a partnership with Charles E. Coggshall, which lasted until March of 1899. Furstnow was known for his fancy leatherwork. He died in 1923. The saddlery continued to operate under Joseph Moreno. They issued their 35th catalog in 1928. They closed the saddle making part of the shop in September of 1946, when maker Pete VerBeck left.

G.S. Garcia

Guadalupe S. Garcia was born in Sonora, Mexico in 1864. He moved to Margarita, California and opened his first shop in 1882, where he made saddles, spurs, and bits. Garcia moved to Elko, Nevada in 1894. There, his unique style and quality of craftsmanship made him famous. Many master craftsmen worked for him at various times—Mike Morales, Juan Estrada, and Raphael (Philo) Gutierrez to name a few. Due to Garcia's failing health, his sons Less and Henry took over the business in 1932. G.S. Garcia died the next year. They moved the business to Salinas, California in 1936 and changed the name to Garcia Saddlery. Matt Klein worked for them in the late 1940s and he described their leatherwork as the finest he had ever seen in one shop. The brothers were very interested in keeping the trade "alive" by passing the "tricks of the trade from one craftsman to another." All leather goods that were sold in the retail part of the store were made in their shop. Their silver-mounted work was also the best Klein had ever seen. Jay Venezula and Jack Kendall also worked for the Garcia brothers.

Hamley & Company

30 SE Court Street • Pendleton, OR 97801
541-276-2321

John and Henry, the sons of William Hamley (an English saddle maker) were the beginning of the famous "Hamley & Company." The first shop was started in 1883 in Ashton, South Dakota. They moved their business to Kendrick, Idaho in 1890. In 1893 Henry died and John moved the business to Pendleton, Oregon in 1905. Around 1909 his two sons, Lester H. and John M. went to work in the family business. John M. died in 1937 and his father in 1939. The firm was left in the very capable hands of Lester H. and his son David. This fourth generation partnership kept the company going. Lester H. died in 1963. The Hamley Company is a landmark in Pendleton. They were associated with the famous Pendleton Roundup Rodeo from its beginning in 1910. They are still in business today.

Dale Harwood

876 E 1500 N • Shelley, ID 83274
208-357-3803

Dale Harwood/Trail's End Saddle Shop in Rigby, Idaho in the 1980s and presently in Shelley, Idaho.

Hermann Heiser

Hermann H. Heiser was born in Germany in 1836. He was educated in the National schools, after which he worked in a bookbindery until 1854. After coming to the US, Heiser began an apprenticeship with a Platteville, Wisconsin saddle and harness maker. About two years later, Heiser moved to Highland, Wisconsin to open his own saddlery. In March of 1864 he moved to Colorado and opened a shop in Black Hawk. In 1866, while still keeping this shop, he opened another shop in Central City. In 1870 he sold the Black Hawk shop and moved to Central City, where he remained until 1874. Heiser then moved to Denver. In May of 1874 he bought the William Merchant shop on Blake Street. In October of 1877 he married Mathilde Wolter and had four sons. Heiser died in Germany while visiting his sister in 1904. In 1904, his saddlery amassed about $40,000 in total sales. By 1917 the amount had increased to $600,000 in annual sales. In June of 1917 the Heiser Saddlery merged with Heiser Brothers Investment Company to become the Hermann H. Heiser Manufacturing & Selling Company. Around 1919, his some Ewald bought his brothers' interests in the saddlery part of the business and ran it until 1945, when he sold it to the Denver Dry Goods Company. They used the Hermann H. Heiser name and trademark. The Keyston Brothers bought the company in 1950 and they too kept the Heiser name and trademark. Heiser's work was always stamped with the famous "H.H.H.", the ninth registered trademark in Colorado. The Heiser Quick Draw Holster was patented in 1906.

Hoggan Custom Leather

2165 S 1800 E • Gooding, ID 83330
208-663-4646

Contemporary leather and saddle shop, Nancy Hoggan.

Ray Holes

213 Main Street • Grangeville, ID 83530
208-983-1460

Ray Holes was born in 1911 in central Washington. He opened his first saddle shop in Cottonwood, Idaho in 1936. Soon after he moved near Grangeville, where his shop is still located today. Ray's son Jerry grew up in the shop and is now a master craftsman of the trade. They started making their own saddle trees in 1955. Ray also invented tools for carving leather that are still used today. Ray, himself a master carver, considers Jerry's work to be even better than his own.

King's Saddlery

184 North Main Street • Sheridan, WY 82801
800-443-8919

Bruce Donald King learned saddle making from his father Don. Bruce is now a master saddler. Donald "Don" King learned to build saddles from Rudy Mudra in Sheridan, Wyoming in 1940. King opened his own shop in 1947 in Sheridan. He has made many trophy saddles, including ones for the Rocky Mountain Quarter Horse Association, R.C.A., Cheyenne Frontier Days Rodeo, Walla Walla Stampede Rodeo, and the Pendleton Roundup Rodeo.

King Ranch Saddle Shop
(see Running W Saddle Shop)

Knox & Tanner
Los Angeles, California from 1915-25 and Rawlings, Wyoming from 1920-30.

Lawrence & Company
Clayton, New Mexico, circa 1890-1910.

M.L. Leddy's
2455 North Main Street • Fort Worth, TX 76106
888-565-2668
M.L. Leddy opened a shop in Brady, Texas in 1921 and in Fort Worth, Texas in 1923 and in San Angelo, Texas in 1936. The latter two stores are still in operation today. They employ eight saddle makers. All of the stores are running under the same name—M.L. Leddy Boot & Saddlery. Wilson Franklin is the current president and grandson of M.L. Leddy.

Donn Leson
2883 Williams Highway • Grants Pass, OR 97527
541-476-4218
(1980s-90s)

Main & Winchester Saddlery
Charley Main and Ezra H. Winchester established their saddlery in San Francisco in 1849. They made all types of saddles—pony express, polo, army, muley (hornless), pleasure, and Western. At one point they offered over 100 styles. They merged with L.D. Stone in 1905 to form Main, Winchester, & Stone. In 1912, they were bought by the Keyston Brothers of San Francisco. The Arizona business directory of 1907-8 listed the Main-Winchester-Jepsen Company as being saddle makers in Los Angeles. Main and Winchester were considered to be two of the most famous saddle makers ever.

Frank A. Meanea
Frank A. Meanea was a nephew of E.L. Gallatin. Meanea helped open the Gallup & Gallatin Saddlery in Cheyenne, Wyoming around 1868. By 1873 Meanea was the sole owner of the Frank A. Meanea Saddlery. He used the famous Gallatin stamp until 1881. By this time the Meanea name was popular in its own right. He was a pioneer in the mail order saddle business. He designed and made the Cheyenne style chaps. He only used the saddle trees that were made by his brother, Theodore E. Meanea in Denver. Frank died in 1928. After 1881 Meanea's earlier saddles were marked "F A MEANEA MAKER CHEYENNE WY." Meanea never stamped his mark in the fenders of his saddles. Beginning in 1995, the F.A. Meanea Company of Cheyenne started producing the complete line of Meanea products and is located at the site of the original shop. The Meanea family is also involved in the company, as it is a continuation of the Meanea Saddle Company of the 1920s. These saddles and other leather goods are being marked as the original products. In the late 1930s and 40s numerous saddles were sent from Texas to Cheyenne and stamped on the fenders by Tony Holmes Saddle Saddle Shop with the FA Meanea mark. These saddles were sold through the Western Ranchman Outfitters as the "Meanea" Cowboy Saddle. They all show the low cantle of the 1940s and are found plain, embossed, basket stamped, and full tooled.

Miles City Saddlery
In 1909 in Miles City, Montana, the Miles City Saddlery was formed by Bert Coleman as president, Charles E. Coggshall as a silent vice president, Clem Kathmann as superintendent, and Frank J. Jelinek as secretary-treasurer in 1909. That day they bought the C.E. Coggshall Saddlery for $9,515.55 and Coggshall was given one share of his stock for the rights to use the famous Coggshall name on the saddles. Bert died in 1917, Clem died in 1936. Joe Conway, the bookkeeper, bought shares in the company that year and in 1939 he bought Frank's shares as well. Ray Wilson, from Broadus, Montana purchased interest in 1938. From 1938 to 1944, Wilson was president, Pete VerBeck was vice president and Joe Conway was secretary-treasurer. Joe Conway and his three sons had all bought interest in the shop in 1944 and owned it until May of 1961 when Carl Wilson purchased the shop and the firm stamp "Maker of the original Coggshall Saddles." He closed the saddle shop in December of 1982.

Blake Miller
Blake Miller, Cheyenne, Wyoming, early 1900s-1920s. He moved to Denver in 1927.

Sam Myres
Samuel Dale Myres, lovingly called "Tio Sam" in his later years, was born in Texas in 1871. He served a three-year apprenticeship with T.R. James and Sons Saddlery in Cleburne, Texas. In 1893 Myres went to work for M.B. "Doc" Kouns in Weatherford, Texas. There he honed his skills in stamping leather. In 1897 he was finally able to buy his first shop from J.K. Polk in Sweetwater, Texas. He developed the Myres Quick Draw Holster, which was used by many law officers and even the FBI. From 1919 to his death in 1953, he lived in El Paso, Texas. At one time or another, these saddle makers worked for Myers: Herbert Camel, Bob Flynn, John Kemp, Albert Prince, Mike Rogers, Earl Massey, Joe Merino, Earnest Meyers, Shorty Saylor, Clyde Taylor, R. Lloyd Davis, Bo Hubble, and Clair Dudley who carved the $10,000 saddle.

Olsen-Nolte
Al Nolte was born in the late 1870s in Los Angeles. Nolte was a fine saddle maker; John E. Olsen was not a saddler. He provided financial backing and an extensive business background. Their combined talents produced a booming business that was founded in 1937 in San Francisco.

Nolte died in 1942. The company continued to run through the 1950s. Before 1937, Nolte worked for Main & Winchester, D.E. Walker, J.H. Wilson, H.H. Heiser, and the Great West Saddlery. He is thought to have had a short-lived partnership with Steve Ybarra as well. The business was also known as Nolte-Olsen.

Padgitt Brothers
Jesse D. Padgitt and William C. Padgitt made saddles in Dallas, Texas from 1885-1900. The sons of William C, Charles and Thomas, continued the business into the 1940s.

Ricotti Saddle Company
PO Box 10, Highway 88 • Clements, CA 95227
800-742-6884
Contemporary shop owned by master saddle maker, Rick Ricotti.

Running W Saddle Shop (King Ranch Saddle Shop)
PO Box 1594 • Kingsville, TX 78364
877-282-5777
This business had its beginning in 1867 as a little shop originally established for making saddles and other equipment used on the great King Ranch in Texas. This ranch was famous throughout the state as one of the largest individually owned ranches in the US. In 1929 it spread out over one million acres. The Kingsville Lumber Company took over the saddle shop around 1910 and kept the Running W Brand Saddles, manufactured and guaranteed by "The Running W Saddle Shop, a department of the Kingsville Lumber Co." They issued their number 30 catalog in 1930. Today they are still in business as the King Ranch Saddle Shop in Kingsville, Texas.

Sean Ryon Saddle Shop
2707 North Main Street • Fort Worth, TX 76106
800-669-7966
Contemporary shop, established in the 1950s.

Sentinel Butte Saddle Company
This shop was founded by W.F. Lucas on his Rafter E Ranch about 12 miles northeast of Sentinel Butte, North Dakota, circa 1900. Lucas moved the shop to Sentinel Butte where he employed a few saddlers. In 1910 he sold the shop to Lewis F. Crawford. Lucas stayed on as the foreman of the shop. The new corporation quickly expanded, establishing branches in Beach, Belfield, and Dickinson, North Dakota as well as in Glendive, Terry, Baker, and Lewiston, Montana. They put out their 11th catalog in 1916. The Sentinel Butte shop closed in 1918 and moved to Billings, Montana where the company operated for only a few more years.

Severe Brothers Saddlery
PO Box 1453 • Pendleton, OR 97801
541-457-2561
Bill and Duff Severe started making saddles at Hamley's. After WWI they went out on their own and the shop is still in business today in Pendleton, Oregon. They are noted for their fine contest saddles and braiding.

Charles Shipley
Charles (Chas) P. Shipley was a saddle and spur maker in Kansas City, Missouri. He was born in 1864. He established his business in 1885 and incorporated in 1910. After his death in 1943, his sons, Clyde and Charley, kept the business going. Clyde died in 1956 and Charley continued until 1970.

Lucius Stone
Lucius D. Stone Company, San Francisco, California was established in 1852. In 1894 they issued a catalog with 430 pages. They merged with Main & Winchester in 1905.

Visalia Stock Saddle Company
5135 N Blackstone Avenue • Fresno, CA 93710
559-227-3419
Visalia Stock Saddle Company had its beginning with David E. Walker and Henry G. Shuham in Visalia, California in 1870. After much buying and selling, and several moves, William "Bill" Majors bought it in 1964 and opened another location in Grass Valley. He then sold it to David L. Stidolph in 1977. Stidolph sold the business to William "Bill" Cutting in 1982 and it is now located in Fresno, California.

D.E. Walker
D.E. Walker (see Visalia)

Chas Weldon
4950 Austrian Pine Drive • Billings, MT 59106
Chas Weldon, 1980s. Master saddle maker and carver who worked for Don King Saddlery in Sheridan, Wyoming.

H & M Wyeth
H & M Wyeth, St. Joseph, Missouri, 1840s-1950s. They made the mochilas for the Pony Express eastern divisions. Their 196th catalog was put out in the early 1930s and their 220th was issued in 1939.

Other Books from Stoecklein Publishing

The American Quarter Horse
Dude Ranches of the American West
Western Fences
The Cowboy Boot
The Western Buckle
The Spur
Cowgirls in Heaven
Ranch Style
The Performance Horse
Lil' Buckaroos
Cow Dogs
Spirit of the West
The American Paint Horse
The California Cowboy
The Idaho Cowboy
Cowboy Gear
The Montana Cowboy
Don't Fence Me In
Cowgirls
The Texas Cowboys
The Western Horse
Sun Valley Images
Sun Valley Signatures I, II, III

Technical Notes

I use Kodak film and Canon cameras and lenses for all the photography in my books and in my commercial work as well. I use a variety of different cameras from Canon, mostly the EOS 1N and the 1V. As for lenses, I use the 300mm and 400mm f/2.8L IS USM and the 16-35mm and 28-70mm f/2.8L USM and 70-200mm f/2.8L IS USM zooms. I also use prime lenses like the 20mm f/2.8 USM, 35mm and 50mm f/1.4 USM. I use the Canon Image Stabilizer lens whenever I can, which happens to be most of the time.

All of the slide film for this project was processed at the BWC Photo Imaging lab in Dallas, Texas. They have been processing the film for all of my books as well as the 35mm film for my regular assignments for the last thirteen years. We have a great working relationship, one that is essential in this line of work to maintain consistency and accuracy. All of the scans for this book were done at T-graphics/Express Printing in Hailey, Idaho.

I am extremely lucky to have all the good people at Canon USA and BWC as well as the staff at my studio in Ketchum, Idaho as a support team while I fly around the country on assignments. Without all of them, my job would be much more difficult.

—DRS

Thanks to my wife, Mary,
who helped me with most of the
photographs for this book and
is my partner in life.
Love, Dave

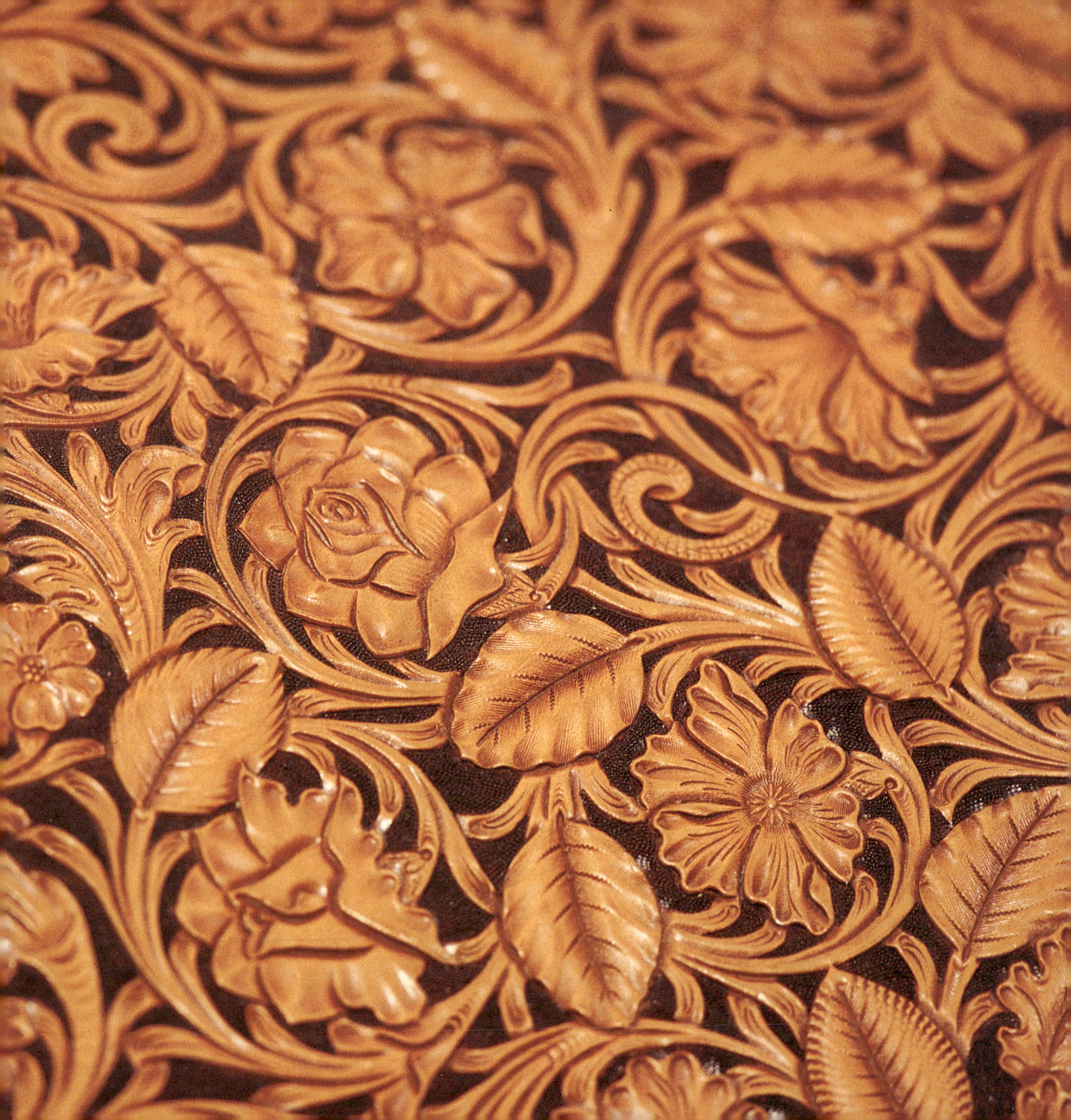

SADDLES OF THE WEST

history, art, culture, function

PHOTOGRAPHY BY DAVID R. STOECKLEIN

TO TOM B. SAUNDERS IV

There are a few people who become important in your life—people who influence you and seem to influence everyone they meet. For me, they are men who possess great wisdom, great compassion, and a great passion for life. They are men who live their lives true to themselves, true to their families, true to their friends, and true to their business partners. These rare men pass on their knowledge to others without question and do not ask for a price. They give it freely with love and care.

Tom B is one of these men. He has touched my life in a very profound and positive way. I only hope that I can live up to all that he has given me. Tom is a true Texas cowboy and a man who lives by the real Code of the West.

—David R. Stoecklein